MW01623589

Cavaliers and Friends

My Two Favorite Things

by Mary Colburn-Green

A Limited Edition

Published by Blue Dragon Publishing, LLC.
www.blue-dragon-publishing.com

ISBN 978-1-939696-32-8
LIMITED EDITION
Library of Congress Control Number: 2017957159
www.blue-dragon-publishing.com/authors/mary-colburn-green

Graphic Design: Jill Little Design, St. Andrews, New Brunswick, Canada

For information about custom editions, special sales, premium and corporate purchases, please contact Blue Dragon Publishing, LLC at BlueDragonPub@cox.net.

TO ORDER:
www.blue-dragon-publishing.com/books/cavaliers-and-friends-my-two-favorite-things

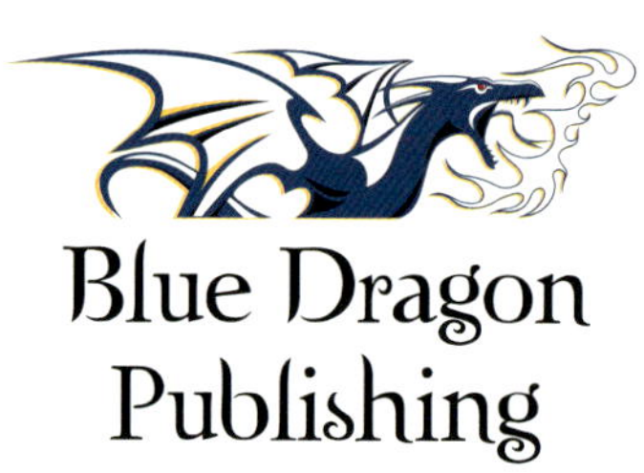

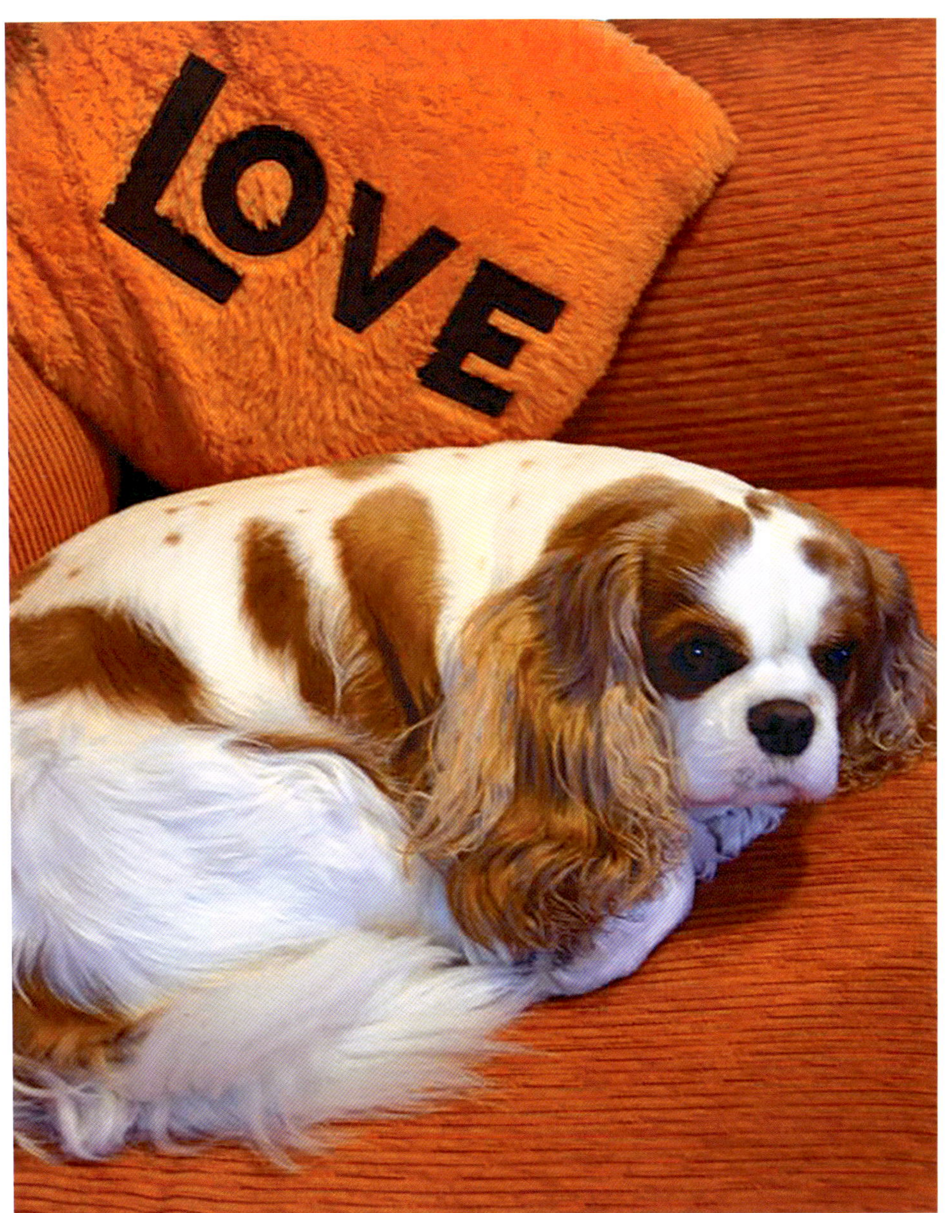

To Callie, and all the Cavaliers like her, who teach us about Love and Courage.

"This amazing book has brought together Cavalier King Charles Spaniel lovers from every corner of the world!

Gaynor Davis, Breeder, Laranna Cavaliers, Milan, Italy

"Cavalier breeders and owners alike are excited about this book."

Claudia Hänsch, Breeder, Erlenbacher vom Hemmerich Kennel, Germany

"The love of Cavaliers comes though on each and every page in this captivating book."

Heather Marino, Breeder, Marino's Precious Cavaliers, Athens, Tennessee

"Finally, a book about Cavaliers that's pure Nirvana for the Soul. Love it!"

Michele Matheson, Breeder, Elswyth Cavaliers, British Columbia, Canada

"This book illustrates the pure joy of owning Cavaliers."

Sandrine Camer, Breeder, Des Cavaliers de Corence, La Teste-de-Buch, France

Acknowledgements

Rather surprisingly, this book moved rapidly from a fun idea into an obsession for me. It was facilitated by the convergence of my two addictions: Facebook and Cavaliers. Once I started to write and collect the photos seriously, I saw it as a Calling. Perhaps, in retrospect, I compiled the book too quickly — in less than three months — sometimes not going to sleep at night.

At times, the pace took its toll, making me tired and irritable. So, I must first thank my husband, Ken, for allowing me to have a pack of fur babies and pursue my dreams. Also, for putting up with my obsession with getting this published in record time. He truly kept me going by feeding me and listening to my daily trauma with photo resolutions, permissions, and computer glitches during this marathon. I also appreciate that my dogs, Callie, Moonbeam, Dolly, and Honey Bea Jones loyally stayed by my side on the couch 'til all hours of the morning, putting up with that wicked laptop. My fur babies' snuggles and kisses at regular intervals inspired me to push onward.

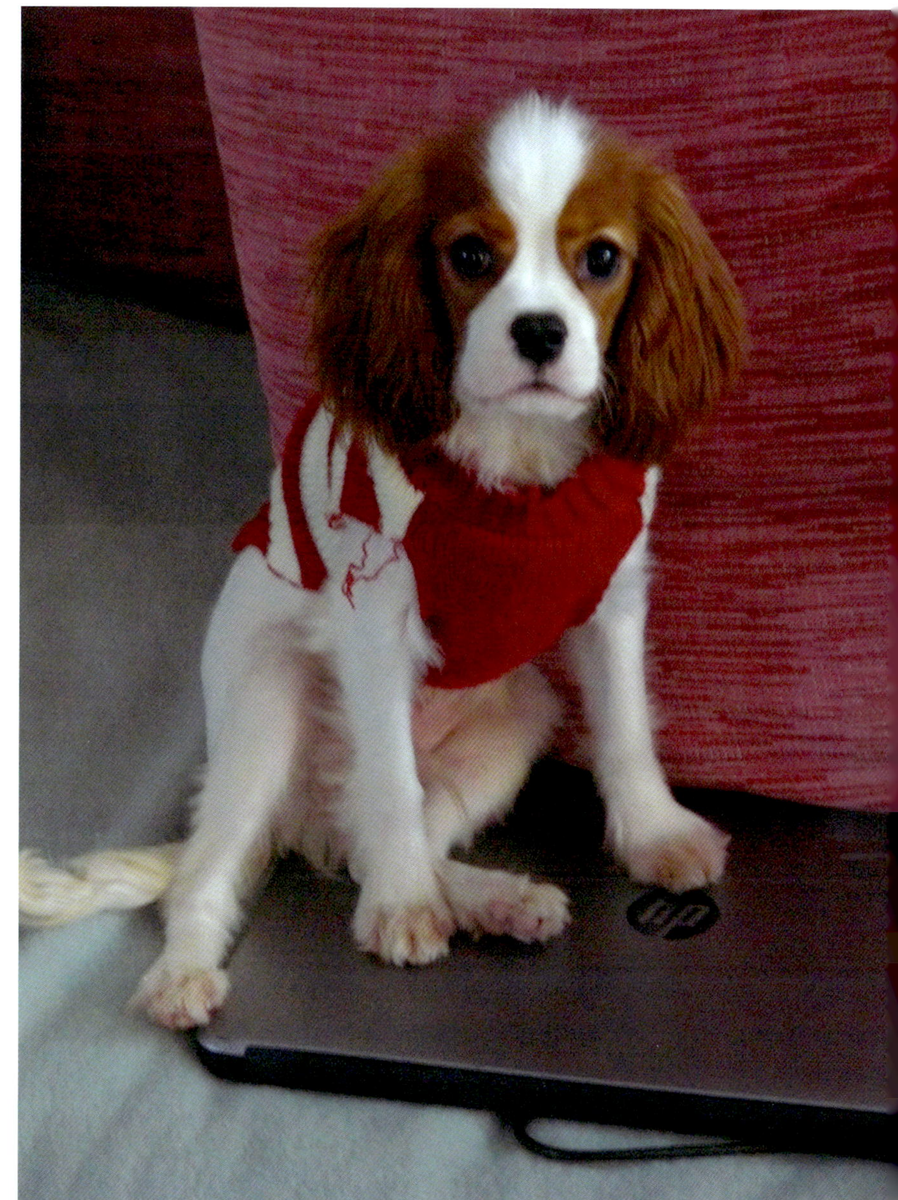

Come to bed, Mom!

Two amazing people in the World of Cavaliers helped me immeasurably. Veronica Hull and Dennis Homes contributed sage advice and profound insight while I was researching and writing this book, not to mention a tremendous amount of time and support. In addition to being a fine breeder of numerous champions and dogs with amazing longevity, Veronica is a respected Show Judge and Director of the Cavalier Club. She served as a brilliant mentor teaching me so much about Cavaliers and about graciousness. Her patience with my learning and mistakes was phenomenal, and I'll never be able to repay her kindness. As all who know her will attest, Veronica truly loves the breed and has dedicated most of her life to Cavaliers. She also contributed her expertise to the rescue and resource chapters.

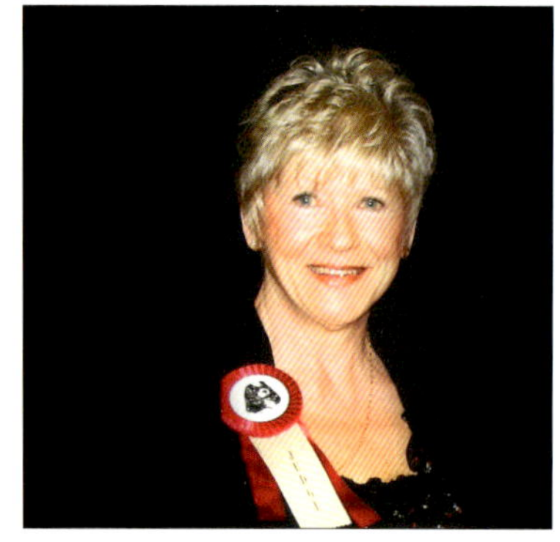

Veronica Hull

By the same token, another exceptional Cavalier champion and acclaimed historian on the breed Dennis Homes encouraged and helped me greatly throughout this writing. He read my rough manuscripts more than once and provided me with valuable materials and contacts. His wife, Tina, and co-author of *The Cavalier King Charles Spaniel: The Origin and Founding of the Breed*, also took part in the manuscript readings. This gentile couple, breeders of champions for more than 30 years, epitomizes the selfless devotion of today's breeders to revive and improve the Cavalier bloodline. What's more, they embrace newcomers like myself, and thanks to their pioneering work, we're able to follow meekly in their giant footsteps.

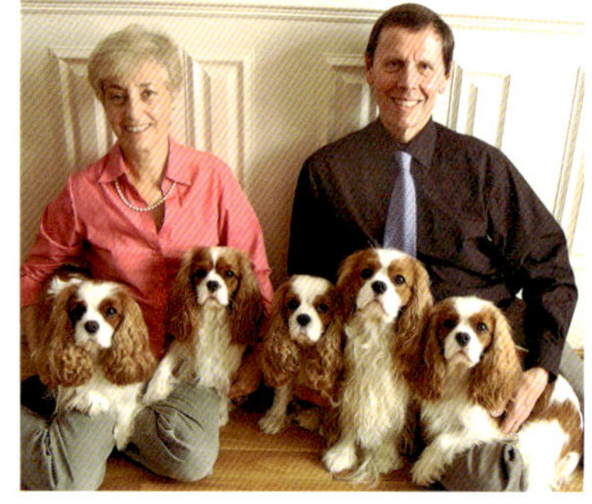

Tina and Dennis Homes with five Leogem Cavaliers

I thank the American Cavalier King Charles Spaniel (ACKCS) Rescue Trust, Inc. and all the other rescue organizations worldwide, and their devoted volunteers for their phenomenal work to provide caring homes for deserving Cavaliers. I especially thank ACKSC Rescue Trust Director Renee Bruns for a guiding hand with the content of my book. I hope that this book will benefit the rescue effort in North America and abroad and continue to serve as a bridge between the Cavalier community of breeders and owners.

I greatly appreciate the help of my dear friends Mary Bray and Mary McNally, who read the manuscript many times. The former was a client turned dear friend. The latter I met here in France walking her Cavalier Charlie, who became Callie's buddy just as Mary and I became friends. Both Marys were kind enough to cheer me on, critique my words, and review my photos (repeatedly). My son Cameron, a writer and photographer in his own right, was also generous in his advice and editing.

My publisher, Dawn Brotherton, President of Blue Dragon Publishing, LLC, was truly a Godsend. I had a contract pending from a big international publisher, but had decided to self-publish to be able to donate more to Cavalier Rescue. Little did I know at the time that this would have been a disaster. Dawn literally fell into my lap due to a referral from an accomplished publisher of children's books in New York City. All I can say is Dawn is phenomenal. She listens, solves problems, saves money, and is the best team-player I could wish for in publishing my first book. Moreover, her fee structure is reasonable, and she totally understands what I'm trying to accomplish for Cavaliers. If you ever want to publish a book, she's the one who will make it happen for you. Thank you, Dawn, for living with my photo resolution nightmares and the 400 photos that turned out to be 800 when I finally stopped long enough to count.

I'm so grateful that my former graphic design consultant and friend from St. Andrews, Jill Little, was able to fit this project into her busy schedule. I have worked with many excellent graphic designers over the years, and Jill, by far, is the best. She is reliable, responsive, and knowledgeable. Her repertoire of design expertise ranges from logos and brochures to promotions, and even books. Jill's vision and touch has graced every page of this book.

However, the lion's share of the credit goes to all my wonderful Facebook Friends. They showed such amazing excitement over the writing of this book, sending me photos and emails, and so much good will. I posted once that this book had turned into a circuit of love between those of us who are fortunate enough to have Cavaliers in our lives.

My ultimate acknowledgement must extend to exuberant King Charles II, and the long line of successors including relatives and breeders, who also recognized the special qualities of these Royal Toy Spaniels. As this book clearly illustrates, I, and a world of others, share his passion for the Cavalier King Charles Spaniel.

Foreword

We're very excited to be a part of this beautiful book that clearly shows the love we all share for Cavalier King Charles Spaniels. It's a charming and telling depiction of the breed that gives so much love to those of us who are blessed to have them in our lives. This book will definitely be treasured and on coffee tables amongst our dedicated volunteers. Mary is to be commended for her efforts and dedication.

Renee Bruns
Oklahoma City, Oklahoma, USA
A Trustee and National Director
of the Cavalier Rescue Trust

The Cavalier King Charles Spaniel is often described as being a big dog in a small jacket. This is a very appropriate description, as although they are a toy breed, they are also very sporting. They are equally at ease going on a lengthy trek across rugged countryside as they are snuggling up on their owner's lap by the fireside. In her book *Cavaliers and Friends*, Mary Colburn-Green, a devoted Cavalier owner, has shared her love of the breed and put together a wide range of photographs that depict the many sides of a Cavalier's character—from young puppies to veterans; from show dogs to rescue dogs; and from sporting dogs to those getting into mischief and having fun. For the Cavalier lover, this book is indeed a tapestry of delights.

Dennis Homes
Herefordshire, UK
Co-author of *The Cavalier King Charles Spaniel: The Origin and Founding of the Breed*

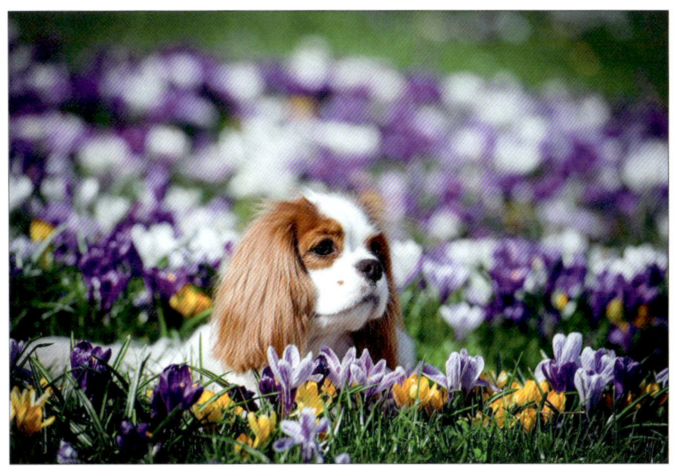

Cover photograph credit:

From Wodzislav, Poland, Anna Derleta is a well-known professional photographer who specializes in studio and outdoor photographs of dogs and cats, as well as dog show reportage. She can be reached at www.pet-photography.pl.

Derleta explains, "I always loved capturing and preserving moments of my life on paper. That's how my pet photography business began... just to save some memories of my first puppy in pictures. But simple photographs weren't enough for me. I wanted to be better as a photographer and as an artist, so I worked hard to improve my skills, using my Cheryl as a model and trying my best at dog shows. Now I'm working with breeders and pet owners. What's more, many clients have become my friends. So my journey with the camera goes on, with Cavaliers, dog shows and friends."

Table of Contents

Introduction by the Author

Like anyone who knows the Breed, I'm enamored with Cavalier King Charles Spaniels (CKCS or Cavaliers). Ever since I saw my first Tri-Color sitting in his owner's lap on a restaurant porch, I was hopelessly hooked. As I learned more about these dogs' loving, playful, easy-going qualities, I knew this was the breed for us. For in our sixties, my husband and I had plans to travel extensively during our pre-retirement years. *(Little did we know then that we'd be splitting our time between three homes in Canada, France, and Spain, and traveling for work.)*

I reasoned a small, loving, lap dog would be perfect. What's more, I knew a Cavalier would be nothing like the frenetic family of five Jack Russell "terrors" we had previously. I immediately started to search online for a puppy.

This book is inspired by my experience with my first Cavalier, Callie, which totally changed my life. It reveals the depth of dedication and commitment people all over the world have for these special pets, as well as some of the issues that affect the breed. I hope you enjoy taking this voyage into the world of Cavaliers with me. I know that it has inflamed my passion, resulting in a new life mission.

According to The Kennel Club survey of 2010 Statistics and the American Kennel Club survey of 2017, Cavaliers are the sixth most popular dog breed in the UK. They are also very popular in the US. The Royal Toy Spaniels range from 13 to 18 pounds and are just 12–13 inches tall. Cavaliers are not to be confused with a similar, but smaller, royal breed with a more extreme pug nose, the King Charles Spaniel.

People call Cavaliers "love sponges" because they're extremely affectionate, attentive, and fun to be around. Their amazing beauty, coupled with comical antics and soulful expressions, bring out the love in people. Frequently, they serve as therapy dogs, uplifting the spirit of everyone they meet.

Ironically, in France, Cavaliers are the mascot for the association for children with heart disease, a problem these little dogs unfortunately may share along with having other genetic problems. Nevertheless, with responsible breeding and systematic health-testing protocols, Cavaliers can be free of debilitating defects and live to a ripe old age of 18 or 19.

Because this breed makes such wonderful pets for families as well as older adults, ensuring that Cavaliers have good health and longevity are important breed priorities, as with all canine companions.

The passion of King Charles II of England (1625-1649) was clearly Cavaliers (and the ladies)...hence, the Breed's name and royal designation. The original English spaniel was crossed with a short-nosed breed to achieve a stylized flat nose. Cavaliers then became "au courant" among European aristocracy and the upwardly mobile in the 17th and 18th centuries. However, the Breed was almost lost in the 20th century due to the hardships of World War II. After the era of King Charles II, a concerted effort to bring back the longer nose of the earlier spaniels came about, and thus the split occurred between the Cavalier King Charles Spaniels and the King Charles Spaniels, which are recognized today as two separate royal spaniel breeds.

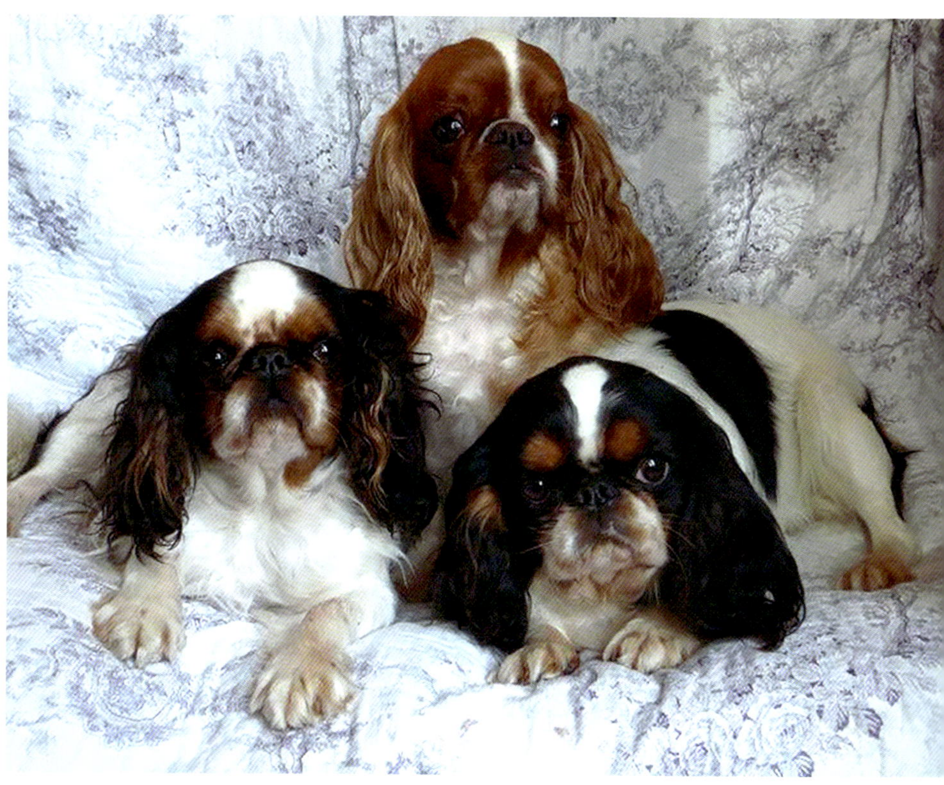

King Charles Spaniels have shorter noses and smaller statures.

Photo credit: Roger Medec, Cavaliers de la Geode, Seine-et-Marne, France

Both breeds have the distinctive four colors: the Blenheim in Cavaliers or the Prince Charles in King Charles Spaniels (mahogany and white with a dot on the Blenheim's crown); the Tri-color (black, white and brown markings inside the ears, on the eyebrows, and legs); the Ruby (all reddish or blondish brown); and the Black and Tan (predominantly black with touches of brown under the ears, on the eyebrows, and legs). The colors are also referred to as split colors (the two colors with white) and solid colors (the two colors with no white).

The four Cavalier colors are shown below in Breeder Claudia Hänsch's dogs: Ruby, Tri-Color, Blenheim, and Black and Tan.

Photo credit: Breeder Claudia Hänsch, Von Erlenbacher Hemmerich Cavaliers, Neubrunn, Germany

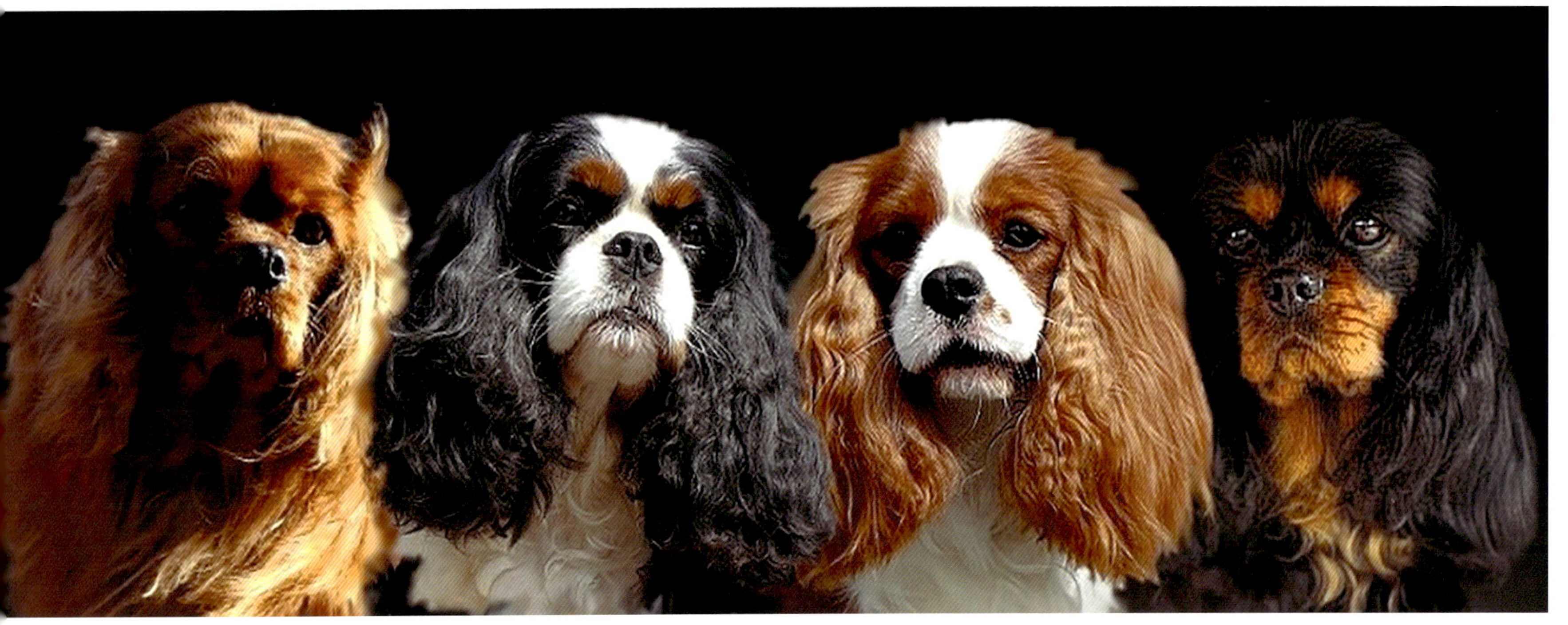

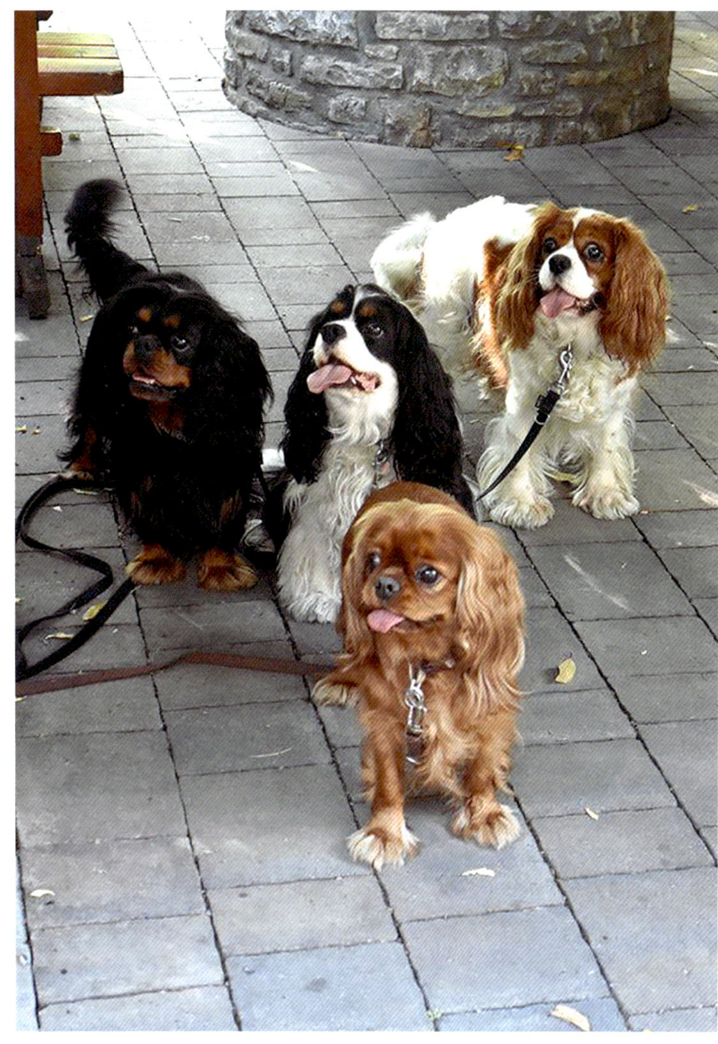

Here's another group of all the colors from Astrid Cavaliers.

Photo credit: Astrid Zigliotto, Trieste, Italy

Histories of the Breed are fascinating and full of lore, but suffice it to say that the King was often accompanied by scores of his Cavalier pups. He was even criticized for dereliction of duty due to the inordinate amount of time he spent with his many dogs. For more information on the history and other aspects of the breed, see the resources chapter at the end of this book. Many aficionados of the breed also seem to collect a pack of Cavaliers, much like the royals, because they're so easy to love, and they get along so well together. *(Hint of what's to come—we now have four Cavaliers.)*

Perhaps, because of their early affiliation with royalty and remarkable beauty, Cavaliers today possess an innate regal quality. They love luxury, food, sleep, grooming, affection, play, and do well with just a little exercise. Over the years, they've been called Comforter Spaniels, Carpet Spaniels, and Little Cocking Spaniels – the latter for their hunting virtues. They have both the cuddling nature and the sporting abilities that make them extremely adaptable.

Rest assured, Cavaliers waste no time wrapping their human companions around their little paws. So, don't bother covering your best furniture or coveting your place in bed, because you'll spend your life gladly spoiling and catering obediently to your Cavalier fur baby, or babies, as the case may be. This saying fits the breed to a tee, "Most dogs have owners, but Cavaliers have staff." Nonetheless, being indentured to a Cavalier is a delightful labor of love.

This book is dedicated to the loving Cavalier owners around the world who rescue, adopt, breed, groom, show, photograph, paint, and pretty much dedicate their lives to these sweet little pets. The following Facebook post from a friend about losing her Cavalier companion typifies just what these dogs mean to their families.

> *Our sweet Chloe passed suddenly this past Tuesday ... There is absolutely no way to describe our years with her. She was our family's world. She snuggled, hiked, traveled, helped me recover after foot surgery, loved her backyard, loved chicken, and she most of all loved us. Our hearts are broken.*
>
> *- S.B., USA*

And here's another recent Facebook post from a Cavalier owner.

> *On a very wet day here in London, I've just been sitting reading with all my dogs snuggled up around me. Many of us who show are proud when we achieve big wins in the show ring, but at the end of the day it's their companionship as pets that really highlights the joy of owning dogs. They have infiltrated the very fabric of our lives. They are loyal and trusted friends, quick to forgive and eager to please. They do not judge us; all they want is food, time with us and affection. Their empathy with human emotions has certainly created a unique canine/human bond, which is a thing to treasure.*
>
> *- D.H, England*

I found the same devotion among the many people who enthusiastically shared their photos and stories for this book. These are real stories and mostly amateur photos taken by Cavalier owners. Whereas the quality of the photographs may not be picture-book perfect, in my opinion, their authenticity makes up for any shortcomings. Both the stories and photos reveal just how much these dogs are adored by their humans and how much fun and enjoyment they bring to people's lives. In fact, quite a few of my Facebook friends post photos of their Cavalier fur babies every single day, just as they would a beloved child.

This book is also written for those of you who'd love to have a Cavalier, but must wait for personal reasons. At least for now, you can enjoy looking at the photos and dreaming about the day when you can finally have your Cavalier. Hopefully the last chapter, featuring resources to learn more about the breed and locate a reputable breeder, will help you find the perfect pet. Surely, they may keep you from making the mistake we did with our first Cavalier, Rivermead Callista Berkeley Girl "Callie," who supposedly came from a good breeder in Saskatchewan, Canada.

I found the breeder on the internet and had many phone and email conversations with her prior to buying Callie. I asked specifically for a health-tested dog on the small side, so we could take her on the airplane with us when we traveled. The breeder assured me that Callie came from the best Irish lines free of heart disease and that her parents and grandparents were tested for any genetic defects.

Furthermore, she assured me that Callie would be small, as the runt of the litter. Well, to make a very long and painful story short, Callie is 30% larger than the breed standard; she went deaf before two years old; she has spinal arthritis, severe Mitral Valve Disease, ruptured tendons in her back legs (necessitating remaking her back legs at seven years old), dry eye, and possibly syringomyelia; and had a cerebral stroke at seven years old.

The fact is, I never saw the breeder's health tests! I was naïve and simply believed what the breeder said. After all, she had photos online of her showing her dogs and was a member of the Canadian Kennel Club. All her cute photos and affirmations convinced me I was getting a good dog. Looking on the bright side of things, I guess if I hadn't been cheated out of a healthy dog, I wouldn't have written this book. For Callie's valiant and loving spirit—in spite of her health issues—has engendered in me a love of the Breed. Consequently, I feel compelled to share this love with the world. Additionally, I want to help people find a healthy, pet Cavalier that can bless their lives as Callie has blessed ours.

I also dedicate *Cavaliers and Friends* to the veterinarians, geneticists, and reputable breeders worldwide working tirelessly to free Cavaliers from debilitating diseases. Cavaliers are not unique in this respect, as most highly bred, pedigreed breeds have their own health weaknesses. For that matter, Cavaliers are not even on the Kennel Club's list of the top at-risk breeds. Through conformation showing, selective breeding, and strenuous health-testing, reputable breeders of all pedigreed dogs are striving to counter their breed's deficiencies.

In the research I've done to compile this book, I've been particularly impressed by the reputable breeders of Cavaliers I've come to know. They love their dogs as pets first. Their breeding dogs live in their homes and experience a comfortable, loving family life. The breeders grieve as we do when they lose one of their dogs, and they celebrate the birth of a litter as if it was their own babies. Puppies from these kinds of breeders are well-socialized and cared for, unlike the pitiful offspring of callous backyard breeders and cruel puppy mills.

To enjoy the companionship of the healthiest, best-adjusted pet you can find, I urge anyone looking for a CKCS to seek out an experienced breeder who gives you written evidence of two generations of health testing for heart, eyes, and patella and a DNA test for genetic diseases along with your puppy's pedigree. There is more on the health-testing protocol in the last chapter of this book. If the breeder has a reputation for showing and socializing superior dogs, all the better. Lastly, most reputable breeders do not breed their dogs before the age of two-and-a-half to be sure they're free of genetic defects. Therefore, also check the age of your prospective puppy's sire and dam.

A wonderful alternative to purchasing a puppy from a breeder is to rescue a Cavalier (although rescues may have special needs). We have devoted a chapter to Cavalier rescues, and in CKCS Resources, you'll find a list of rescue organizations and breed information. Moreover, by purchasing this book you've unwittingly made a financial contribution to Cavalier rescue because I'm donating half of the proceeds to this worthwhile endeavor.

We feel fortunate to have Callie still with us at eight and a half; each day with her is like a celebration. She's the undisputable Alpha of the household and pretty much takes care of herself, demanding very little of us other than affection and food. I communicate with her through sign language and massage, and she has her way of grunting as if to talk. She seems to be able to read my mind and certainly knows well ahead of time if we're going out or going to travel. She continues to be the sweetest and bravest creature we know. From the start, she's wanted only to be our loving companion and enjoy copious affection, tasty indulgences, and interesting adventures along the way. She's been a perfect traveler living between three countries not to mention frequent visits to family in the States and lots of pleasure travel. In fact, Callie's been to 15 countries with us, either snoring contentedly under airplane seats (thanks to her Emotional Support Animal status) or riding proudly in her raised car seat. What's more, I believe Callie has been in more restaurants than most *gourmands!*

Callie is a Superstar, but all Cavalier owners think that about their dogs! Everywhere our "stuffed animal" with the big brown eyes goes, she brings smiles to people's faces. Thanks to her, we've made some incredible lifelong friends in our travels, and she's probably the reason we settled in France, with its dog-friendly attitude.

When Callie is riding in the stroller we use in crowded markets and for long walks, the paparazzi (i.e., anyone with a mobile phone) is drawn to her like a magnet. Hence, Callie may also be the most photographed dog in the world. She's certainly one of the most adored. Kids can't resist her. And nowadays, when all our dogs are sitting in the window sill in France, people stop their cars to take pictures and neighbors come by daily to pet and talk to them.

Cavaliers may very well be the most social dogs in the world. They love everyone and also enjoy all the human attention they can get. Wherever you are, there they are, even following you to the bathroom. Just by being their affectionate comical, selves, they naturally bring joy and richness to people's lives. They are full of empathy (or perhaps ESP) for your moods and needs, and should you ever be sick, they won't leave your side. What more can you ask of your best friend?

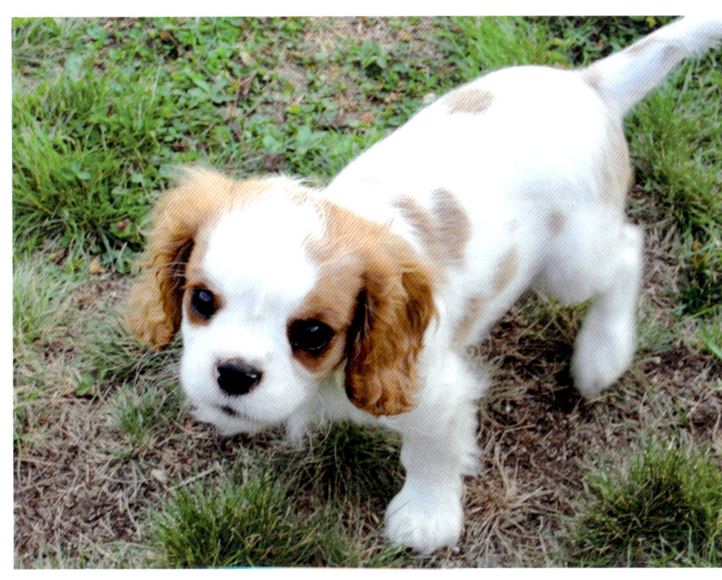

At nine weeks old when Callie arrived at our home in Canada.

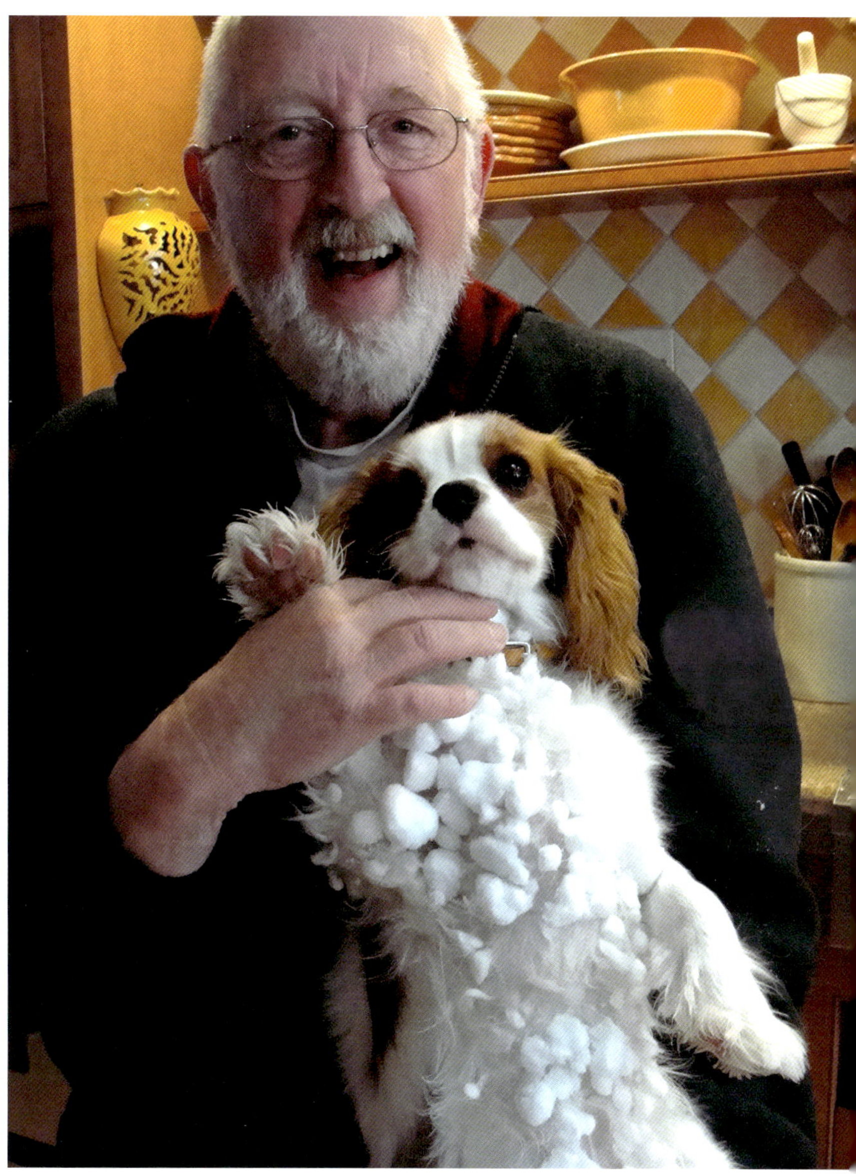

Daddy Ken's girl...from day one and for always.

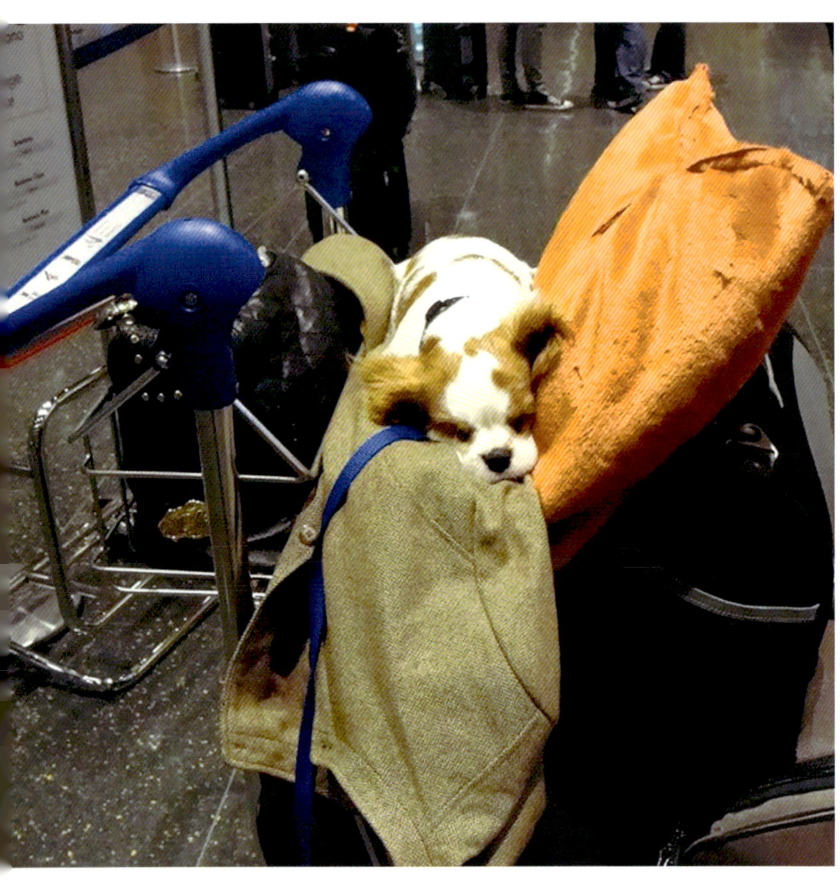

En route from Canada to our home in France at four months.

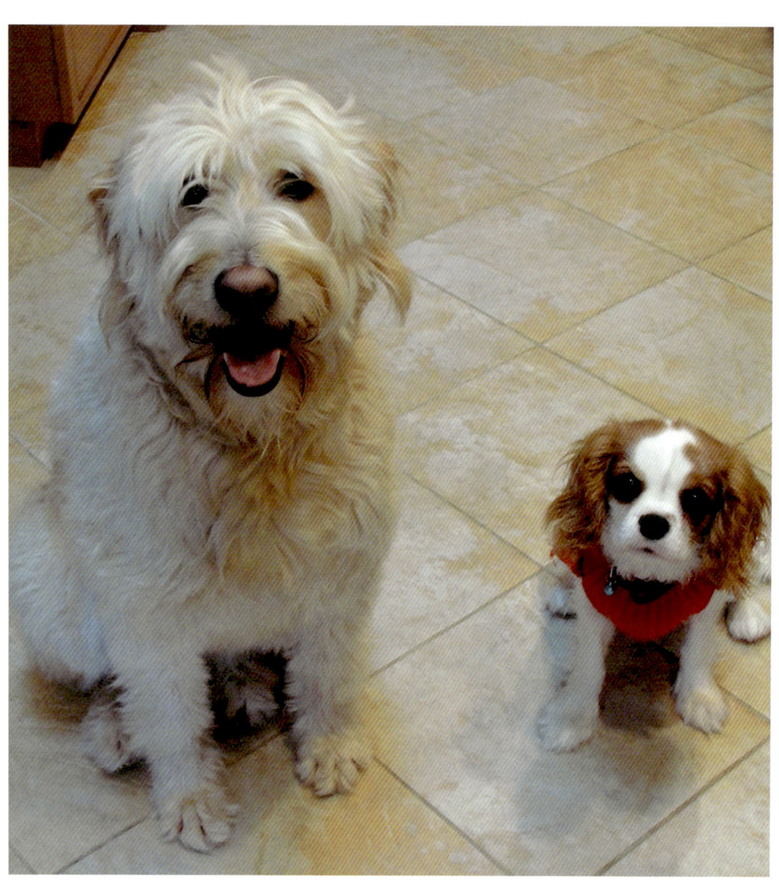

Daily visits in Canada from our neighbor's Goldendoodle, Bella, Callie's Best Friend Forever (BFF)

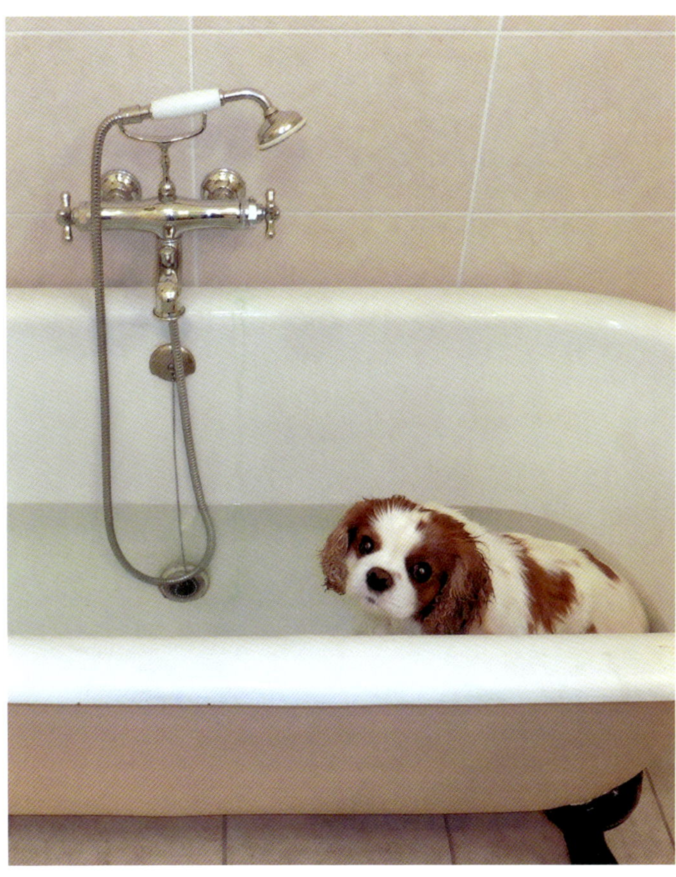

Looking a bit lonely at two in her clawfoot tub in France.

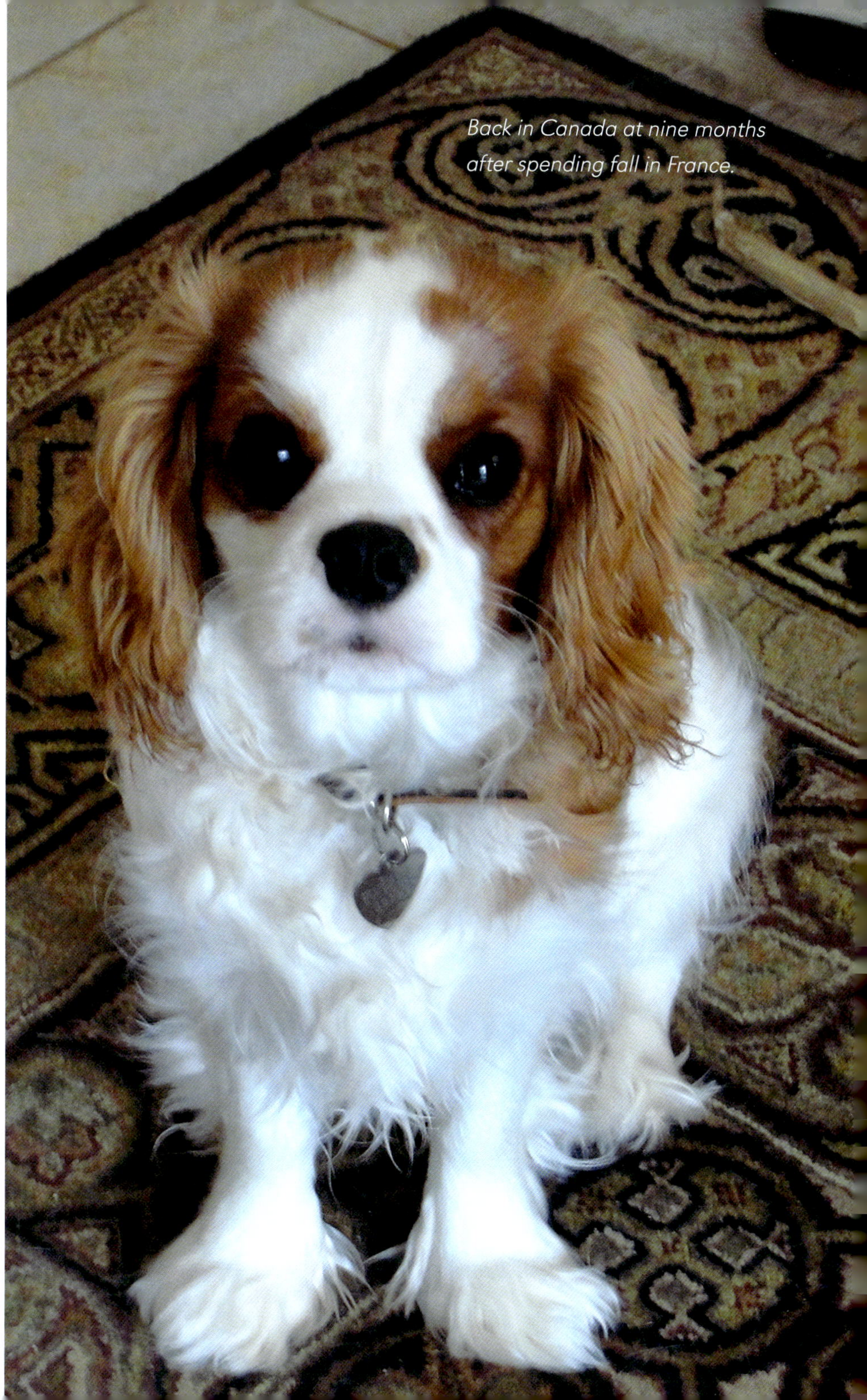

Back in Canada at nine months after spending fall in France.

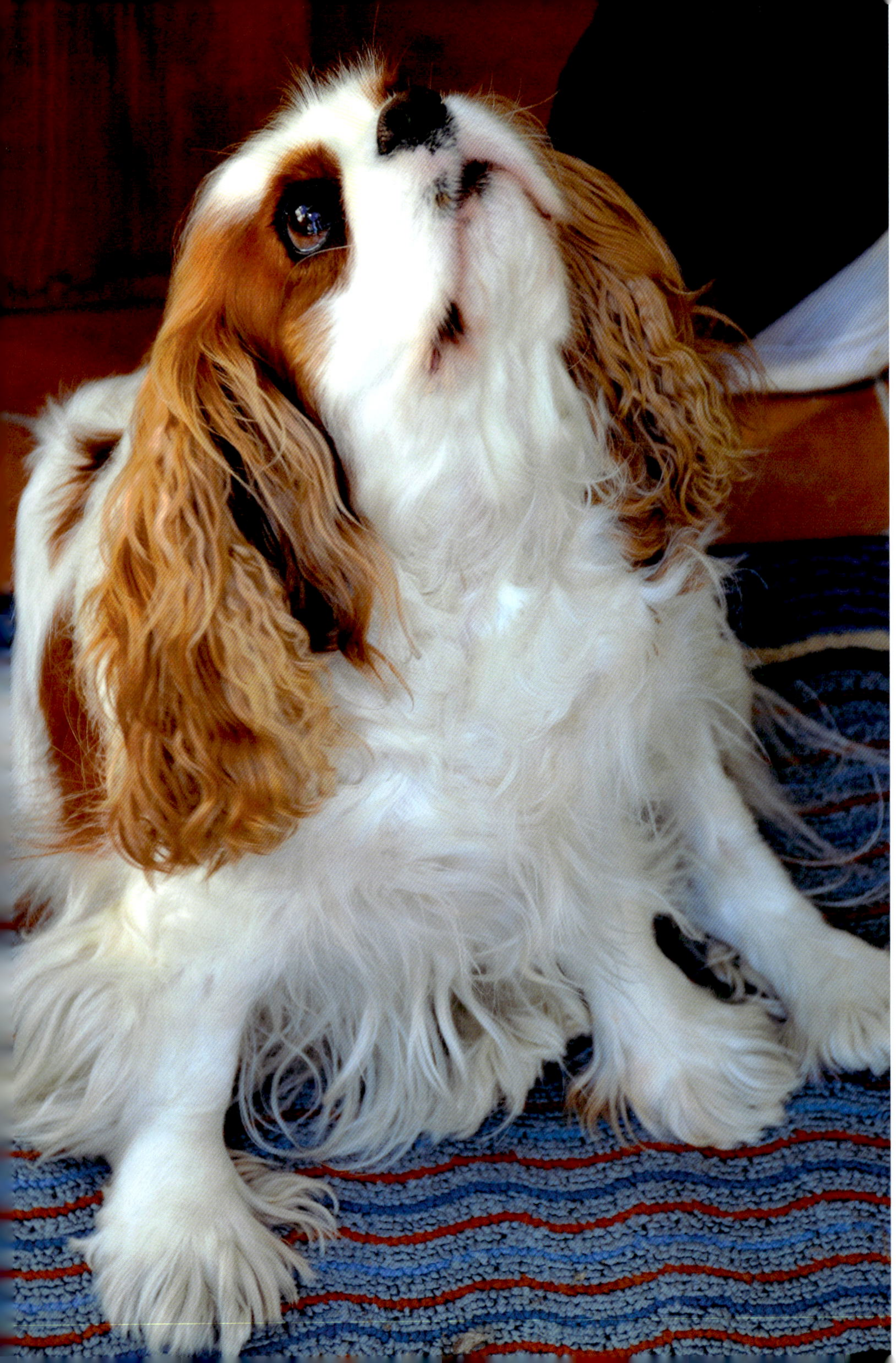

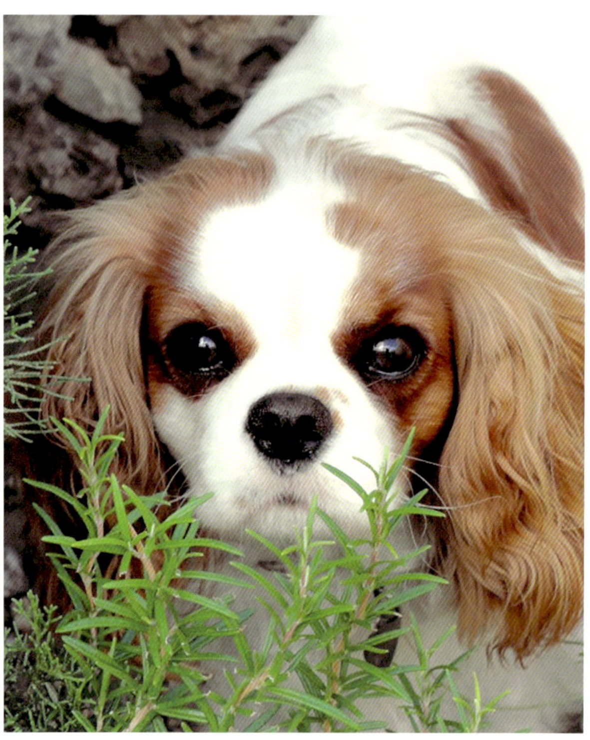

At four, after spending more time in France and developing a taste for French cuisine.

Hard to resist those pleading eyes.

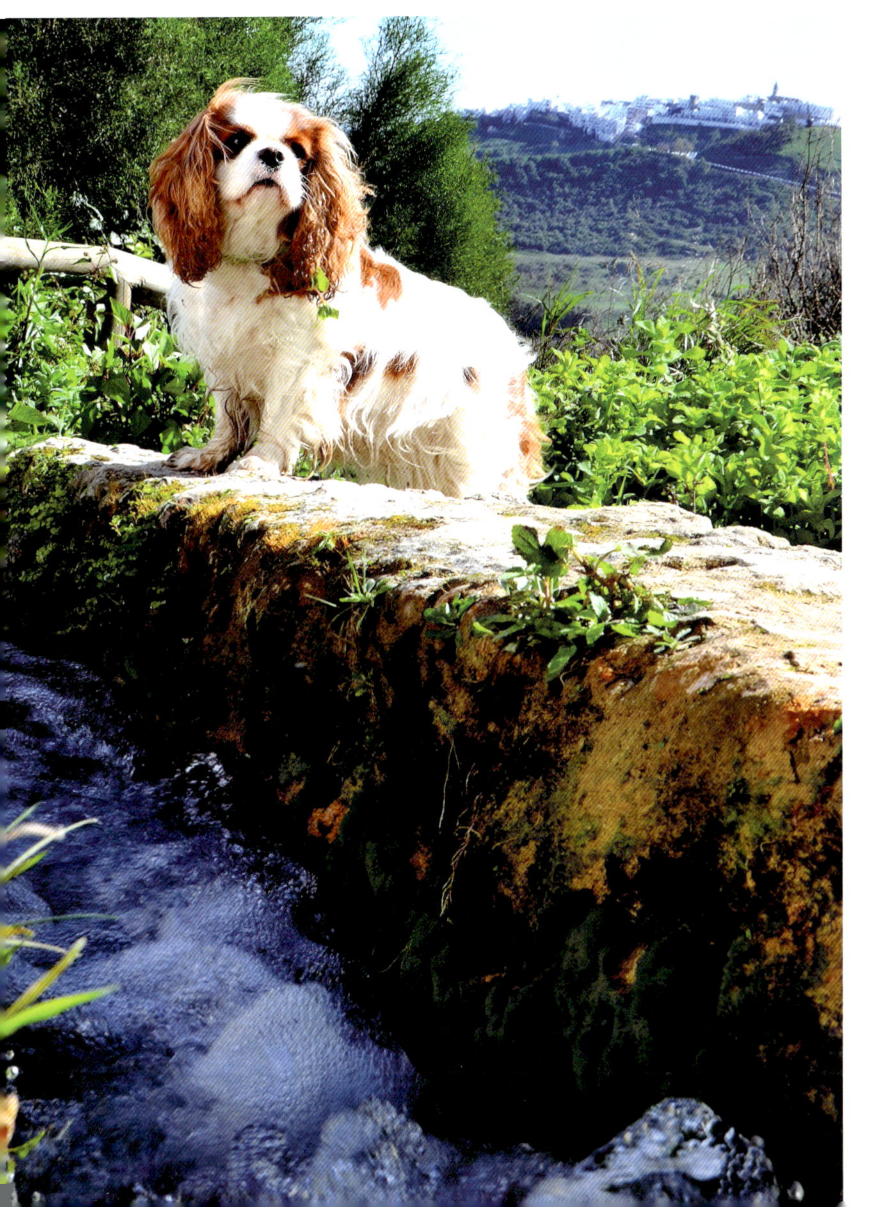

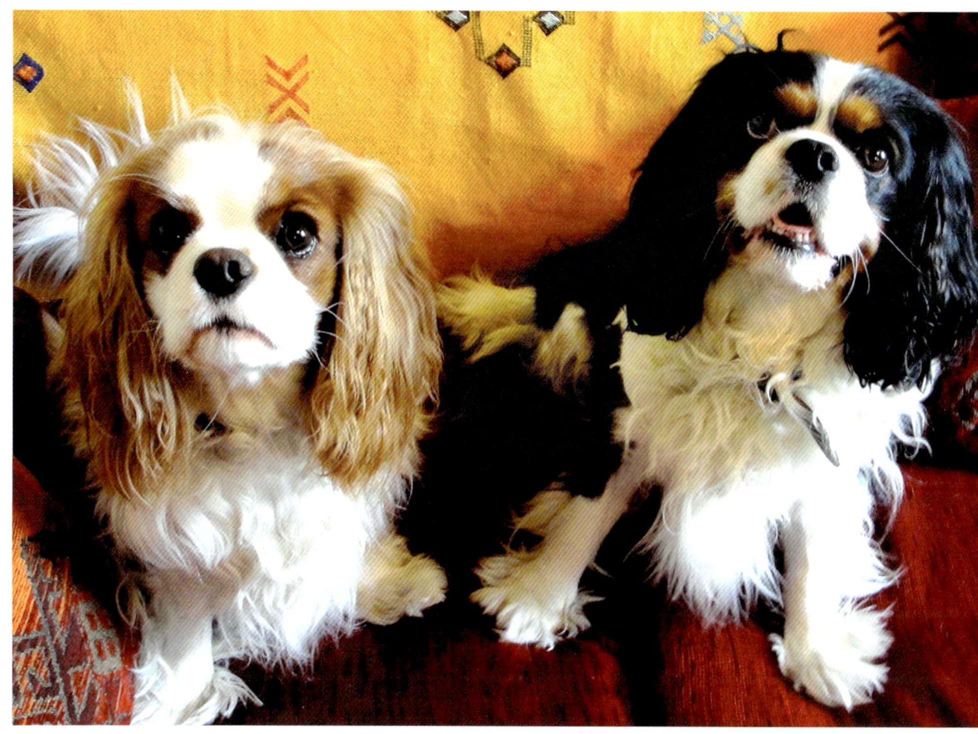

With her French beau, Charlie (but no wedding due to her genetic issues).

At five, walking on the Roman aqueduct near our pueblo blanco.

Photo credit: Cameron Green, New Jersey, USA

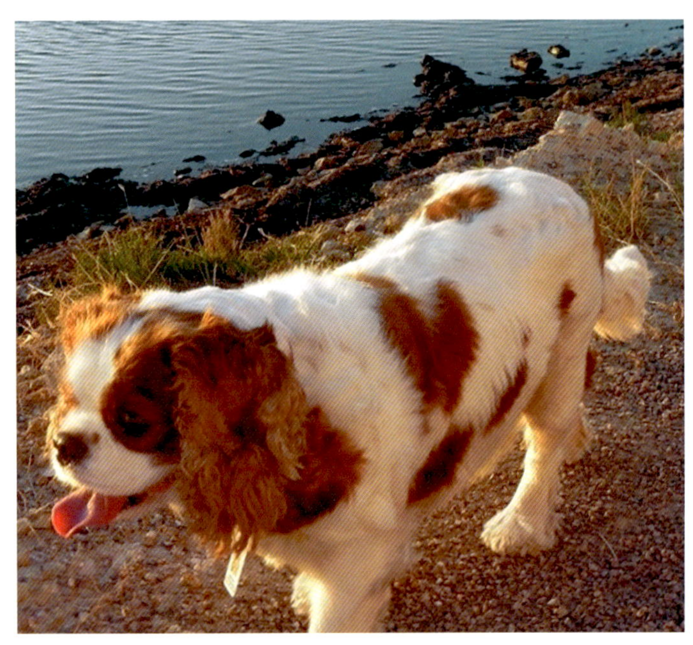

At six and super-sized at 13 kilos (30 lbs.) exploring a Mediterranean l'etang (marsh).

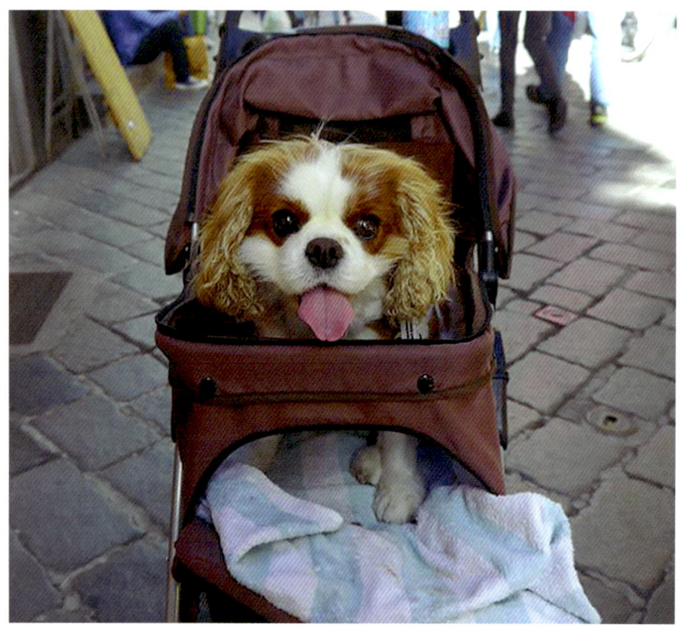

After major surgery on her back legs at seven, appreciating her stroller on vacation in Italy.

And then I got the breeder's bug! I'd so wanted to breed a litter from Callie, but with her early on-set deafness and ensuing health problems, that dream was impossible. So along came Moonbeam and Dolly, whom I found from a European breeder.

We were apprehensive about how Callie would accept the two little ones after being our only fur kid for seven-and-a-half years. Callie had started sleeping all the time and was not at all interested in life. I thought the young dogs might peak her interest. After about a month of transition, she accepted them beautifully, although she still hordes the chewies. Nevertheless, she loves to go for walks and stays around them all of the time. In turn, they absolutely adore her and recognize her status as Alpha "Auntie." Strangely enough, Callie has the same birthday as Moonbeam, and personality-wise, the two of them are like two peas in a pod. Dolly, however, acts like a mellow princess, affectionate to a fault, but she knows her place as lowest in the pecking order.

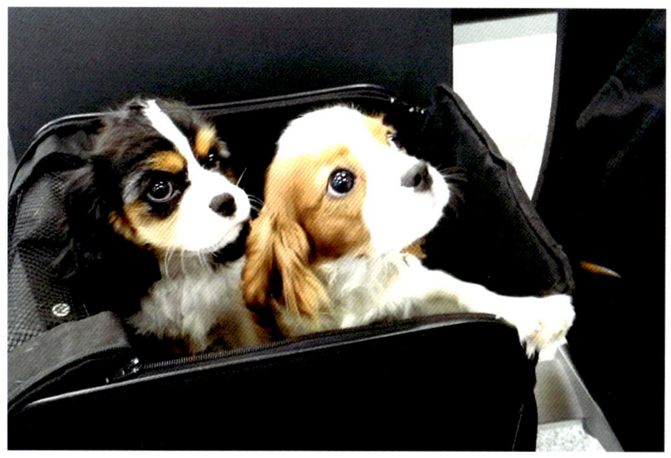

Hand-delivered to Barcelona, Spain, Dolly, and Moonbeam, the author's new fur babies.

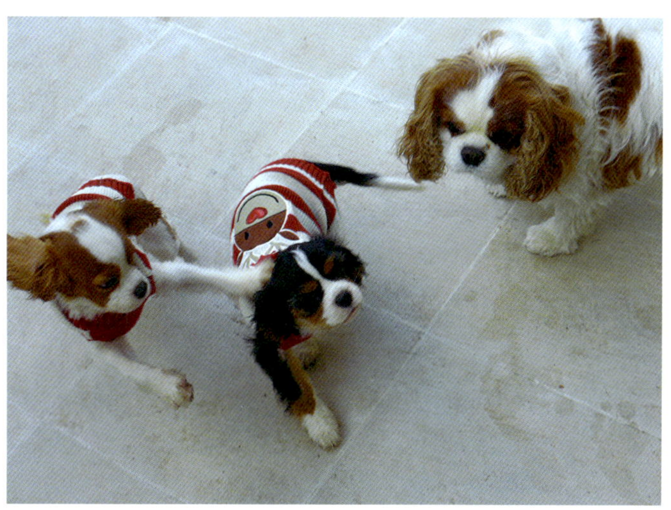

Callie keeping an eye on the new kids.

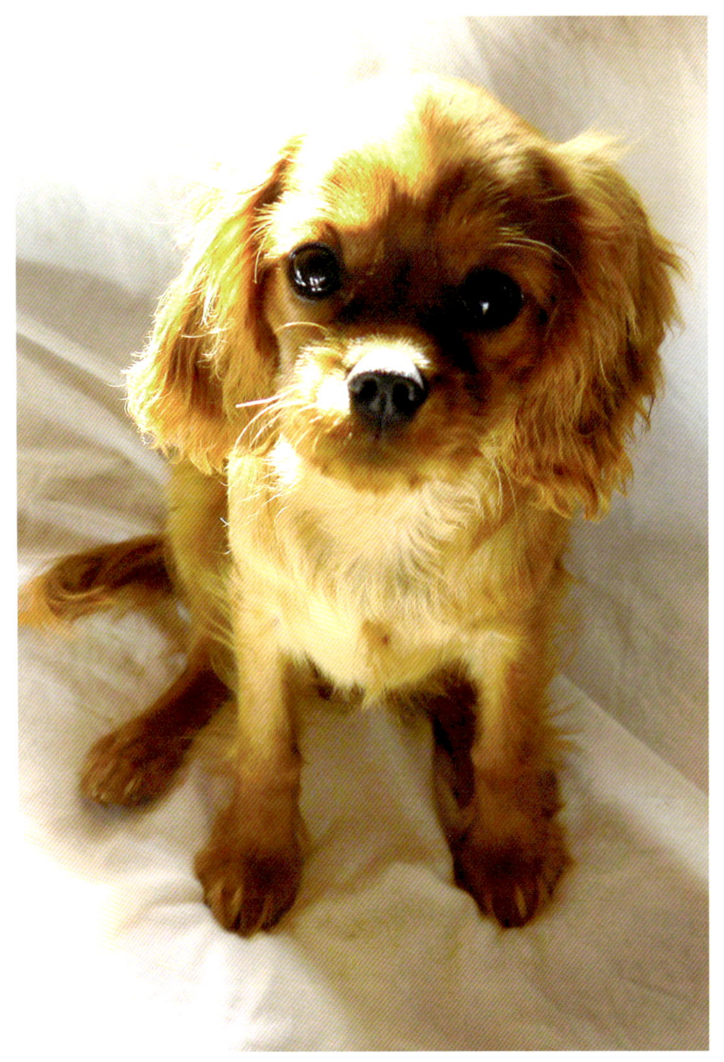

A year later we got Honey Bea Jones. At just six months, we call her "Code Red" as she is the nurse of the family, licking all of us *ad nauseum* and running around full of *esprit de joie*. I love her playfulness, beautiful auburn color, and pretty face. Plus, having an active puppy around is amusing for the whole family. I just wish I hadn't decorated our home in France with white Berber carpets! But to my defense, when we purchased them in Morocco a year ago, I had no idea we would amass a family of four fur-kids.

Honey Bea Jones from Germany.
Her pedigree name is "Funny Fresh."

These three new Cavaliers will form the foundation of Sweet Love Cavaliers when I begin the breeding phase once they're two-and-a-half and fully health-tested. My husband acquiesced to us having a young family of Cavaliers for my final career. Over the last year, I've learned so much about the Breed. It's truly a pleasure to be involved with multiple Cavaliers and to have the opportunity to allow them to produce a few healthy litters.

As I mentioned, Callie has come alive because of her new brother and sisters. She still hoards the bones, but she clearly enjoys their company. Getting the young'uns has been good for all of us—more family, more love. We laugh all the time at the dogs' antics and having them fills our nest with contentment.

When we travel, we have to arrange for responsible babysitters, but my Irish friend Mary is glad to help. Frankly, with all these love sponges as company, I prefer to stay at home if they can't go. However, we still have plans to vacation by car with our precious fur family in Europe.

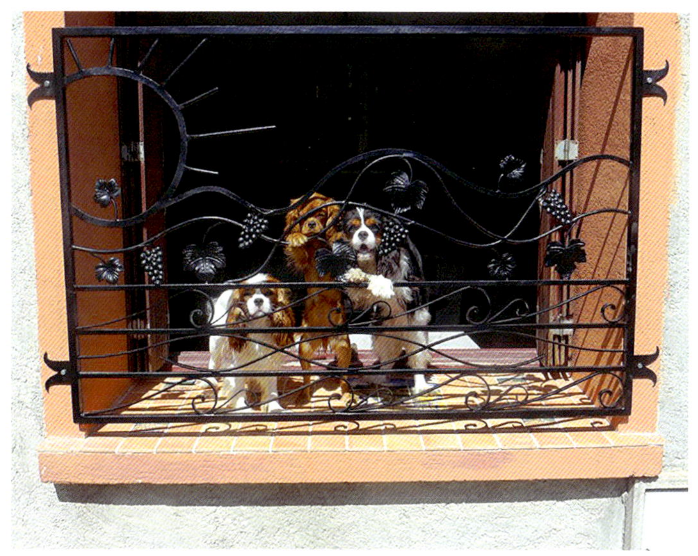

Our three new loves, Moonbeam, Honey Bea Jones, and Dolly greeting the villagers.

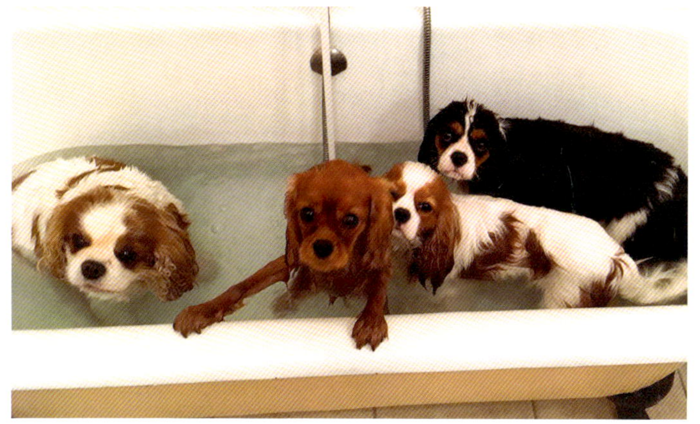

One big happy family now (no more lonely Callie).

Part of breeding is showing your dogs to gain affirmation from a variety of judges that they're ideal prototypes meeting breed standards. Thinking back, barely a year ago, I was a complete novice to dog showing and all the intricacies of titles, grooming and training that are a part of it. Of course, as a dog lover I'd always watched Westminster and Crufts on TV, but I'd never even attended a professional show. The whole idea of professional showing was pretty scary at first.

Callie had participated in fun community dog shows to raise money for animal shelters in Canada, but professional shows are a whole world apart...serious, competitive, and yet a super way to meet others devoted to Cavaliers and learn about the Breed. So, through self-study and help from breeders, I've started showing a bit, and to my great surprise, my new dogs have won Best of Breed in an international and national dog show in Spain and France (in the puppy and young dog divisions). I have to say, showing for amateurs like me is really a lot of fun, as long as you keep everything in perspective and do it for your and your dogs' enjoyment. So far, my pups seem to love the excitement of getting groomed, seeing other dogs, and showing off a bit. Callie enjoys the shows too, as a spectator and fan club director for the pups. What's equally amazing to me is that Moonbeam and Dolly have been so easy to train. Showing seems to be in their blood.

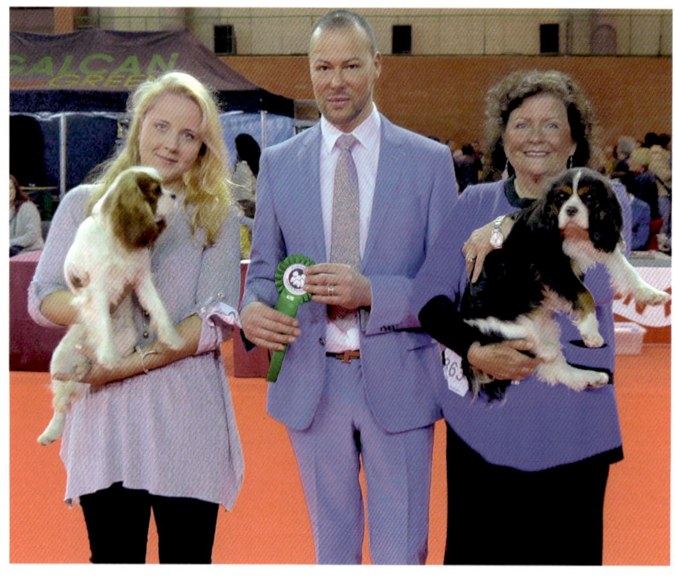

Urska Longar, grooming and handling expert from Slovenia, showed me the ropes at the international dog show in Seville, where Moonbeam and Dolly both won their puppy classes and Moonbeam was awarded Best of Breed Cavalier Puppy. Thanks for getting me off on the right foot, Urska. Thank you especially to Seville Show Cavalier Judge Laurent (Luxembourg) for recognizing my dogs.

Now you know the story of why Cavaliers have become my passion, just like a certain King's and millions of Cavalier owners around the world. It's been an incredible journey thus far and something I never anticipated when I first got cute little Callie, as a companion.

I hope you enjoy this multi-faceted portrait of the Breed as much as I enjoyed compiling it. If the pictures touch your heart, I encourage you to join our special club of Human Cavalier Companions, but only if you have the time, resources, and commitment to care for a lifelong pet.

Cavaliers, like all dogs, want above all to be with their owners; it's their instinctual job. If you decide to be a Cavalier companion, please find a reputable breeder or adopt a dog through a rescue organization. Rescue organizations do a beautiful job of finding, fostering, and helping new owners succeed with a rescue pet, all with trained volunteers. Additionally, plan on making your dog a central part of your life for the next decade and a half.

But rest assured, you'll treasure each and every day of pet companionship, for your Cavalier will return your love ten-fold and enrich your life in ways you never imagined.

Where does life go from here for me aside from breeding and writing? I hope to raise funds for rescuing Cavaliers and support the worldwide movement against puppy mills... although I'm sure the biggest challenge ahead will be not to keep all the puppies I breed!

Hugs from France!

Mary, Ken, Callie, Moonbeam, Dolly, and Honey Bea Jones (and hopefully more to come)

Disclaimer Errors and Erratum: With hundreds of photos, captions and permissions from photo owners, photographers and/or artists, this book has been a complicated, labor-intensive process to research and assemble. Working online with people from around the world and gleaning photographs primarily from Facebook has required a tremendous amount of sleuthing to create complete captions and secure permissions. I've made every effort to present factual, correct information, but dealing with many thousands of factoids is bound to result in errors. I apologize, in advance, if there are misspellings of names, incorrect locations, or errors in canine and/or people's names, dog titles, or mistakes of any nature. I request that you notify me by email (marycg1948@gmail.com) of any correction that need to be made. I'm also not responsible for incorrect information provided to me by the suppliers of photographs. This book would not exist now if I had taken the time to triple-check every fact, so I hope you will forgive any errors and help me make it right for subsequent editions.

All for Cavaliers, Mary Colburn-Green

Chapter 1- Precious Puppies

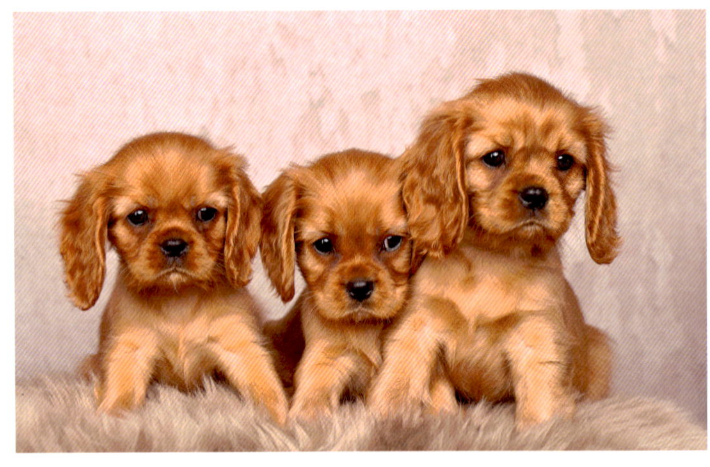

These Spark of Hope Ruby puppies are Conny Meiboom's special babies.

Photo credit: Conny Meiboom

Photography: Dr. Christian Bömke

While all puppies are cute, Cavalier puppies are exceptionally adorable. The pink-nosed and pink-pawed puppies are born in litters on average from one to seven puppies, although they can also have litters of 11 and 12. The puppies' eyes open at about two weeks, and at four weeks they're starting to interact with their littermates. The real fun starts at six weeks when they become quite mobile and start to wrestle and play.

Cavalier puppies love to kiss and snuggle, just like human babies. They especially like to be held and cuddled. They are generally quite the gourmets and will gladly tuck into your food. In fact, Cavaliers may be the best little beggars in all the world, with those heart-melting eyes and endearing personalities. Cavalier puppies are mischievous, playful and so precious to behold, as you'll see in the photos that follow. They are delightful, even when they do naughty things. It's difficult to get mad, because they're just babies after all.

It's amazing to watch Cavaliers mature and witness how beautiful they become as they get their luxurious coats and long "feathers." By two years old, they're decked out in their full regalia. So best get them used to grooming while they're little, because that's a part of owning this regal breed.

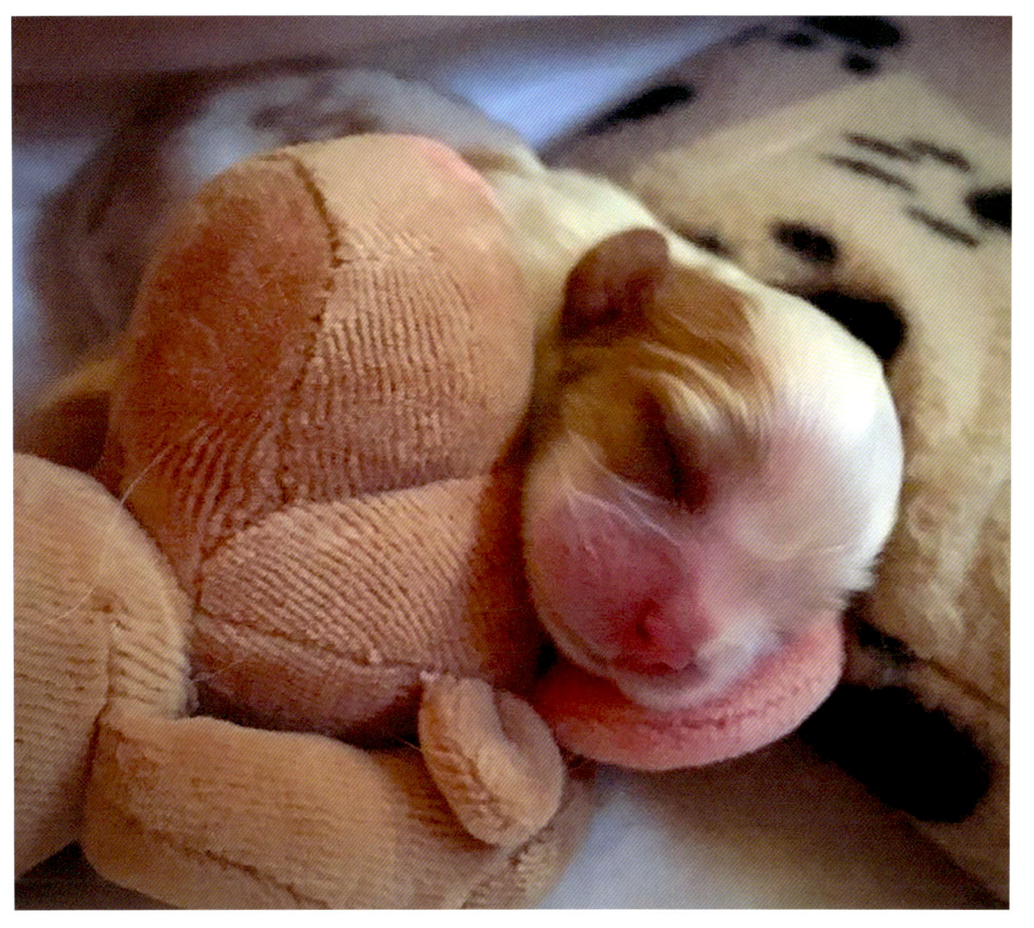

Hello, world! I'm Elswyth's Molly, all of four days old.

Photo credit: Michele Matheson, BC, Canada

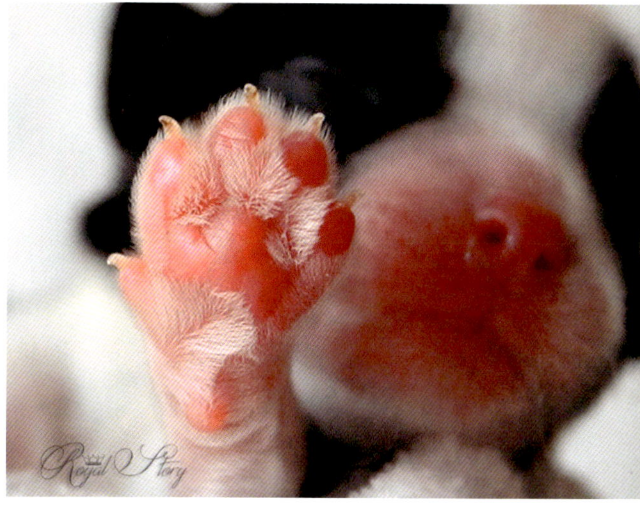

It's pink perfection from Royal Story Cavaliers.

Photo credit: Kasia Klein, Dublin, Ireland, UK

Photography: Kasia Klein

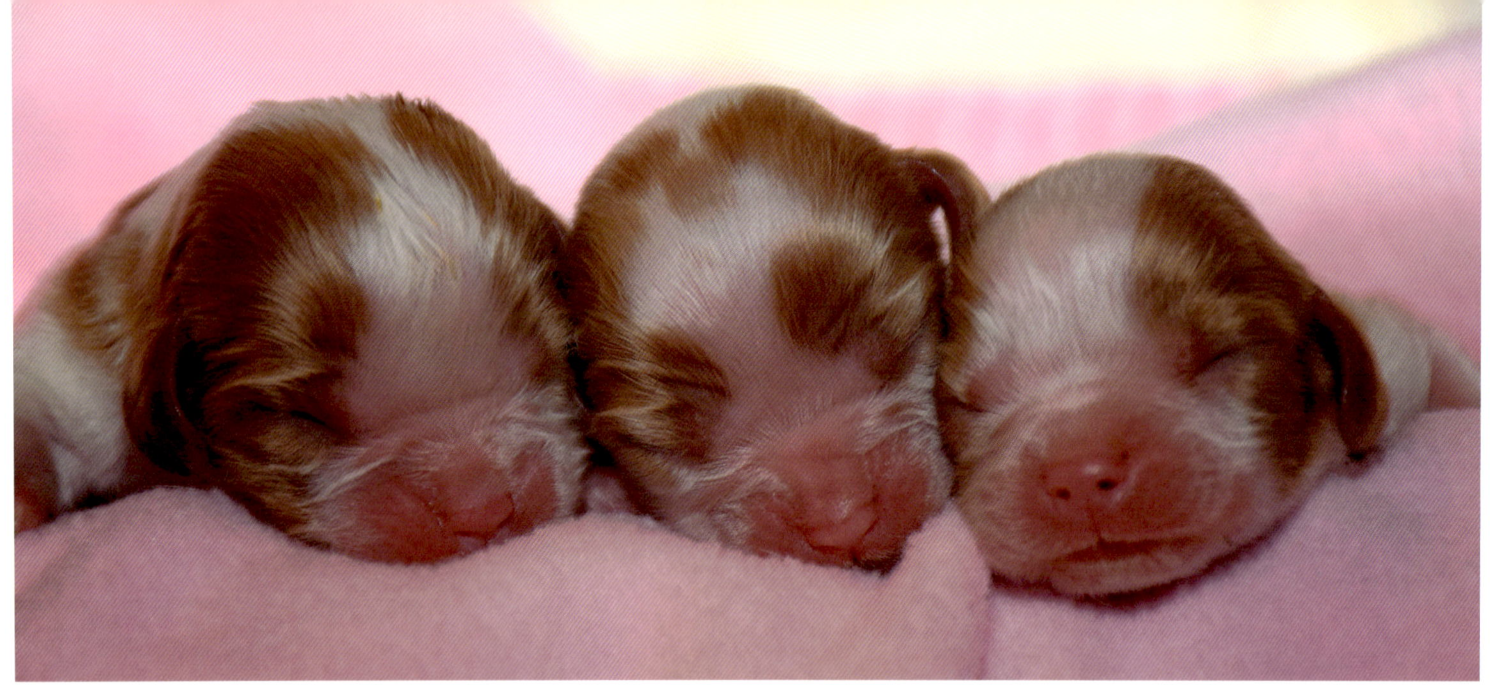

Meet newborn Blenheims, Nicky, Nayan, and Magic.

Photo credit: Stephanie Fernandes, Paris, France

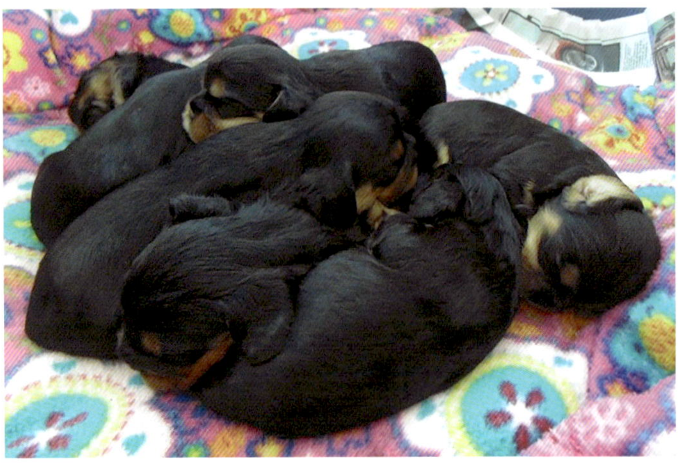

This Black and Tan litter is from Svena Whole Colour Cavaliers' (parents: Svena Moonlight Shadow x Svena Hocus Pocus).

Photo credit: Bridgette Evans, Wales, UK

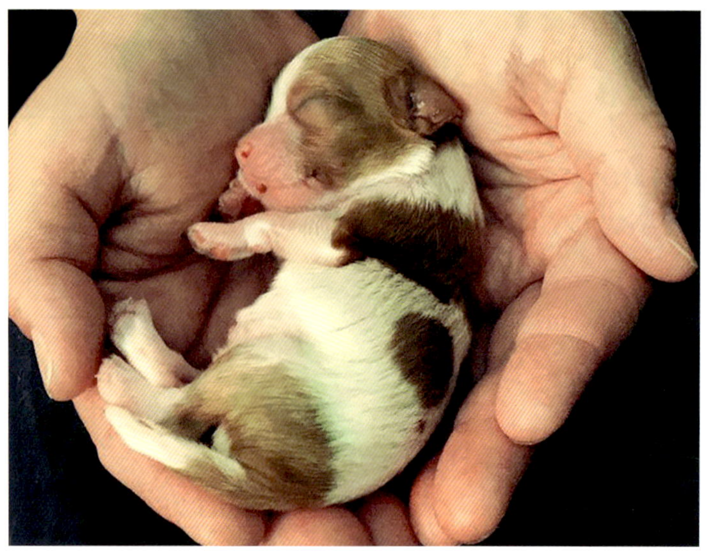

It's magic to hold a new life, so full of promise.

Photo credit: Lynwood Cavaliers, Linda Baird, Illinois, USA

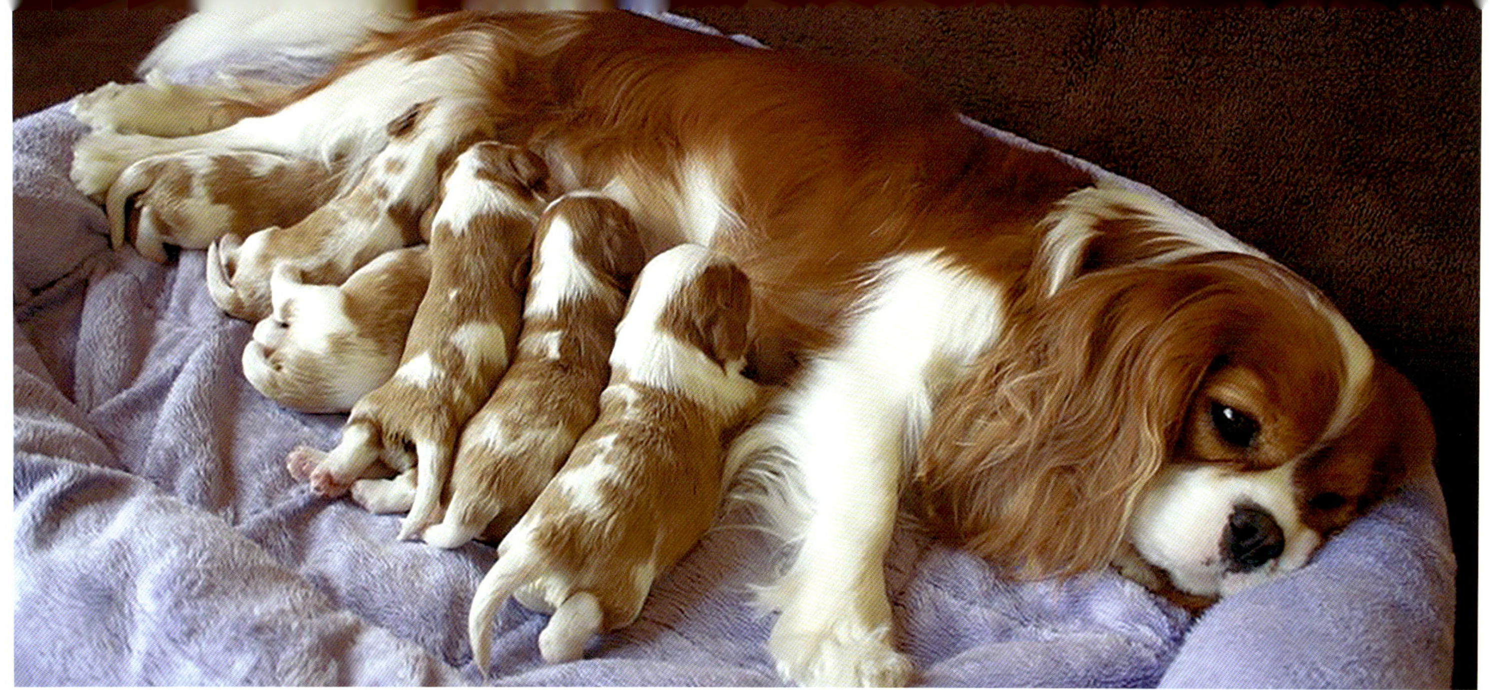

Home White Wings litter feed lustily.

Photo credit: Paola Martini, Savona, Italy

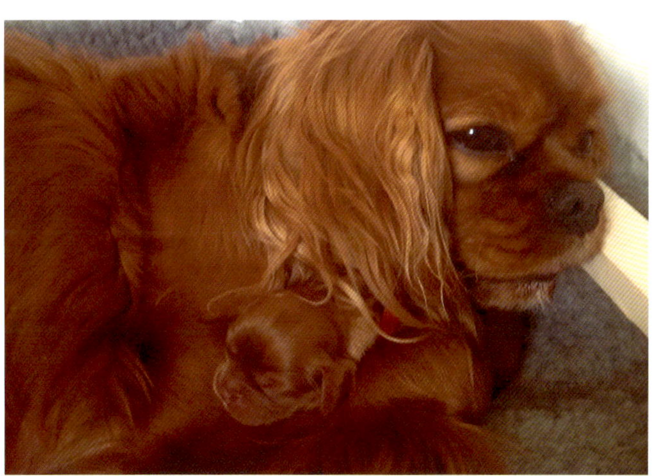

Mommy Tiley cuddles Teddy, her brand-new bundle of ruby joy.

Photo credit: Denise Blackie, Beaminster, UK

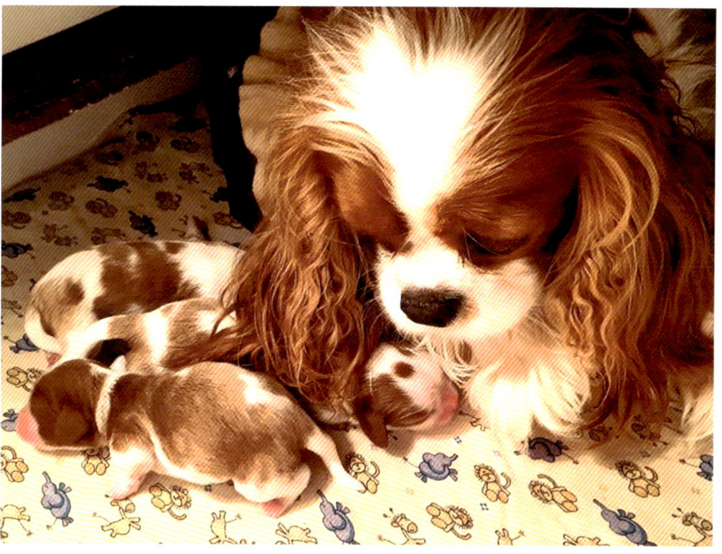

Mamma "Lola" Samba Gorska Fantazja is not letting her precious puppies out of her sight.

Photo credit: Malgorata "Meg" Mlynarska, Illinois, USA

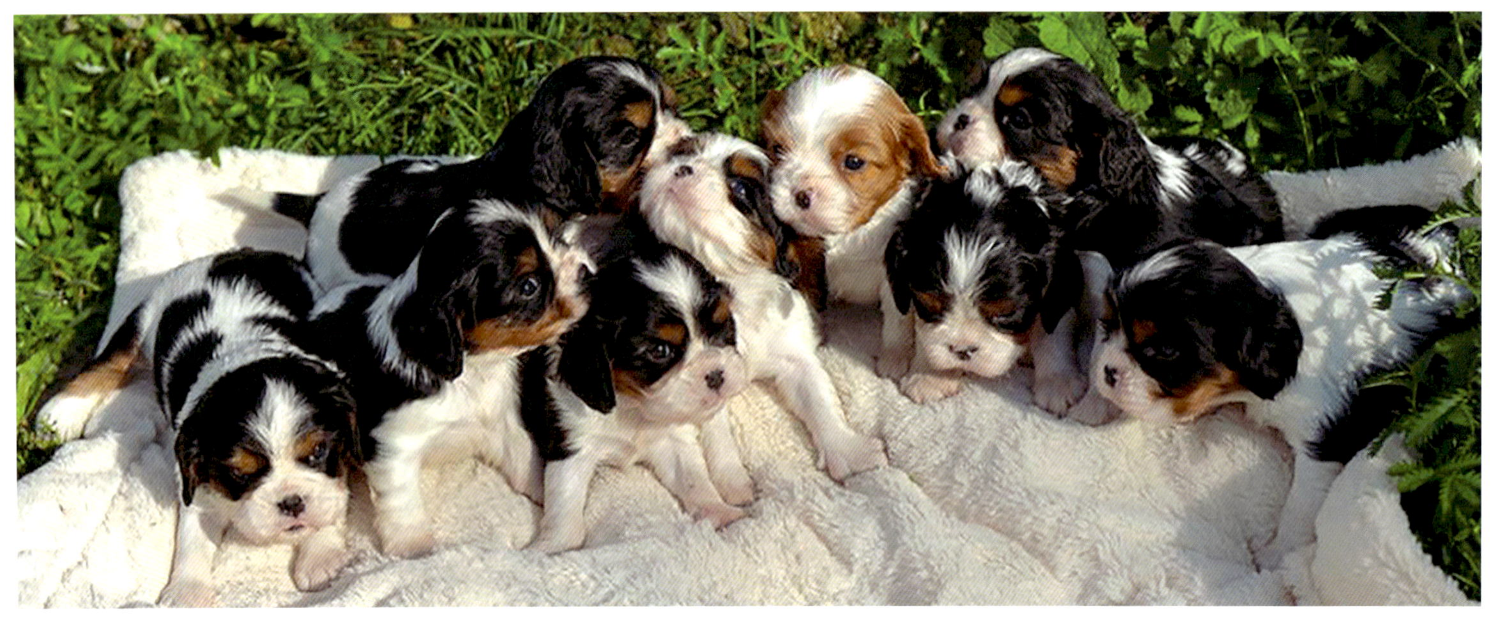

Nine beautiful puppies from Father Milbu Lordship and Mother Milbu Call Me Queen Victoria.

Photo credit: Milda Busa, Jelgava, Latvia; Photography: Gederts Buss

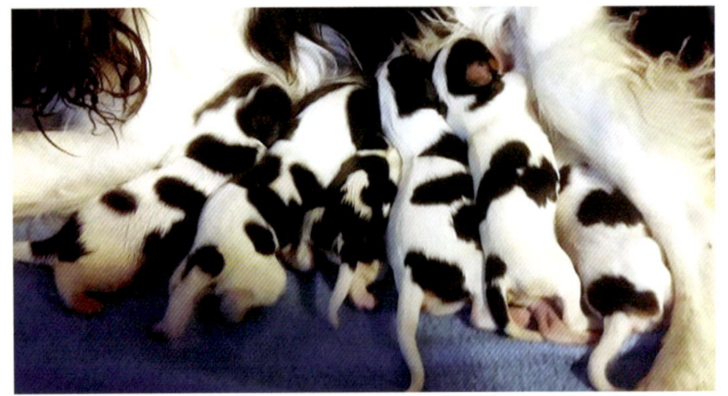

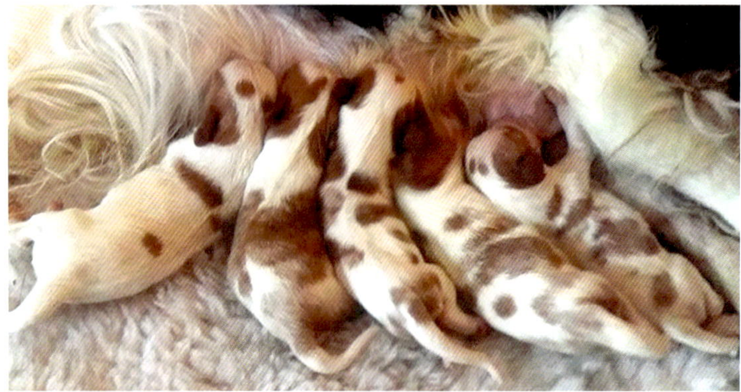

Bottom left and right: There are 11 puppies in this litter! All with beautiful broken colors.

Photo credit: Marielle Johansson Milljas, Bengtsfor, Vastra Gotalands, Sweden

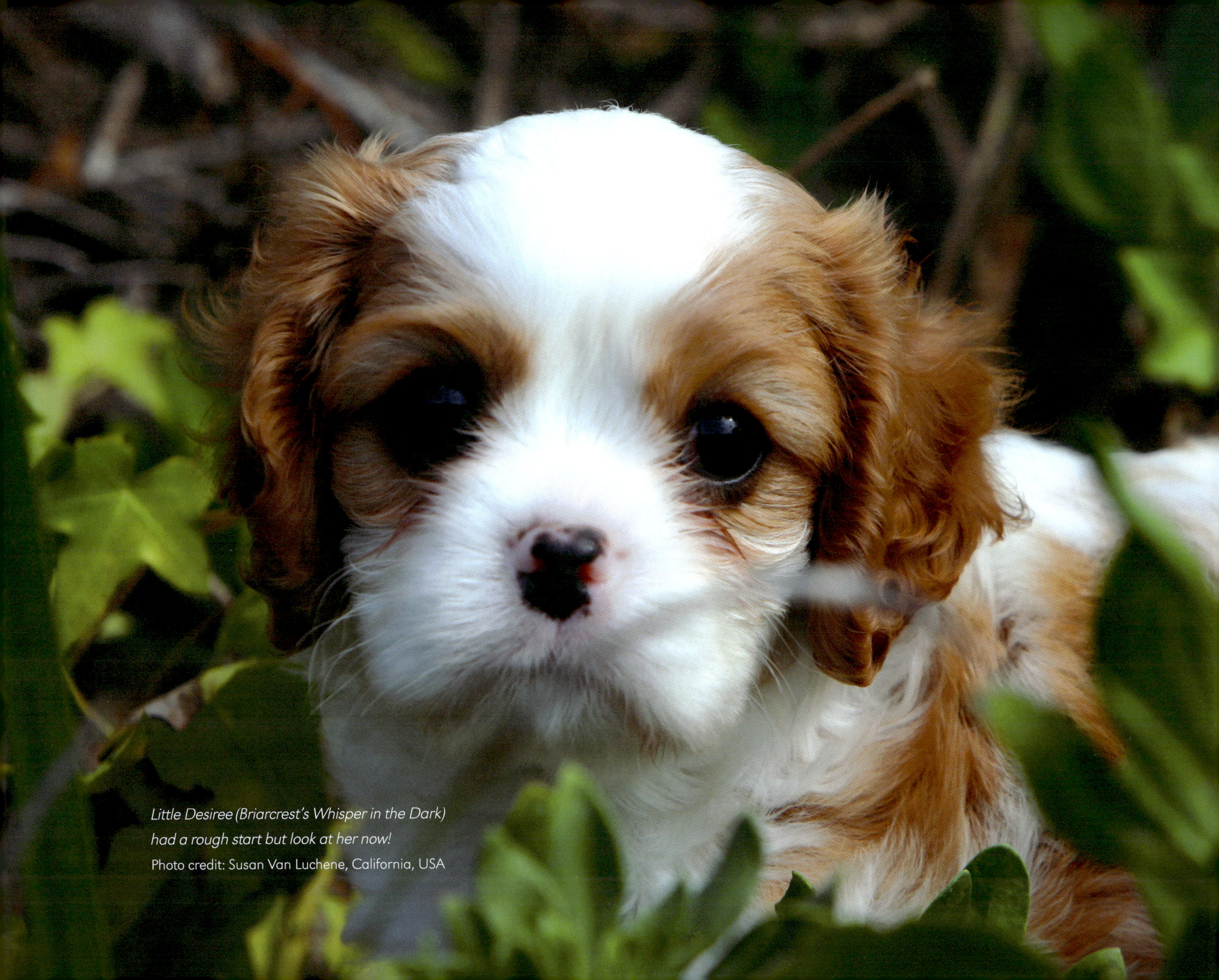

Little Desiree (Briarcrest's Whisper in the Dark) had a rough start but look at her now!
Photo credit: Susan Van Luchene, California, USA

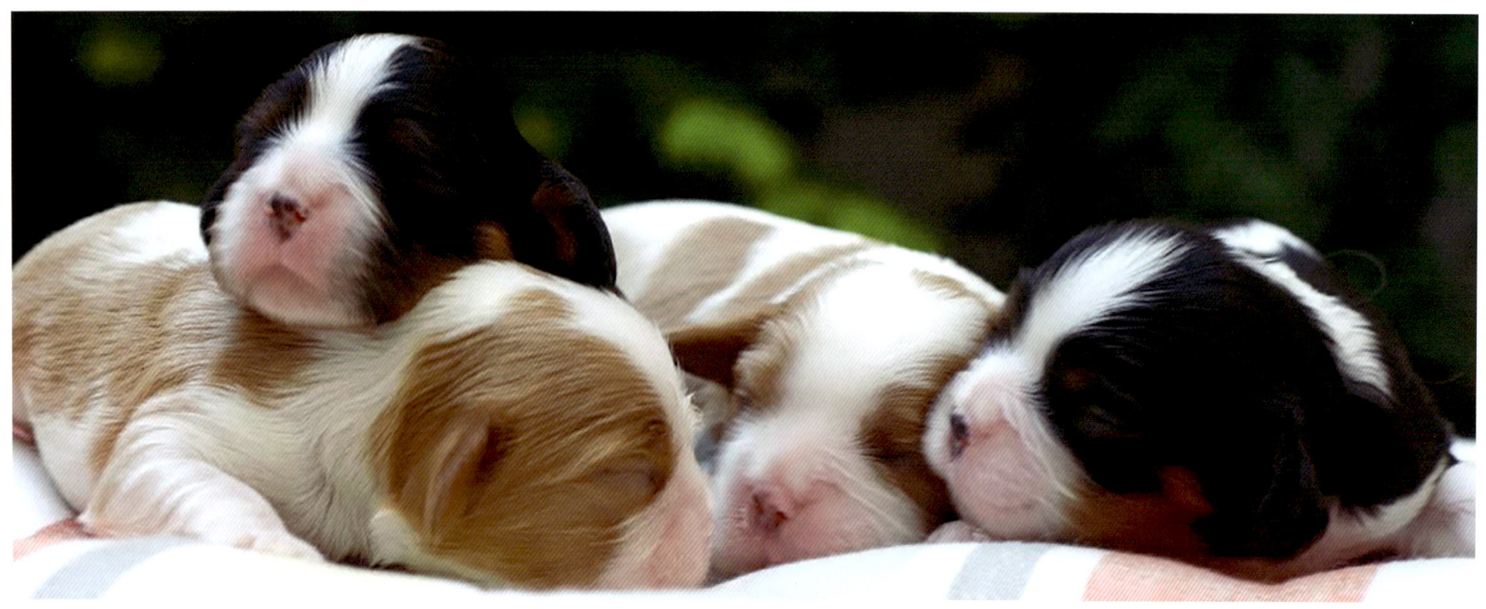

This litter is perfectly balanced with two Blenheims and two Tri-Colors.

Photo credit: Sofia Salazar Leite, Lisbon, Portugal

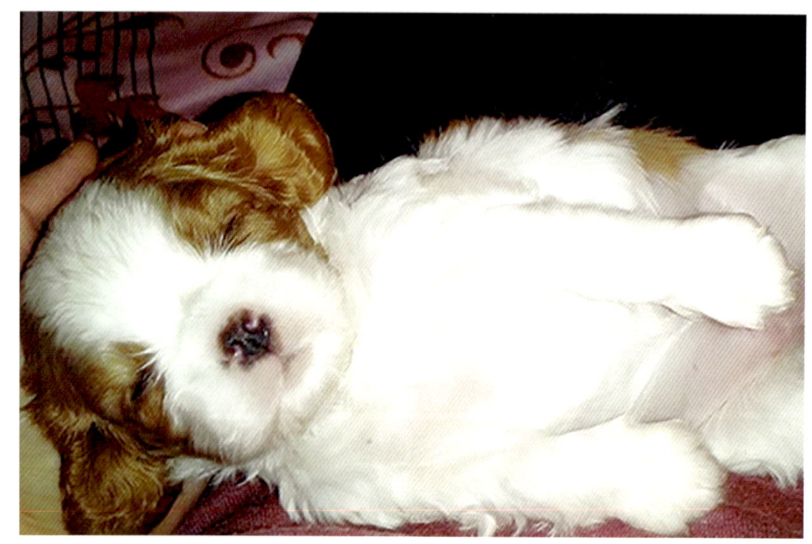

Puppies sleep a lot.

Photo credit: Beate Schages, Nordheim Westfallen, Germany

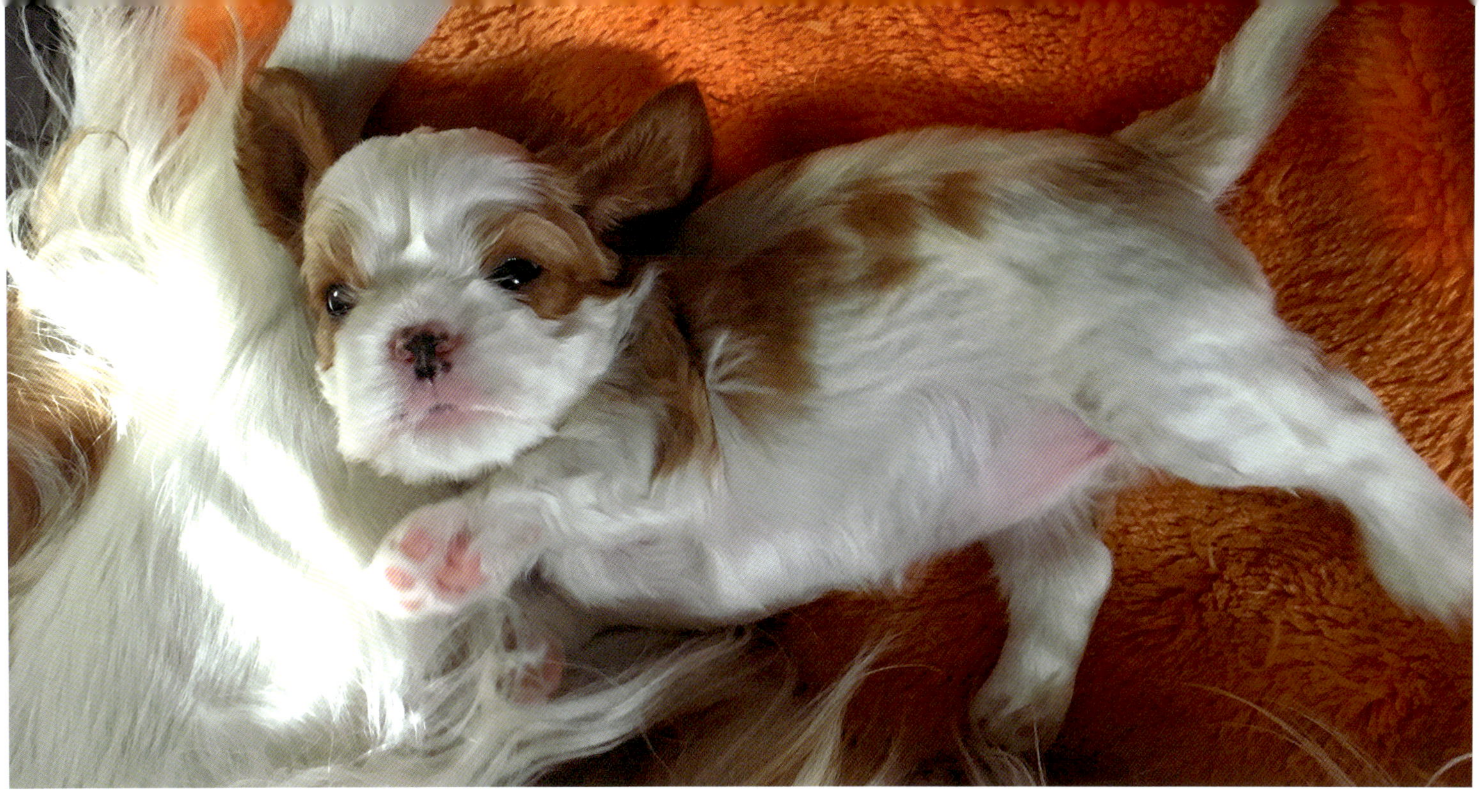

Molly's an only puppy who's sure to be spoiled by Mother Cwem.

Photo credit: Michelle Matheson, British Columbia, Canada

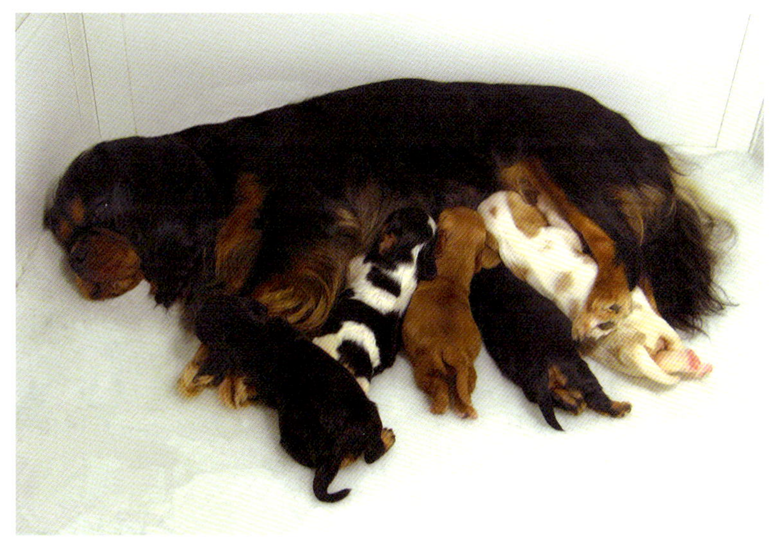

Telvara Cavalier Velvet's litter has every color of Cavalier.

Photo credit: Veronica Hull, London, UK

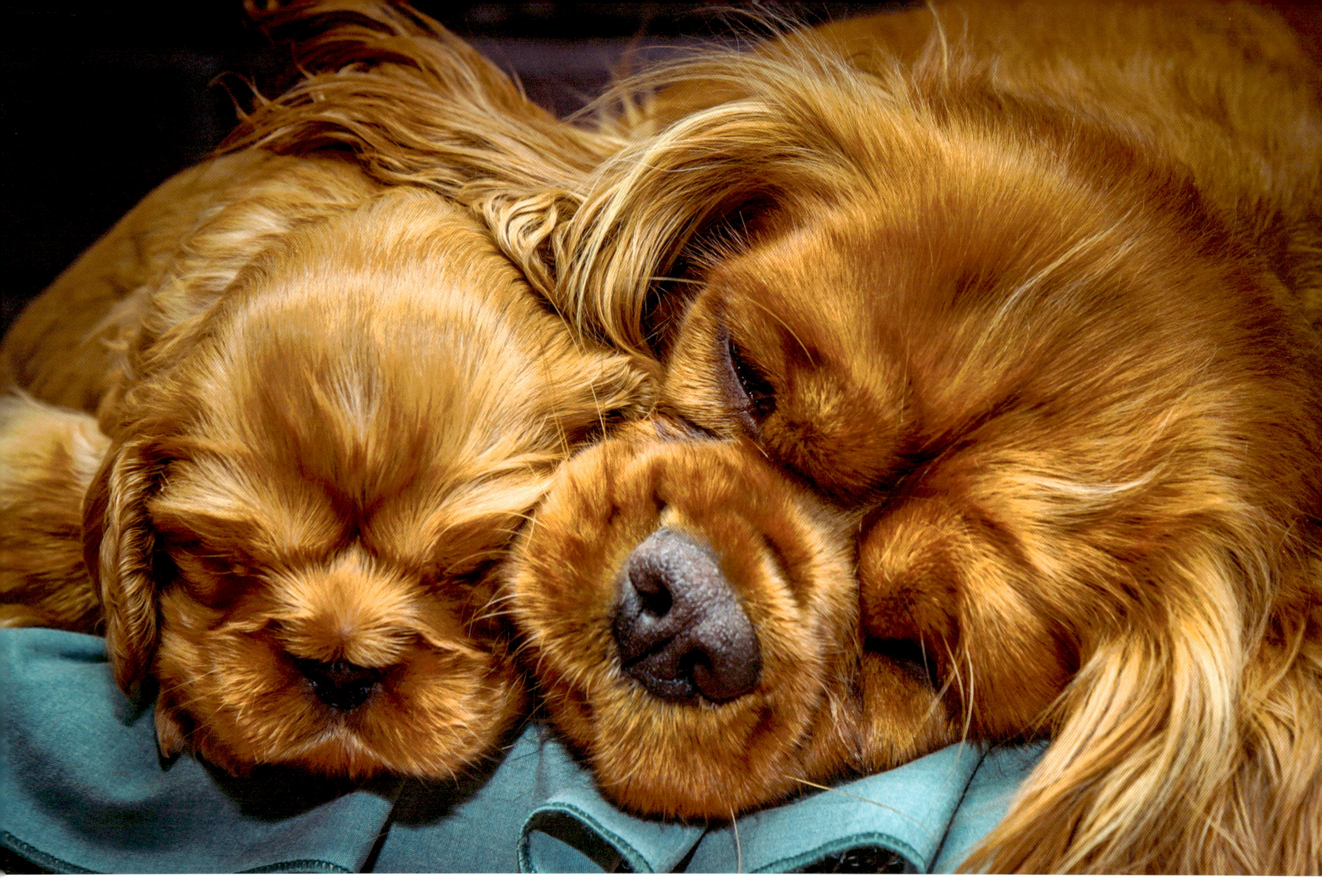

Elke, bred by Chris Darwen, Edenridge Cavaliers, cuddles her puppy, Mia.

Photo credit: John Harvey, Lower Blue Mountains, NSW, Australia

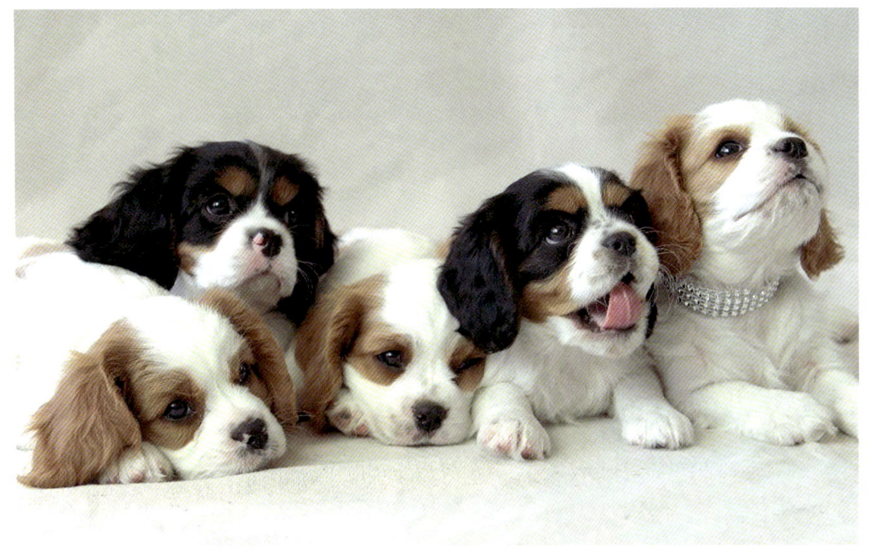

Sanders Sweet Cavalier puppies are getting very sleepy.

Photo credit: Gail Sanders, Arizona, USA

Photography: Cathi Cenatiempo

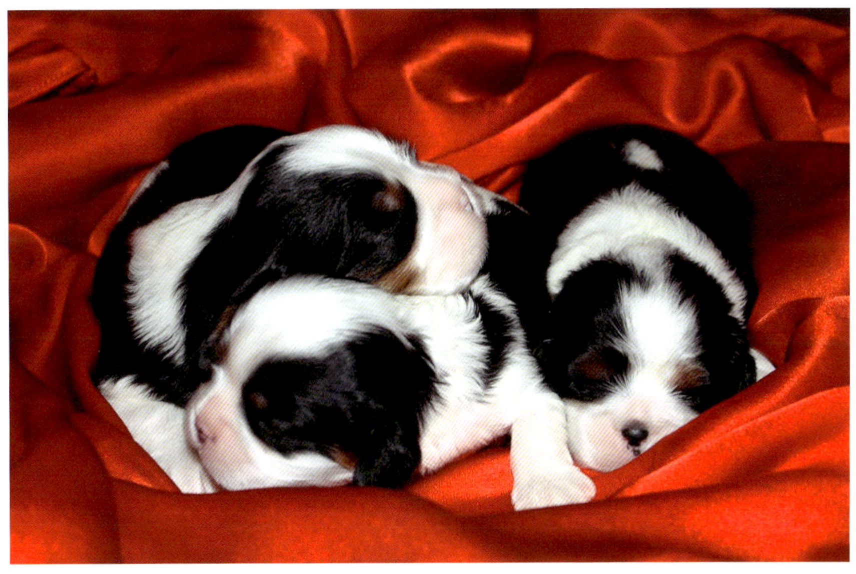

Elegancijo Kristalas' stunning Tri-color litter is out of Jasmin tik Herkus and Lambert Love Me.

Photo credit: Vladyslav Vinogrodskim

Photography: Dominyka Win, Vilnius, Lithuania

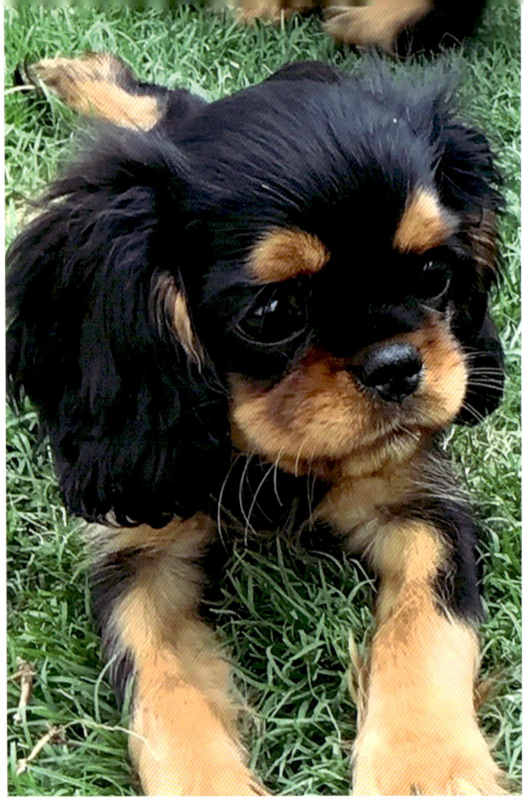

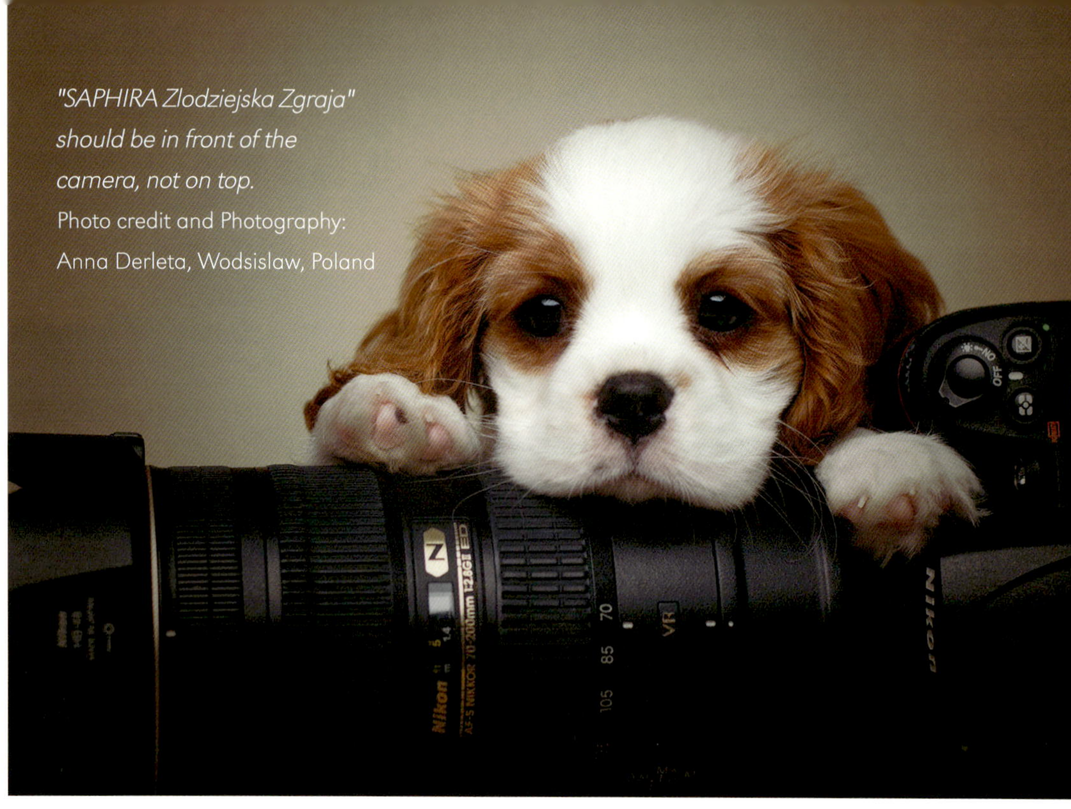

"SAPHIRA Zlodziejska Zgraja" should be in front of the camera, not on top.
Photo credit and Photography: Anna Derleta, Wodsislaw, Poland

Look at the size of those "peepers" on Black and Tan Harper!
Photo credit: Stephanie Jones, Melbourne, Australia

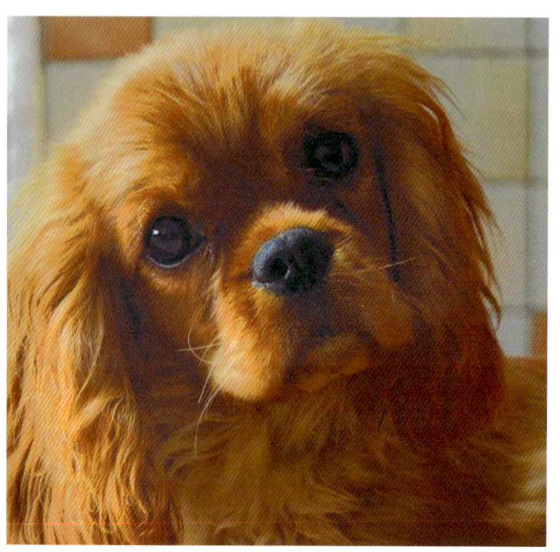

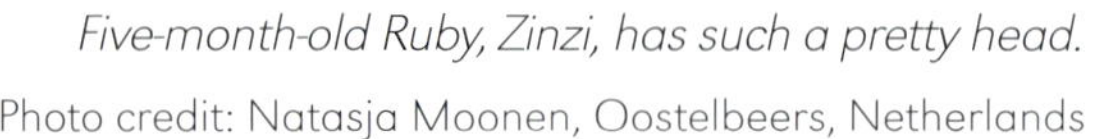

Five-month-old Ruby, Zinzi, has such a pretty head.
Photo credit: Natasja Moonen, Oostelbeers, Netherlands

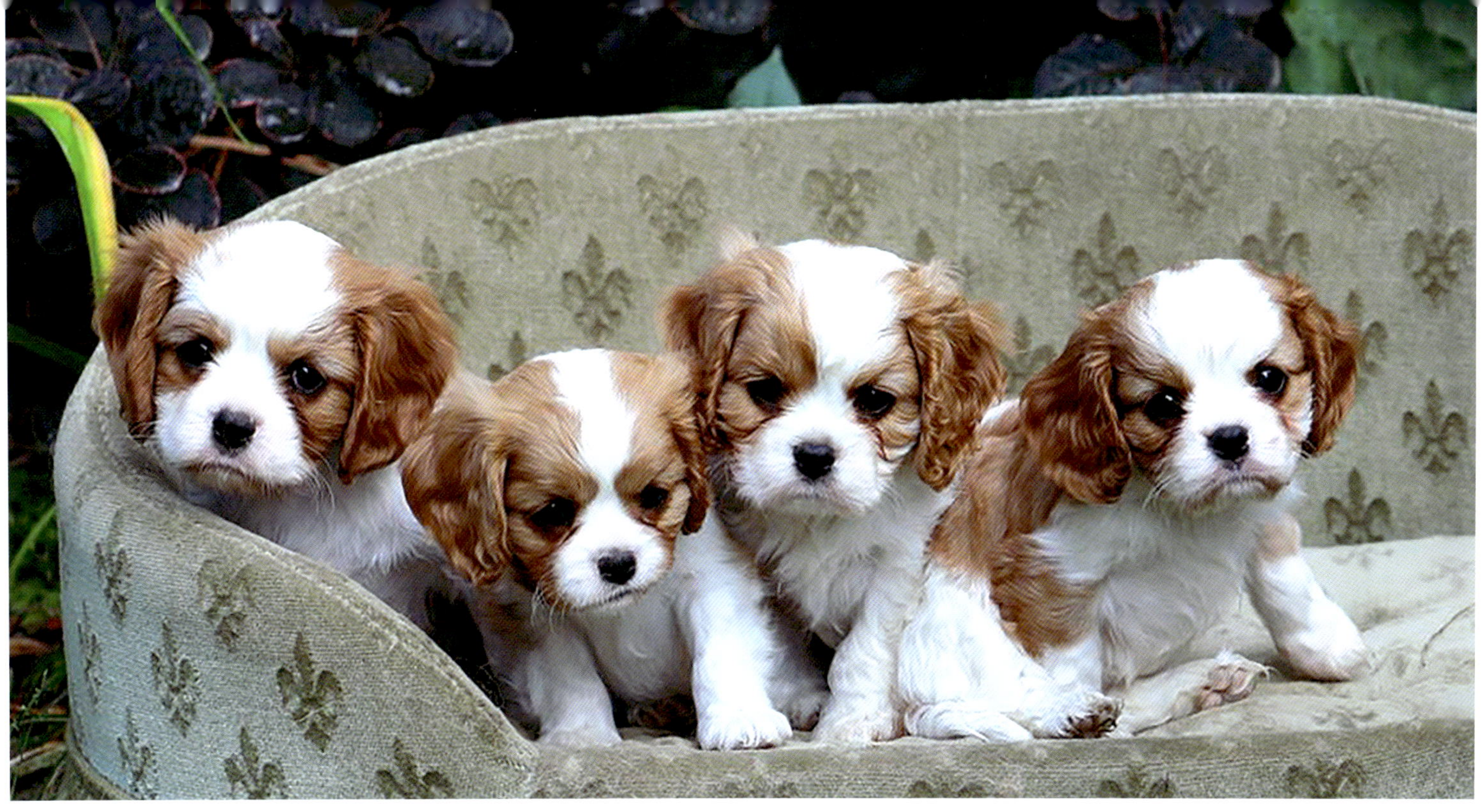

Lovely puppies of Orchard Hill's Just Enough Cash and Angel's Pride Isabella.

Photo credit: Monika Lauritsen, Norway

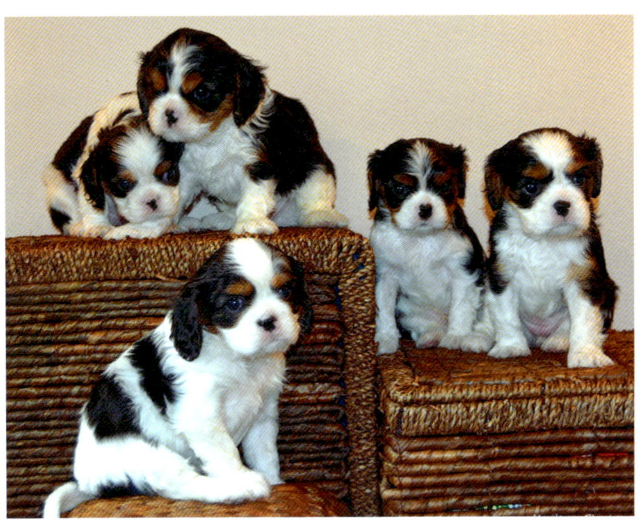

Introducing D Litter of Telperion sired by Lincoln Abraham de los Ursidos Kodiak x Jamaica Reggae Silver Capricorn

Photo credit: Martina Hartmannová, Poland

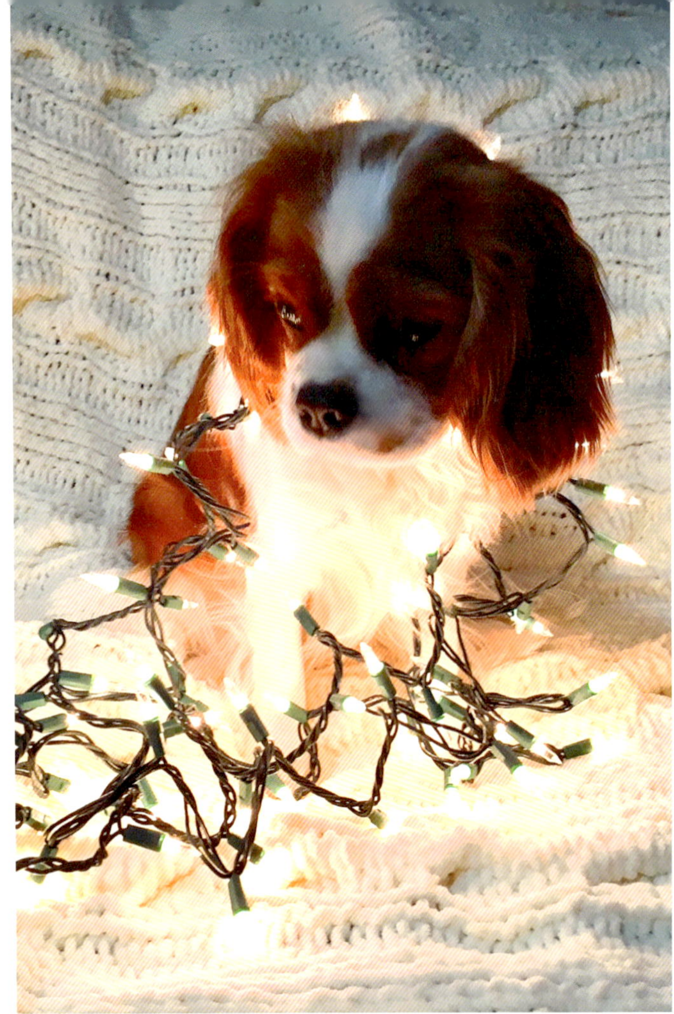

It's beginning to look like Christmas for this puppy.

Photo credit: Michelle Matheson, British Columbia, Canada

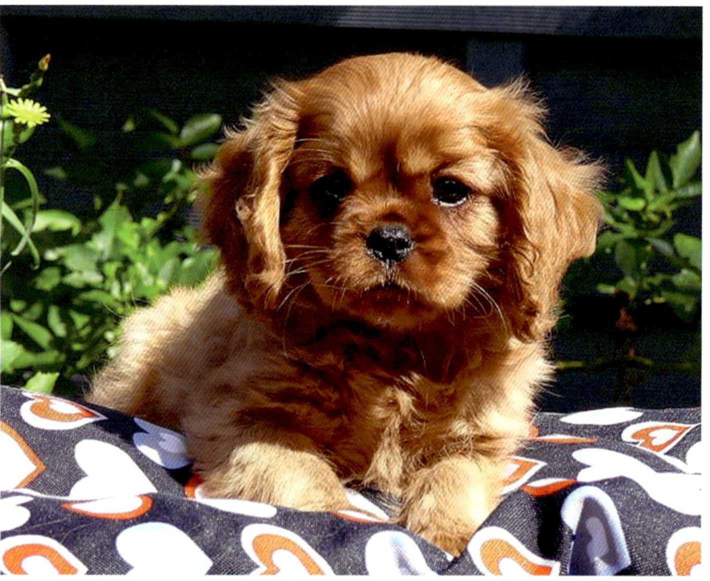

Adorable nine-week-old Betty from von Erlenbacher Hemmerich's B-Littter is a creation of Delicious and Paddington.

Photo credit: Claudia Hänsch, Neubrunn, Germany

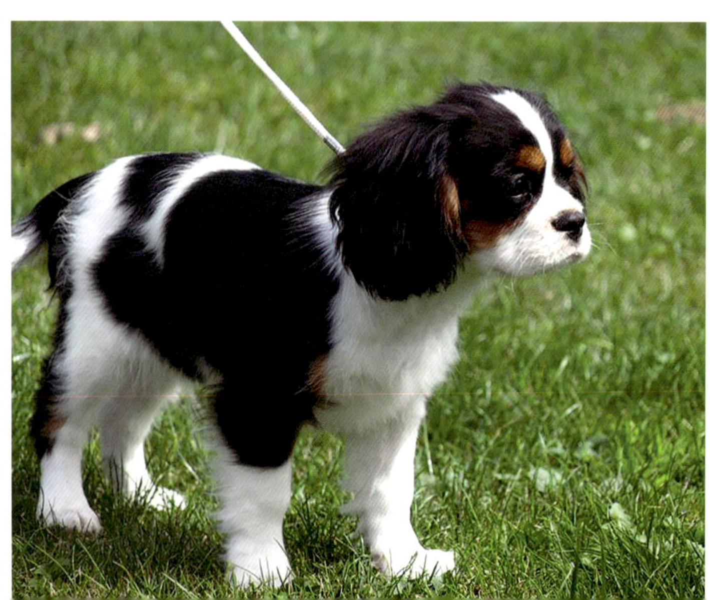

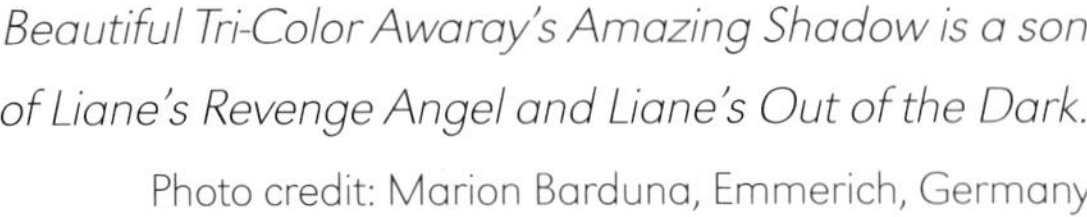

Beautiful Tri-Color Awaray's Amazing Shadow is a son of Liane's Revenge Angel and Liane's Out of the Dark.

Photo credit: Marion Barduna, Emmerich, Germany

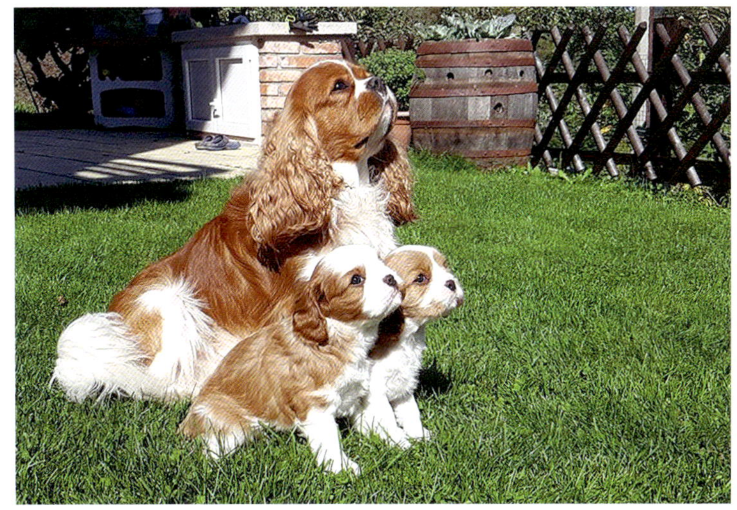

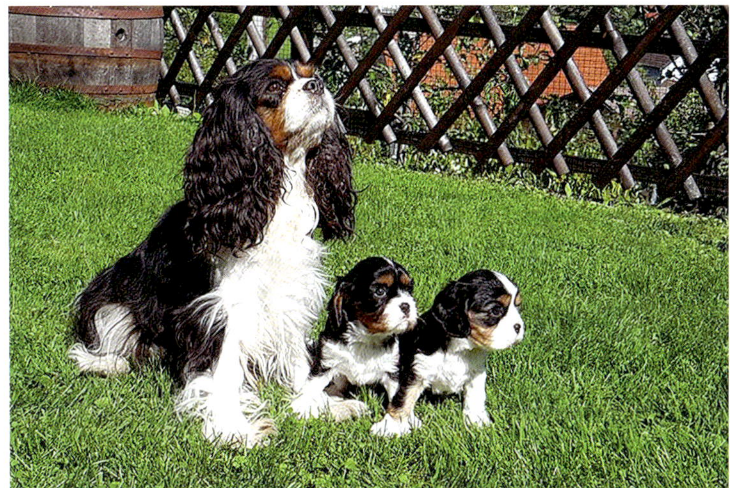

Family Portrait: on top, Papa Aranel Everlasting "Johnny" with Din and Daisy, and on bottom, Mom Gracie with Luna and the author's, Dolly.
Photo credit Anja Trcak, Maribor, Slovenia

Unforgettable May di Corte Naonis is incoming.
Photo credit: Betty Tomasi, Pordernone, Italy

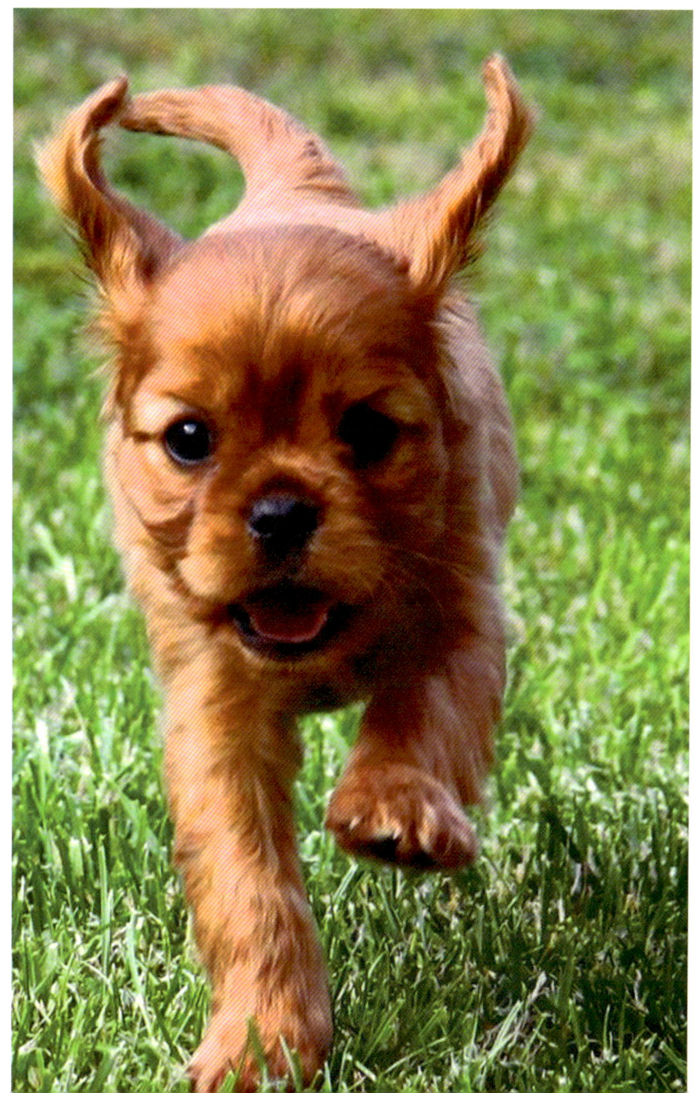

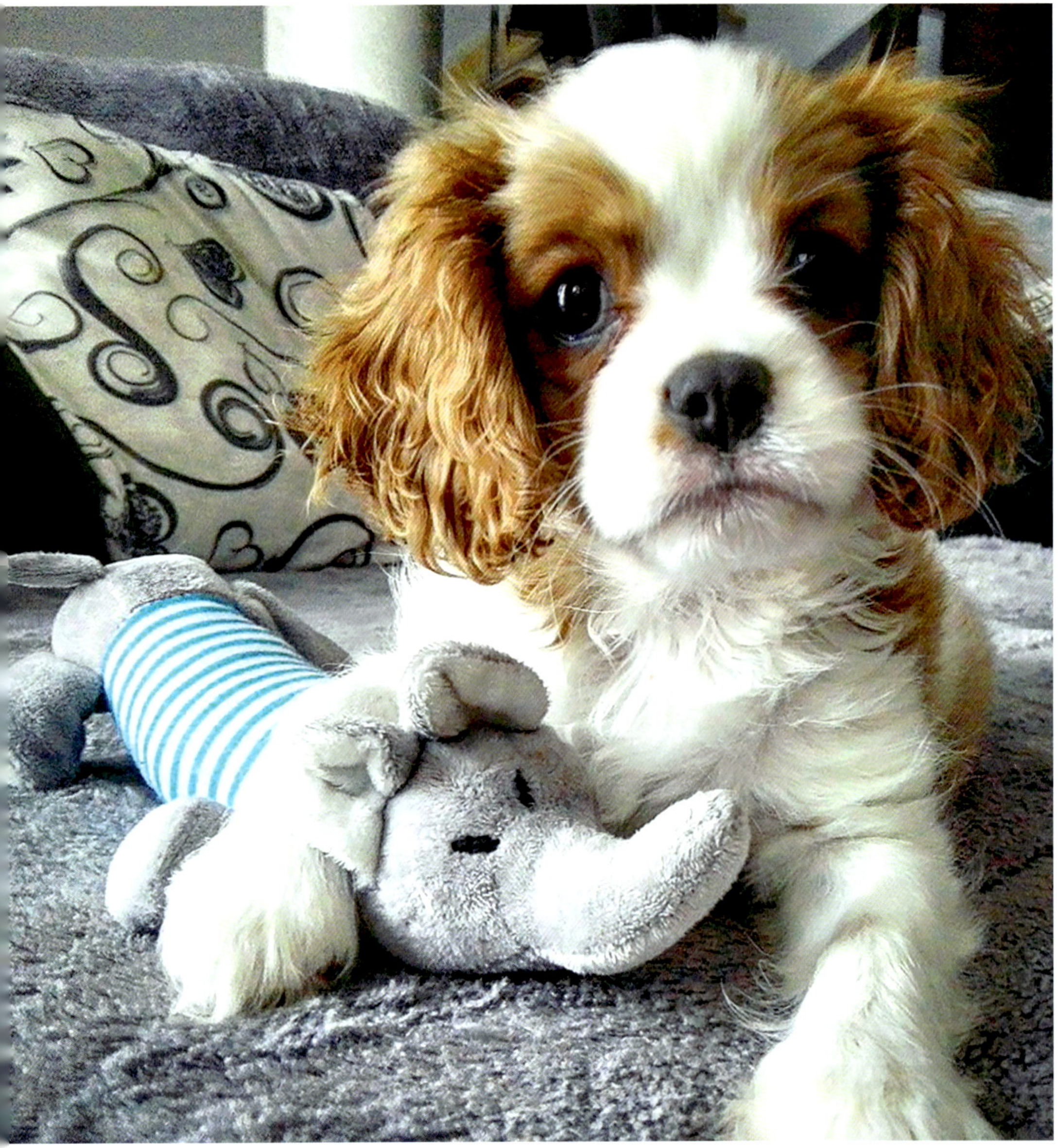

Baby Noah and his elephant.

Photo credit: Tania Mainolfi, Montearchio, Italy

Baby Winston Brough deep in thought about what's for dinner.

Photo credit: Christine Medway, Nottingham, UK

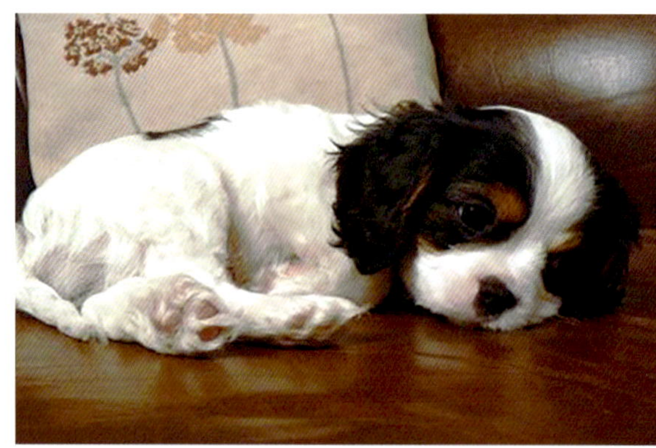

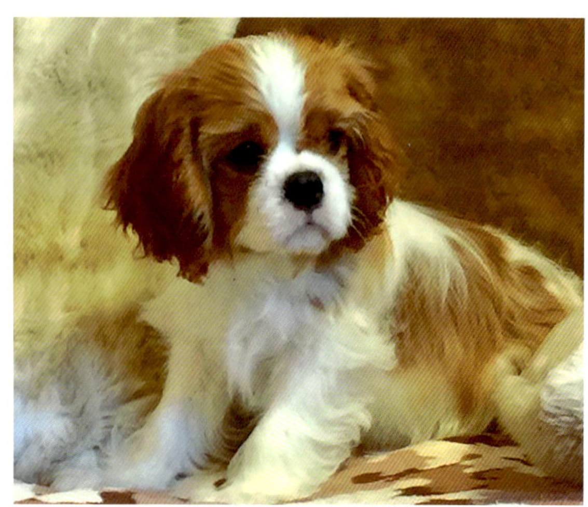

Cassandrina is as pretty as a picture.

Photo credit: Paola Martini, Savona, Italy

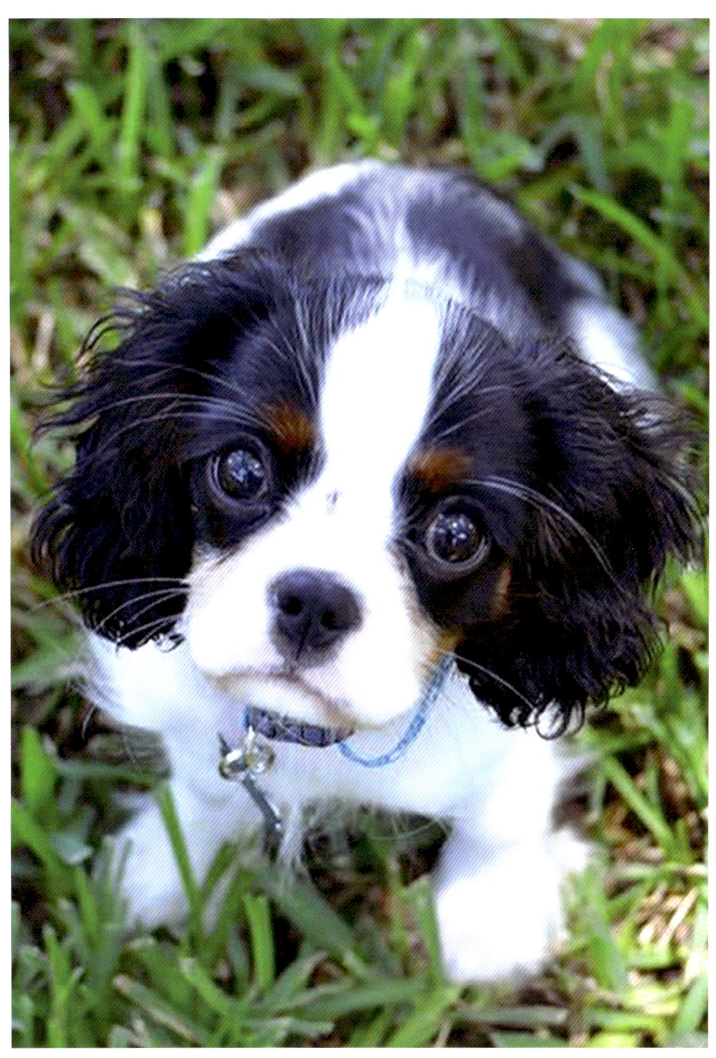

Aren't I the cutest thing?

Photo credit: Carol Casey, Texas, USA

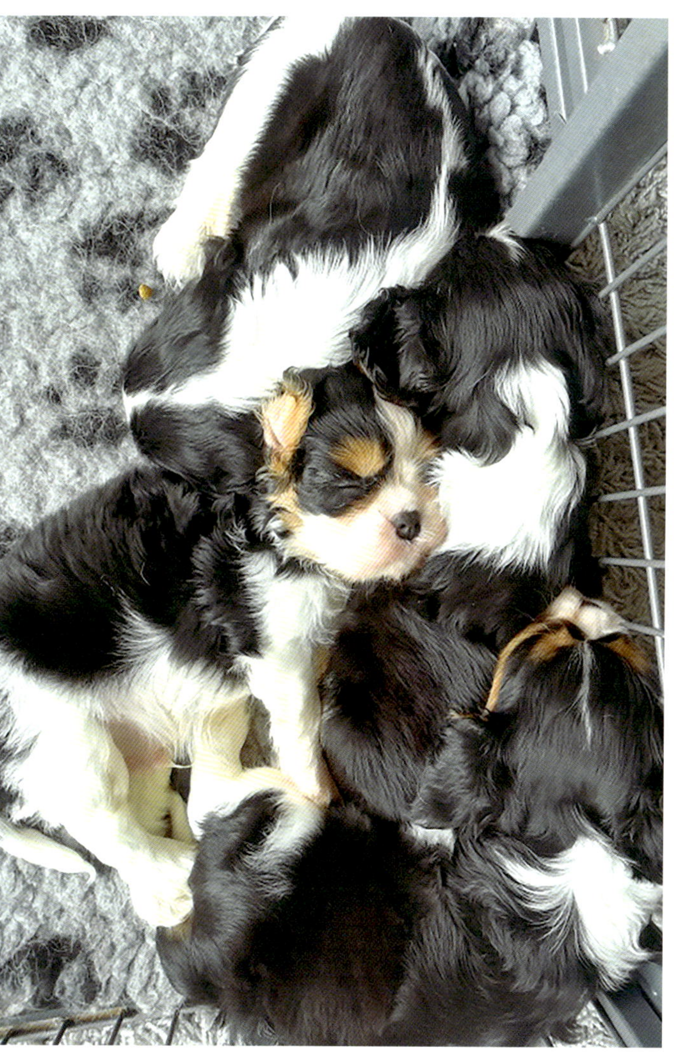

This is an adorable puppy pile from the litter of Lady Britania des Cavaliers de Corence and Malo des Cavaliers de Corence.

Photo credit: Sandrine Corence, la Teste-de-Buche, France

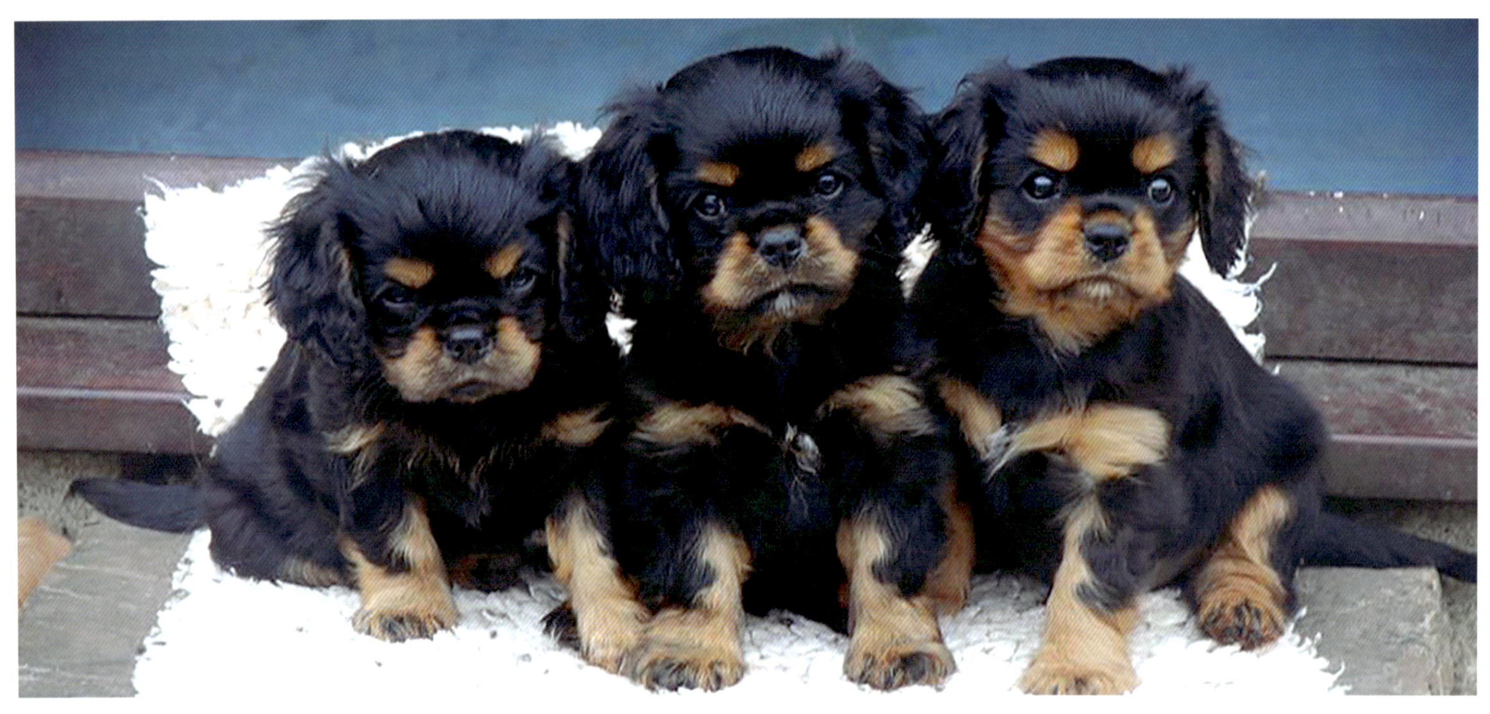

Black and Tan litter motto: Hear no evil, see no evil, speak no evil.

Photo credit: Sharon Slobody, Ohio, USA

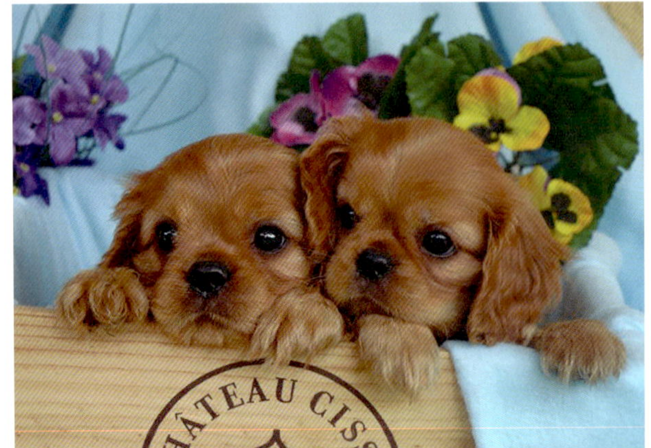

These perfect Rubies are Maisey and Martha.

Photo credit: Breeder Katie Sloan, Perthshire, Scotland, UK

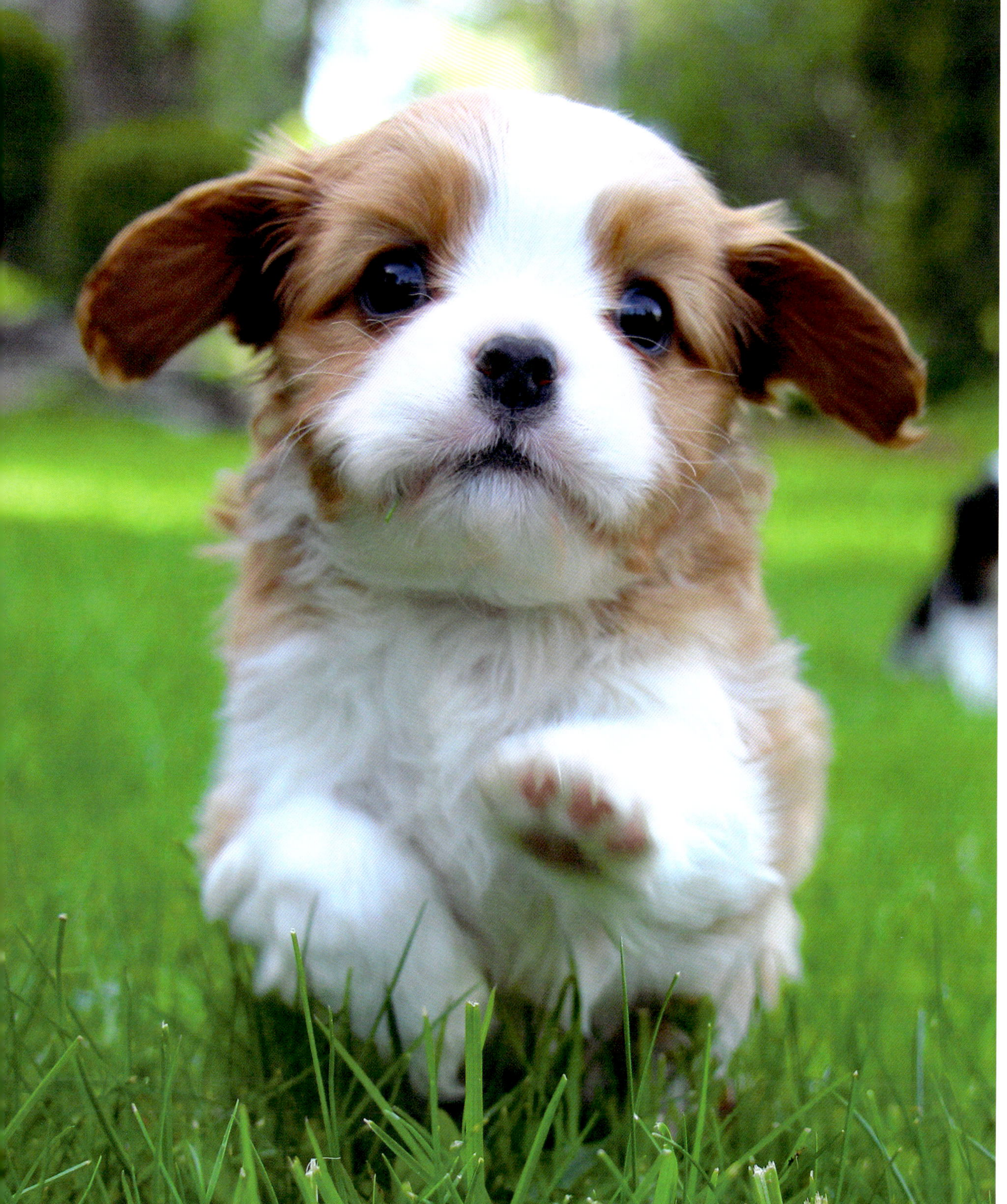

Royal Fantasy Emerald Cut (Harley) runs as fast as the wind.

Photo credit: Urve Tipp, Viljandi, Estonia

Chapter 2 - Cavaliers and Kids

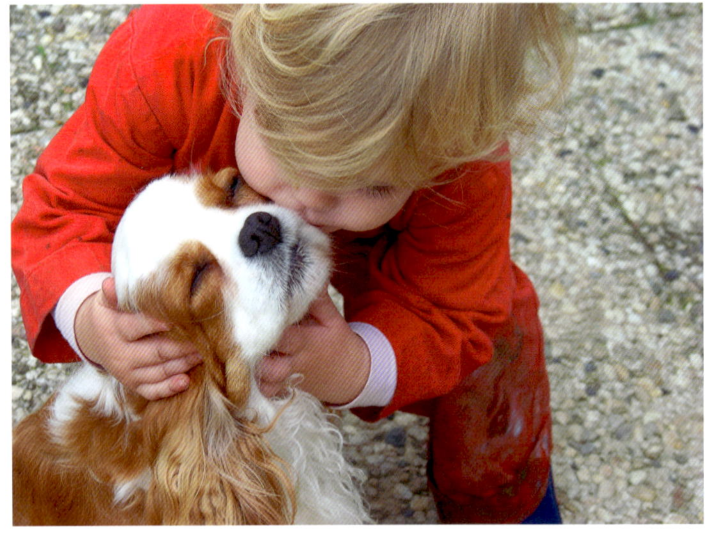

Breeder Marieke's daughter, Bente, lavishing pup Vanilla, m v.h. Lamslag with kisses.

Photo credit: Marieke Hillhorst, Hummelo, Netherlands

Cavaliers and children are cute, playful, and affectionate, so it's not surprising that they have an unspoken affinity for each other. It's usually love at first sight. In fact, you could say that Cavaliers are kid magnets! Even the puppies recognize a child and tend to be extra gentle and also a bit curious. Cavaliers have never met a stranger, and with kids around, their tails never stop wagging.

Whenever we take Callie out on her leash or in her stroller, it isn't long before she is encircled by children. Here in France, the village children come to our house and ask to walk her. My granddaughter, Sienna, who has her own dogs, is totally smitten with Callie. When Sienna was small, I told her that she and Callie were princesses so she would treat her with great regard and gentleness.

Cavaliers make super therapy dogs and emotional support animals because loving and empathy come so naturally to them. The following photographs of Cavaliers and their human siblings and/or young friends illustrate this special relationship between Cavaliers and kids.

Archie and Tobie are guarding newborn baby, Luca.

Photo credit: Sandra Ireland, Hereford, UK

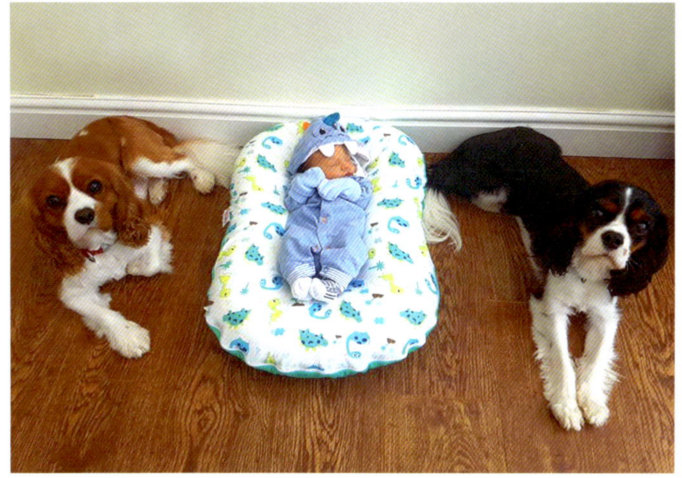

Floris is wondering what's making baby Jarin smile.

Photo credit: Marieke Hillhorst, Hummelo, Netherlands

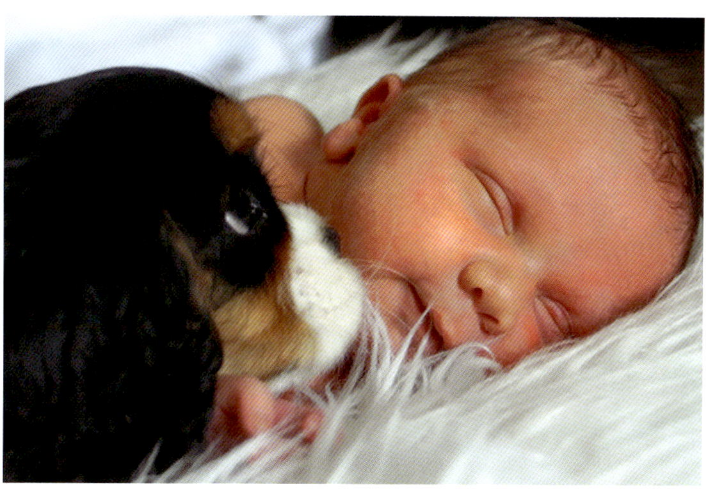

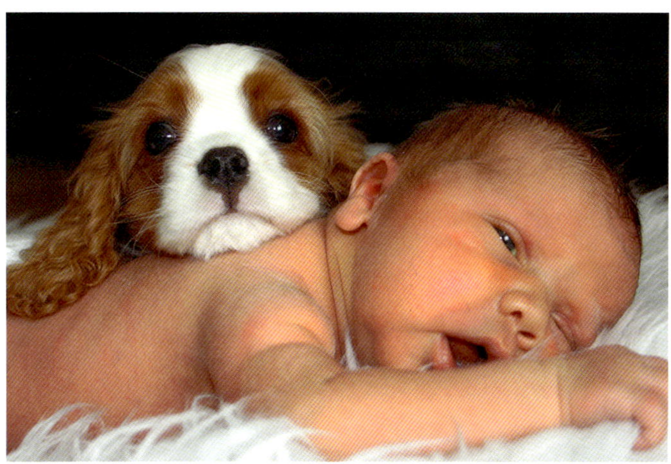

Louise has "got this." She's keeping Jarin warm while actually photobombing the shot.

Photo credit: Marieke Hillhorst, Hummelo, Netherlands

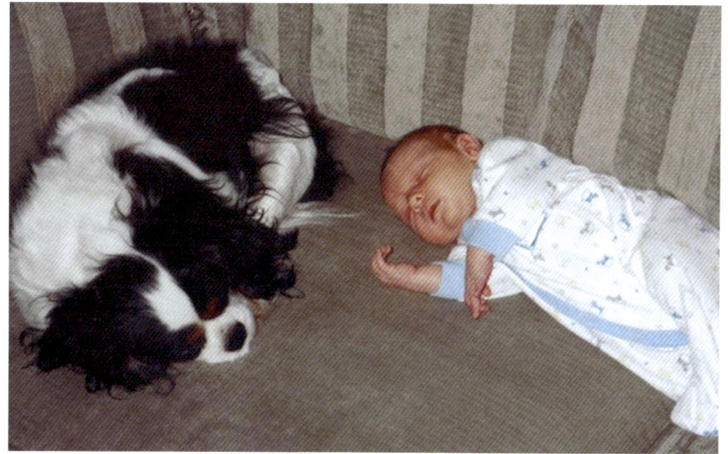

Kewpy's Moonman won't leave grandson Josh's side.

Photo credit: Karen Wills, Alberta, Canada

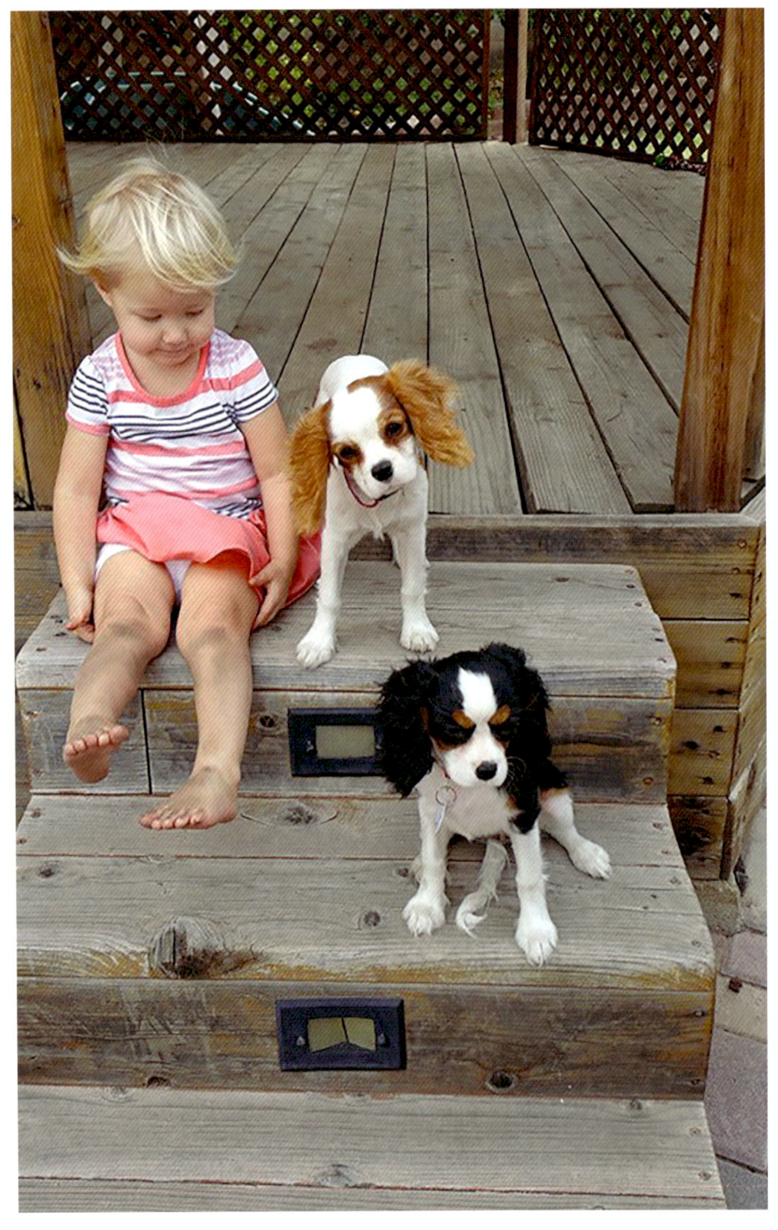

We're just chillin' together on the steps.

Photo credit: Heather Marino, Tennessee, USA

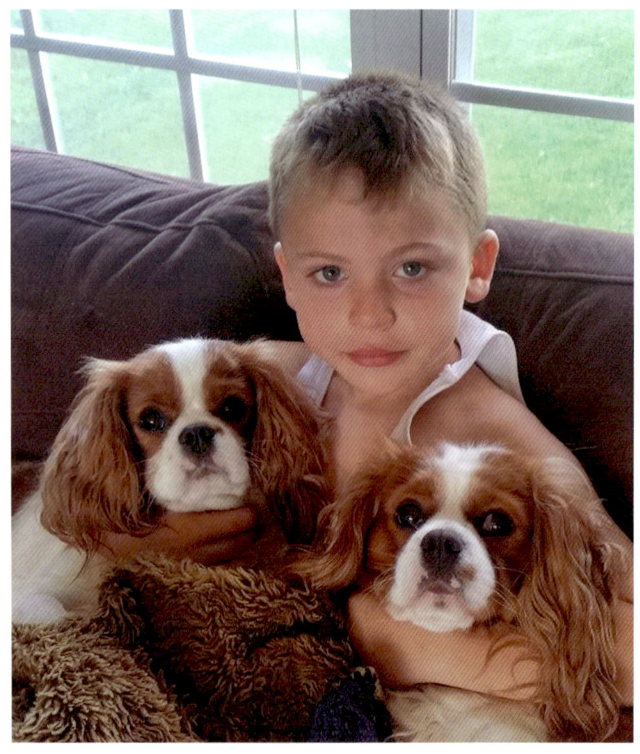

Great-nephew David doing couch time with Gini's Blenheim brothers, Finnegan and Tully.

Photo credit: Gini Locurcio, New York, USA

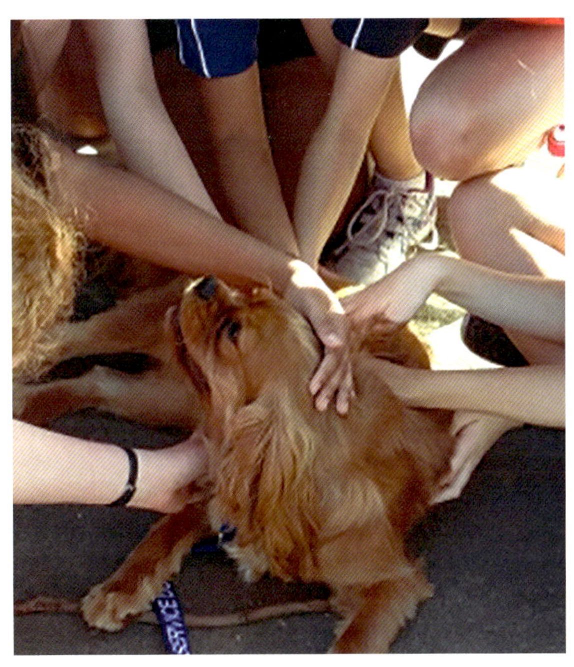

Ruben attracts a lot of affection when he visits the playground.

Photo credit: Margie Ruben Beange, Kurrajong, Australia

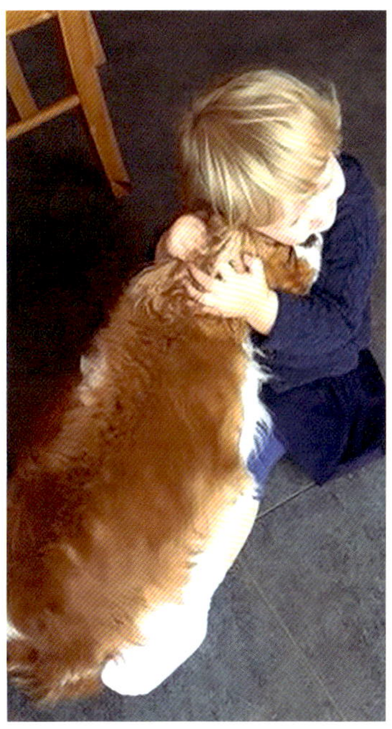

Katie Sloan's granddaughter Rebecca just loves Blenheim Viva.

Photo credit: Katie Sloan, Perthshire, Scotland, UK

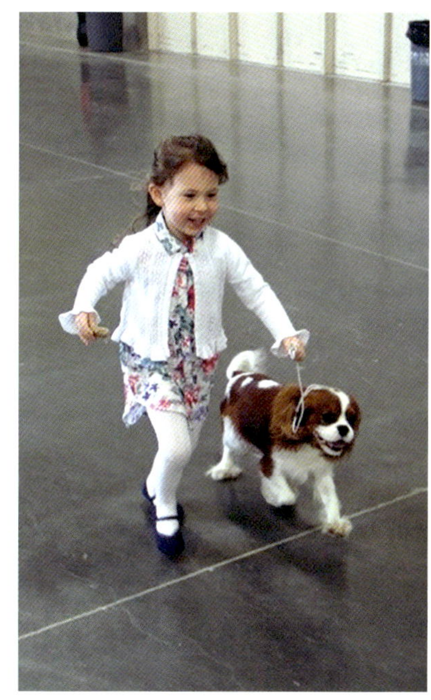

Alisha Lockleer's four-year-old daughter Allie, shows Benjamin - BISS GCH Orchard Hill Toy Money (owned by Julia Johns and Erica Venier).

Photo credit: Alisha Lockleer, Washington, USA

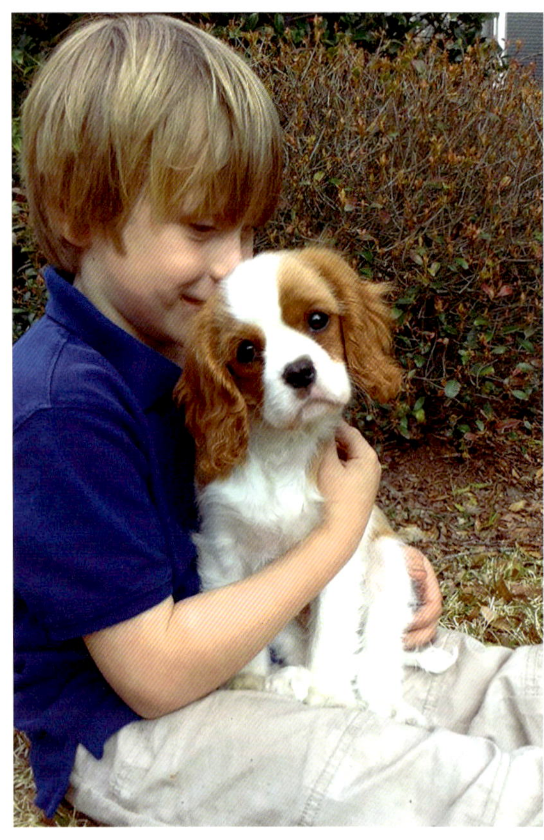

Bentwood Wonderstruck "Riley" likes cuddles from Breeder Heather Borton's son, Noah.
Photo credit: Heather Borton, North Carolina, USA

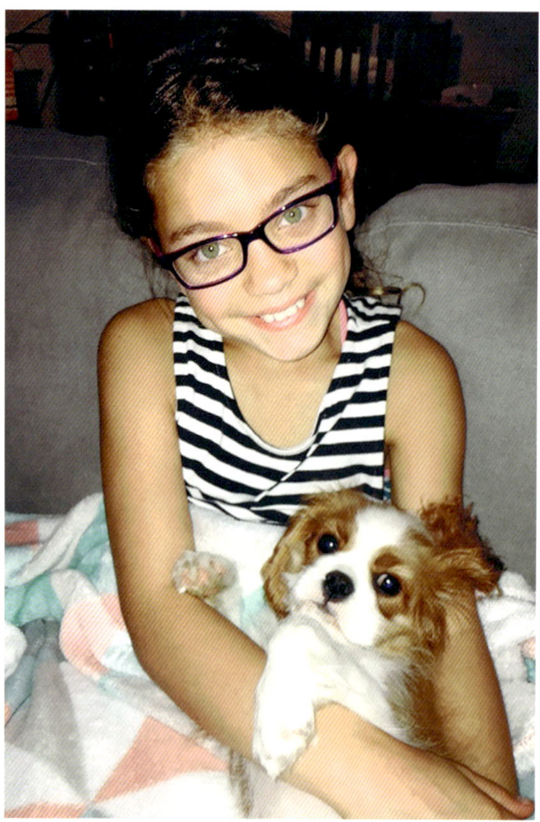

Ava Patane is most enamored with baby Leo, bred by Barbara Martin (sire is Charnell Hogan (JW) (UK) and the dam is Breshaad Candle In The Wind).
Photo credit: Barbara Martin, Adelaide, South Australia

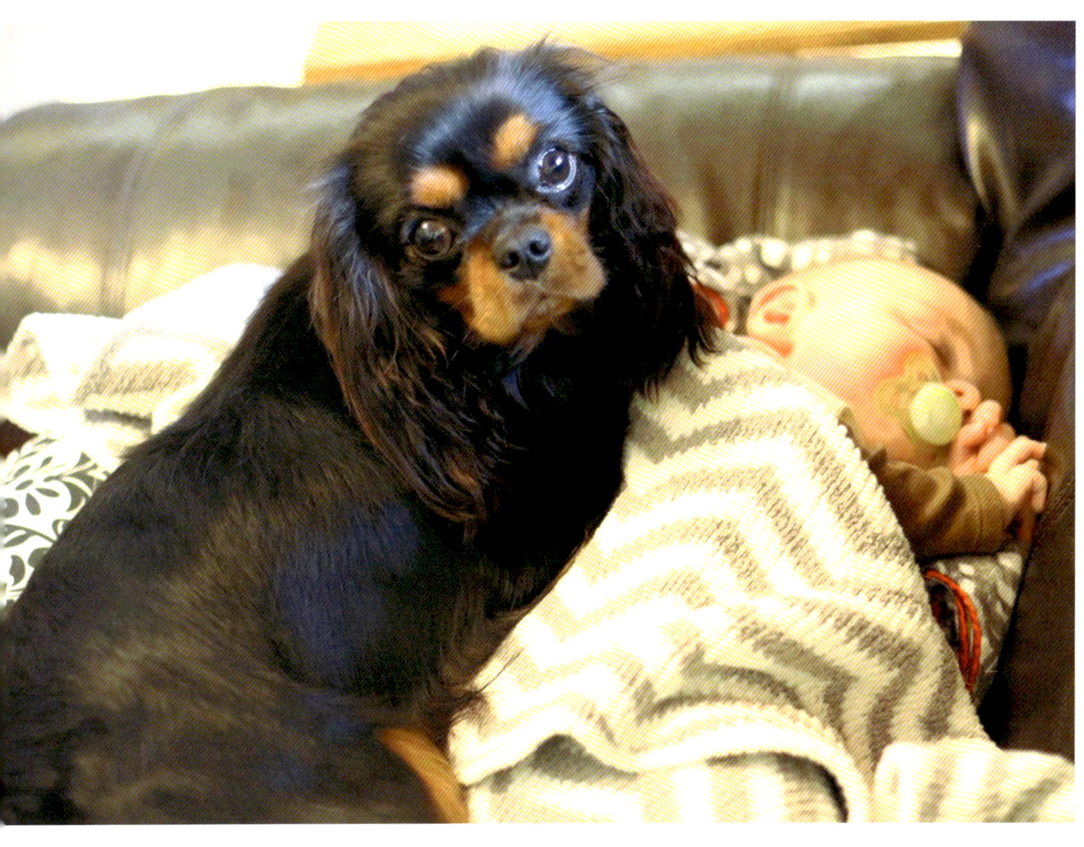

Inka Love Me is on-guard over napping Rylin.

Photo credit: Heather Marino, Tennessee, USA

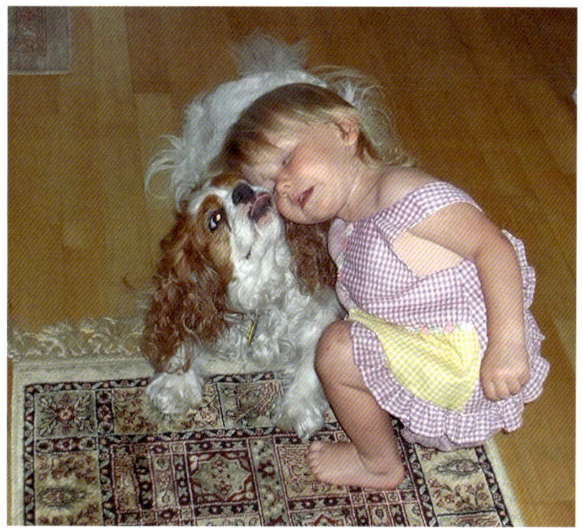

Rachel adores getting kisses from Abby.

Photo credit: Lisa Falchetti, California, USA

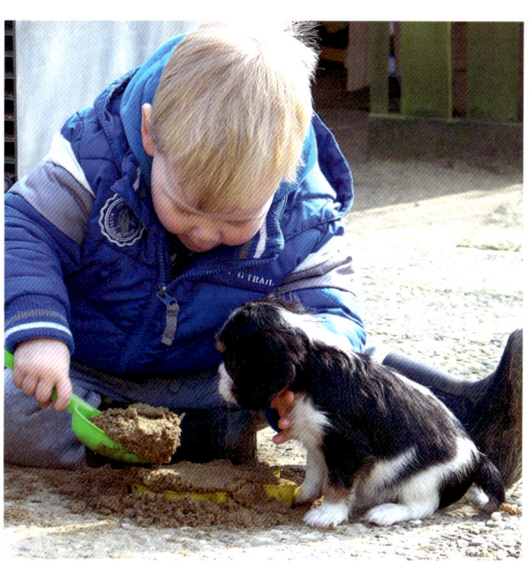

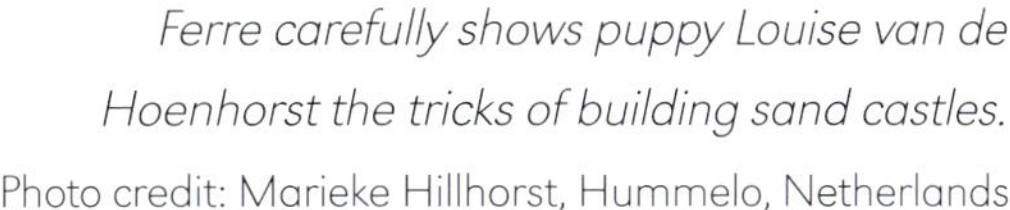

Ferre carefully shows puppy Louise van de Hoenhorst the tricks of building sand castles.

Photo credit: Marieke Hillhorst, Hummelo, Netherlands

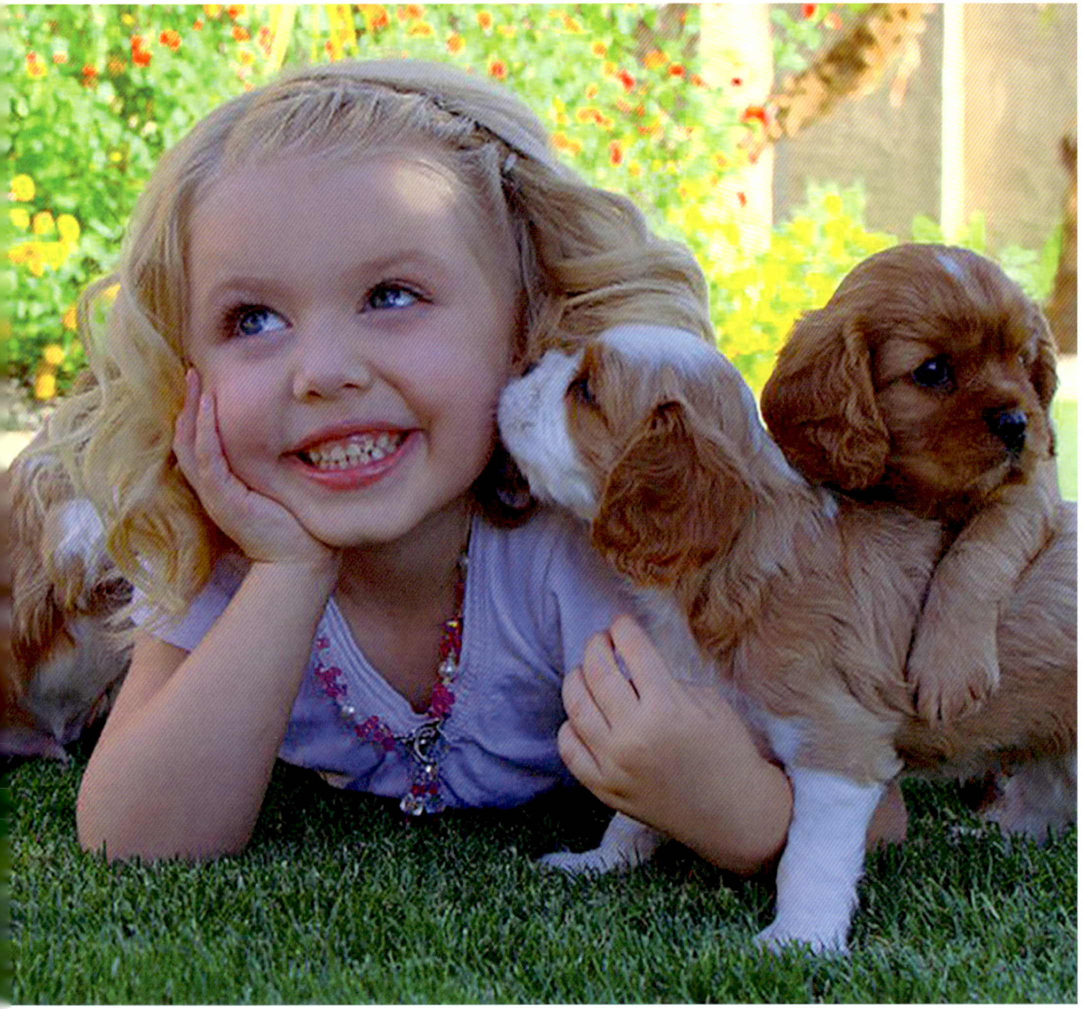

Kameryn Helms with Breeder Gail Sander's first litter.

Photo credit: Efnor, Alberta, Canada

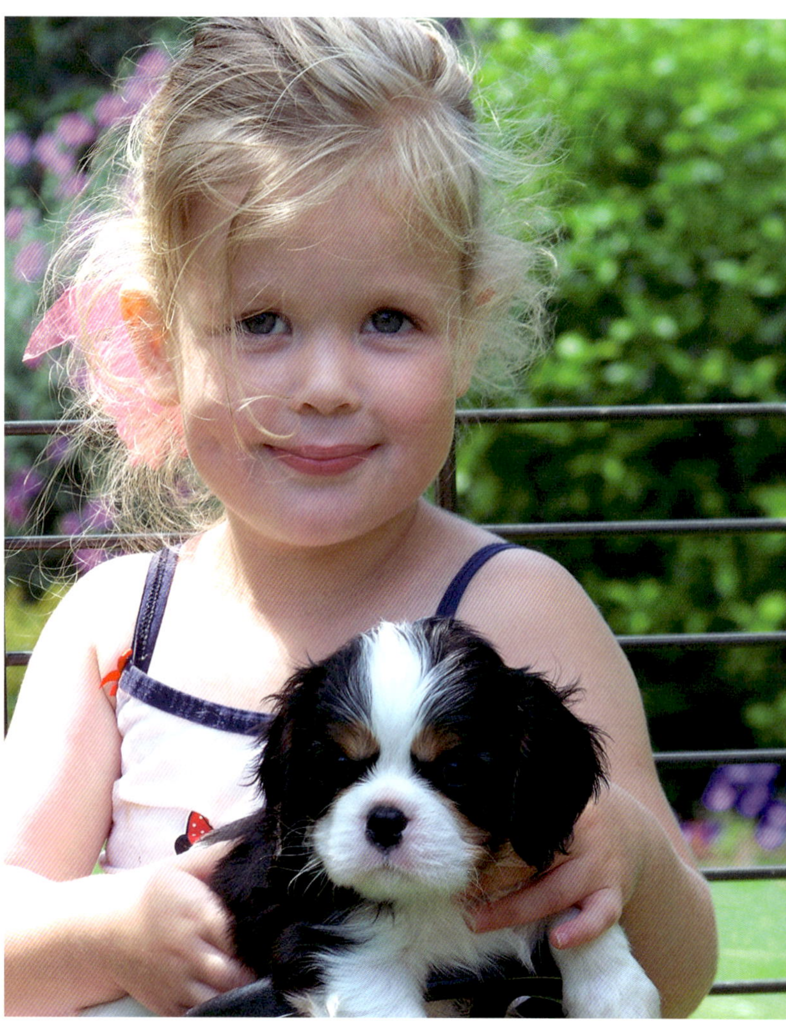

Pretty Breeder Marieke's daughter
Bente is holding Vanilla v.h. Lamslag.

Photo credit: Marieke Hillhorst, Hummelo, Netherlands

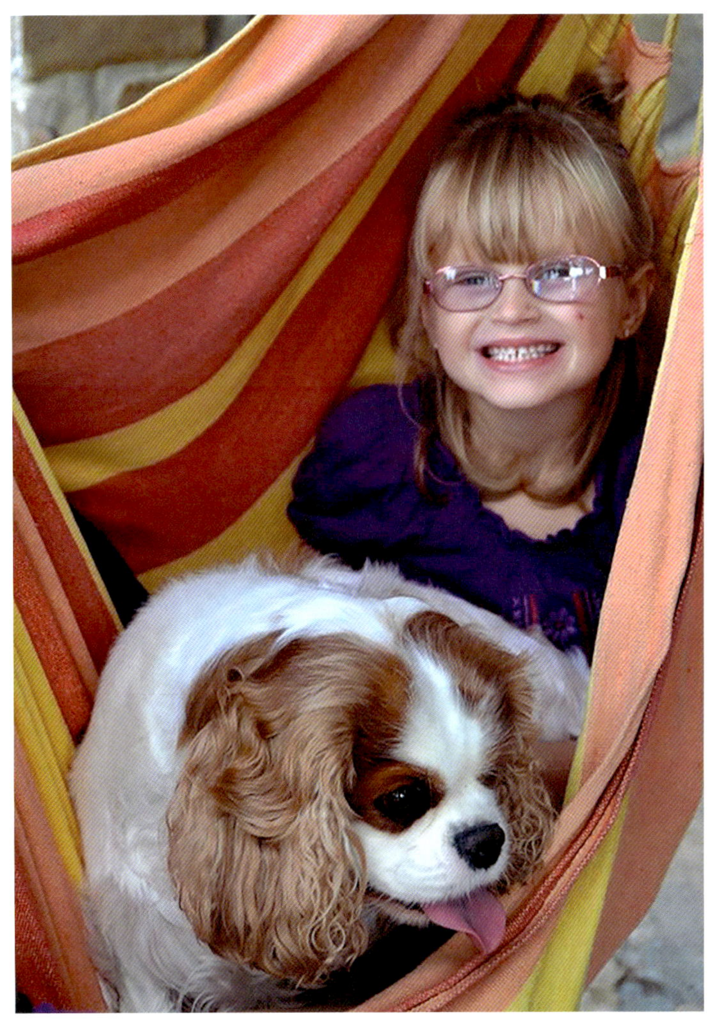

Sienna and Callie are sister princesses.

Photo credit: Mary Colburn-Green, L'Aude, France

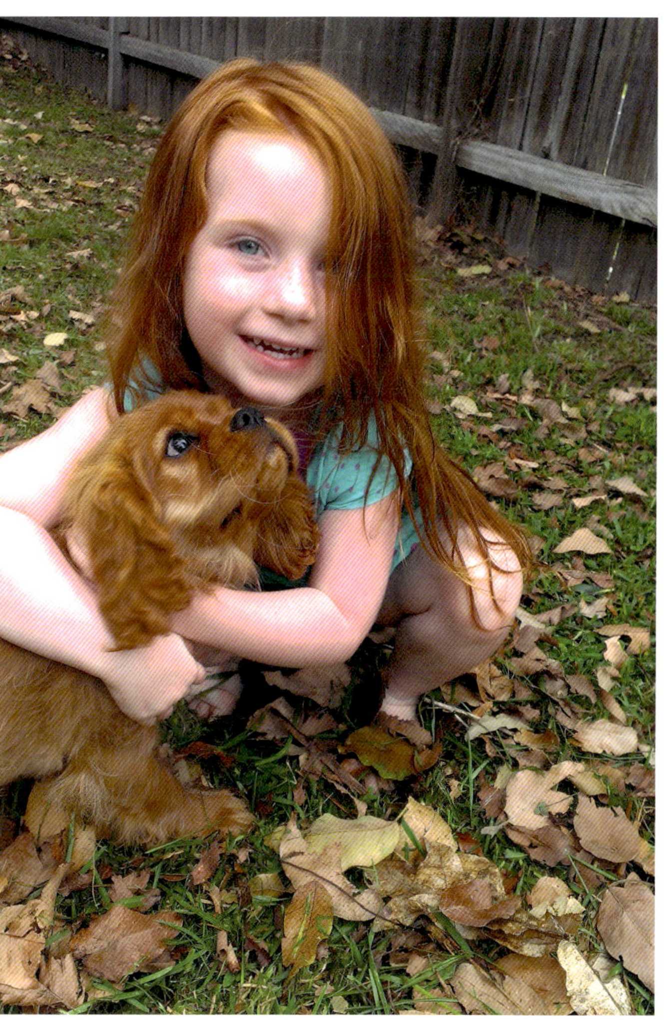

Stunning Rubies, Granddaughter Grace and Ruben.

Photo credit: Margie Ruben Beange, Kurrajong, Australia

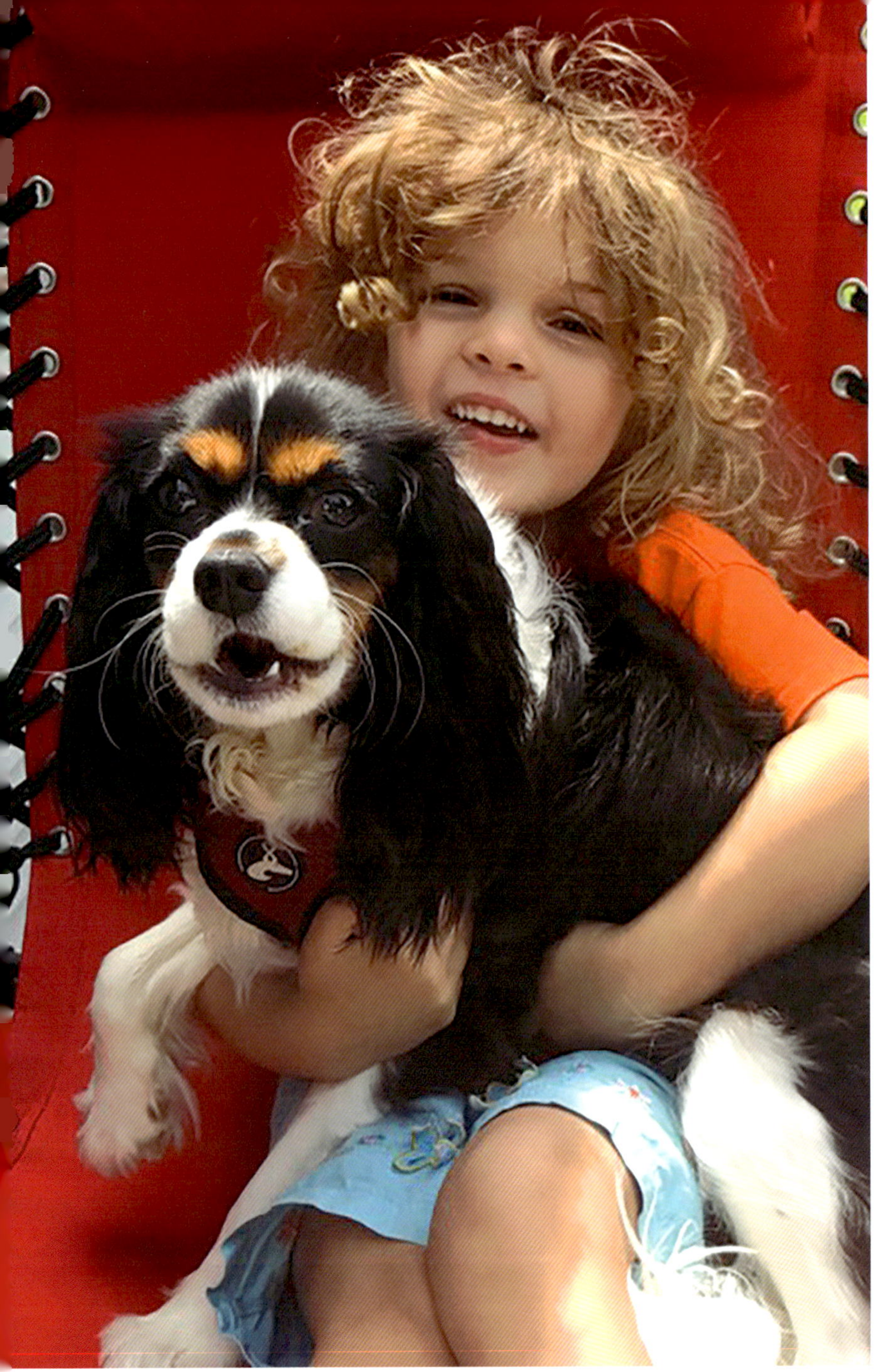

Tri-Color Raggedy Anne (Annie) is best friends with Pamela Stewart's granddaughter Anne.
Photo credit: Pamela Stewart, Michigan, USA

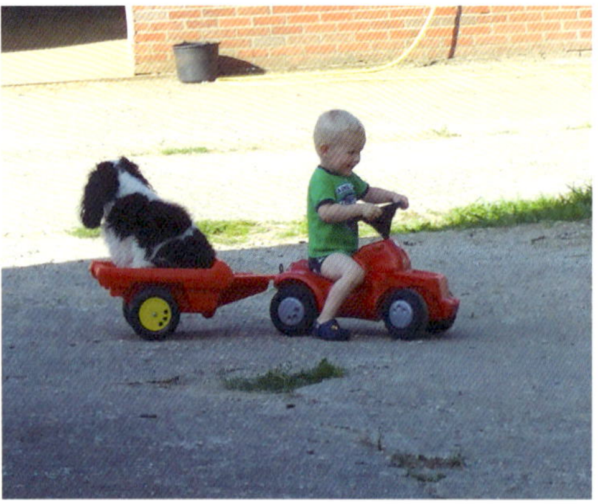

Marieke's son, Milan, giving Blenheim Joachem a lift at the Kennel de Hoenhurst.
Photo credit: Breeder Marieke Hillhurst, Hummelo, Netherlands

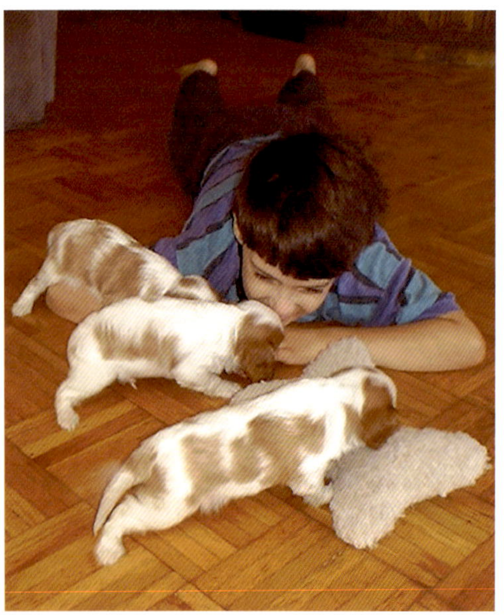

Zach Wehking plays with Lucy's pups. What kid wouldn't relish having a house full of Cavalier pups all his own?
Photo credit: Jennifer Wehking, Georgia, USA

"Snuggles" and his new siblings.

Photo credit: Heather Marino, Tennessee, USA

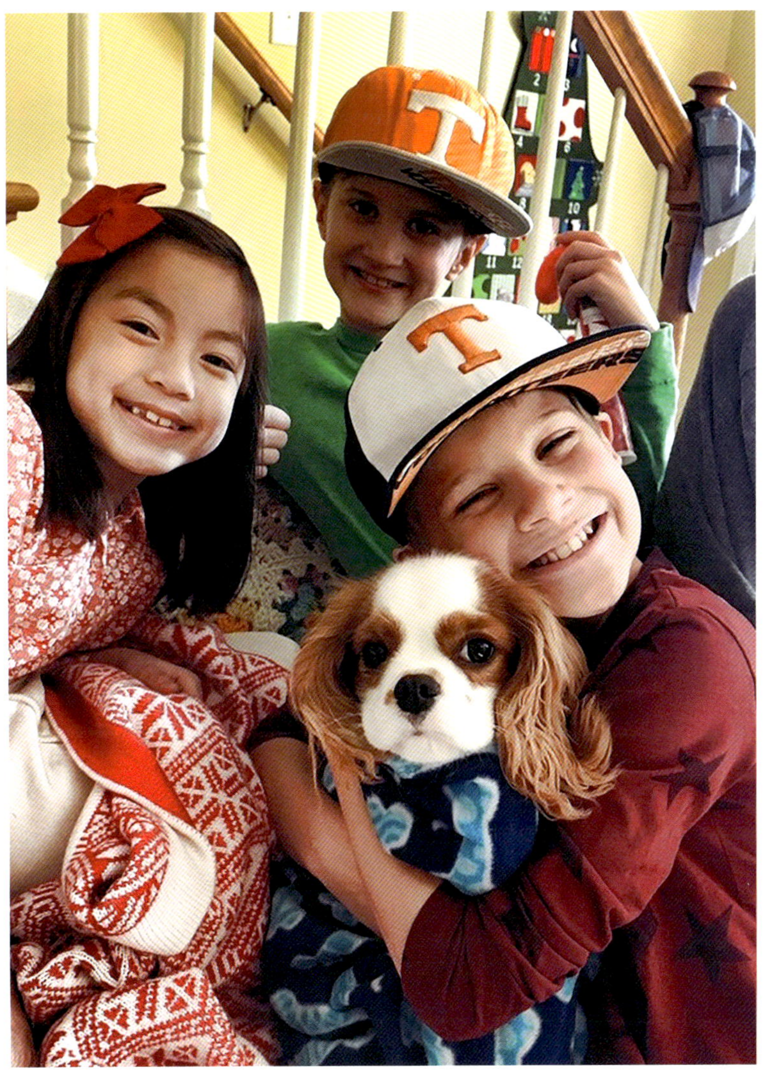

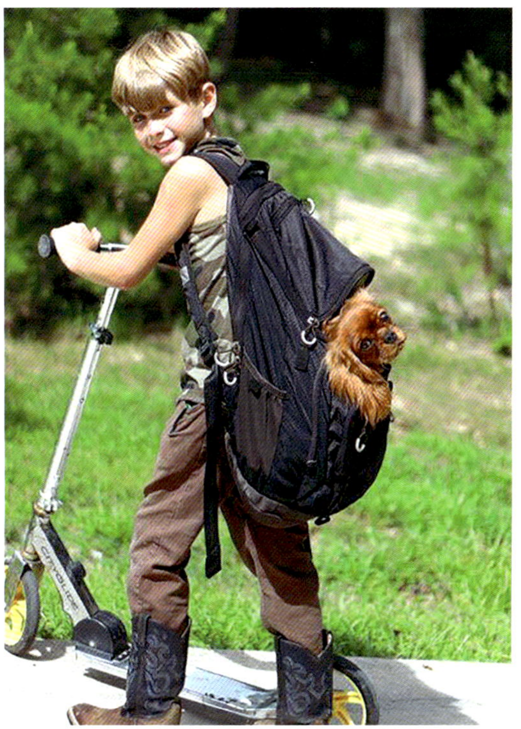

Gavin Marino had a little lamb, and everywhere Gavin went, Tasha was sure to go.

Photo credit: Heather Marino, Tennessee, USA

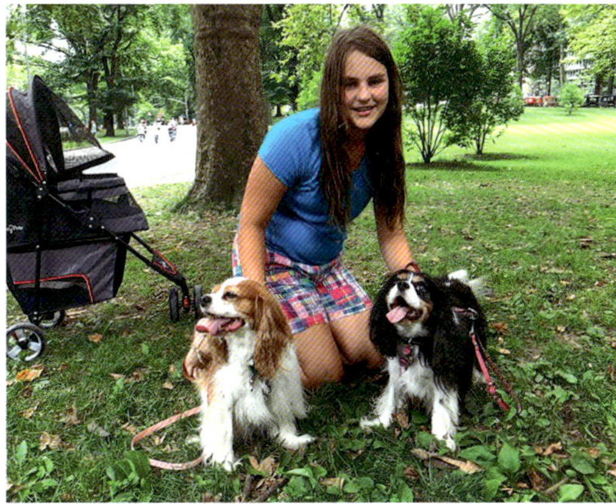

Christy Pully Berry's Cavaliers Sophie and Maggie, and their girl Sarah.

Photo credit: Christy Berry, Indiana, USA

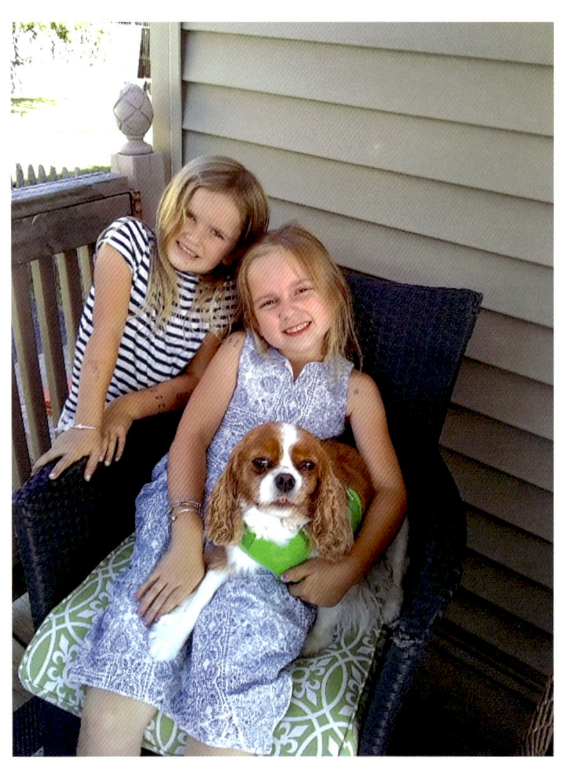

Ella and Olivia love to visit their grandmother so they can play with Lizzie.

Photo credit: Janet Fritsch, Massachusetts, USA

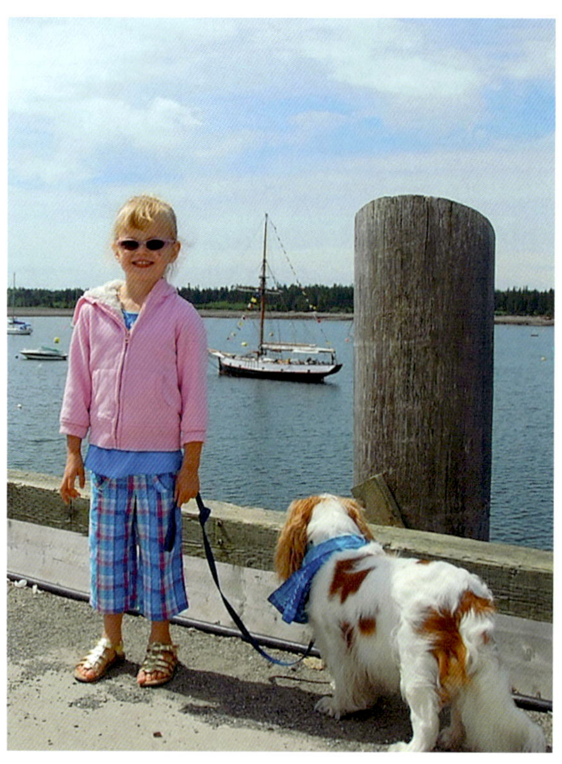

Sienna, the author's granddaughter, walking Callie on the St. Andrews, New Brunswick Pier.

Photo credit: Mary Colburn-Green, L'Aude, France

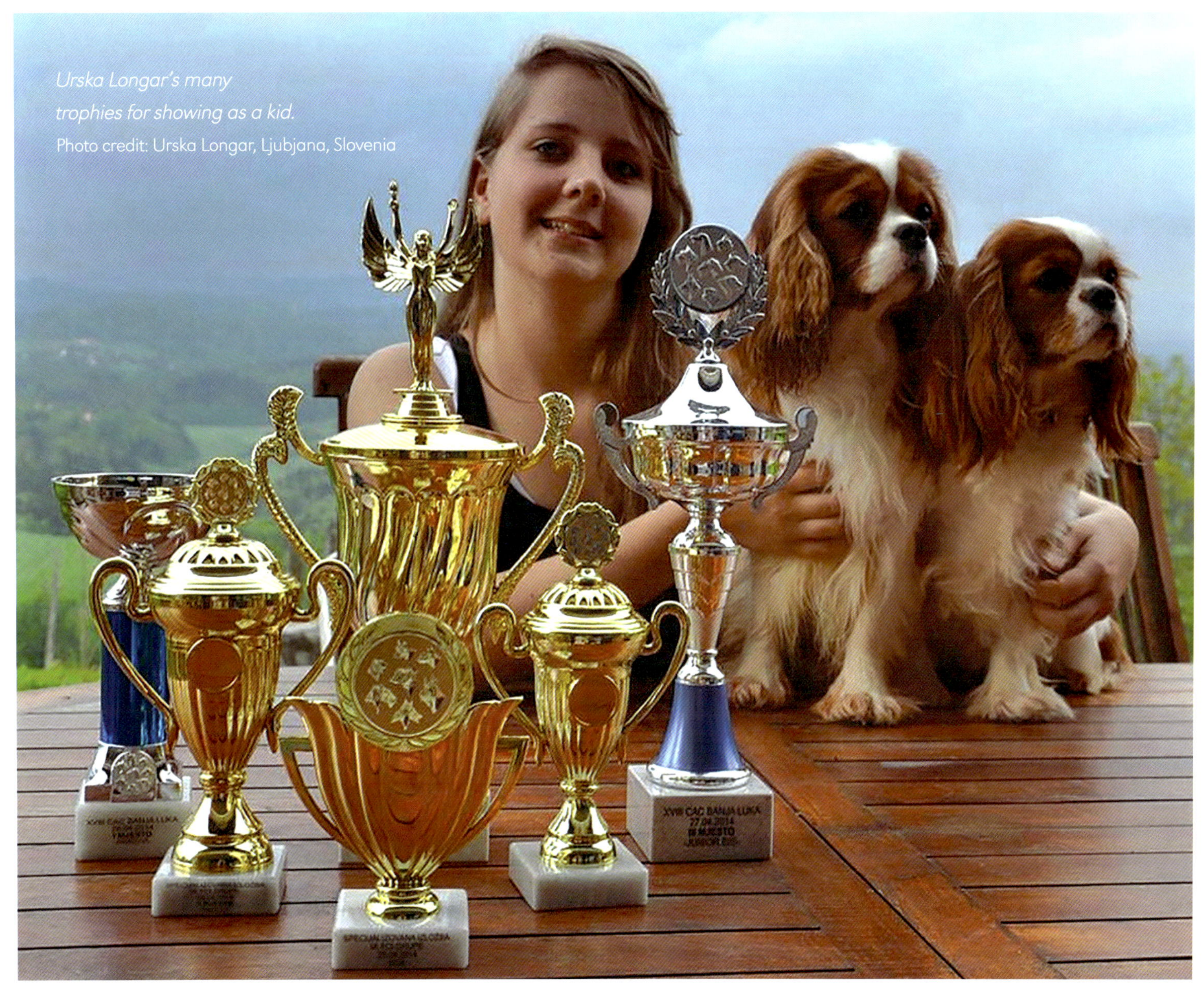

Urska Longar's many trophies for showing as a kid.
Photo credit: Urska Longar, Ljubjana, Slovenia

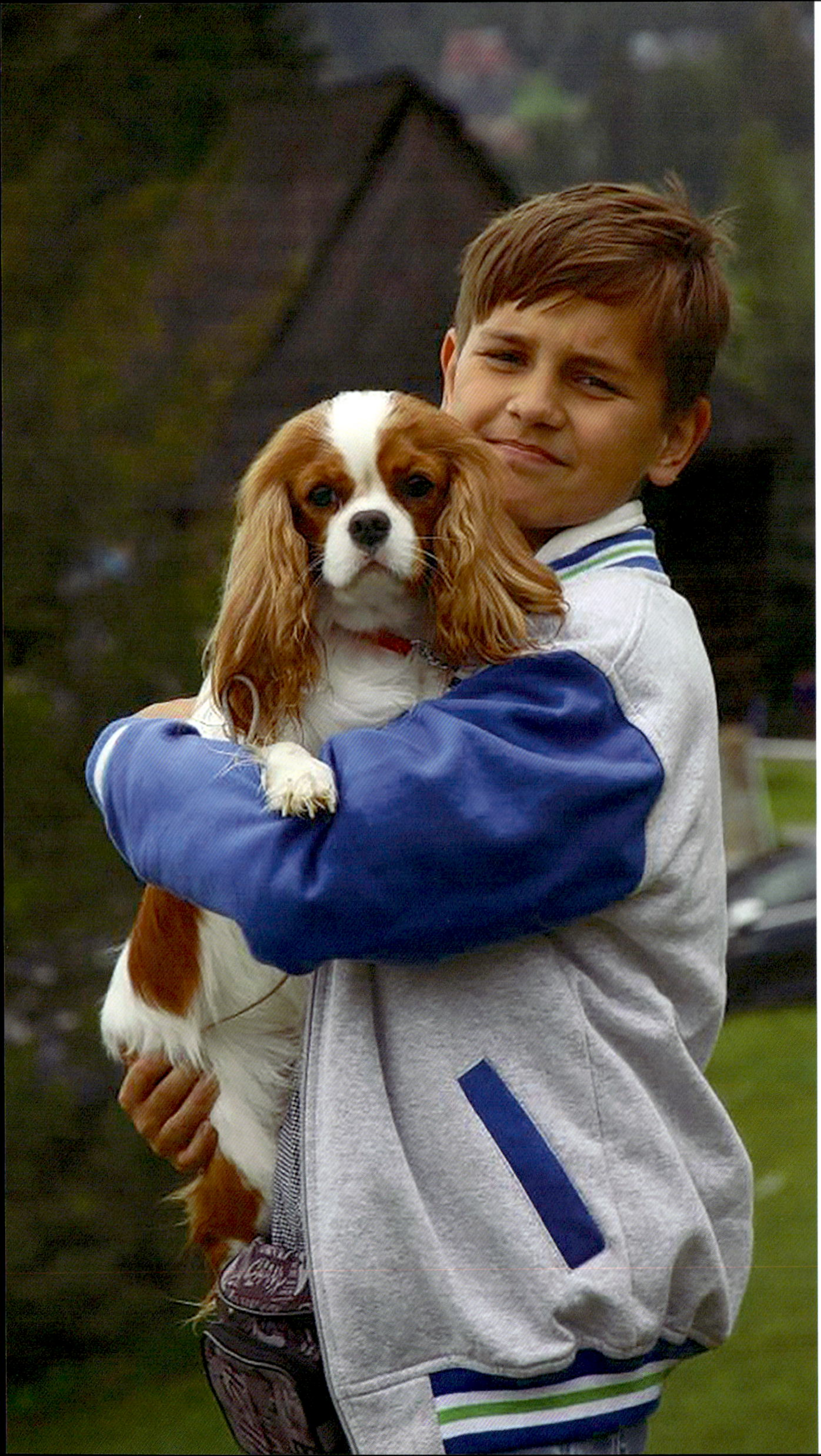

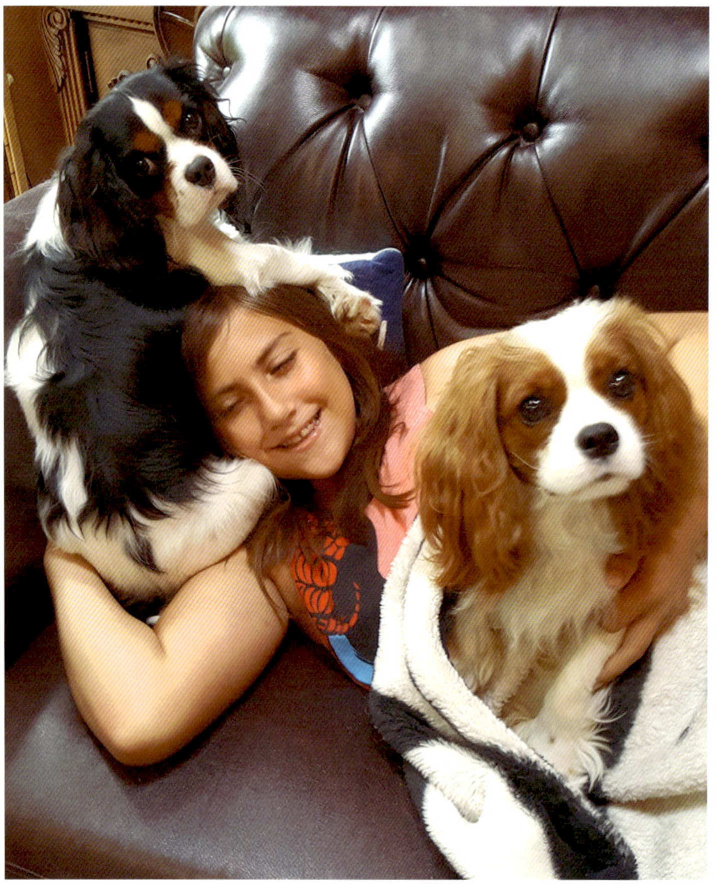

Zoe Wilk and Cavaliers Zorro and Dr. Watson are fast friends.

Photo credit: Irina Wilk, Pennsylvania, USA

Fabian, son of Breeder Alexsandra Kubica, is proud of his fur friend Blue Moon Cavaliers Unbreakable Spirit.

Photo credit: Zlota Manolia, Katowice, Polland

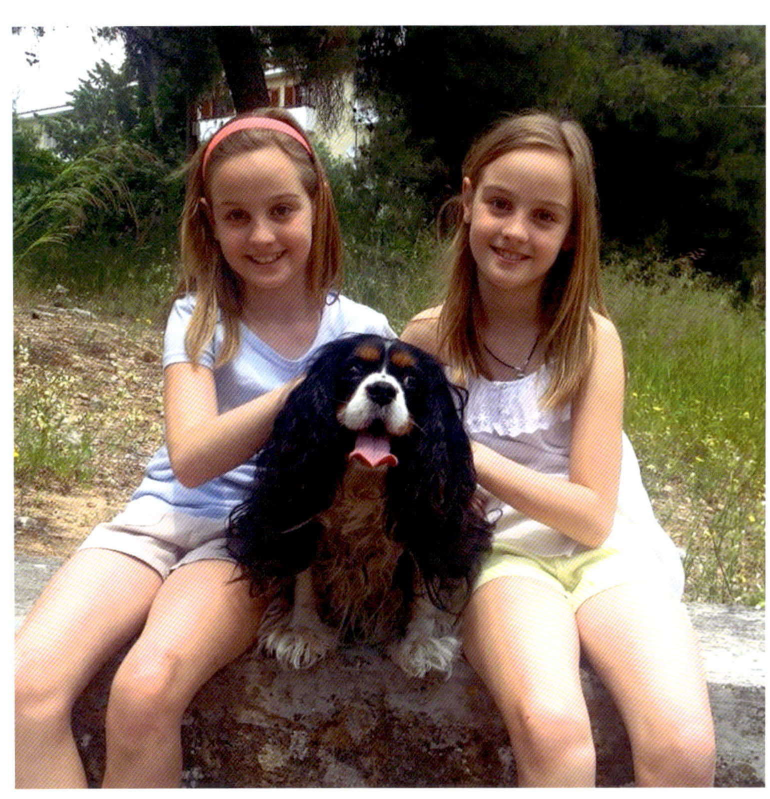

Twins, Johanna and Helen, simply adore Emma.
Photo credit: Rena Gallou, Athens, Greece

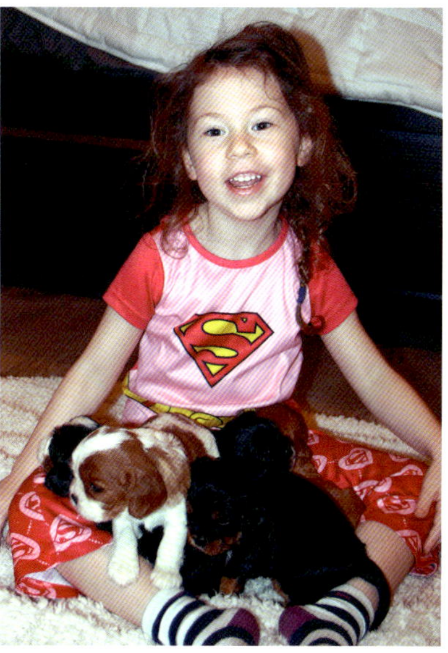

Allie is loving her lap full of puppies, bred by her mother.
Photo credit: Alisha Lockleer, Washington, USA

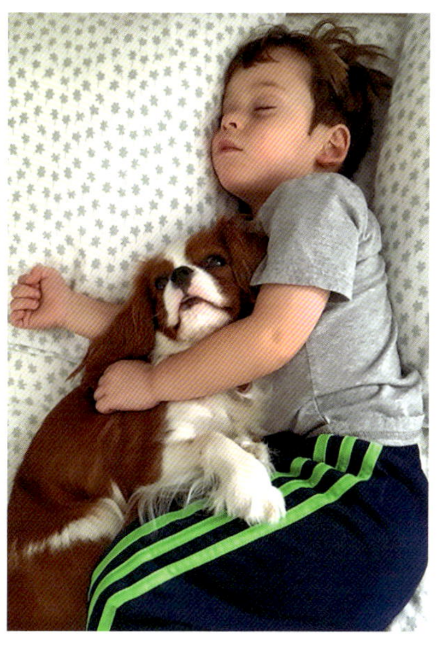

Grandson Teddy and Violet Button take every opportunity to cuddle.
Photo credit: Mary Padgitt, California, USA

Sabrina Ritter won a community dog show with her best friend, Callie!

Photo credit: Mary Colburn-Green, L'Aude, France

Neighbor Markella adores Emma, the Tri-Color.

Photo credit: Rena Gallou, Athens, Greece

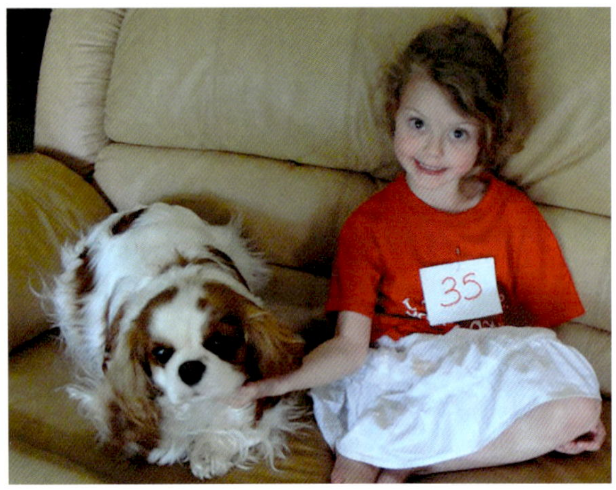

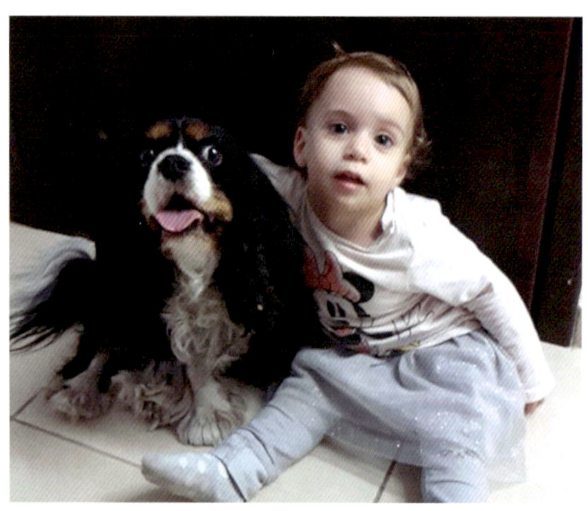

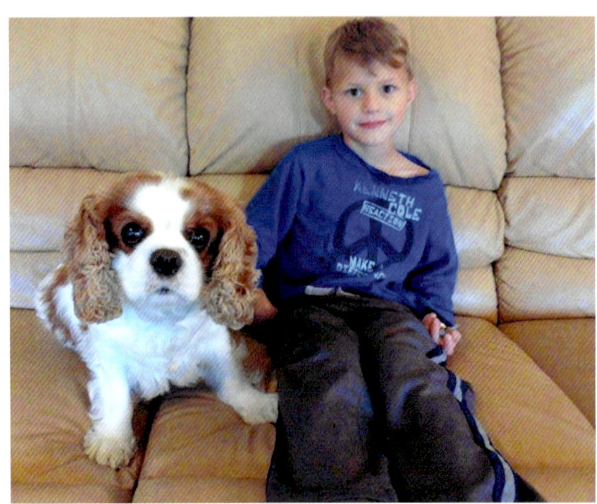

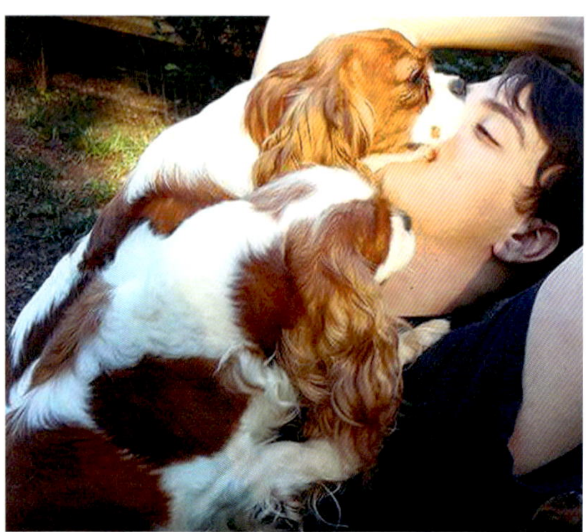

Mathias Ritter and Callie, like brother and sister.

Photo credit: Mary Colburn-Green, L'Aude, France

Given half a chance, the family Cavaliers will smother Zach with love.

Photo credit: Jennifer Wehking, Georgia, USA

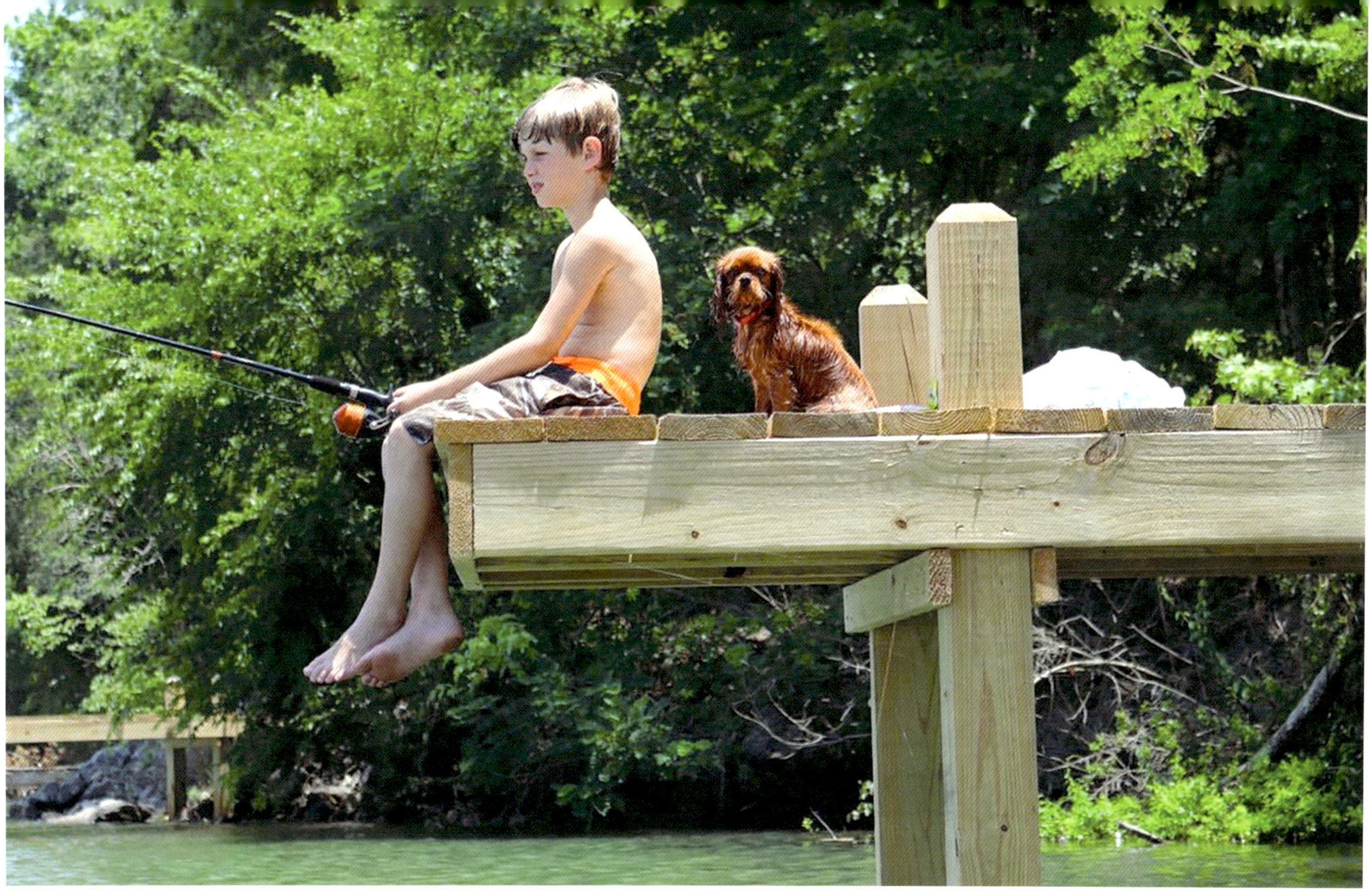

"Huck Finn," aka Gavin Marino, and his trusty girl, Tasha.

Photo credit: Heather Marino, Tennessee USA

Carey, Henley, and Grace overseen by Dylan and Mahogany (with clown Henley up front saying, "cheese please").

Photo credit: Shirley Coyle, New York, USA

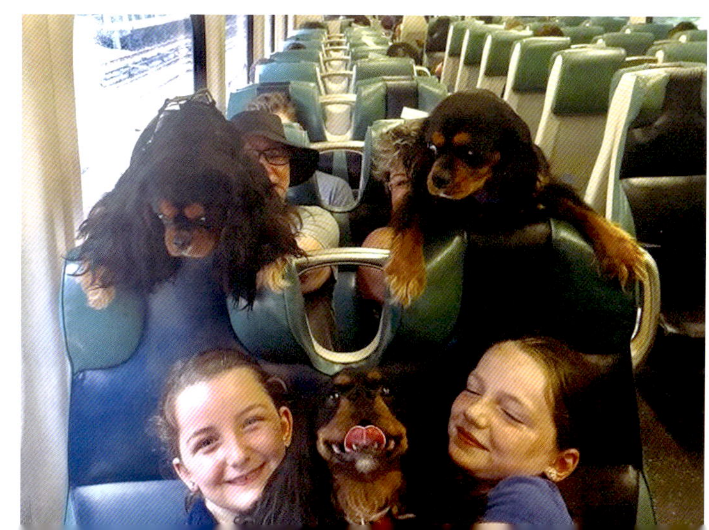

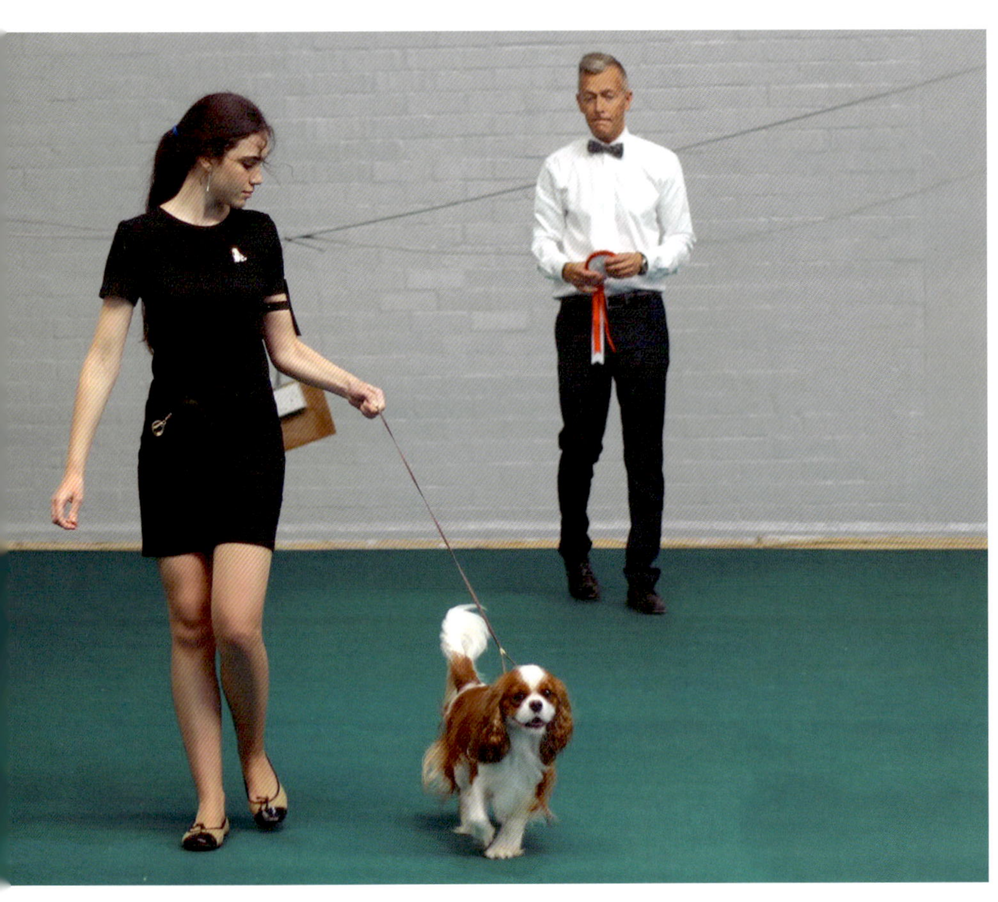

Well done, Lucia Cobos (15), daughter of breeder Maria Jose Molina, for showing Kingdom Ravenna's George at the Gibraltar International Dog Show and winning 1st Exc GCC CACIB.

Photo credit: Maria Jose Molina, Cordoba, Spain

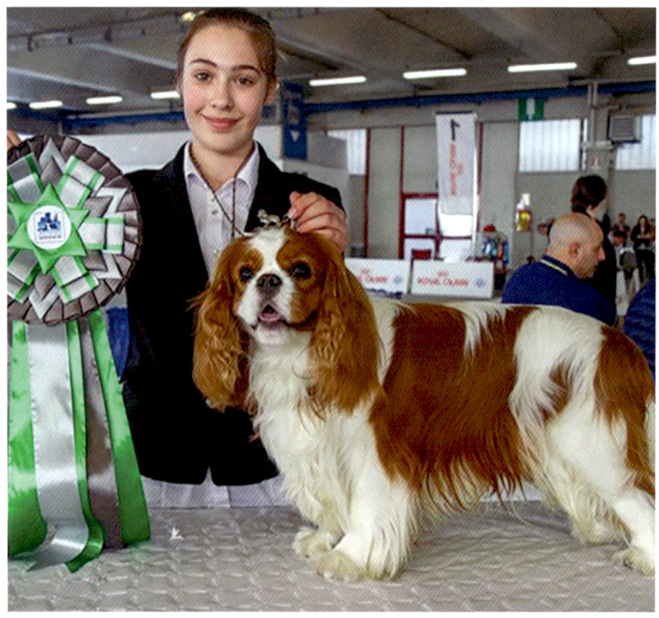

Amelie (12) shows her dog London, from Breeder Visintini Valter, as a junior and wins the big prize.

Photo credit: Vanessa Rocca, Sonorio, Italy

Even teenagers like
Amelie love Cavaliers!
Photo credit: Mary Colburn-Green
L'Aude, France

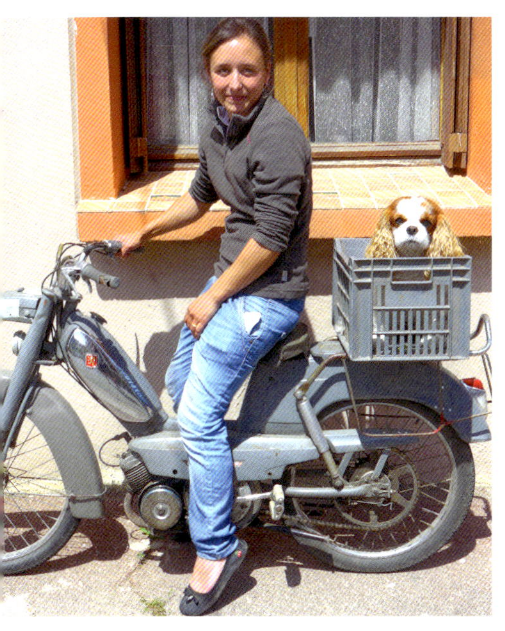

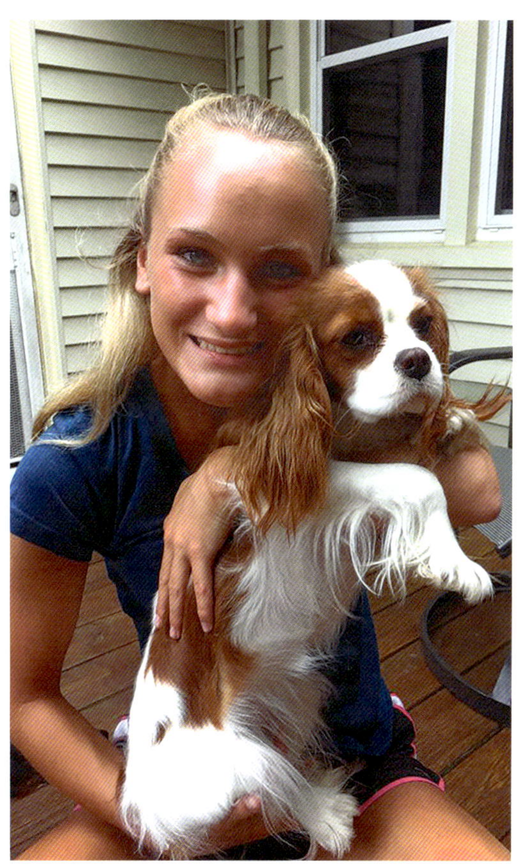

Kate (17) can't fathom leaving
her beloved Gracie (2) for college.
Photo credit: Tracey Draveck, New York, USA

No child can resist Callie in her stroller
looking like a sweet peluche (stuffed animal).
Photo credit: Mary Colburn-Green, L'Aude, France

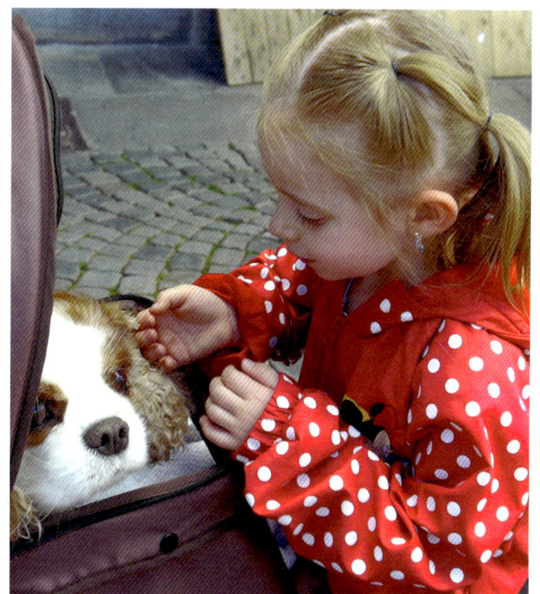

Chapter 3 - Rescue Cavaliers

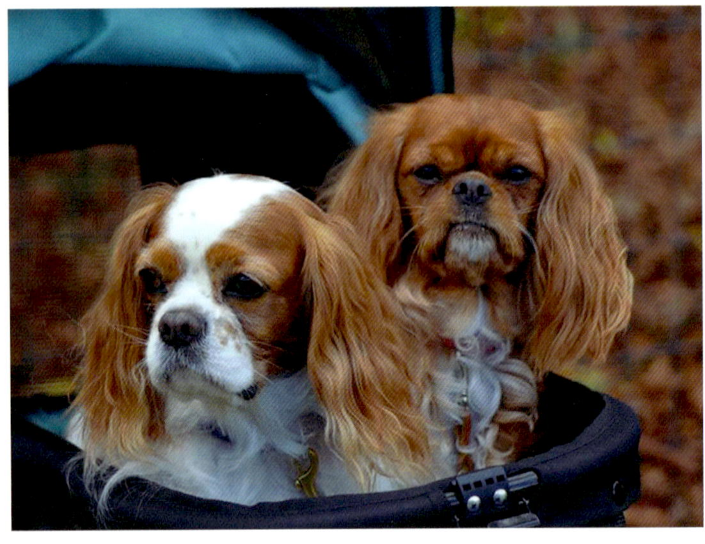

April and Tanner, beloved rescue Cavaliers, enjoy riding in style.

Photo credit Jennifer Walking, Georgia, USA

Like other popular purebred dogs, Cavaliers are pricey and attract profiteers such as puppy mills, backyard breeders, and internet scammers. Luckily, there is a movement under way to stop these profiteers from selling their dogs to retailers, and rescue organizations are only too willing to find good homes for dogs released from these dreadful conditions.

People may have to give up a beloved Cavalier due to the owner's death, disability, or other situational change. Moving abroad or to an apartment that doesn't allow pets, or perhaps an allergy may instigate the alteration. Often a Cavalier is surrendered because of its difficult health issue. Then, there are the lost Cavaliers who end up in shelters or those for whom the owners cannot afford care.

The reasons for a Cavalier being in rescue may be myriad, but the worldwide network of rescue fosterers and adopters, as well as organizations removing dogs and puppies from horrendous breeding mills, is active, committed and commendable. ACKCS Rescue Trust, Inc. and Cavalier Rescue USA rescue and place about 1,000 rescue Cavaliers in suitable pet homes every year.

A list of rescue organizations is located in the Resource Section in the back of this book. Owning a rescue Cavalier earns you double the points for entry to heaven and extra large angel wings. More importantly, you'll be amply rewarded here and now as your tender, loving care nurtures your foster fur baby into a happy, well-adjusted member of the family.

Enjoy this sample of Cavaliers who have been rescued.

The first story I received about the rescue of Sparkle, a senior Cavalier, will touch your heart.

I just recently adopted this sweet, senior, special needs girl from Cavalier Rescue USA. She was surrendered to Rescue by a homeless woman living out of her car. The woman took out a Craigslist ad to give her away, which is how Rescue found out about her.

This poor little girl was skin and bones, matted, and had been heavily flea-infested for so long that she was anemic. She had embedded foxtails in her paws and had serious health issues like an enlarged heart with a grade 5 heart murmur and painful bone spurs on her spine (spondylosis).

Her name is Sparkle and the name fits. In spite of everything she's endured, she's still sweet, affectionate, trusting, and her tail is always in motion. Her foster mom, Sarah, had her bathed, treated for fleas, groomed and got her in for a long-overdue vet visit soon after she was surrendered.

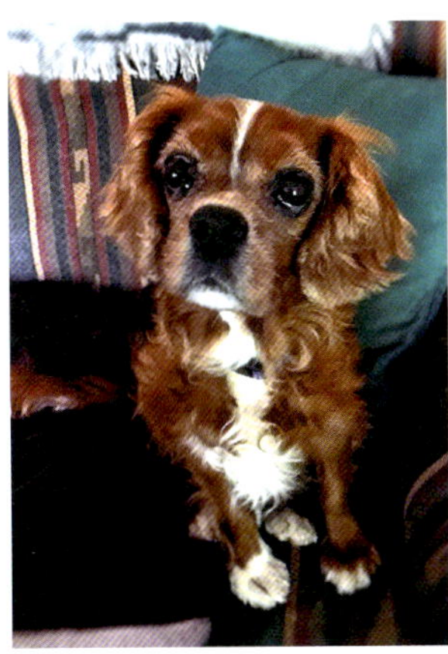

Sparkle is now on a high-quality diet (with plenty of red meat to improve her anemia). She gets her pretty auburn coat brushed daily, receives dietary supplements, takes several Rx medications, and gets all the cuddles and lap time she wants! She deserves to live out her last years being loved and cared for. I am so fortunate to have her. She puts the sparkle in my life! ♥

Catherine Novak's special needs rescue Sparkle lights up her life.

Photo credit: Catherine Novak, California, USA

This rescue story is from Sarah Knudsen in California.

I fostered Jack and Ladybug several years ago for Cavalier Rescue USA when their owner from Pebble Beach moved east into a high-rise apartment. They felt their dogs would be happier with a family who could offer them outdoor space. Our family fell in love with the two and couldn't part with them. They were young, healthy, completely trained, and totally adorable. Ladybug (on the right) is our rescue 'spokesmodel' at rescue events. She's the perfect advocate to adopt a rescue rather than shop for a Cavalier. But don't let her sweet face fool you. She snores like a lumberjack and rolls in stinky stuff whenever she can. Whereas Jack is our guard dog, protecting us from squirrels and mailmen. They're our little treasures. ♥

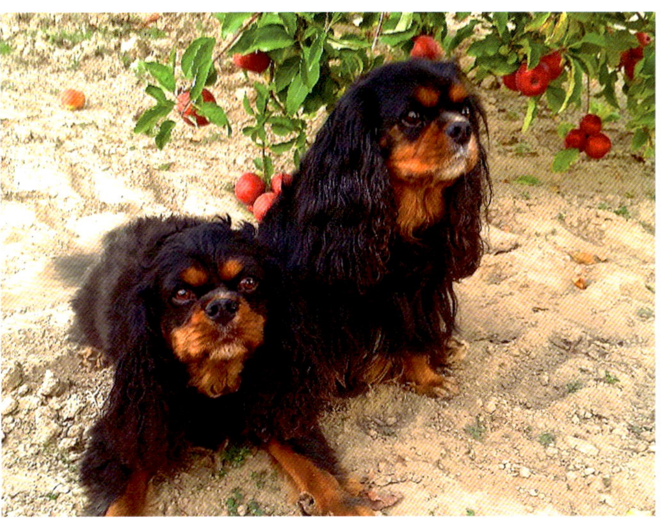

Jack and Ladybug were fostered by Sarah Knudsen,
but they stayed because the family fell in love with them.

Rescue sisters, (from left) Lady Ruby Marigold and Lady Blossom Isabella, now ladies in waiting to Princess Phoebe, the Blenheim, are the fortunate rescues of Pamela Duker, Harrowgate, North Yorkshire, UK.

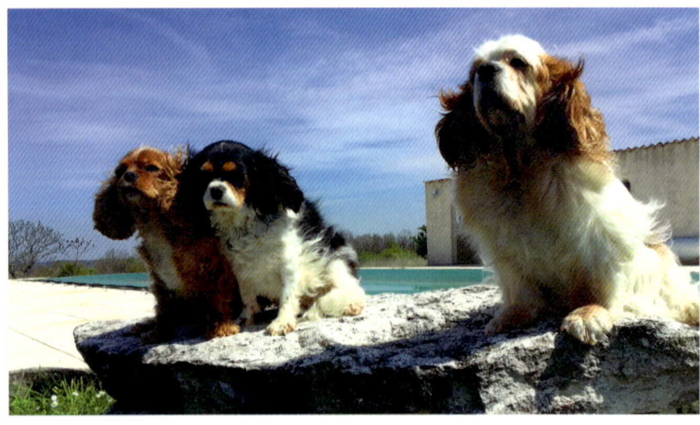

This wonderful rescue of Blenheim sisters from a puppy mill in Leeds is from Pamela Duker, who lives in Harrowgate, UK.

I had been contemplating a companion for Princess Phoebe Angelica as I knew that Willow, her German Shepherd bodyguard, was 14 and a half and so had very little time left. I decided on a puppy from fully health-tested parents and started looking for a responsible breeder to put my name on the probably long waiting list.

At the time, I was a member of Saving Cavaliers UK that purchases Cavaliers considered in danger—usually cheap, unneutered dogs who are likely to be passed on for breeding. I saw a picture of two ex-breeding bitches who were sisters that Saving Cavaliers UK had purchased from a puppy farm near Leeds. As they always do, they had passed them on to a local dog rescue for vet treatment, assessment, and re-homing.

As soon as I saw their picture, I immediately filled in the adoption form—and then broke the news to my husband. Strangely, he too was drawn to the two "flower girls," Blossom and Marigold. So, when Jane from West Yorkshire Dog Rescue rang to talk about the sort of home we could offer, we were both very excited.

The girls had arrived at the rescue thin, matted, ears full of mites, and teeth so bad that they had over 40 removed between them. But the real horror was poor little Marigold; she was covered in old and recent bite wounds around her neck. Her neck was swollen and filled with pus. Both girls had early stages of pyometra, wombs filled with pus from whelping in dirty conditions. These lost souls were terrified of the human touch, had shut down, and had eyes that were so empty. They had been bred when they were only nine months old, so were very small, weighing only 4kg (less than 9 lbs).

A few weeks later we picked them up, healthier, and thanks to Jane, much further along with their education, but they still needed lots of work on their psychological state. I was worried about taking them. My head said, "Don't do it," but my heart just could not say no to having them.

We drove all night—17 hours—to get them home to France. Listening to our voices for that long seemed to have a positive effect on the dogs. We knew we had made a huge leap forward when at one of our fuel stops they both stood up and wagged their tails when we returned to the car. Of course, Princess Phoebe who lives to travel in the car set an excellent example.

They have taken leaps and bounds forward every day since then. Within just a few days I knew why my heart was so besotted with them and why I was so drawn to them. As Princess Phoebe's ladies-in-waiting, they are now Blossom Isabella and Ruby Marigold. They fit into our pack as if they were made for us. They also adore Willow (still with us at 15 and a half) and Phoebe. For sisters, they are like chalk and cheese, and yet are amazingly similar. Blossom has an obsession for my husband and hates to leave the house and garden. Ruby wants to explore the world and loves everybody, even complete strangers.

We are very blessed to have them, and they are the center of our world. ♥

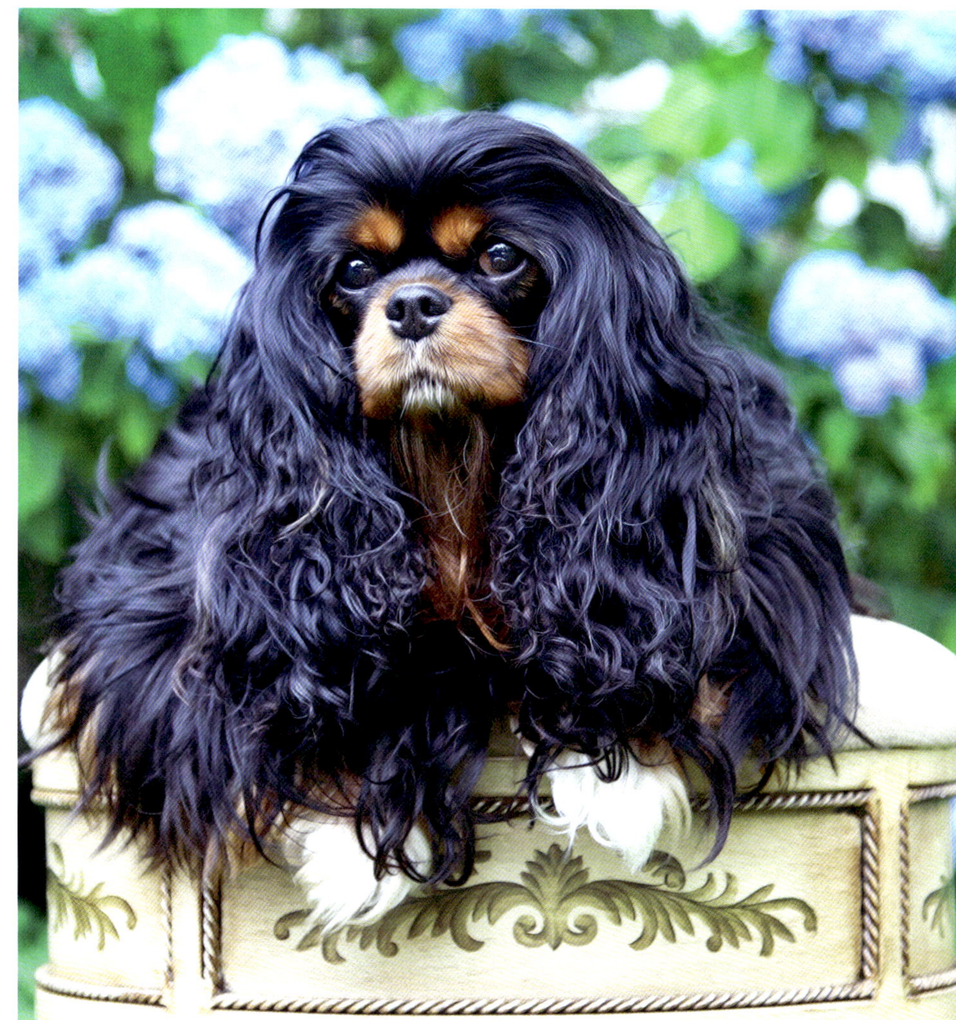

Beautiful Maggie Mae was a rescue from Lucky Star Cavalier Rescue.

Photo credit: Leanne Newman, Tennessee, USA

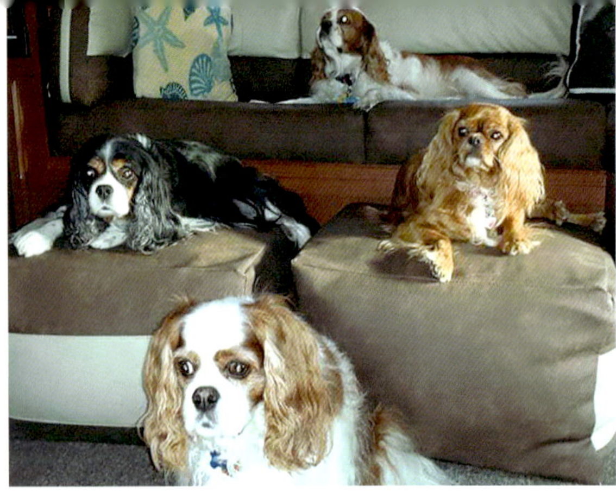

Chuck Andrick's rescue family in Florida.
Photo credit: Jennifer Wehking, Georgia, USA

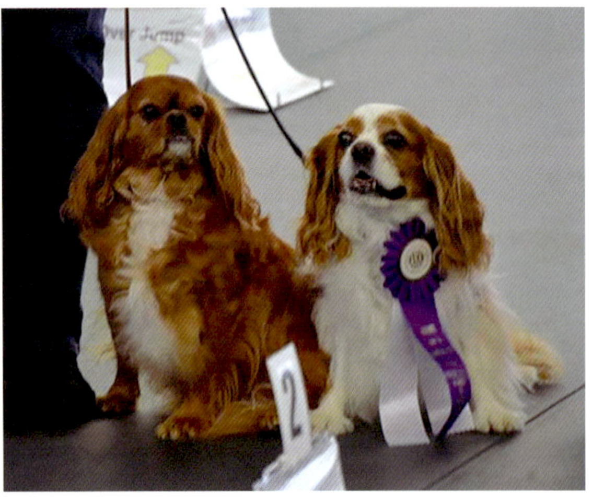

April and Tanner, winning rescue Cavaliers in Georgia.
Photo credit: Jennifer Wehking, Tennessee, USA.

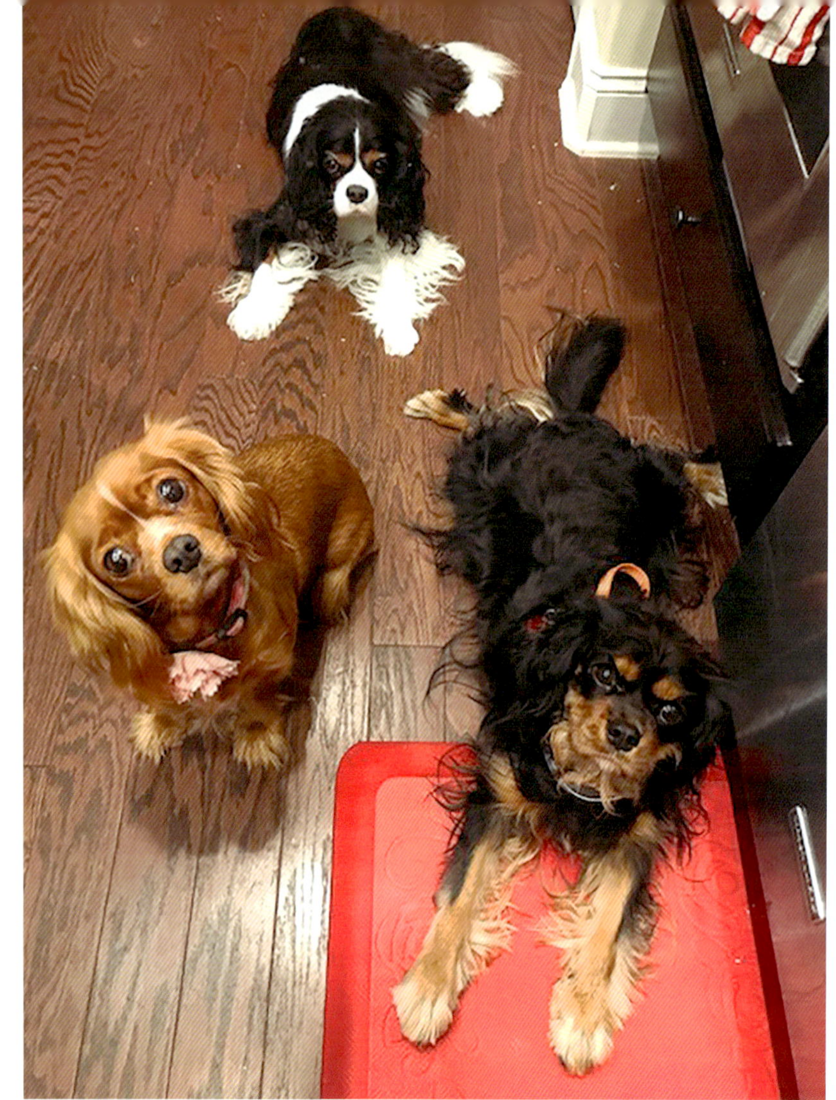

These are Pam Foley's three rescues: the Ruby is Sugar Pup Ginger, the Tri is Jazzie, and the Black and Tan is Scarlet Rose (who hates her picture taken). According to Pam, Scarlett Rose is a two-year-old spitfire with SM from New Orleans, Louisiana, and Jazzie is a rescue from Franklin, Tennessee, who she found on the "RESCUE ME" site 4 years ago.
Photo credit: Pam Foley, Alabama, USA

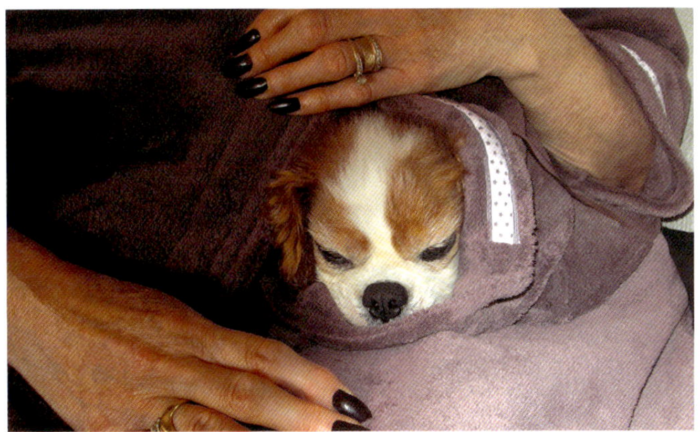

Breeder Veronica Hull's rescue Cavalier Gizmo, suffers from Curly Coat Syndrome, an auto-immune disease, and many other genetic disorders. Yet through her wonderful care and love, he has managed to live to almost 15 year and is still going.
Photo credit: Veronica Hull, London, UK

This rescue story is from Veronica Hull of Telvara Cavaliers, one of the UK's best CKCS breeders, advocates, and Kennel Club leaders. It gives insight into why Cavaliers must undergo the proper health-testing protocols prior to breeding.

My Little Gizmo, a Cavalier rescue, came to me at two weeks of age, having been left by his heartless breeder at a local vet practice for euthanasia following a diagnosis of the auto-immune anomaly Curly Coat Syndrome. I then received a panicked call from the vet nurse who had no way of looking after this little scrap of fur. I agreed to collect and foster him through his first few weeks of life, if he managed to live that long. He has one testicle, was blind by 9 months of age, and any vaccination would probably have killed him, but he is the happiest little soldier as long as he knows I'm close by for snuggles.

Gizmo was diagnosed with Addison's Disease 14 months ago and given an extremely poor prognosis. Following the diagnosis, I was sent on my way with Prednisolone and advised palliative care was all that I could offer my sweet little man, who nature dealt with unkindly. He has every genetic fault in the book, but he's the dearest little soul ever.

When diagnosed with Addison's, Gizmo had lost nearly all the sparse, rough textured coat that accompanies Curly Coat Syndrome, so last summer he was down to bare skin. Dear Darcy of Willowheart Onesies very kindly fast-tracked me a couple of her handmade fleecy PJ sets to help stop poor Gizmo's shivers. His tail is still virtually uncoated, and he has some patches where his coat hasn't quite covered over the skin, but for a 14 & 3/4 years old dog, who was given a diagnosis offering a zero future, he's doing so well...bless him.

For me it was yet another 'heart in mouth day' with a vet check-up for my constant shadow—my Velcro dog, Gizmo. Today my vet didn't hesitate in prescribing a new batch of steroids for my Chihuahua-sized Cavalier with the words, 'whatever you're doing, keep doing it.' And we will! This baby drew the short straw at birth, but he and I have travelled a very special and rewarding journey together. I wouldn't have missed a day of it, and I suspect my little Gizmo would say the same. In fact, he does in his own endearing way every day. This little man was never born to be a show dog, and with all his imperfections, he could never win a prize for external beauty, but he has a heart of pure gold. I'm so grateful we found each other almost 15 years ago. I'm just so very proud of this inspirational, little Cavalier. But he would never have had to suffer if the breeder had tested his parents' DNA for Curly Coat. ♥

Here's another sweet rescue story from Stephanie Sue Barber from Lexington, Kentucky USA.

Chloe is my fifth Cavalier and was owned by a family that consisted of a fireman, a nurse, and four children between the ages of 2 and 12 who had no time for Chloe. She was very neglected with sad eyes, ribs that showed, and hair that had been clipped down to her skin. They didn't want to make her fat, so they only fed her once a day, but the food they fed her was the equivalent of a tortilla chip in terms of nutrition and taste. Despite all of that, she wagged her tail when I greeted her.

I had done Cavalier rescue when I lived in Fort Collins, Colorado, and had never thought about buying a dog from Craigslist without knowing its pedigree. Many prayers for a little companion (as I was lonely here in Lexington Kentucky) led me to Craigslist and an ad for a Cavalier puppy at the price of $200. She is the sweetest little girl, comic with a funny and quirky personality. Her personality rivals the other Cavaliers that I've owned in the past with excellent pedigrees. ♥

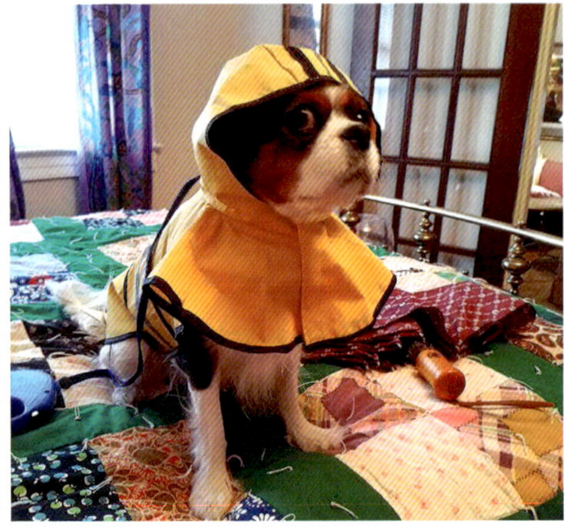

Chloe

Photo credit: Stephanie Sue Barber, Kentucky, USA

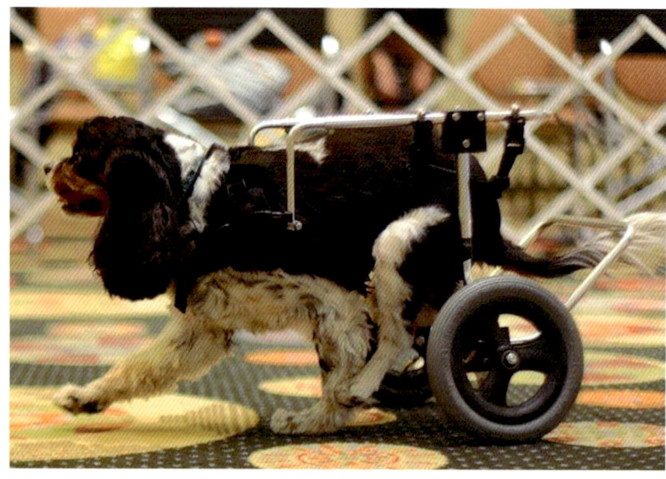

Abby, a rescue of ACKCS Rescue Trust Inc., greatly enjoyed her new mobility.

Photo credit: Chris Weeks, Oregon, USA

This story about Judy and EJ Harank's experience as a volunteer family gives insight into how the ACKCS Rescue Trust Inc. (Cavalier Rescue Trust) helps Cavaliers, including special needs dogs like Abby.

Abby…a Love Story by Judy Harank

(originally published in "The Royal Dispatch" magazine)

Abby, originally called Baby, was an owner-surrender Cavalier who came under the care of the Cavalier Rescue Trust in October 2011. Her paperwork indicates she was approximately 4 or 5 years old. Her condition at the time of her surrender was heartbreaking. She was underweight, her nails were like talons, her hair dull and matted. Her back legs were so deformed from such a severe degree of uncorrected patellar luxation that they literally folded and flopped, useless, behind and underneath her when she moved. Her tummy, hind end, and elbows were covered in scrapes, open sores, and calluses from dragging herself along as she moved from one spot to another. She lived outside day and night. Her environment was a patch of concrete patio, a dirt yard, a worn-out rug for a bed, and a dirty water dish. The one picture I have seen of her in that environment breaks my heart every time I look at it, but at the end of the day, the owner did the right thing by surrendering Abby to the Cavalier Rescue Trust for a chance at a better life. It took a village of kind-hearted volunteers to transport Abby to her new home in Arizona. A relay was organized, through California and across the desert to Arizona. At one of the hand-off points, the volunteer recalled crying as Abby was handed off to her, this pathetic looking dog, obviously in bad shape and in need of help. And then Abby was set on a patch of grass to go potty, and the volunteer's tears turned to joy as Abby sniffed the grass and 'crab-walked' around, her unbroken spirit coming to life. In Arizona, Abby was under the care of a veterinarian who volunteered her time to oversee Abby's surgeries and rehabilitation. Not such an easy task, as it turned out. Several surgeons refused to perform surgery on her back legs, saying it would be kinder to euthanize her. One surgeon said he would amputate her back legs. Finally, an orthopedic surgeon agreed to perform the corrective surgeries, but admitted that he was not overly optimistic about the outcome.

By now, Abby had settled in with her devoted foster family in Arizona, Holly and Gale, and their two Cavaliers, Abby and Ruby. Baby Abby was in heaven living with Holly and Gale. She was allowed to sleep inside the house on the comfy human bed. Holly made a soft cloth sling to support Abby's hind end so she could go on short walks. Gale made a cart for Abby so all five of them were able to go on longer neighborhood outings. Holly says that Abby sat up so straight and tall in that cart, so joyful to be out and about! Her hair was getting shinier and her beautiful ears were growing out long and lush. Holly says that Abby's spirit, however, was even more beautiful to behold. She was so happy sitting beside Holly on the sofa, gazing into her eyes, loving her, and telling her how grateful she was for this new life.

In the winter of 2011, while under Holly and Gale's loving foster care, Abby had her surgeries, first on one leg and then the other. The surgeries were funded by very generous donations to the Cavalier Rescue Trust. Abby embraced the required therapy after the surgeries. Holly says you could see her think through the exercises. She would pause, think, and move one hind leg at a time in order to navigate her first steps. She was so proud of each new movement, and loved learning about what her hind legs could do. While she would never be able to walk like a normal dog, at least her legs now lifted her up to the extent where her tender belly did not drag against the ground. She was even able to scratch her ears with her hind legs. Soon it was time for Abby to find her forever-home. Holly says she didn't think it would happen so quickly, as she didn't think anyone would be able to see past Abby's funny legs. Abby was a beautiful dog, inside and out, but who would want a dog that cannot run and play? The surgeries had done wonders, but Abby was still definitely a special needs dog.

My husband EJ, my mother, and I went to visit Abby for the first time at Holly and Gale's house on a sunny spring day. Their two Blenheim Cavaliers Abby and Ruby rushed to the door to greet us, so sweet and friendly. Against their wishes, they were gently but firmly put in the backyard to allow us time to focus on Baby Abby. Although we had been warned that Abby would likely never be able to walk normally, I was still shocked at the extent of her…I hesitate to use this word…disability. (Looking back at this now, I have to laugh. Abby never considered herself disabled—just special.) However, I hid my shock to the best of my ability and settled on the sofa to get to know Holly and Gale, and especially Abby, a bit better.

At that very first visit, it was apparent that Abby was special on so many levels. And she was very proud, as if to say, "Don't you dare feel sorry for me!" She was bright-eyed and alert, a tri-color beauty, who had the most amazing, soulful eyes. Because Abby was unable to jump up on the sofa by herself, Holly lifted her, and she settled in right next to me. Abby looked into my eyes and took a tight hold on my heart. She told me with her eyes that she understood that we were there to possibly become her permanent foster parents. She told me with her eyes that she could tell we were kind-hearted people who would treat her like a queen. She told me with her eyes that, although she couldn't walk like a normal dog, she wouldn't be any trouble at all. And she told me with her eyes that she was a very special girl, and that if we took her, she would fill our lives with joy.

After an hour or so, EJ, Mom, and I said our good-byes to Holly, Gale, and Abby and headed home. It was a quiet ride. When EJ and I first talked about the possibility of a rescue Cavalier, we considered that it might be an older dog, or maybe a dog with a heart condition that needed medication. We hadn't really talked about a true special needs dog, and I think EJ was a bit concerned that we wouldn't be able to give Abby the time and attention she deserved. Abby's special needs and ongoing care would require a true and lasting commitment on our part, not something to be taken lightly.

I waited patiently while EJ thought everything through, back and forth, pros and cons. I tried very hard not to put any pressure on him. After all, he wasn't the one sitting next to Abby on the sofa, so he wasn't able to look into her eyes like I did. She wasn't able to communicate her story to him like she did to me. Finally, after about 24 hours, and to my husband's everlasting credit, he came to the same conclusion I had. That it would be an honor to become Abby's permanent foster parents.

It was such a happy, emotional day when we picked Abby up to take her home. Holly and Gale, who had cared for Abby with such devotion during her surgeries, were sad to see her go. But EJ and I were so excited and so happy to take this extraordinary girl home and call her our own. Well, legally she belonged to the Cavalier Rescue Trust, but in our hearts, she was our dog. We forged a lasting friendship with Holly and Gale, and got together frequently for what we called 'Wine and Cavaliers' dinner parties. When Holly and Gale would come over for one of these dinners, Abby would head straight to Holly, squirming with happiness, look up at her with adoration, and ask Holly to pick her up and hold her. There we would sit at the dinner table, all of us, with Holly holding Abby throughout the meal. EJ and I eventually got two more dogs from the Cavalier Rescue Trust: Archie, a.k.a. Big Lug, a 31-pound, emotional, loveable, Blenheim boy; and Rose, an old gal with the personality of a '60's flower child and a big wart on her forehead that only added to her uniqueness. Abby welcomed our new additions with grace—once they understood that she was the queen. Archie even joined us at the dinner table for our Wine and Cavaliers dinner parties, with his own chair pulled up to the table. Rose preferred to be off by herself in a corner, in her own happy little world.

We had a full and happy life in Arizona. Physical therapy sessions continued for Abby, with the hope her legs would continue to stretch out and become stronger. Our neighbors, Jeff and Melanie, who loved all of our dogs, kindly allowed us to use their pool for Abby's swimming exercises. When they knew Abby was coming over for swim therapy, they would turn on the pool heater to warm the water, set out the plush doggie spa towel, and have doggie treats waiting for Abby. Although Abby was never crazy about her swim therapy, if EJ got in the pool with her, she would tolerate it without complaint.

There were frequent walks on the greenbelt, which were fun for all of us. EJ would get Abby's wheeled cart out, and she would wiggle with excitement while he worked to strap her in. On the greenbelt, she would run like the wind in her cart, easily passing all the other dogs on the path. EJ would shout, "Watch out! Abby's coming up behind you!" Everyone would move to the right, like the Red Sea parting.

Everyone in the neighborhood knew Abby and adored her. Abby took it upon herself to become our guard dog when she saw that Archie and Rose were failing miserably at the task. While in our backyard, she would bark furiously if anyone dared walk by with a dog. The neighbors forgave her that, in fact, instead of scolding or complaining, they would shout out a hello to Abby, which of course made her bark even more.

In the winter of 2014, EJ and I moved to Southern California. For the first time since having the dogs, we were able to install a dog door. (In Arizona where we lived, there were too many wild creatures lurking outside to safely have a dog door.) Abby loved the dog door so much. It gave her such independence to come and go as she pleased. She learned very quickly to keep her back legs tucked in to her sides as she went through the door, so as not to crack her knees against the opening. She loved going outside at will, sitting or lying in the sun with the cool ocean breeze ruffling her hair. At times, she would lie down halfway through the doggie door, with just her head poking out, and fall asleep. Archie would look at me as if to say, "Mom, can't you do something about this? I want to go outside." He knew he would get into trouble if he disturbed her while he tried to get out the door. Well, there was no way I was going to disturb Her Highness, so I would lead Archie to another door, let him outside, and everyone was happy.

Abby also loved going for strolls in her cart down at the harbor. She knew chances were good that Mom and Dad were going to get fish and chips, and she would have a little piece or two of fish, and a pinch of chips.

Thankfully, our new neighbors in Southern California loved Abby...their dogs, maybe not so much. Shadow and Snickerdoodle tried to make friends with our dogs, and succeeded with Archie and Rose, but Abby was a tough nut to crack. With few exceptions, she typically preferred people to other dogs, unless the dog was a Cavalier.

Abby had a series of health problems — strokes, back pain, stomach problems. Still, she had such a strong spirit and will to live that she overcame each illness like a trouper.

In early June 2015, she became sick again, very sick this time. She ended up in a critical care hospital with around-the-clock care. Severe pancreatitis, inflamed gall bladder, and insulin-resistant diabetes were the major problems. Still, under the care of a skilled internist, she started to rally. Her internist was guardedly hopeful.

The hospital staff called Abby a Superstar. EJ and I visited Abby frequently during the five days she was in the hospital. Sometimes she was sound asleep, and we didn't want to disturb her. We would gently lay our hands on her, softly talk to her, and kiss her.

Other times she was awake and alert, and her tail would wag like crazy when she saw us. One day the staff unhooked all her IV's and brought her to us in a room where we could privately visit with her. That room had a window facing outside. A dog walked by, and Abby went into her guard dog mode, barking at that dog, telling him he had better not even think about coming any closer. It made us smile to see her feisty spirit still intact like that.

On the third day of her hospital stay, I went to visit Abby by myself. She was in her cage, hooked up to her IV's, but awake and alert. She was so happy to see me, wagging her tail, trying to stand up with all her bandages, tubes, and whatnot. The hospital staff opened her cage and I put my face in to nuzzle her. She loved to be nuzzled and kissed, but was never the type of dog who kissed back. Unlike Archie, who can't control his licker, Abby was never a licker. Well, this time she smothered me with kisses, licking me all over my face and hands. I kept saying, "Thank you, Girlie, I love you too!" That love-fest went on for several minutes. I was astonished, as this had never happened before. I remember thinking that was Abby's way of asking me not to give up on her, that she was going to fight this health battle like she had fought every other health battle in her life.

After consulting with multiple doctors, the National Director of the Cavalier Rescue Trust authorized surgery to remove Abby's dangerously inflamed gall bladder. It did not appear that Abby was going to survive without this surgery. That surgery was performed on Friday evening, June 12th. Abby survived the surgery but her blood pressure dropped minutes after the surgery, and she passed away. In retrospect, I think what Abby was telling me when she smothered me with kisses two days prior to her passing, was about the love and devotion she felt for us, the humans who cared for her. I think she knew then that she was going to pass over the Rainbow Bridge.

All of those who knew Abby intimately — Holly and Gale, Char and Lamont, Renee, Auntie Cheryl and Grandma, and our close friends knew Abby wasn't just a pet; she was a treasured member of our family. She was so extraordinary, so endearing, and not because of her legs and special needs. She had such a joyful spirit. You would look into her beautiful, dark eyes and see straight through to her heart and soul.

My husband and I talk all the time about how blessed we were to have such a special dog in our lives. Even with her crazy routine and demands, like waking us up at 4:00 a.m. every morning, so eager for breakfast and for the day to begin. She would start out at the end of the bed and then inch her way forward until her nose was 6 inches from our sleeping faces. She would wait and wait while I pretended to be asleep. As soon as I made one little movement, her tail would start wagging enthusiastically...THUMP THUMP THUMP!!! She would wiggle with such excitement that she would wake the other dogs. I would get up and say, "Okay girl, you ready for a boost?" And she would lift her hind end up so I could easily lift her up and carry her to the kitchen. I loved doing that for her. EJ had a similar routine with her.

We would occasionally leave the house without the dogs to go grocery shopping. They, of course, would be anxiously awaiting our return at the back door. They would go crazy, especially emotional Archie, when we walked through the door—as if we had been gone for days, not just an hour. Big Lug would go berserk, jumping, barking, and carrying on so that Abby had to stand back to avoid being trampled. EJ would immediately set the groceries on the floor, pick up his Girlie, and carry her to the kitchen (Leaving me to deal with Archie and the groceries, LOL!).

What has helped EJ and me as we struggle through grief, that is at times, almost unbearable, is remembering the kindness of the hundreds of people posting their thoughts and prayers for Abby on the Cavalier Rescue Trust FB page. And the unbelievable generosity of so many people who donated to pay for Abby's care—thank you, thank you, to all of you.

It also helps to focus on the happy times of Abby's amazing life: her joy at going for the cart rides with Holly and Gale; her ability to scratch her ears with her hind legs after her surgeries; going for a long car ride to see our friends Judy and Gary, and having a fun-filled visit with their Cavaliers Joey and Luna; chasing the lure in her wheeled cart at a Cavalier Fun Day lure-coursing event. (Although in looking at that video now, it's apparent Abby wasn't very interested in chasing that silly lure. She was doing it to appease EJ, who was enthusiastically running with her, shouting encouragement, and to please her cheering fans on the sidelines.) Yes indeed, that dog always knew how to work the crowd.

Perhaps the greatest highlight of Abby's life was her participation in the 2013 Cavalier National Specialty in Arizona. As the ambassador for Cavalier rescues, she spent hours meeting and greeting many very nice people. At times, she was carried around like a princess, other times her daddy hooked her up to her cart so she could get around easily on her own. While in her cart, she flew around the judging ring like a champion, pausing by the 'Best in Show' sign with her daddy by her side, so happy and proud.

A famous photographer was at the show and captured the most amazing pictures of Abby in her glory—head held high, smiling, eyes bright, and her ears (her pride and joy) freshly coifed by Char. Many people were watching her from the sidelines, clapping and cheering, with tears in their eyes.

That night at the Charitable Trust Banquet, her daddy snuck her into the dining room after everyone had finished eating dinner. The auction to raise money for the Cavalier Rescue Trust had begun, and even though Abby was very tired from the exciting activities of the day, she knew it was her duty to be there. Sure enough, whenever the bidding stalled, her benefactress carried her around the room. One look into Abby's beautiful dark eyes, and people felt compelled to dig deeper into their pockets.

On Saturday there was a Rescue Parade. Once again, Abby sailed around the ring in her cart, so happy and grateful to have found her forever home, but wanting to bring attention to all the sweet rescue dogs still hoping to find their forever families. Abby kept glancing at EJ and I as if to say, "Can't we take them all home?" Oh, if only we could.

To Renee Bruns and all the directors and trustees of the Cavalier Rescue Trust—the legal owners of Abby—I know you are as heartbroken as EJ and I are to have lost the Rescue Trust Heart Dog. Thank God you recognized the special spirit of this dog and did so much for her, in so many ways. I can assure you, and all of Abby's supporters, that for the last several years of her life, Abby had a full and joyful life. She knew that she was loved and treasured. She knew that the Rescue Trust was devoted to her wellbeing. When you think about it, how great to cross over the Rainbow Bridge under those circumstances?

With love and gratitude,
EJ and Judy Harank ♥

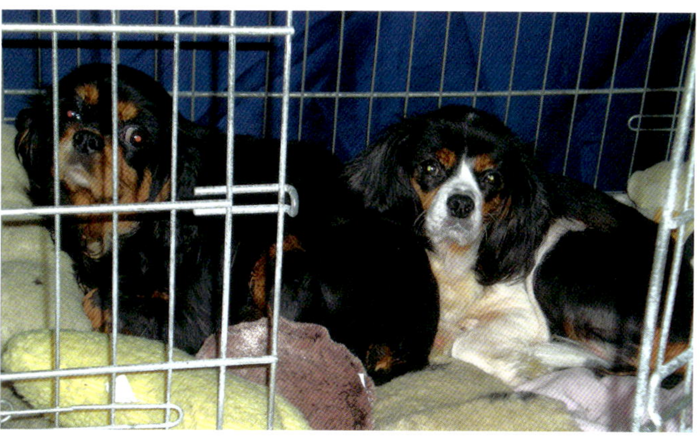

These are the beloved rescues, Dotje and Romy, of Lilly Hoylaerts in Kerkom, Belgium. Lilly says when she first got Dotje, the dog was afraid of the wind in her fur, the grass on her feet, and birds overhead.

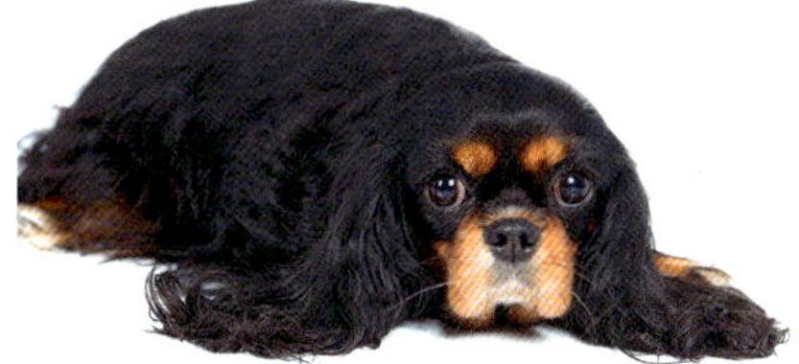

Look at Dotje now. She is doing so well.
Photo credit: Lilly Hoylaerts, Kerkom Belgium

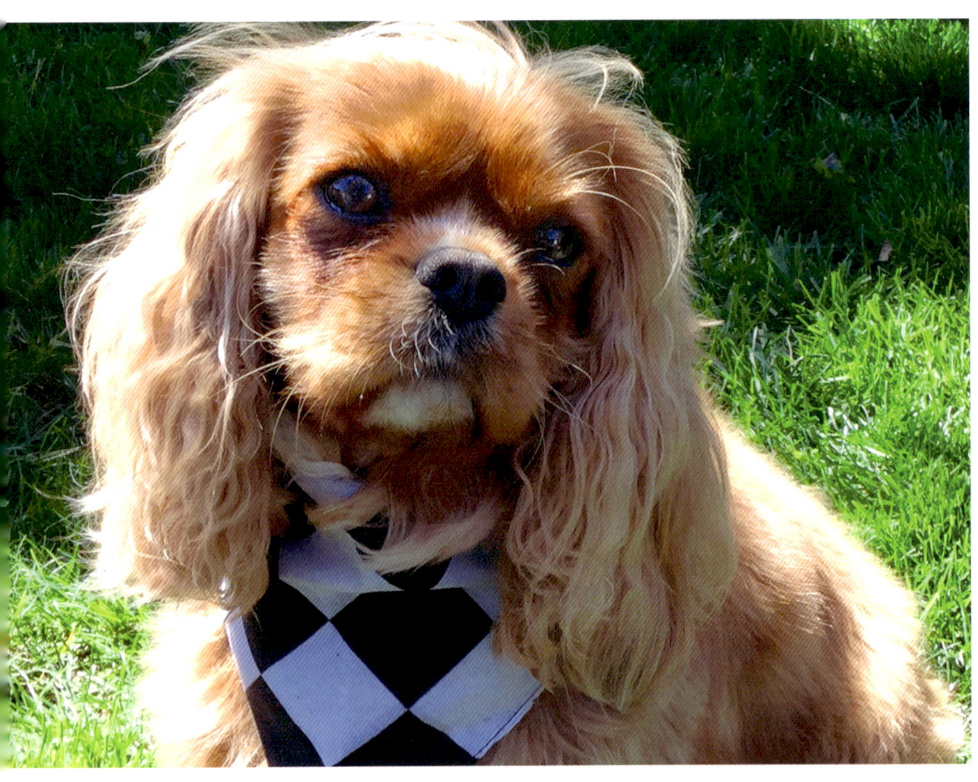

This is Kathy's other rescue Cavalier, Enzo, who is Riley's best bud.

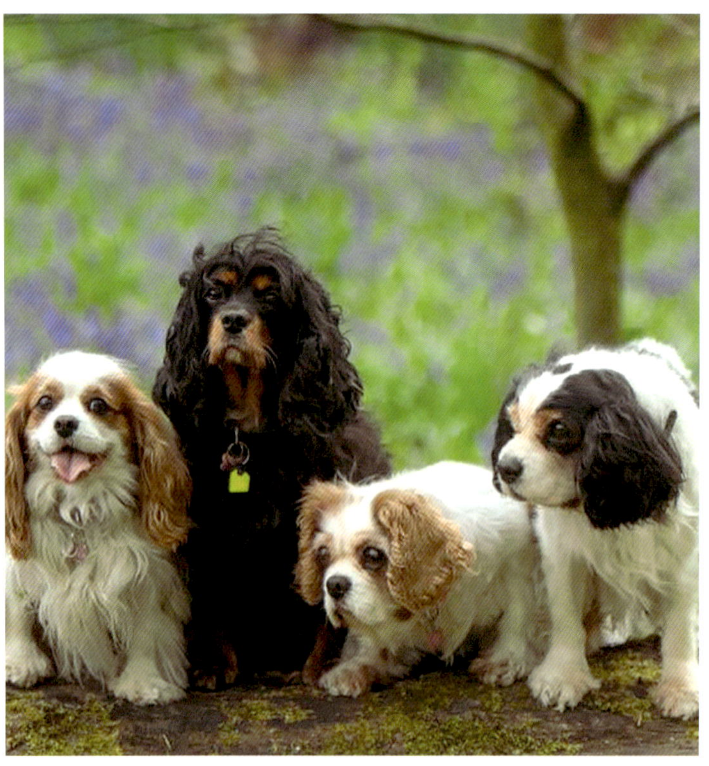

Julie Hargreaves Rescue Cavalier family includes: Nellie, Bonnie, Chrissy and Revvy. Photo credit: Phil Hargreaves, Lancashire, UK

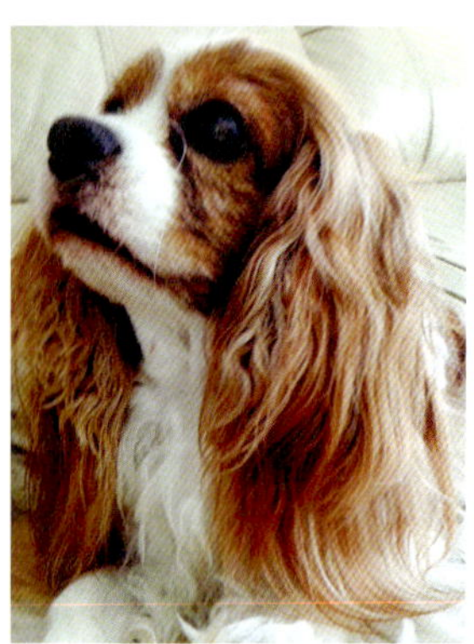

Kathy Vernon adopted Riley three years ago, saving him from a high-kill shelter in Japan. Photo credit: Kathy Vernon, California, USA

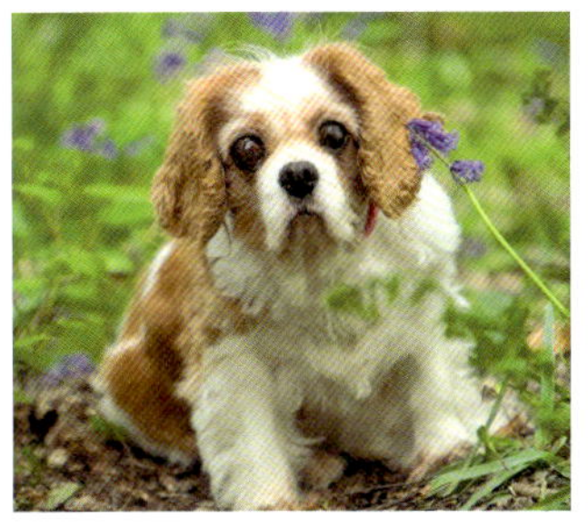

Julie Hargreaves' Rescue Blenheim, blind and deaf Chrissy.
Photo credit: Phil Hargreaves, Lancashire, UK

Julie Hargreaves from Lancashire in the UK wrote this story to commemorate Chrissy and Revvy's "Gotcha Day," which means the day she and her husband Phil brought the rescues home. It says so much about the horrid conditions that puppy mill dogs must endure and what big hearts rescuers like this couple have.

Chrissy and Revvy's Story by Julie Hargreaves

Four years ago today, my husband Phil and I drove to a little village in Lincolnshire to pick up Chrissy Puddin and Revvy. They'd been advertised free on Preloved, and I managed to convince the owner to hand them over to me, backed by Humberside Cavalier Rescue, because the owner trusted me.

We went along with darling Bella, and I was determined to come away with these two little dogs. The owner had said he was retiring and that they were the last of his breeding dogs. When we arrived, what met us were two very stressed little dogs who had clearly never been in his house before. Chrissy was "shortsighted" according to the advert and Revvy was in "good health."

The reality was far removed from that. Chrissy was totally blind and deaf. She was bumping into the furniture as she had no idea where she was and her eyes were horrific. She suffered from dry eye, and they were scarred and covered with green puss. Revvy started kissing them very intently and managed to clean them up. He spent much of his time, as did Bella, cleaning Chrissy's eyes, and I am convinced that he had actually saved them.

Revvy was stressed and overexcited, fussing over Bella and us. He was such a loving dog.

The breeder proudly showed us the chicken run and his carp pond. He also showed us the tiny shed where Revvy and Chrissy had lived in cages along with 20 other Cavs. Revvy was almost 10 and Chrissy was nearly 9. She'd had a pup who had been sold a few weeks before. Her body was absolutely broken, ruined with arthritis and confinement to a cage for years. She broke my heart because Chrissy had lived in a dark, silent and horrific world for so many years. Her loving boy Revvy was her protector, friend, and nurse.

We got the dogs signed over and quickly left before I said something to jeopardize rescuing them.

They had never worn a collar, never been walked on a lead, and never had a comfortable bed. Their whole lives had been spent in cages with wire floors, no blanket, no cushion, no sign of any comfort. Both had bald patches on their tails where they sat on them to give some form of cushioning relief.

Travelling home, I heard an enormous sigh from the back of the car; they never looked back, just lay down and slept.

We took them to the vet, and it was as heartbreaking as you could expect. Chrissy was totally blind, totally deaf, and her bones literally rubbed together. She must have lived in agony for years.

Revvy was even worse! He was deaf as well. Their ears were filled with dirt and infection, which had caused their deafness. Revvy had one ear that was almost closed up, the canal was so infected. His heart was bad with a grade 5 murmur. The vet was actually too worried to chip him at first. He said the shock might kill him! He advised that I take him home and just spoil him rotten for the time I had him. He thought Revvy might have a good couple of weeks, and if he died, then at least it was enjoying his freedom.

It was tragic and absolutely broke my heart, but these little dogs were tougher than they looked. I took them back to the vet and had Revvy chipped so that he belonged to me. They began to thrive and get stronger, enjoying walks and being looked after by Bella.

I stopped crying over their past lives and started looking forward, enjoying seeing them blossom. Chrissy threw herself across my knees from the very start and still lies in this position. Revvy settled and continued to thrive on medication.

We have spent a lovely, funny, chaotic, and content four years together. These little ones have welcomed many other dogs into our home briefly—Revvy with lots of kisses, as every dog received a lot of his loving attention. The love of his life became Bella, who he absolutely adored and who tolerated his attentions with patience. Annie came along all too briefly, also adored by Revvy. Nellie, we adopted, and she was Revvy's running partner.

Sadly, we lost Bella last August, and Revvy began to fade. His heart was broken. So, we made the decision to look for another girl. Bonnie was rescued and immediately Revvy got his mojo back. They became great friends and spent hours kissing each other.

Chrissy is still in pretty good health considering. I clean her eyes twice a day and use cream to keep them moist. She has supplements to help her arthritis and now has a low grade heart murmur that she only developed at 11, but doesn't need medication, thankfully.

We knew that Revvy was going into heart failure; he was on every bit of medication possible to keep him comfortable and happy.

We've enjoyed a few holidays in France with them all. They've also had holidays in Wales and the seaside in England. Our little sweethearts have been the focus of our lives since the moment I first saw their adverts.

Then I saw and fell in love with another cheeky face, a little Tri girl whom I'm convinced Revvy pointed me towards. She has a cloudy eye just like him; she is noisy and daft, just like him. She is a kissing monster and so loving, just like Revvy. So, we adopted Libby.

Revvy was beginning to slow down but was still happy, waggy, noisy, eating like a horse, and wanting to go for walks. He was poorly, but unaware of the fact. I hoped that he would make his 4th Gotcha Day and prayed he would enjoy his 14th birthday.

Last weekend, Revvy rapidly declined. His cough was exhausting him, and he looked tired. He had laboured breathing, didn't want to eat. I looked at him deep in the eyes, while he lay on my knee and I knew. My darling boy crossed the bridge last Tuesday; he broke my heart one final time.

I wanted to share Chrissy and Revvy's 4th Gotcha Day because they came into my home and heart together and will always be connected together. I love them both so very much, and I wanted to share their story because I am honoured and so proud to be a part of their lives.

Please help me to celebrate the Gotcha Day of these incredible, strong, loving and forgiving little dogs who gave me their gift of trust.

Chrissy is across my knees right now, and Revvy is carried in my heart. I promised to love them and protect them for always.

Happy Gotcha Day to my darling, Chrissy Puddin', and my angel boy, Revvy. I love you both with all my heart. ♥

A year ago, Dixie Raby adopted Charlie (r) from Cavalier Rescue USA. She says he's adored by his brother Bentley and "Cavaliers are truly a blessing."

Photo credit: Dixie Raby, California, USA.

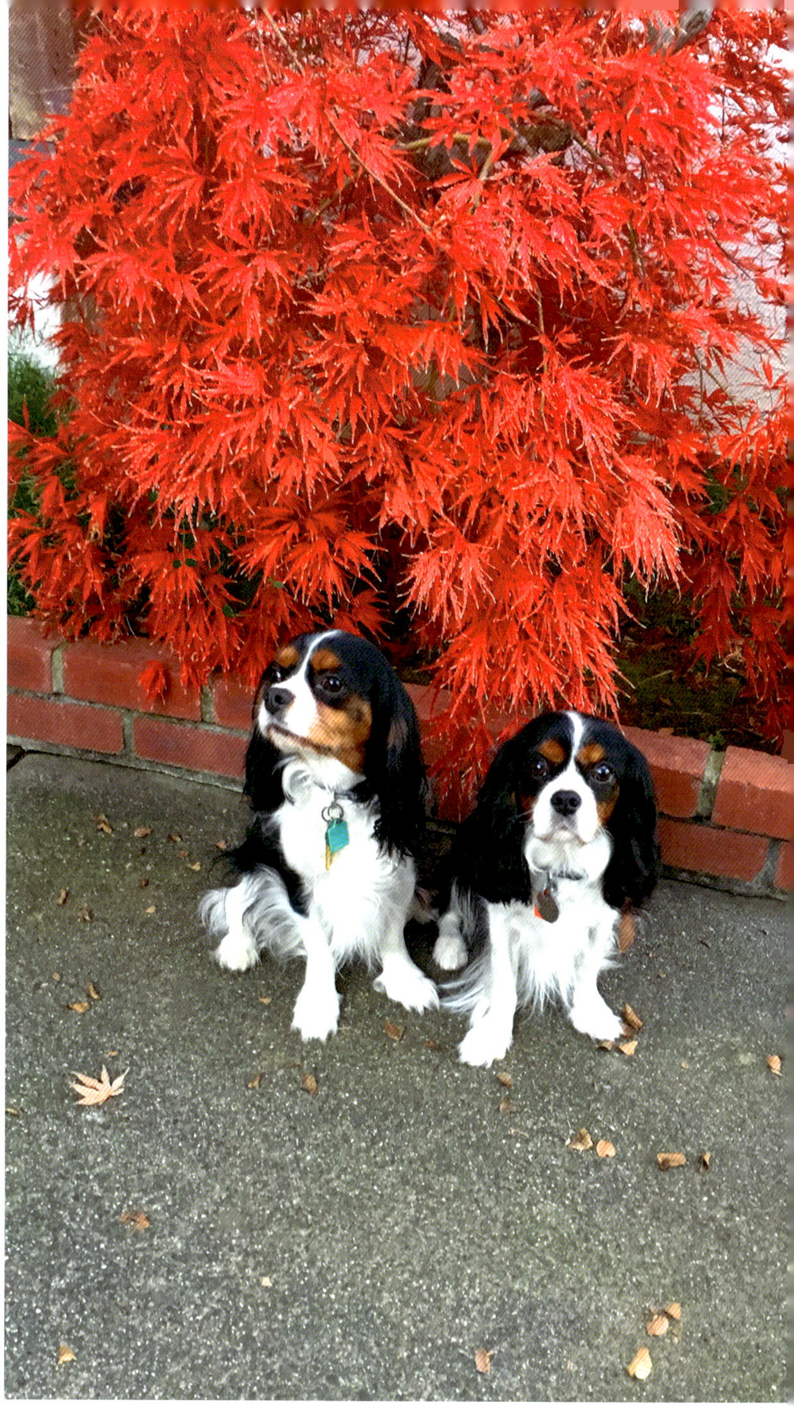

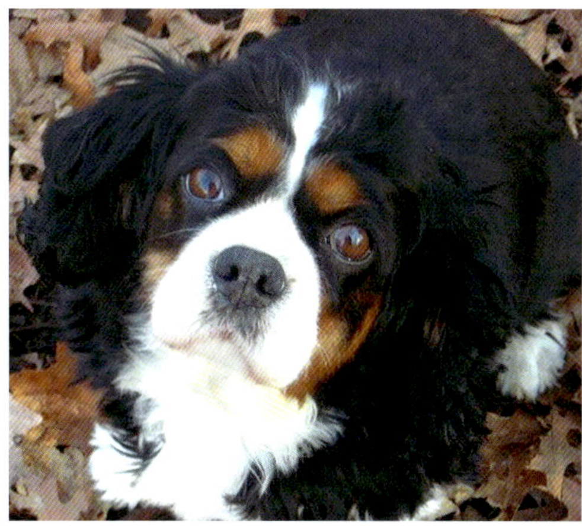

Sharon Kravitz drove 16 hours round-trip, almost to the Canadian border, to pick up her Tri-girl who was living in an unheated trailer with no water. She named her "Hazlenut Café au Lait Moccachino Expresso Prozac" because she's always been so "chill." She's 15 years old now.

Photo credit: Sharona Resnick-Kravitz, Connecticut,USA

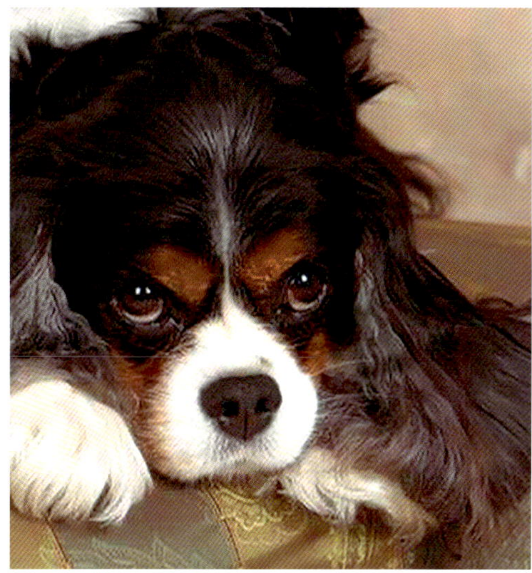

The Andrick's rescue boy, Riley.

Photo credit: Chuck Andrick, Florida, USA

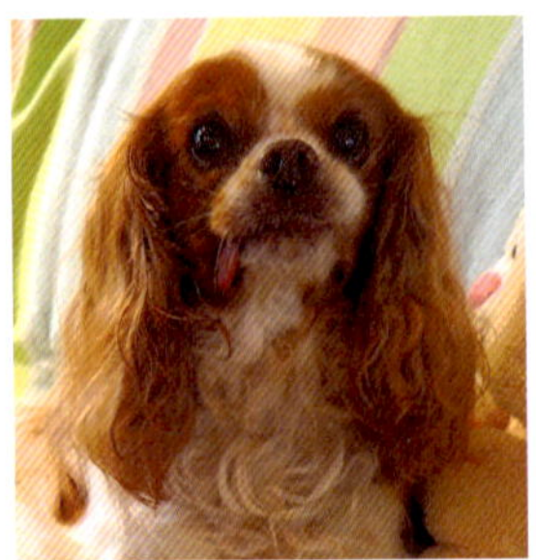

Barney was rescued by Carol.

Photo credit: Carol Casey, Texas, USA

"Wings for Barney" from Carol Casey is a touching story of how she came to terms with releasing her dear friend to fly free over the Rainbow Bridge. RIP Barney 8/15/2017

So many have asked, what happened? As I struggled with Barney's health, I wrote a letter to Barney to work through things. I'm going to share it with those who have asked. My heart hurts. But he went to sleep peacefully; he was so tired because he couldn't rest due to his pain. I'm going to miss him terribly. But I know he is now at peace and free of his worldly struggles.

Barney,

They tell me I should know. "You will know; you will just know." You came into my world afraid of your own shadow, unable to bark or be heard. Your little mouth was so rotted that you lost jawbone as well as all your teeth. Your little legs were so bowed from years of lying in a cage and so short that you couldn't stand and extend your legs. This caused you to have a unique, little walk that served you well. You have never trusted a toy or treat. Over time though, you learned to trust people...the arms of a child were always your favorite, but you allowed me to hold you and cuddle with you for brief moments. I knew this wasn't your favorite, but you tolerated it without complaint.

Over time, you began to insist on being in the same room as the humans, and I accommodated. Every room had a safe zone—a Barney bed. You even became brave enough to venture into the kitchen for a taste of what was cooking. All those safe zones will feel so empty now.

You are the reason I stepped forward and started the rescue mission, Barney. It's to make sure others like you find good homes and some peace. You are their legacy. For every small scared soul I touch will remind me of your fearless, unwavering heart.

So when I ponder, is it time? Is it peace that you have lost? I look back at the promise I whispered in your ear the day we became your family. I promised no one would ever hurt you again, and I will keep my end of this promise. I will not be the cause of your suffering, so I tell myself. But I am human, and as a human, I'm selfish. I've held on to you, waiting for that sign. But, Barney, you don't complain, and you keep holding on to life because I want you to. You can barely tolerate to be touched, much less picked up. It causes you such pain, your little body tightens, and your respirations and heart rate go up. Yet you don't complain; you allow me to pick you up and carry you out to the yard, to hold you up to potty. Then, because you want to show me you are still independent, brave, and strong, you manage to make it back to the door to wait for me to pick you up and take you inside. Or do you head back on your own because it hurts less to struggle to walk than to be picked up?

As I watch you as each day passes, I'm beginning to understand it's the latter, though I have not wanted to see it. I watched, looking for a sign, but you will give me no such sign. Because you're brave and fearless, you'll never complain.

My friend, I'll release you from the pain of this world. I'll give you your freedom to run and play and fly like the wind.

My friend, you've earned your wings. Until we meet again, may you watch over me and keep those that follow you safe and greet those before you with a loud strong bark and a skip in your step.

My prayer now for me is that the tears will lessen and the pain will dull, and that I never forget my sweet Barney's soul.

I know we've all gone through this, but I struggle with tomorrow. What do I do when I wake up and know it will be the last time I hear him snore? When I get in the car and raise his head so he can hang it from the window. When we share our last soft serve ice cream from Dairy Queen? And when he looks me in the eyes and takes his last breath. What will I do then?

I will cry, hang my head, and cry. Feel the deep realization that you will no longer be coming home with me. But between those tears and my gasps for air, I will hold you close as you leave this world. I will know that you're finally free of the worldly pains put upon your little body and soul.

No one ever knew your entire story, but at least we made the latter half of your life as loving and happy as we could. May you enjoy your journey, Barney...until we meet again. ♥

Always yours, Mommy

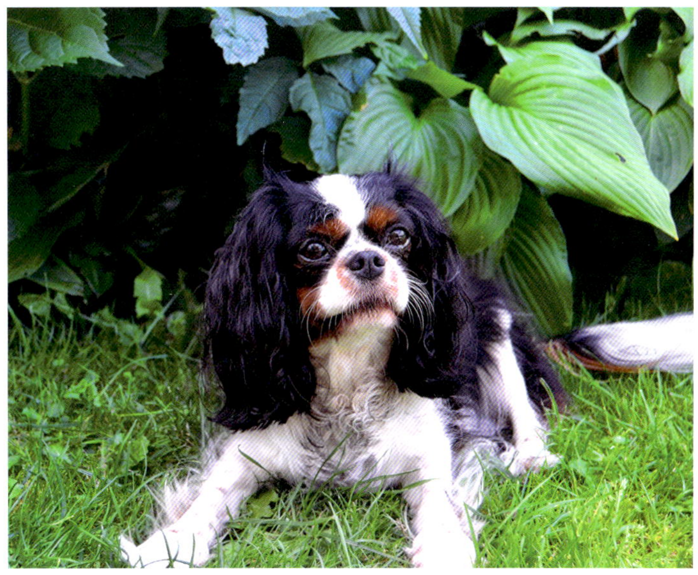

Katerina Kretkova rescued her beloved Emilka four years ago through Nadeje Kavalira — Charlie, an organization active in three Eastern European Countries that rescues about 200 Cavaliers a year. Unfortunately, Emilka suffers from hip displacia and chronic digestive disorders and weighs only 5 kilos.

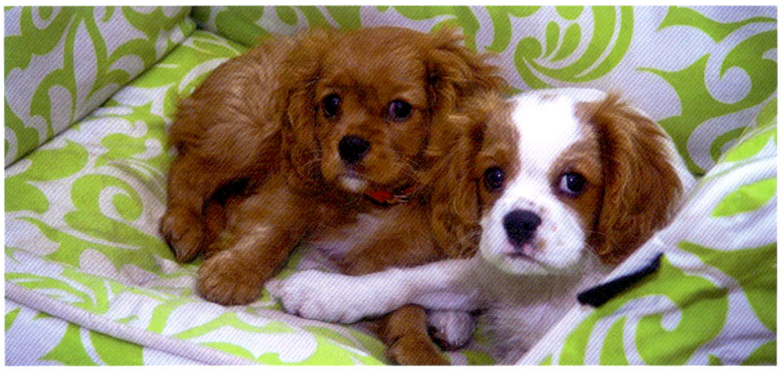

Suzy Stidham, N. California Coordinator of Cavalier Rescue USA fostered these two 11-week old pups, Tori and Darby. She says she "failed" with Tori because she just had to keep her. Her three older rescue Cavs also insisted.

Photo credit: Suzy Stidham, California, USA

Chapter 4 - Sporty Cavaliers

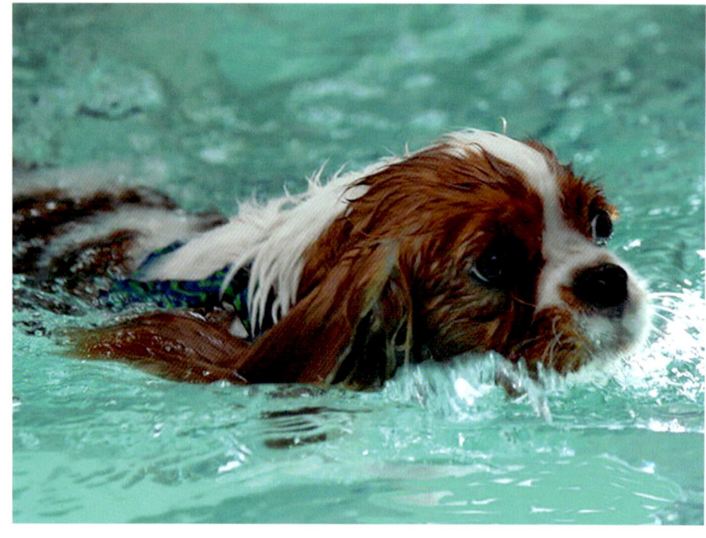

There's nothing like a refreshing swim after a hard workout, right Jemma?

Photo credit: DanaLynn Young, Oregon, USA

If I've painted a picture thus far of Cavaliers as being fussy, spoiled "foo foo" dogs, nothing could be farther from the truth. Actually, they were used as hunting dogs by King Charles II and his ilk and can be quite the competitors in agility meets. Like other spaniels, they revel in nature and the outdoors. Many love to swim, go boating, and take arduous hikes. A lot depends on their conditioning, health, and especially whether their human companions are active people.

Cavaliers adapt to their environments beautifully, so if you want an active, athletic dog, that's what you'll get. If you work at your computer or paint, like I do, your dogs will be content with a romp in the garden and short walks, and perhaps a few bouts of chasing bubbles every day. The literature says that Cavaliers need 30 minutes of exercise a day, but when my Callie was one year old, we took a 10-km hike through hilly vineyards with our monthly walking club in France. As I mentioned, we aren't that athletic, so Callie was not highly conditioned or accustomed to long treks, nor were we. Naturally, before the hike we were apprehensive and wondered whether we'd end up carrying her. Well, "quelle surprise," she outdid all of us, leading our group of 30 walkers all the way, bouncing from side-to-side of the trail with the other dogs who came along.

So, don't underestimate the sporting ability of the Cavalier or their love of the Great Outdoors. They're spaniels after all. Even the most sedentary Cavalier may astonish you with her speed and stamina if a rabbit or squirrel should wander by, or the neighbor's cat, for that matter.

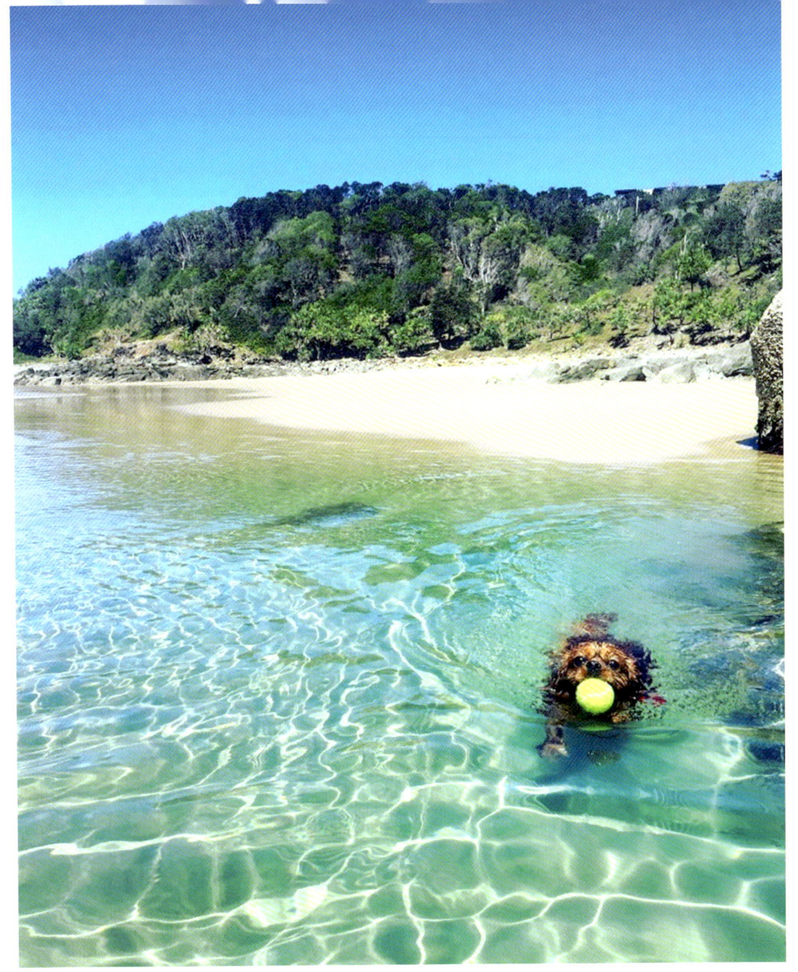

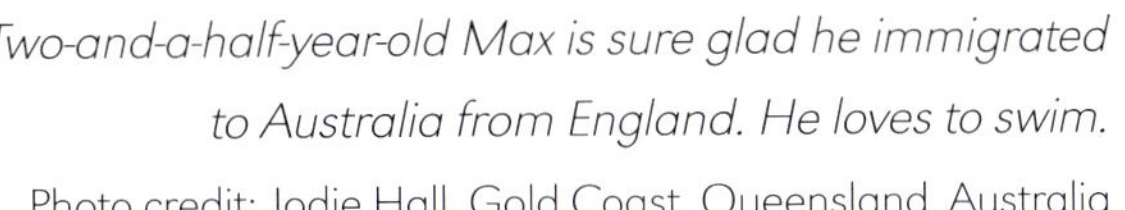

Two-and-a-half-year-old Max is sure glad he immigrated to Australia from England. He loves to swim.

Photo credit: Jodie Hall, Gold Coast. Queensland, Australia

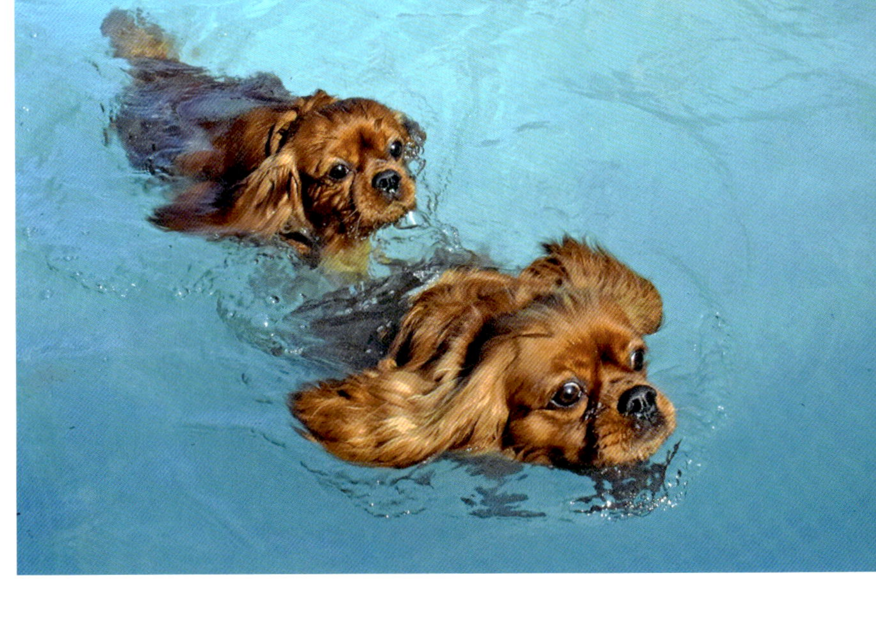

They look intent on their destination.

Photo credit: Michaela Lunini, Placenza, Italy

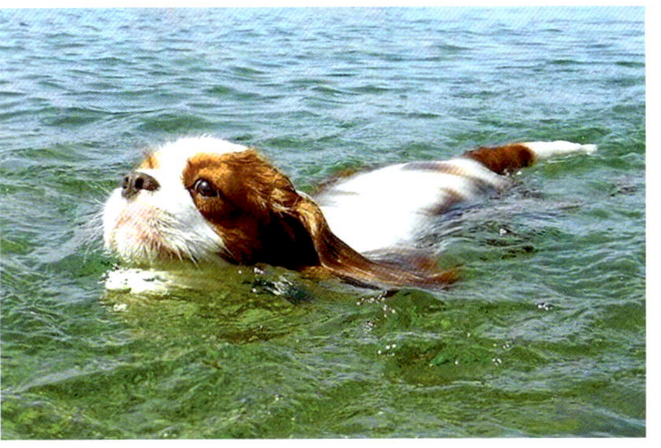

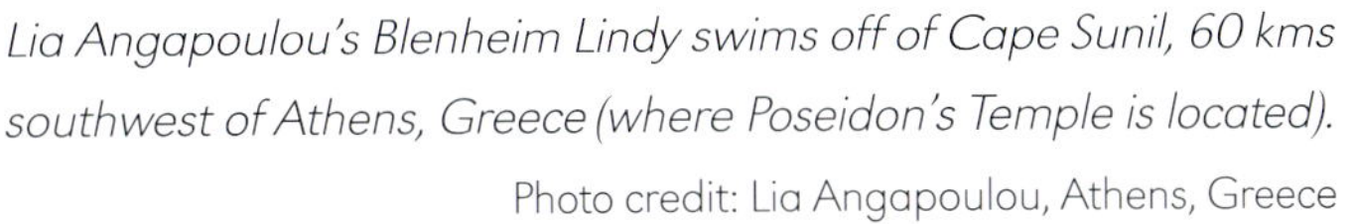

Lia Angapoulou's Blenheim Lindy swims off of Cape Sunil, 60 kms southwest of Athens, Greece (where Poseidon's Temple is located).

Photo credit: Lia Angapoulou, Athens, Greece

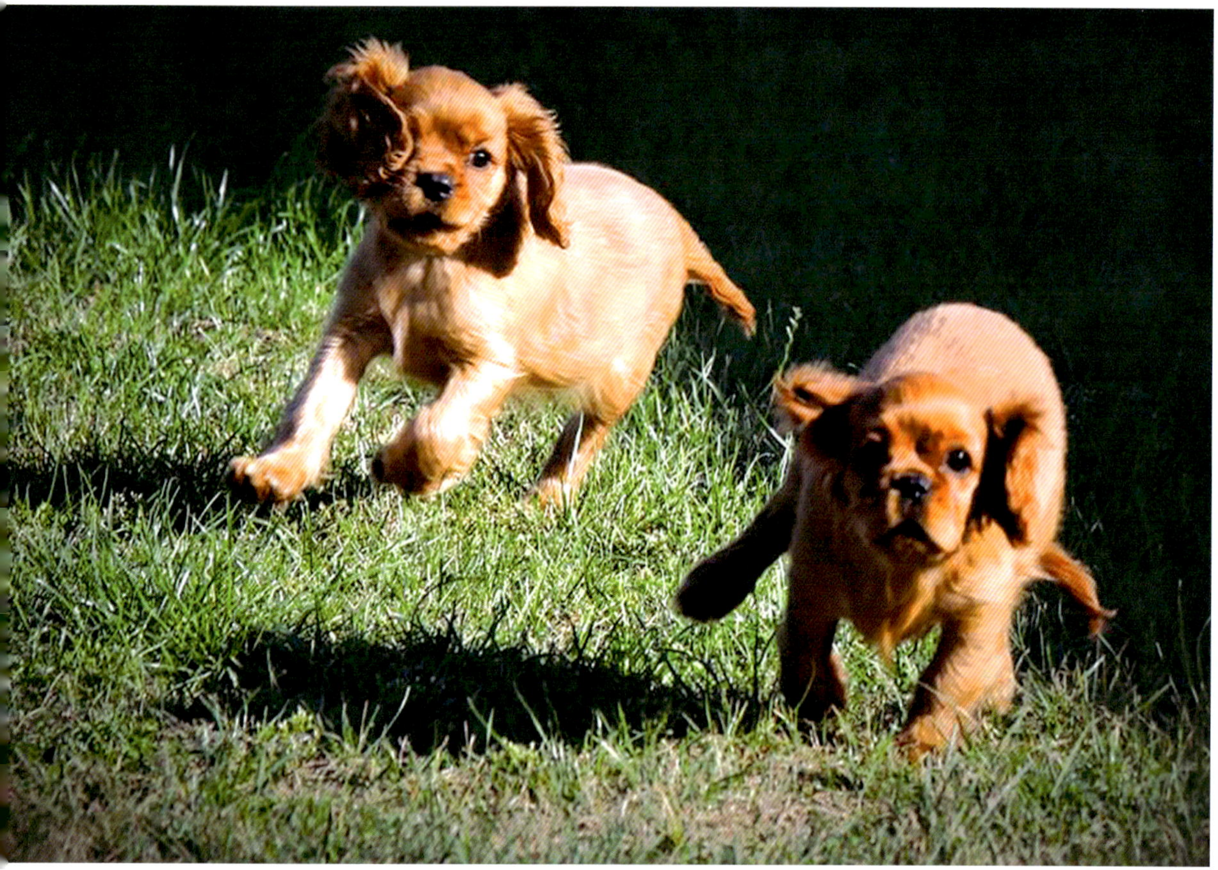

Zygmut and Zofia von Paulinenhof racing through the garden.
Photo credit: Heidi Junghans Mecklenburg, Vonpommern, Germany

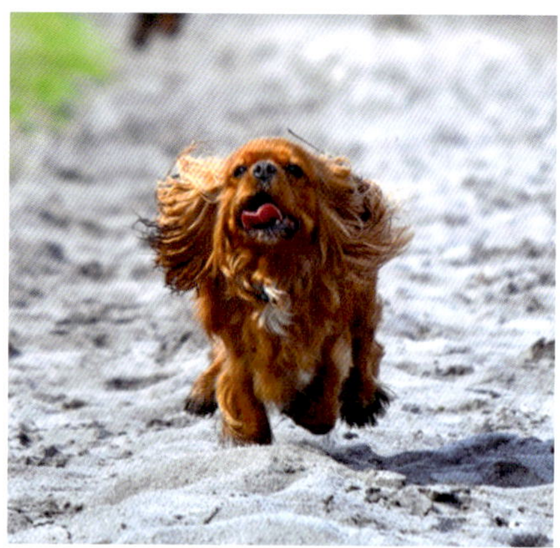

Zelda the hotrod from Spark of Hope Cavaliers.
Photo credit: Conny Meiboom, Xanten, Germany

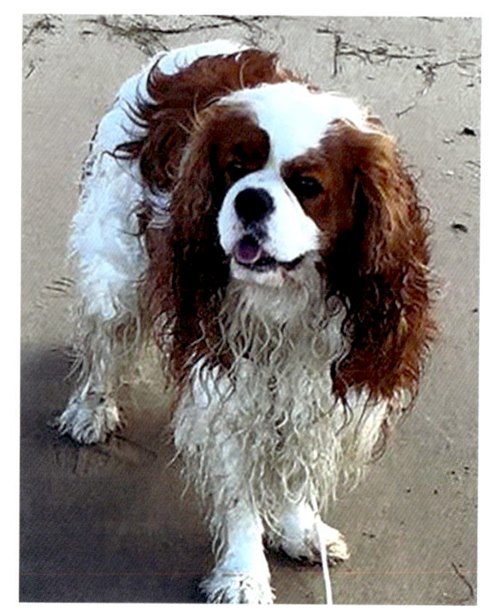

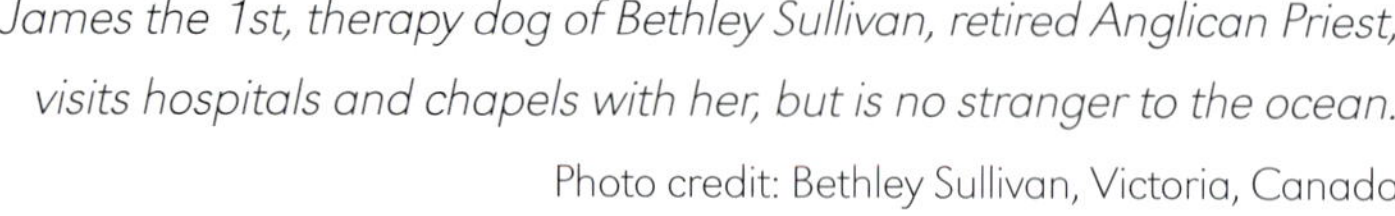

James the 1st, therapy dog of Bethley Sullivan, retired Anglican Priest, visits hospitals and chapels with her, but is no stranger to the ocean.
Photo credit: Bethley Sullivan, Victoria, Canada

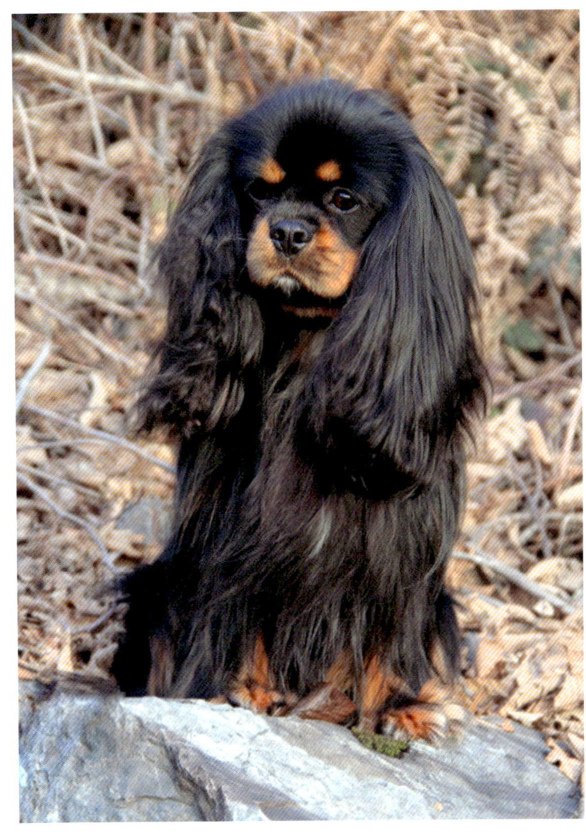

"Ammo," the only son of Coco, spends his time attending Washington State University as Service Animal for his primary owner Malynn Johns.

Photo credit: Alisha Lockleer, Washington, USA

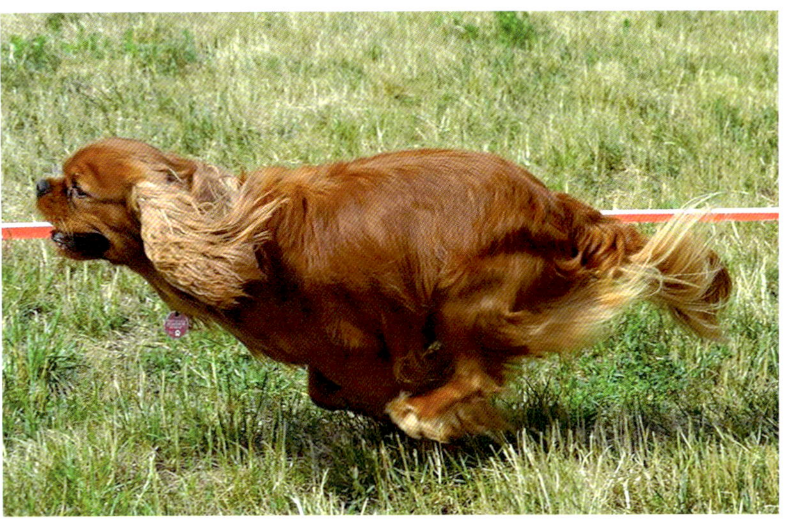

Nothing as fast as this Ruby chili pepper.

Photo credit: Martina Hartmannová, Domazlice, Czech Republic

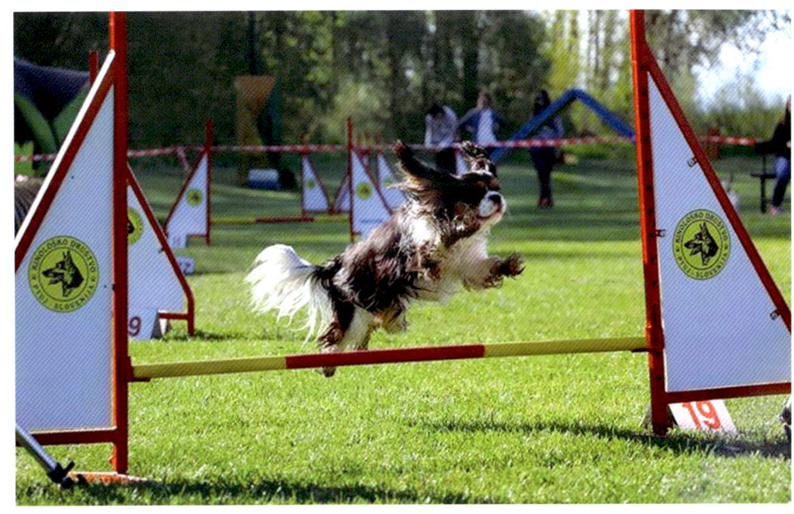

Anja Trcak's dog Gracie works hard at an agility meet in Slovenia.

Photo credit: Anja Trcak, Maribor, Slovenia

Callie's true passion was playing in the snow with best friend forever Bella. Minus 20 Celsius? No problem!

Photo credit: Mary Colburn-Green, L'Aude, France

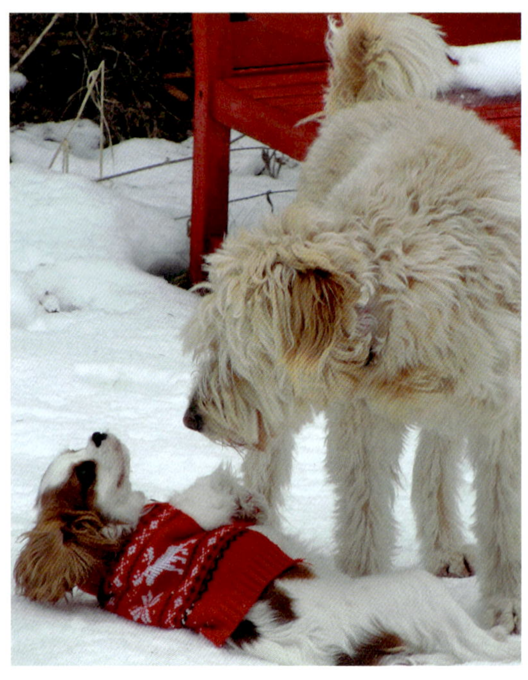

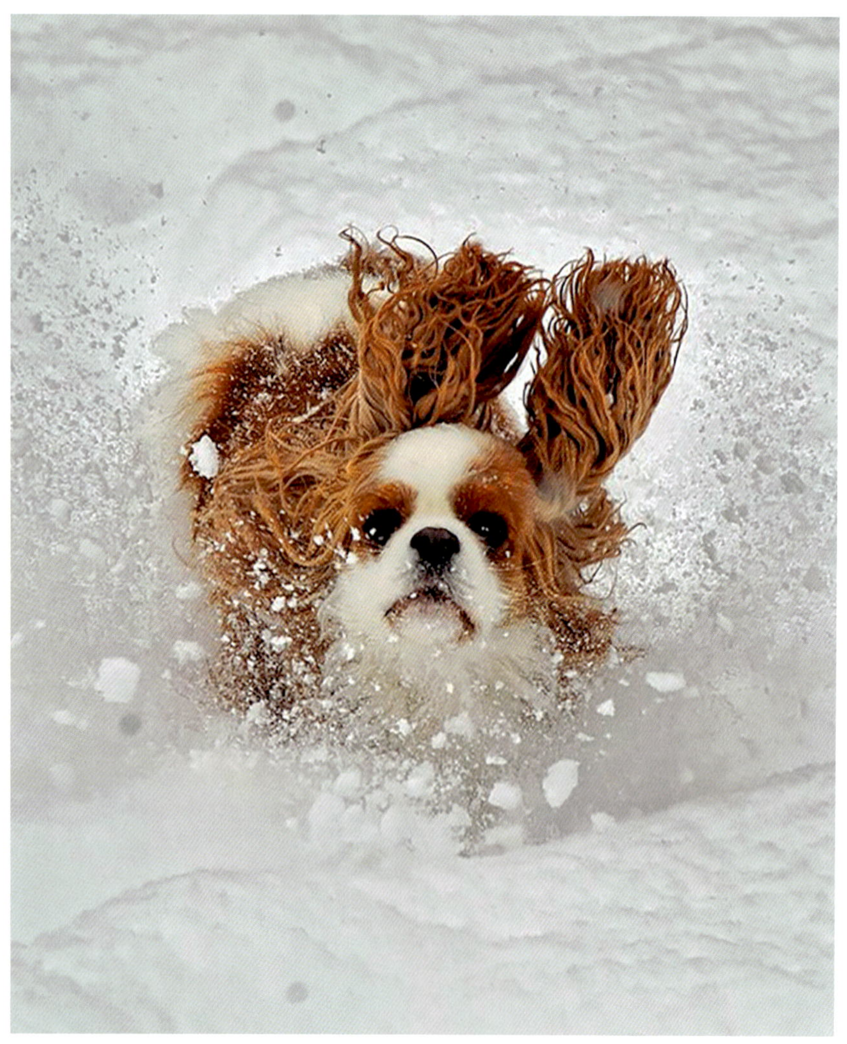

Nellie (O'Nellie Royal Dream vom Erlenbacher Hemmerich at Diorchavon) loves bounding through the deep snow. Owner Dorota Bialek.

Photo credit: Jan Wilusz, JW Kennel Photography, Massachusetts, USA

Kitt Huntington's Merlin and Ludo enjoying their run along the Atlantic.
Photo credit: Kitt Huntington, Wakefield, England

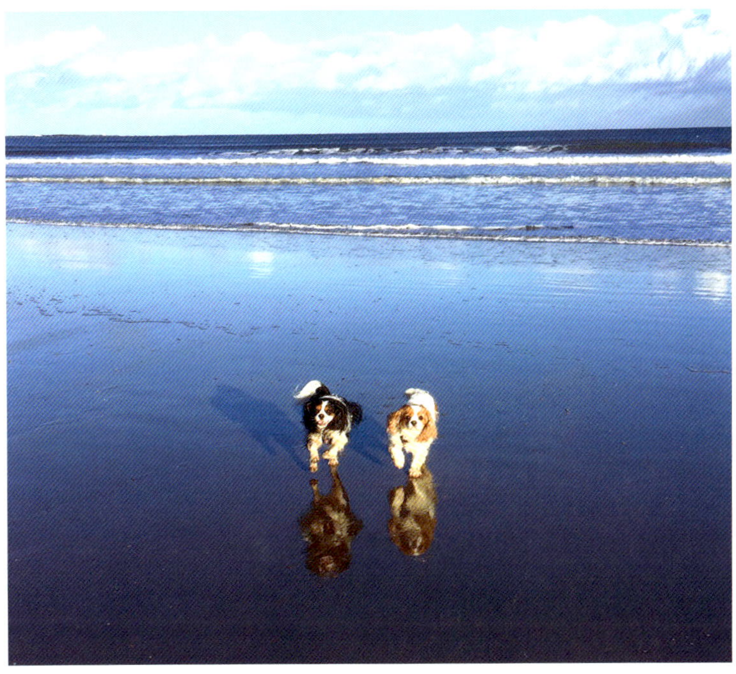

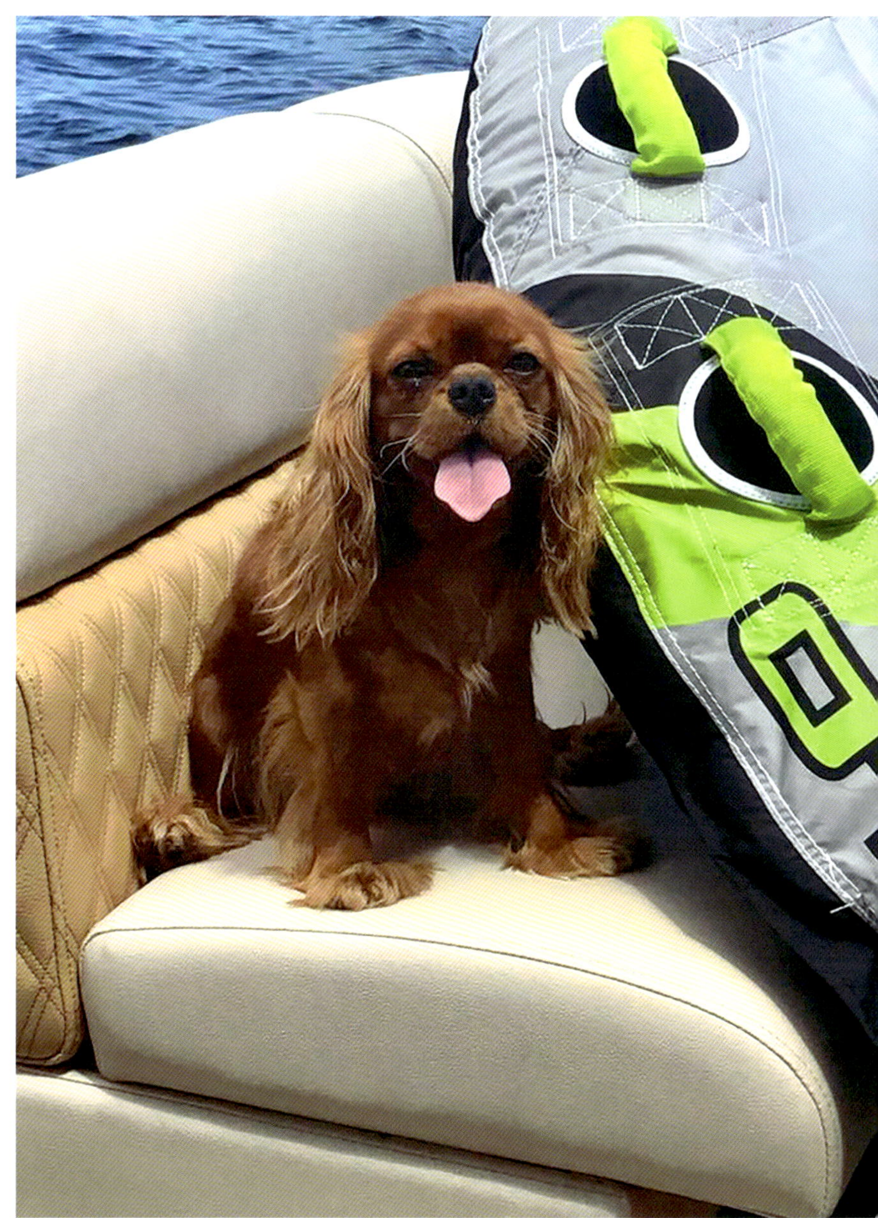

Gavin Marino's inseparable sidekick, Tosh, loves boating as long as Gavin is along.
Photo credit: Heather Marino, Tennessee, USA

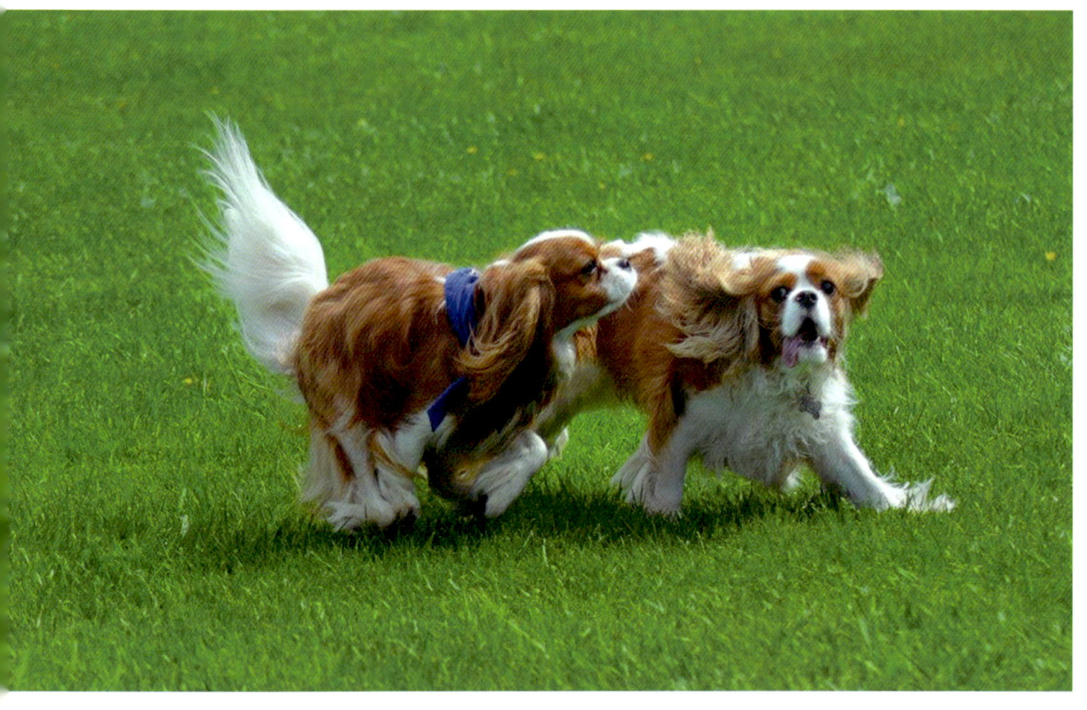

Louis, in the blue bandana, finds a matching friend while out for a run.
Photo credit: Evelyn Slack, Glasgow, Scotland

Amazing CeCe won her agility event and AKC title after months of illness. She's the comeback girl.
Photo credit: Anita Penford Alexander, Alexas CKCS, Saskatoon, Canada

Coco showing off her herding talents.
Photo credit: Alisha Lockleer, Washington, USA

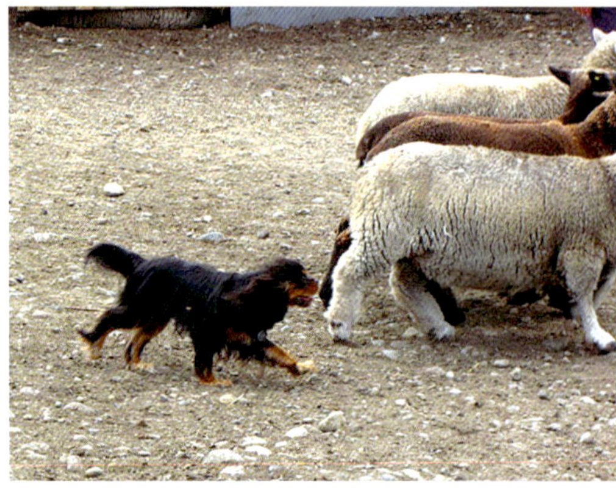

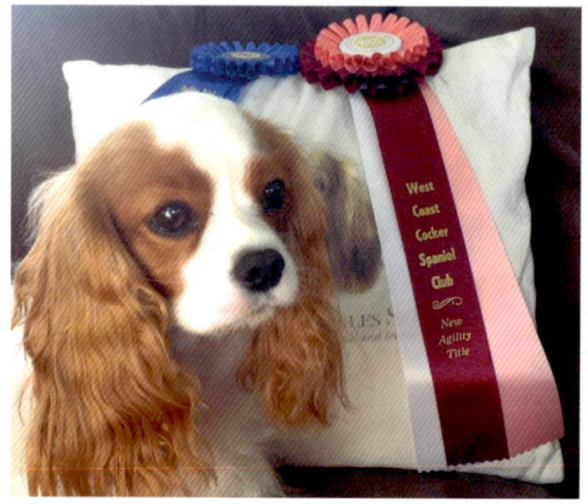

Water is a pleasure for Kasia Klein's big love, her first Cavalier, Janis Joplin Snukraina.
Photo credit and Photography: Kasia Klein, Dublin, Ireland

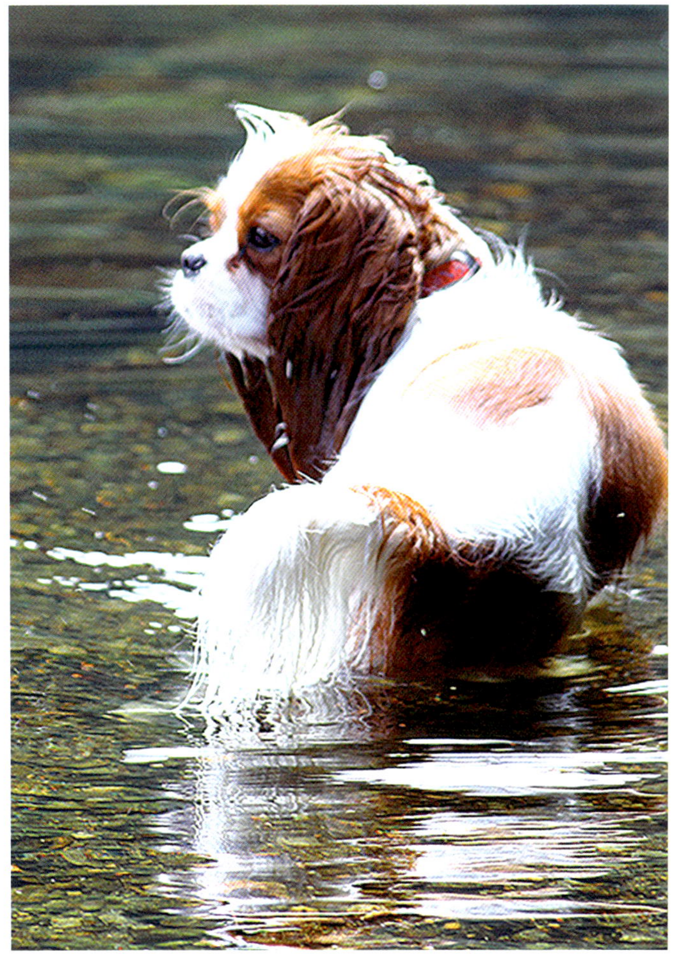

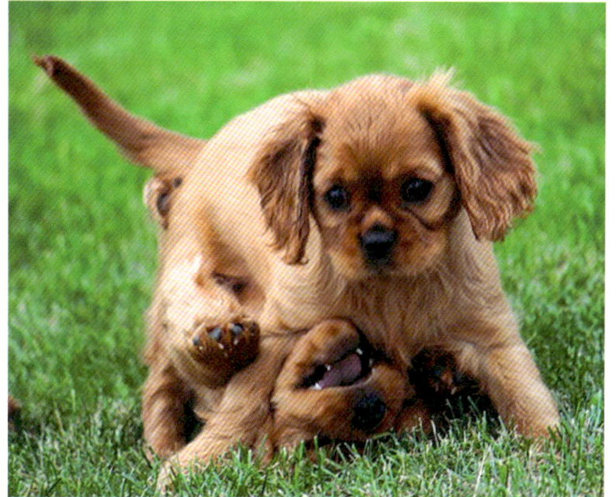

A busy little ruby devil who can't stop playing.
Photo credit: Heidi Jungans, von Paulinenhof Cavaliers, Vonpommern, Germany

Nothing like a good game of ball for Breeder Michele Matheson's Owen and Halo.
Photo credit: Michele Matheson, British Columbia, Canada

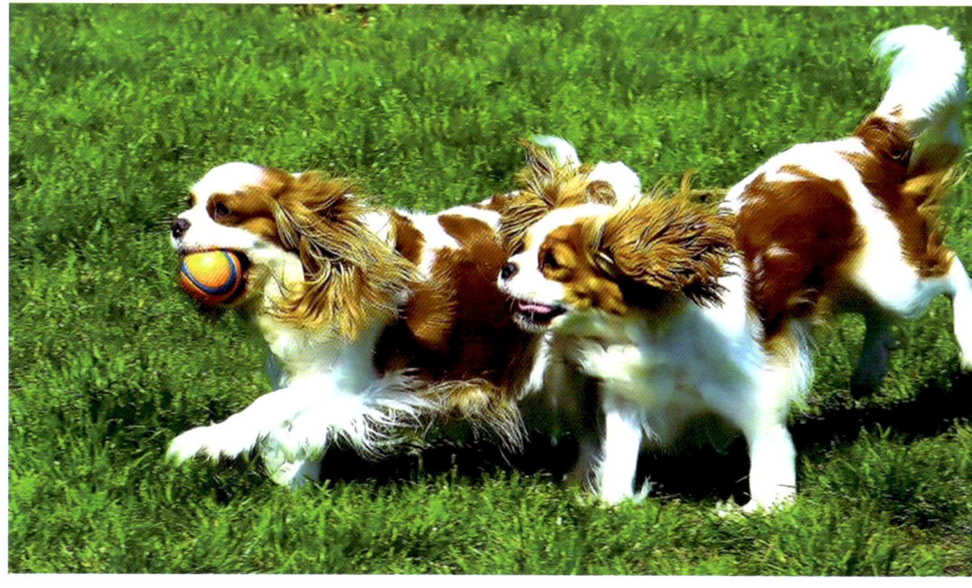

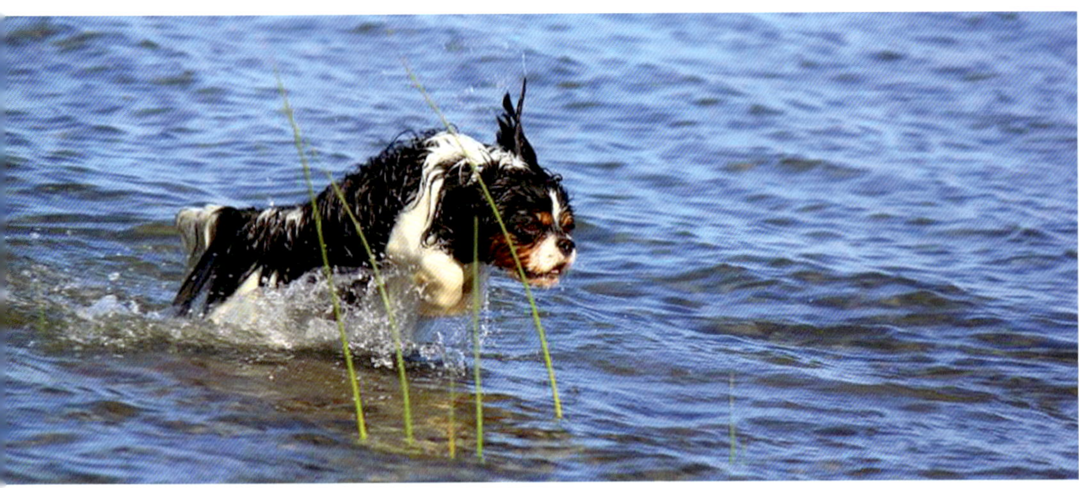

Diamond, loved by Crystal Scheibel, is a water maniac.

Photo credit: Tina Rak, Saskatchewan, Canada

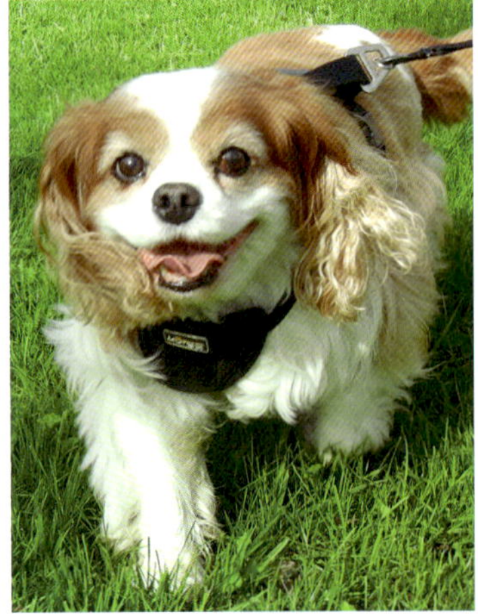

At 105 in human years, Elvis isn't about to slow down.

Photo credit, Christy Berry, Indiana, USA

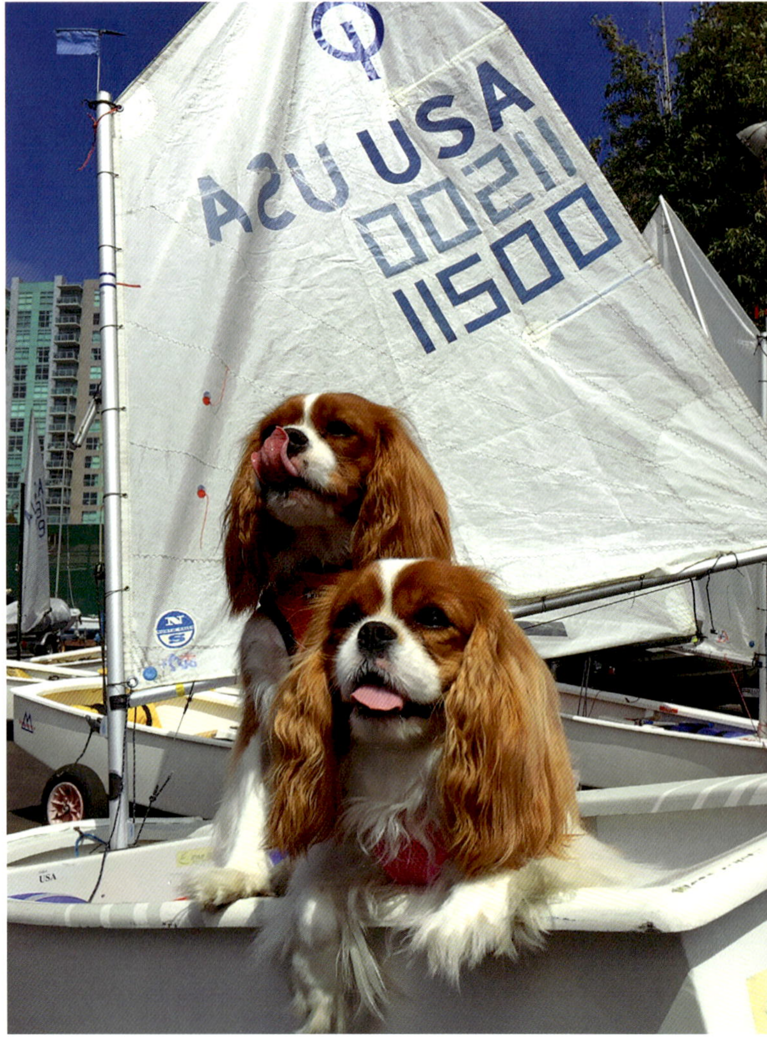

Gracie and Riley think sailing may be their sport.

Photo credit: Jill Prives, California, USA

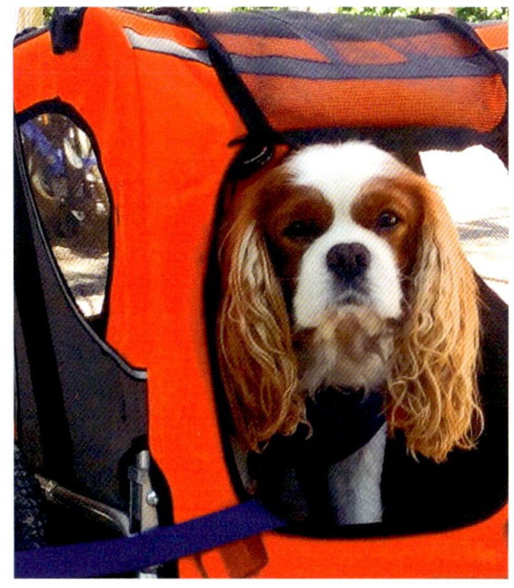

Jack Humphrey, I'm not sure this counts as exercise.

Photo Credit: Christine Medley, Nottingham, UK

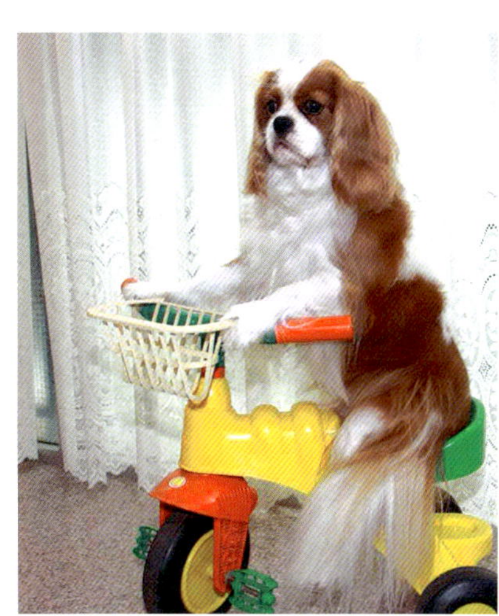

I'm not sure Duke on his bike counts as exercise either.

Photo credit: Nekane Garcia, San Sebastian, Spain

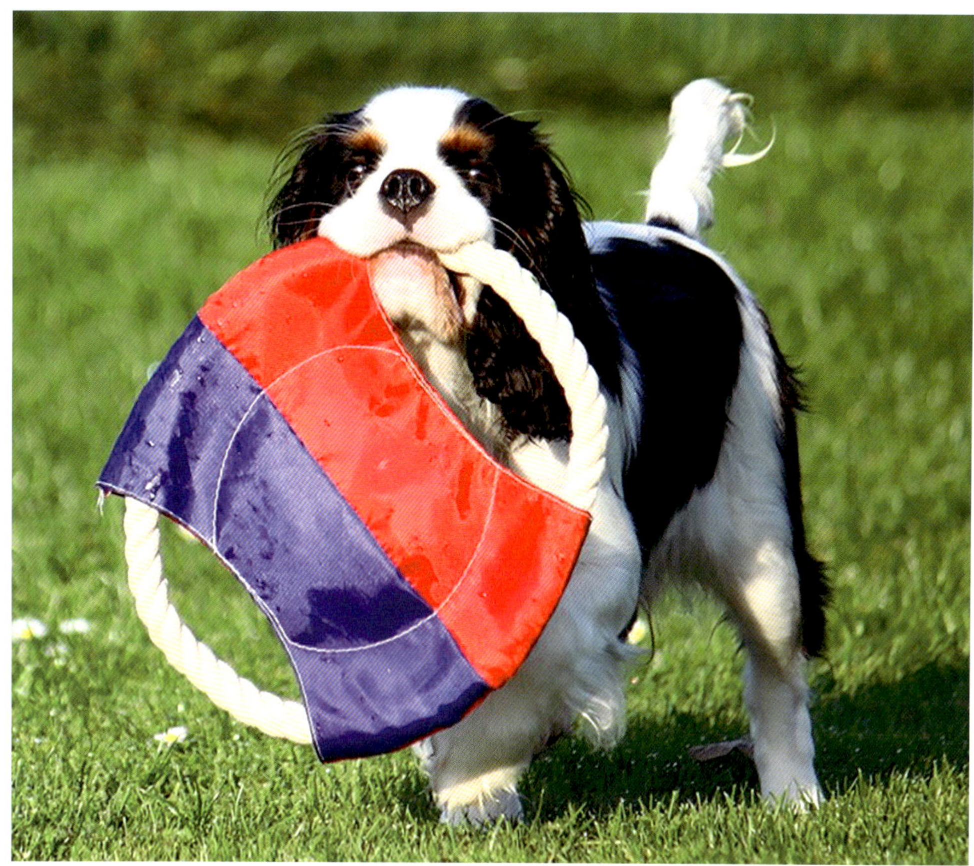

This adorable Beate Cavalier Tri-Color loves his toys.

Photo and Photography credit: Gaby Kottmann, Erwitte, Germany

Chapter 5 - Show Cavaliers

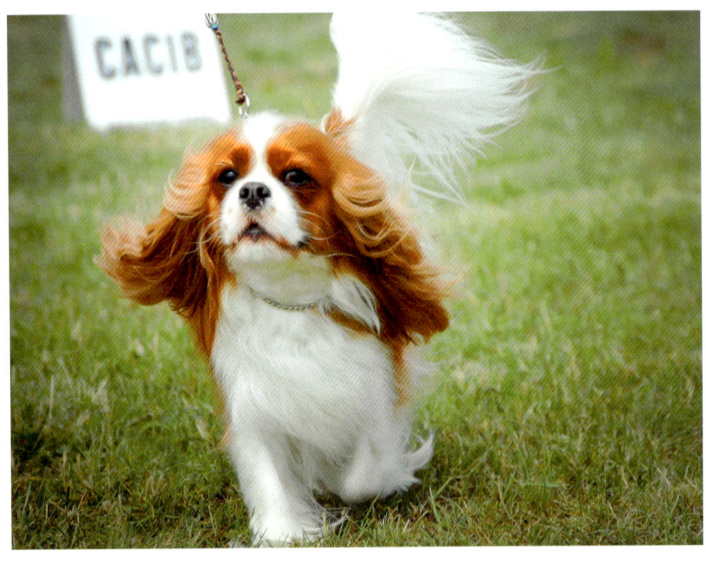

Agata Rozbiewska's "Margot" Collare di Diamanti was awarded Exc 1 CAC, reserve CACIB at CACIB SOPOT 2017.

Photo credit: Kamila Smolska, Szczecin, Poland

Cavaliers are shown in the Toy Group at professional conformation dog shows sponsored by the CKCS Clubs of each country and in the all-breed shows held by The Kennel Club (KC) in the UK, American Kennel Club (AKC), Canadian Kennel Club (CKC), and the international equivalent, Federation Cynologique Internationale (FCI). Athletic Cavaliers who have extensive training can participate in agility events. There are many different types of shows—from the fun community fundraisers open to all dogs to the competitive national and international dog shows only for pedigree dogs.

The professional shows judge beauty, sociability, and breed standards, agility and/or obedience. Winning at the professional shows gives individual dogs points toward becoming champions, international champions, multi champions, and grand champions. It's a rather complicated scoring process, but with enough wins, they not only get championship titles, but also access to the top shows like Crufts, Westminster, and/or the FCI World Dog Show held in a different country every year. More than 20,000 pedigree dogs compete at the week-long World Dog Show.

Vital in advancing the breeds and establishing pre-eminent breeders, conformation dog shows have been held since 1859 in England, although more informal shows of hunting dogs were held before that time.

Cavaliers take a lot of grooming to be show-ready. Moreover, serious showing is very expensive with all the travel and equipment involved. Still, having trained judges evaluate a dog helps serious breeders know its potential for producing exceptional puppies that conform to the breed standard.

Note: The photo credits may refer to the person who provided the photo and not necessarily the breeder of the dog.

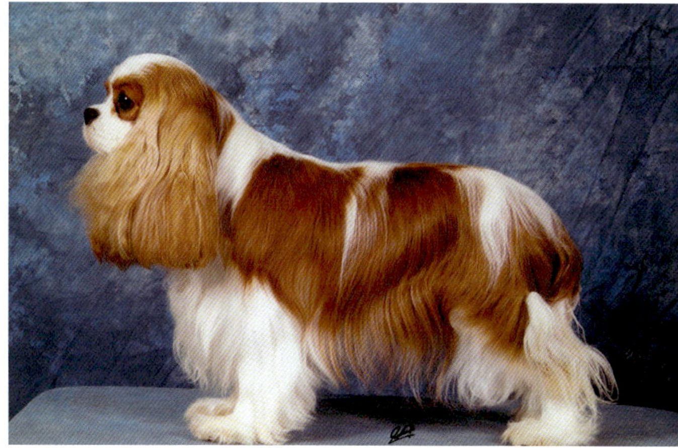

Aranel Scrumptuous, sired by CH Keyingham Branwell with dam Aranel Bubblicious.

Photo credit: Rick Aldous and Mark Smith, Suffolk, UK

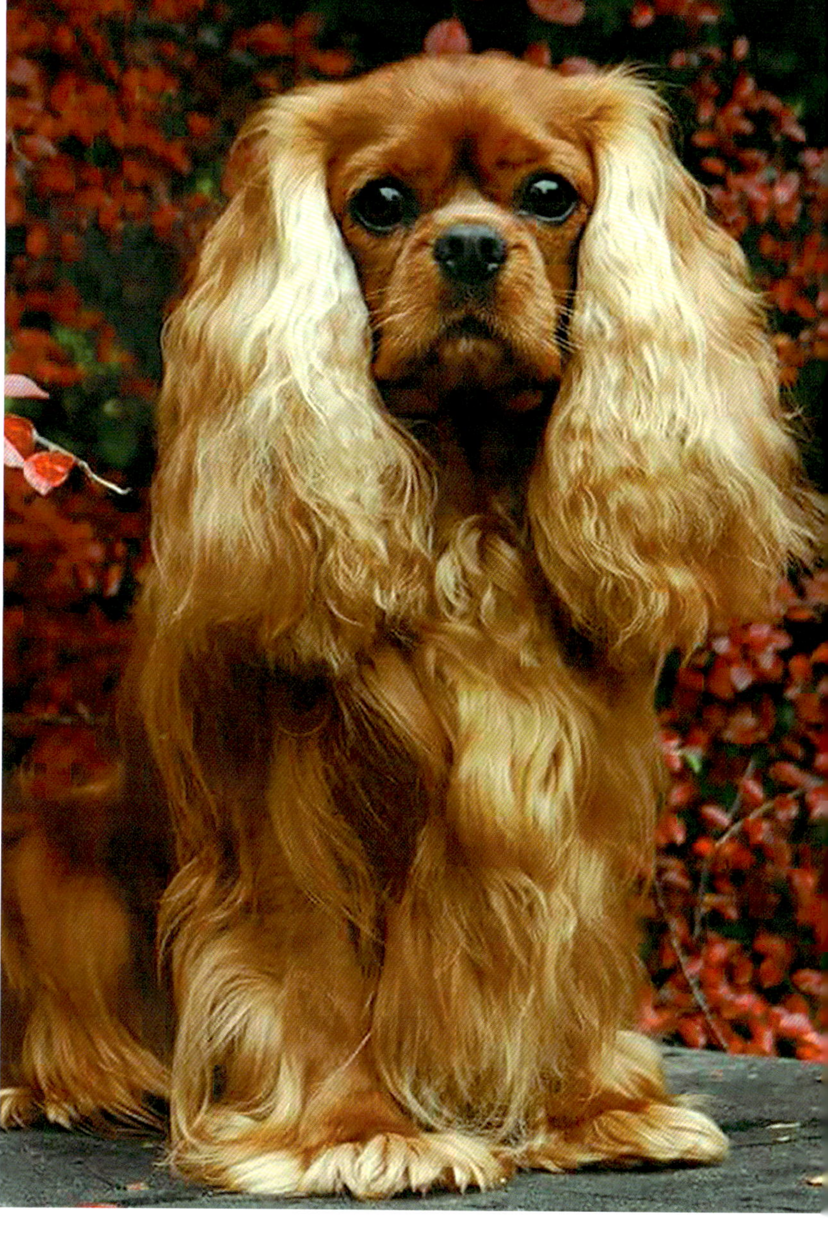

"Dante," Tibama's Rainbow Poet from Sweden.

Photo credit: Marielle Johansson Milljas, Bengtsfor, Sweden

Photography: Nina Lindstrom

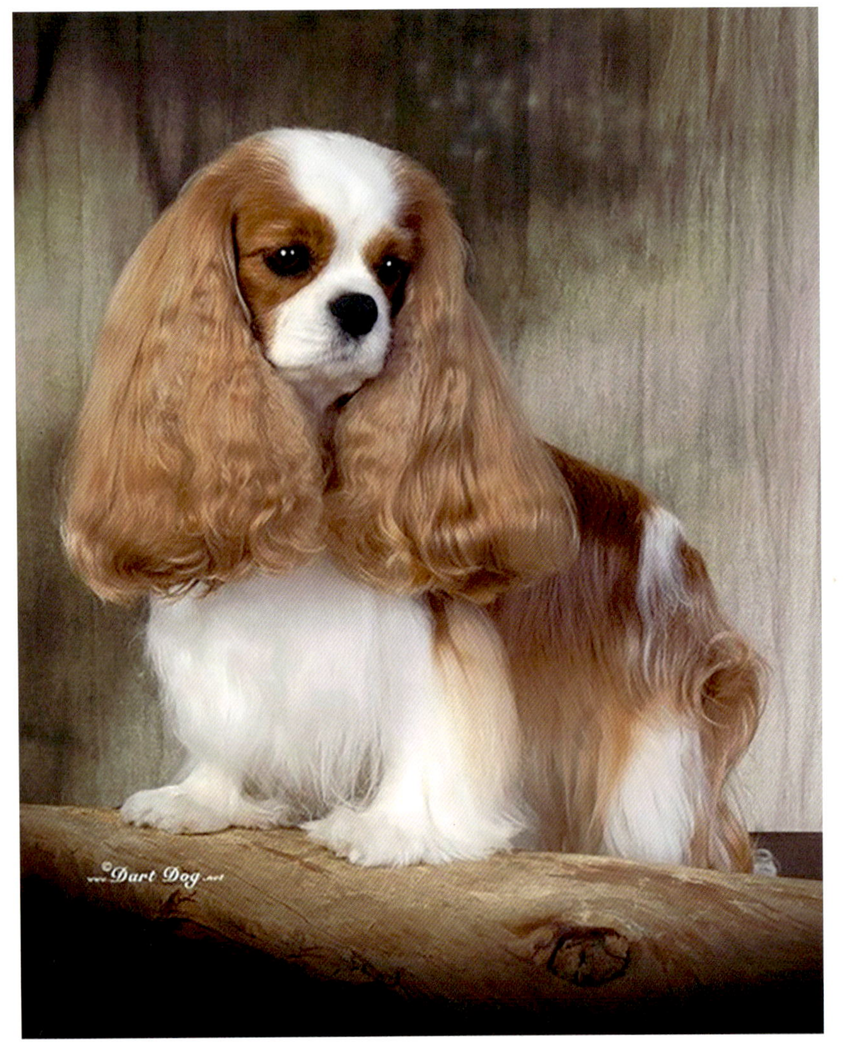

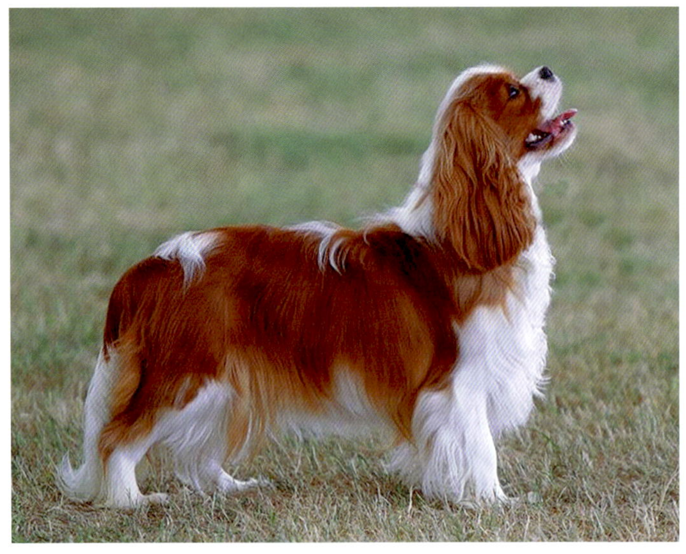

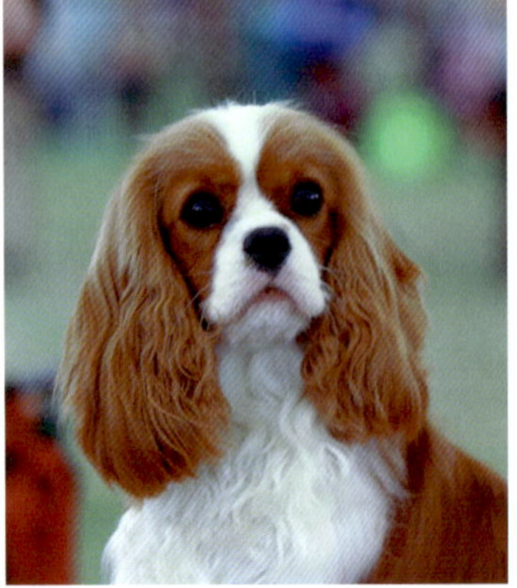

Top right & bottom: Leogem Ginestra —Junior and Novice Bitch-Class Winner-CC and BOS. Bred and owned by Leogem Cavaliers.
Photo credit: Dennis and Tina Homes, Herefordshire, UK
Photography: Ninka Wladzimiruk

CKCSC USA and AKC CH Rosscrea Summertime, "Summer," bred by Wendy Taylor, owned and shown by Jennifer Flowers Foster
Photo credit: Jennifer Flowers Foster, California, USA

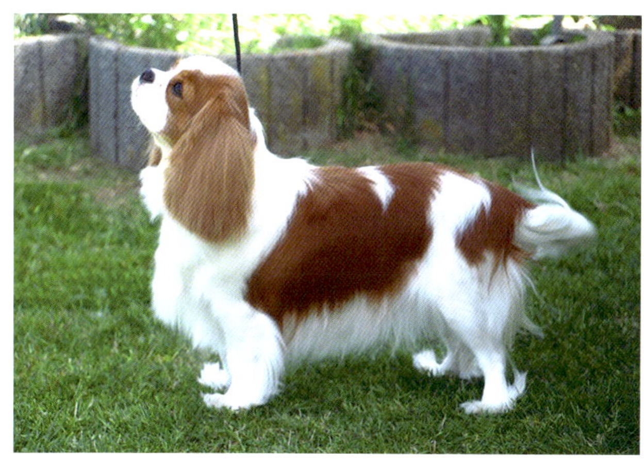

Multi. CH Aranel Aramis (out of UK CH Aranel Genesis & UK CH Aranel Electra), owned by Joachim Julio.

Photo credit: Maria Jose Molina

Photography: Lucia Cobos

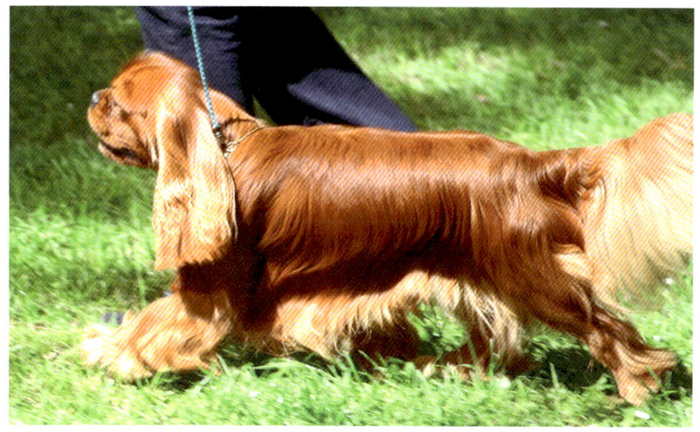

"Brownie" Multi CH James Brown of Sevijean's, CACIB and BOB, Champion de France 2017.

Photo credit: Severine Abraham-Sevijean, Gelannes, France

Photography: Stephan Constant

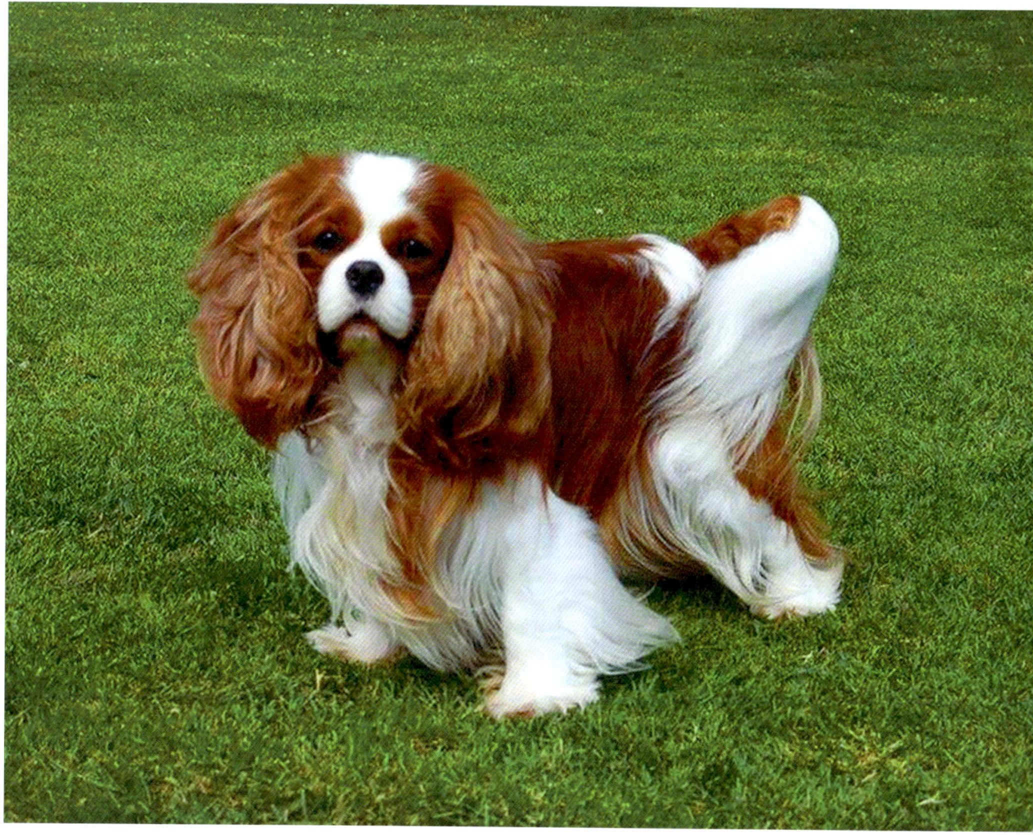

"Oscar" Chantismere Push My Button JW, ShCM at Tangledwood, UK CH with 3 x DCC (2 with BOB) 7 X RDCC with Crufts RCC. Owned by Ian GibbStuart.

Photo credit: Ian GibbStuart, Mauchline, Scotland, UK

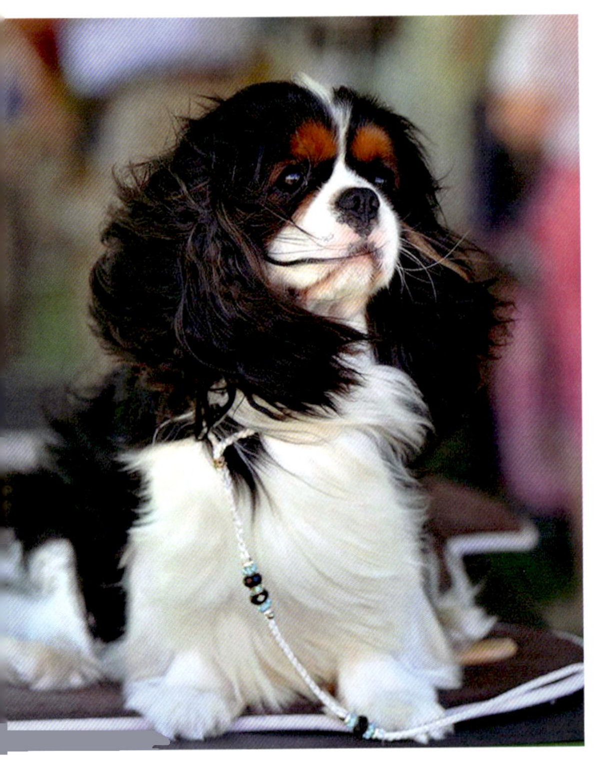

US CKCS Champion Bonitos Companeros Nothing Compares at Diorchavon.
Photo credit: Jan Wilusz, JW Kennel Photography

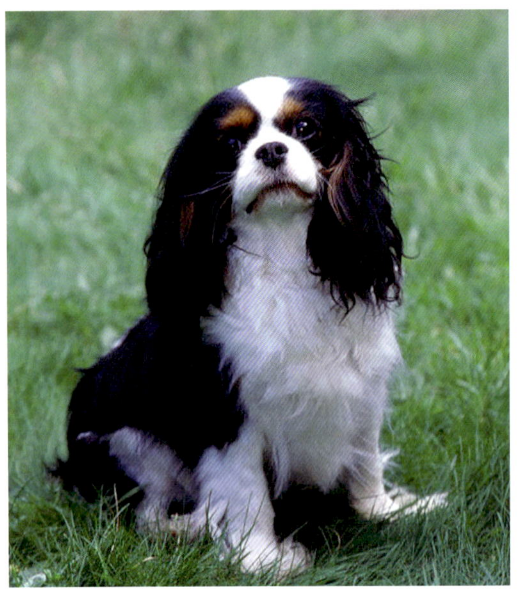

"Amy" CH Kewpy's Ain't Misbehavin'
Photo credit: Karen Willis, Alberta, Canada

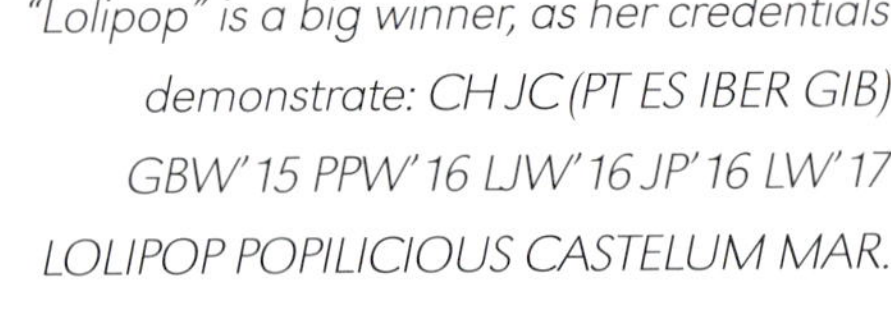

"Lolipop" is a big winner, as her credentials demonstrate: CH JC (PT ES IBER GIB) GBW'15 PPW'16 LJW'16 JP'16 LW'17 LOLIPOP POPILICIOUS CASTELUM MAR.
Photo credit: Sofia Salazar Leite, Lisbon, Portugal

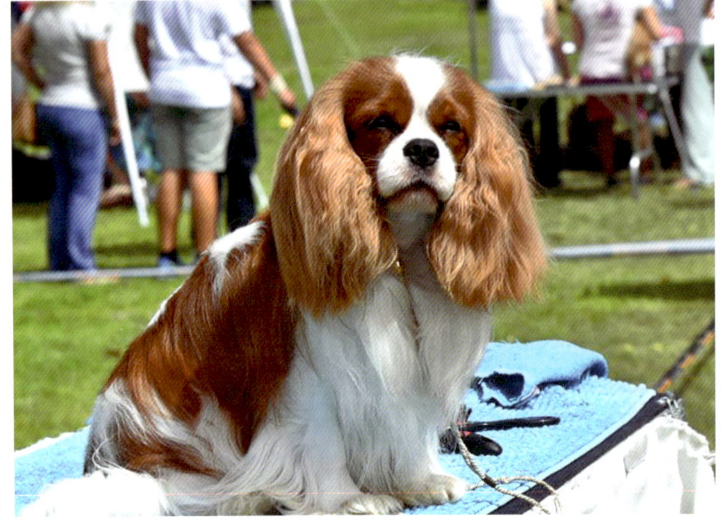

"Honesty" Chelby des Cavaliers de Corence from CH Collins de Contemplations and Filipine des Cavaliers de Corence. Cotation Recommendee.

Photo credit: Sandrine de Corence, Gironde, France

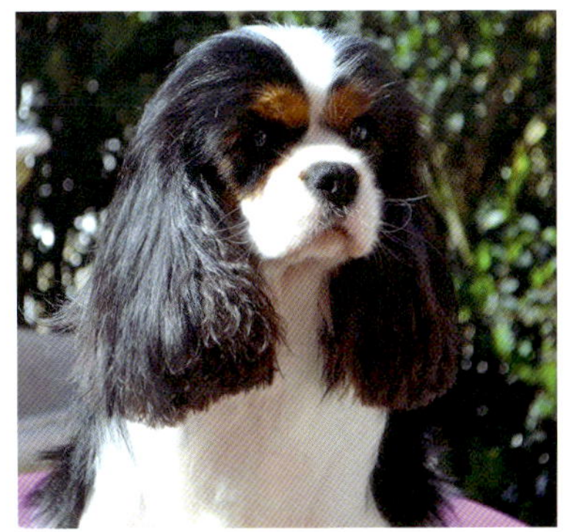

"Monika", European Winner '17 BIS CH Milbu Joy and Pride from Charalier Dress to the Nines for Charlesworth & Milbu All in Sun. Bred by Milda Buša/Latvia, owned by Bojan Cukic, Gentle Star Cavaliers.

Photo credit: Bojan Cukiac, Belgrade, Serbia

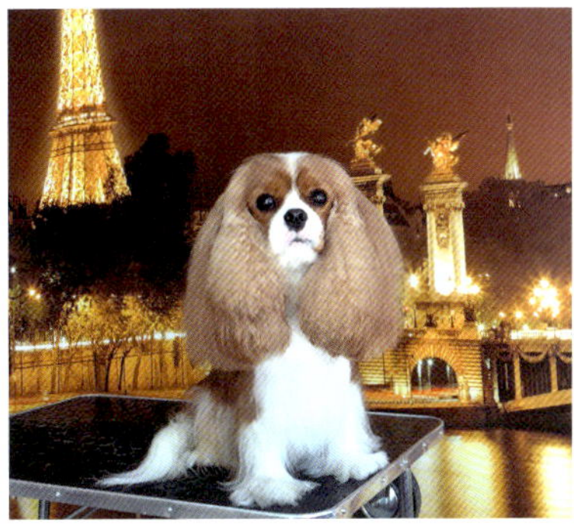

Intl CH FR LUX BE Esley McGregor de Cavaliers de Corence.

Photo credit. Sandrine de Corence, La Teste de Buche, France

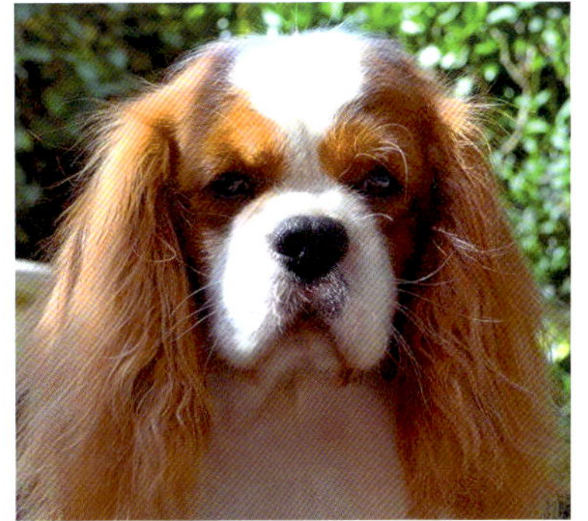

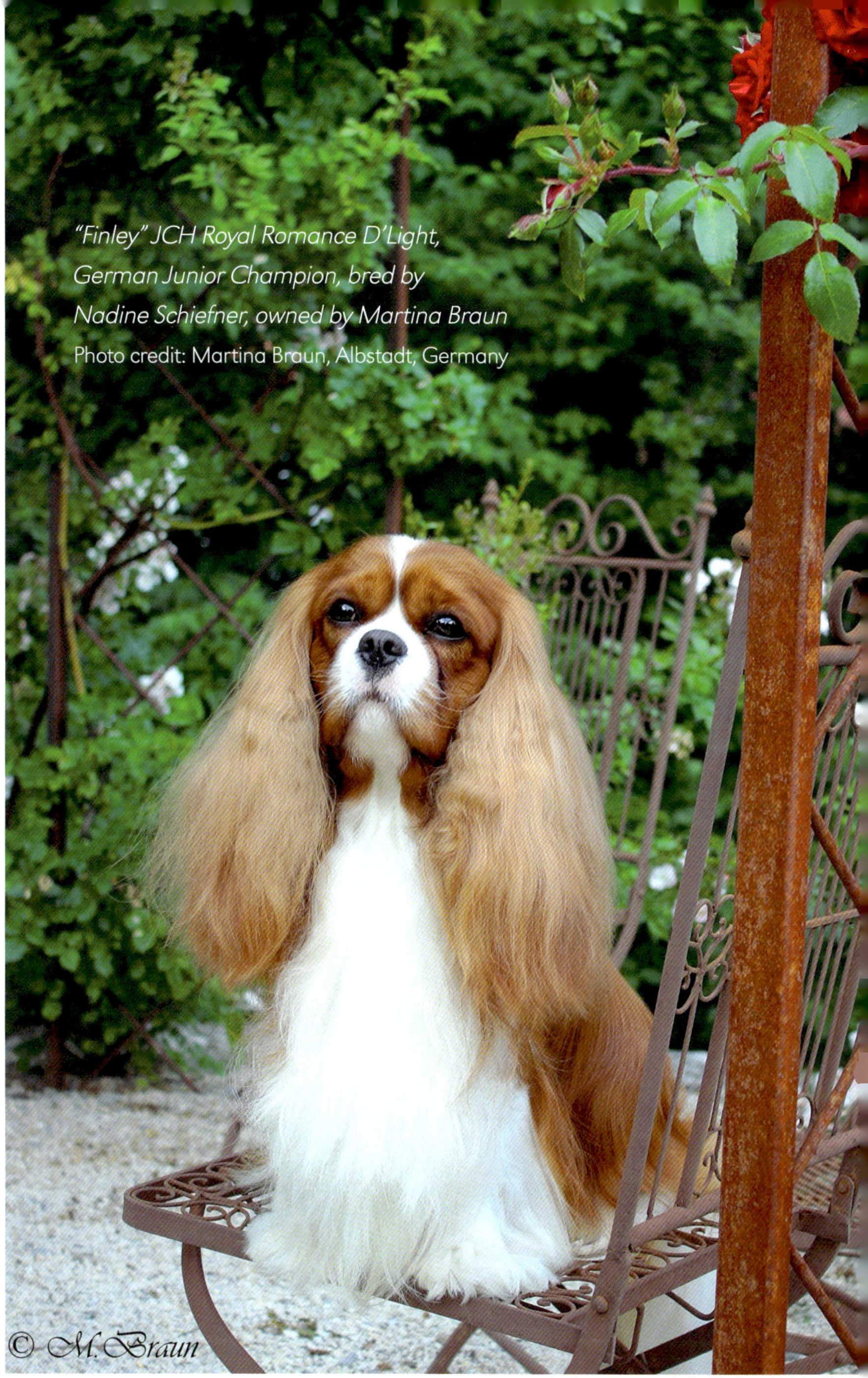

"Finley" JCH Royal Romance D'Light, German Junior Champion, bred by Nadine Schiefner, owned by Martina Braun

Photo credit: Martina Braun, Albstadt, Germany

© M.Braun

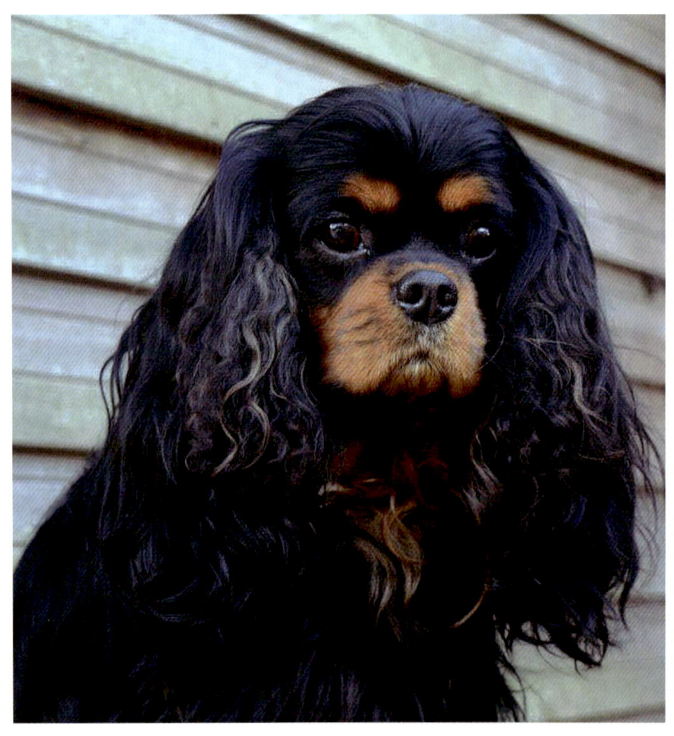

"Murphy" Tangledwood Little Big Shot, son of Oscar, Champion of Holland and Belgium.

Photo credit: Natasja Noonen, Oostelbeers, Netherlands

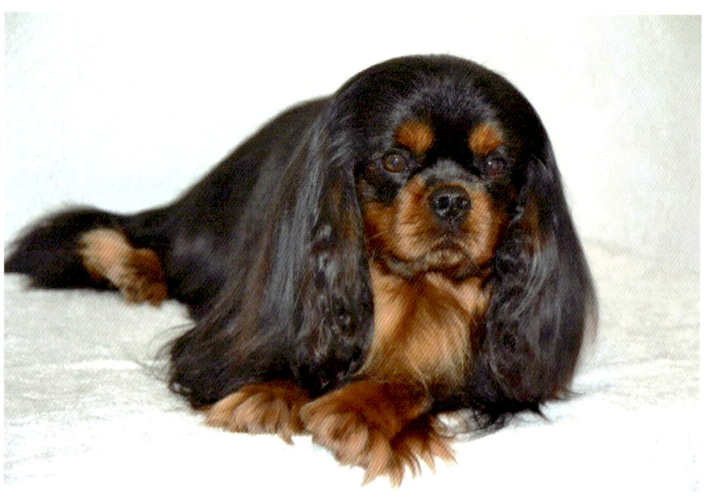

"Roy" CH Blue Moon Cavaliers Rabymar Midnight Express.

Photo credit: Urska Longar, Ljubljana, Slovenia

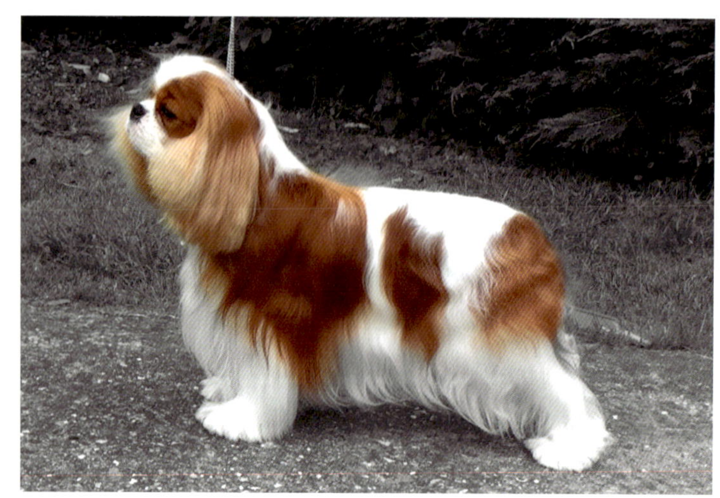

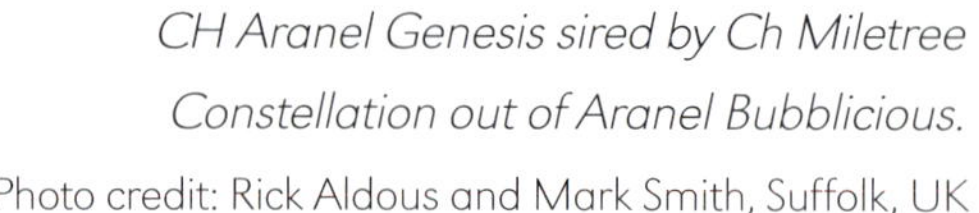

CH Aranel Genesis sired by Ch Miletree Constellation out of Aranel Bubblicious.

Photo credit: Rick Aldous and Mark Smith, Suffolk, UK

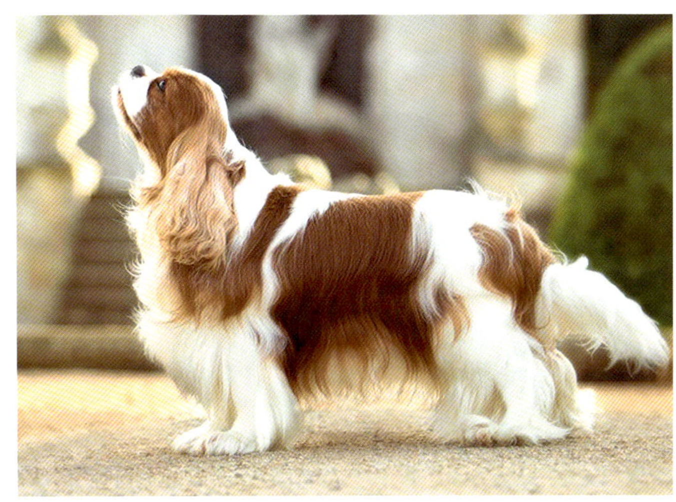

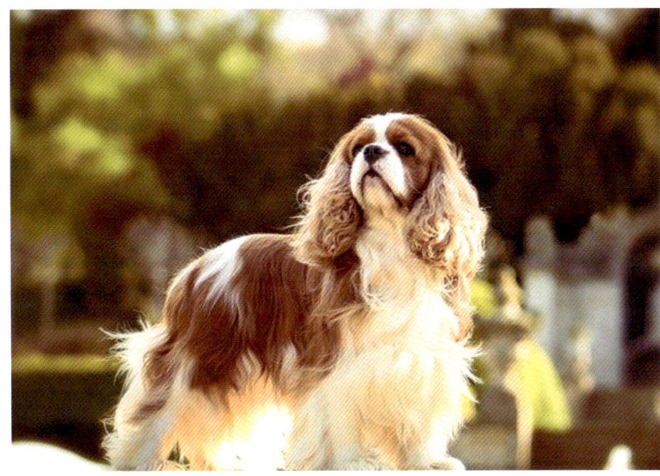

Left top and bottom: German Champion Miletree Soloman, bred by Peter and Ruta Towse, owned by Marlen Blessman.
Photo credit: Marlen Blessman, Castleville Cavaliers, Germany

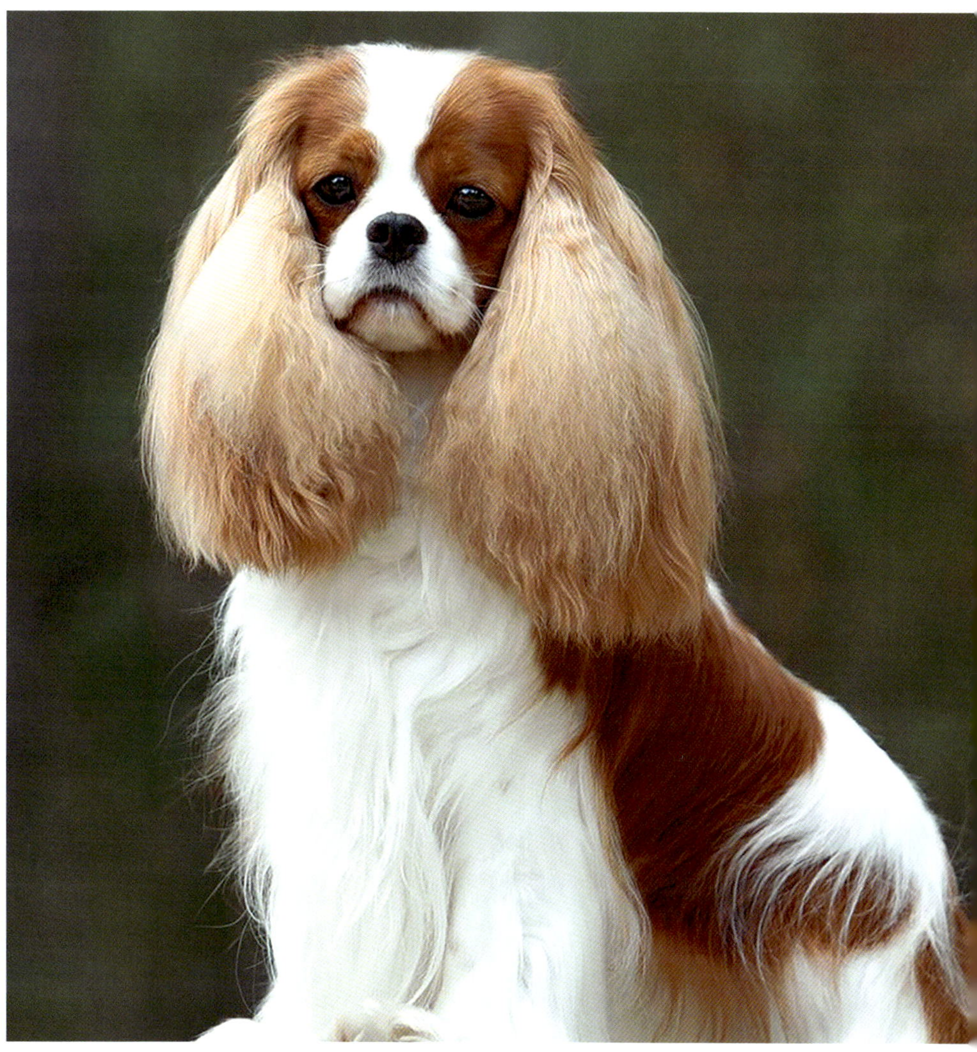

"Penne" MBISS CKCSC, USA CH & AKC GCHG Carmas Penne Pasta at Crizwood. Owned by Susan van Luchene.
Photo credit: Susan van Luchene, California, USA

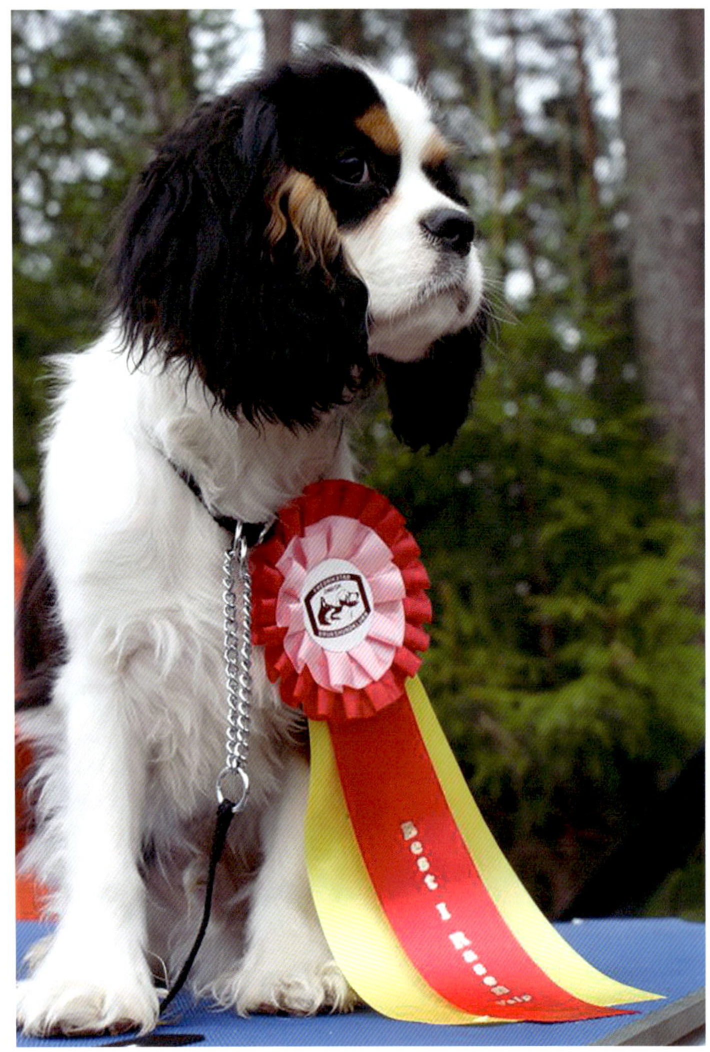

Bacardi du Monaco "Theo" is a two-time puppy winner in Norway.
Photo credit: Angelique Plessis Bobrikova, Banksa Bystrica, Slovakia

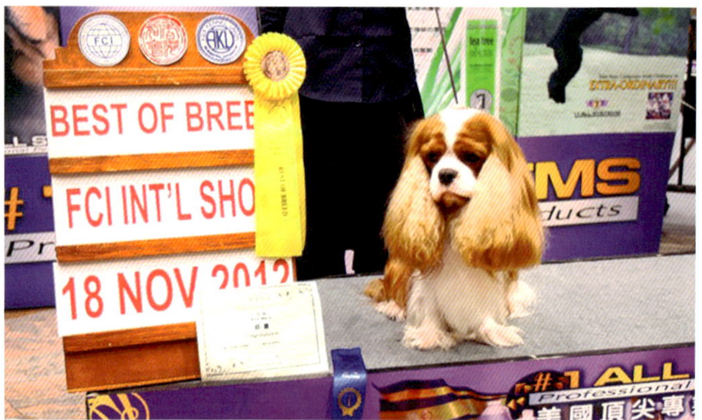

RBIS Multi Champion Liane's Highlander "Bruce," bred by Liane Berger, taking FCI International Show honours.
Photo credit: Jenny Ip, Hong Kong, Peoples Republic of China

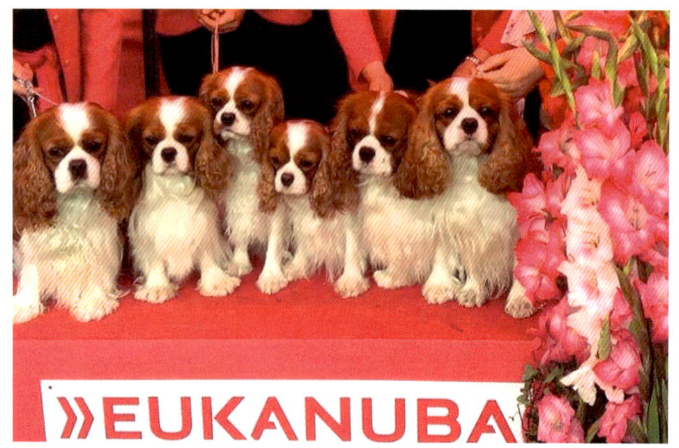

All six puppies from CH Aranel Galaxy "Abbie's" first litter are Finnish Champions, bred by Pauliina and Eveliina Lantta.
Photo credit: Eveliina Lantta, Kouvola, Finland

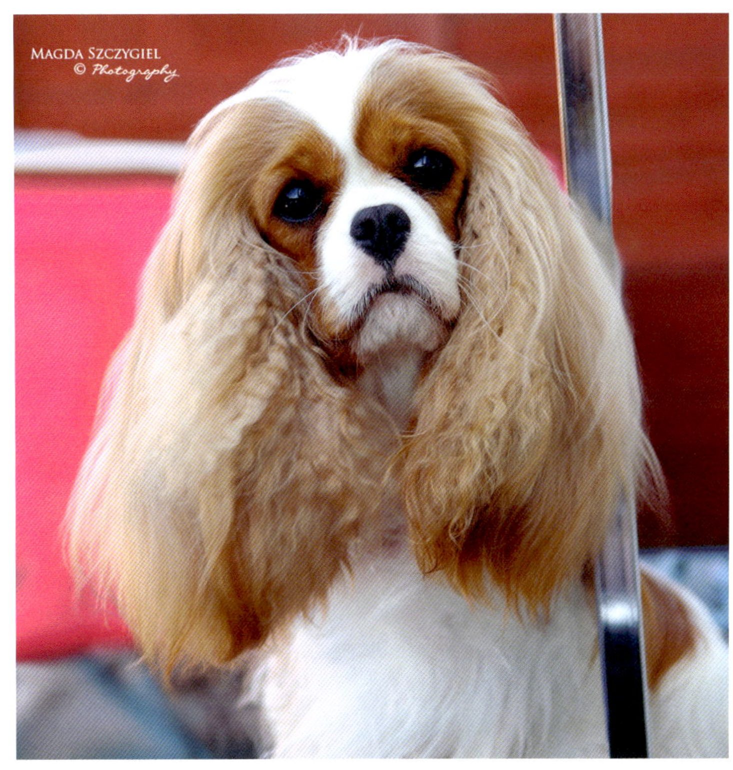

Loli Castletoy Crazy Lollipop, Jun CH, RBIS Irish Cavalier Club '16.

Photo credit: Magda Szczgiel, Dublin, Ireland

Photography: Magda Szczygiel

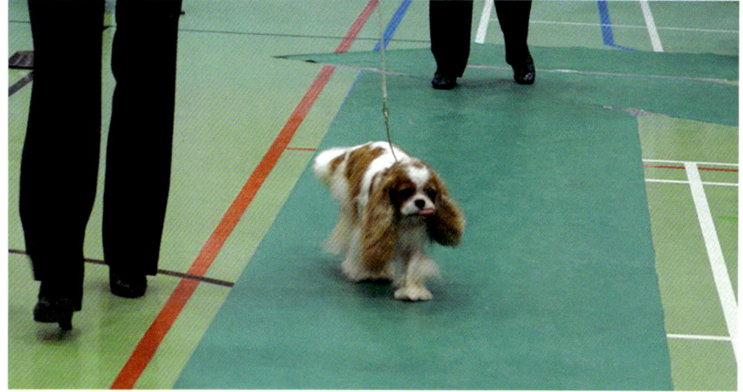

Breeder Veronica Hull of Telvara Cavaliers showing "Lilibet" Telvara Krstiana at almost 13 years old, daughter of CH Telvara Top Hat (a champion Telvara Casanova son) and Dam Telvara Karrina (a champion Telvara Top Hatgrandaughter).

Photo credit: Veronica Hull, London, UK

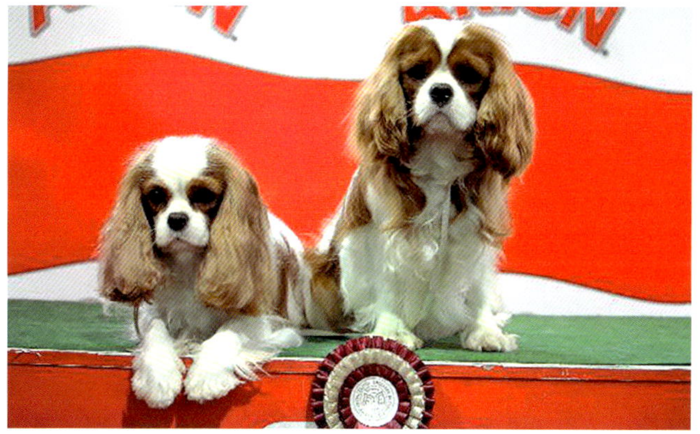

Blue Moon Cavaliers Aphrodite winning BIS, and Nicolai for Aranel winning JR. BOB at Budapest Grand Prix Show.

Photo credit: Urska Longar, Ljubljana, Slovenia

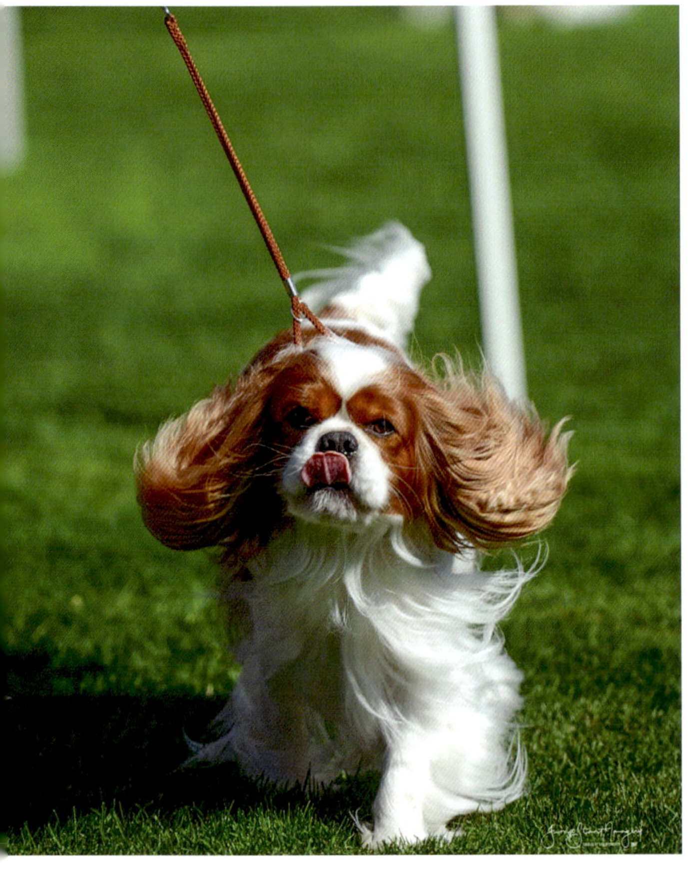

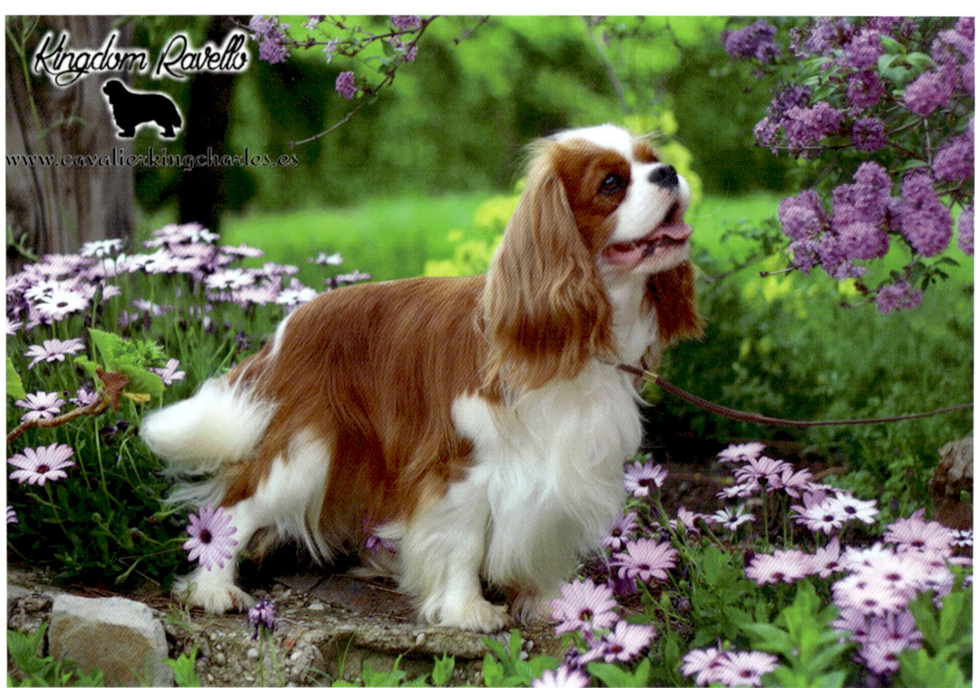

Champion of Spain and Gibraltar, Glamorous Greg Magnolia Passco from Kingdom Ravello Kennel.
Photo credit: Maria Jose Molina, Cordoba, Spain

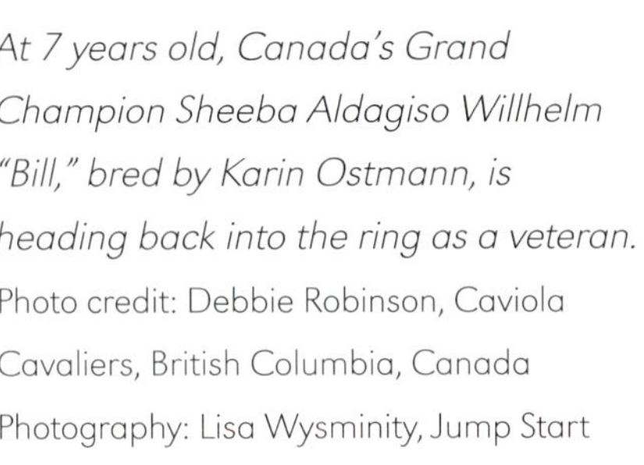

At 7 years old, Canada's Grand Champion Sheeba Aldagiso Willhelm "Bill," bred by Karin Ostmann, is heading back into the ring as a veteran.
Photo credit: Debbie Robinson, Caviola Cavaliers, British Columbia, Canada
Photography: Lisa Wysminity, Jump Start

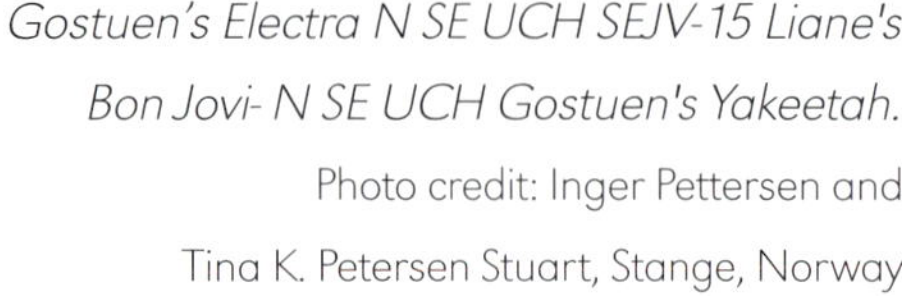

Gostuen's Electra N SE UCH SEJV-15 Liane's Bon Jovi- N SE UCH Gostuen's Yakeetah.
Photo credit: Inger Pettersen and Tina K. Petersen Stuart, Stange, Norway

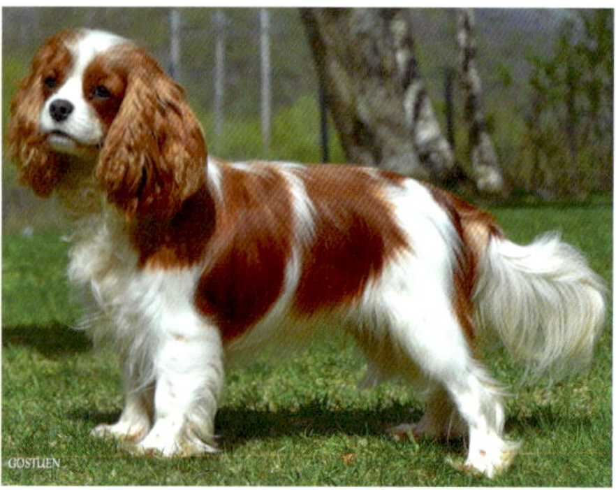

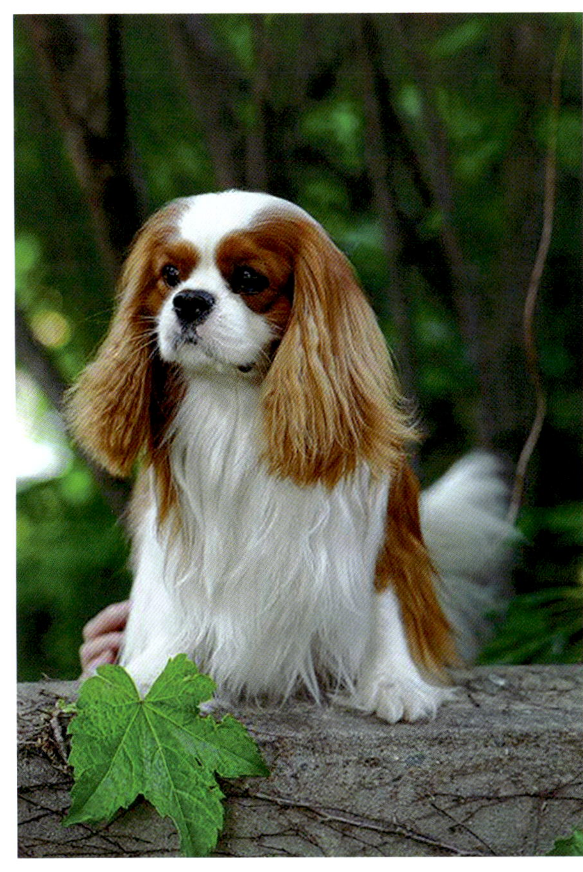

"Leo" CKCS-USA CH & AKC-GCH Bonitos Companeros Kaleo at Diorchavon. Owned by Dorota Bialek.
Photo credit: Jan Wilusz, JW Kennel Photography, Massachusetts, USA

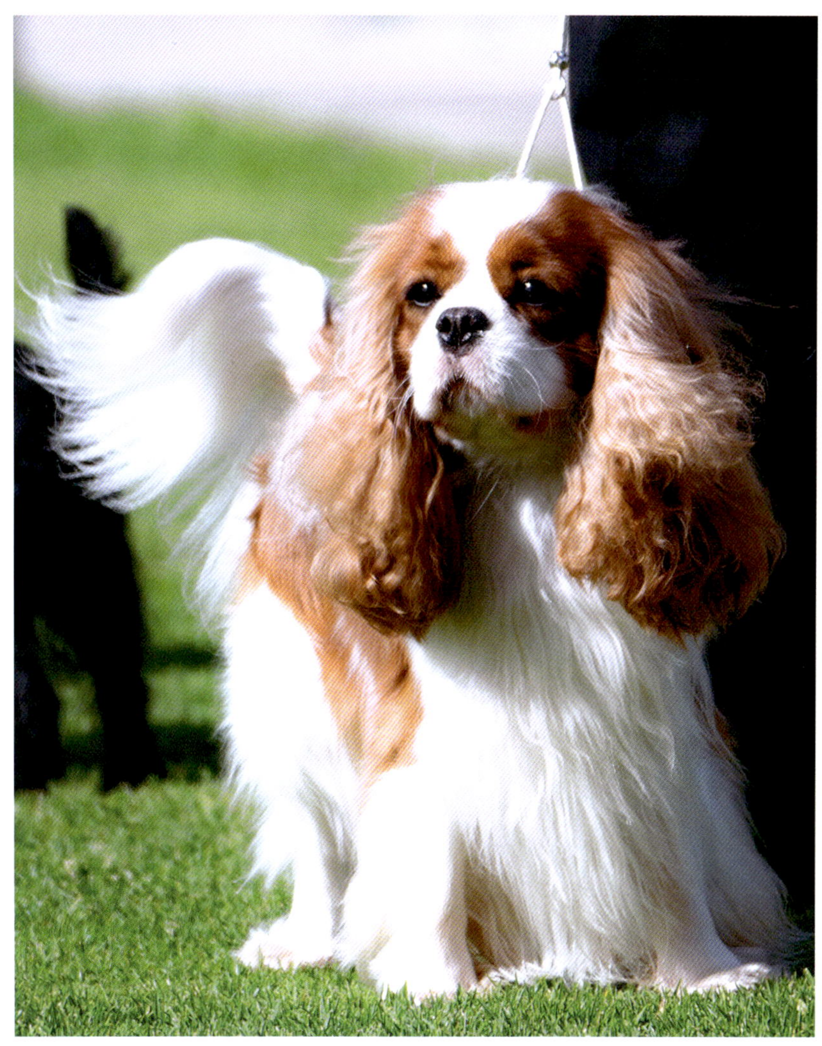

The pedigree name of Australian Champion "Nathan" is Aust. CH Cavashon Pistols at Dawn.
Photo credit: Kym Brooksby, South Adelaide, Australia

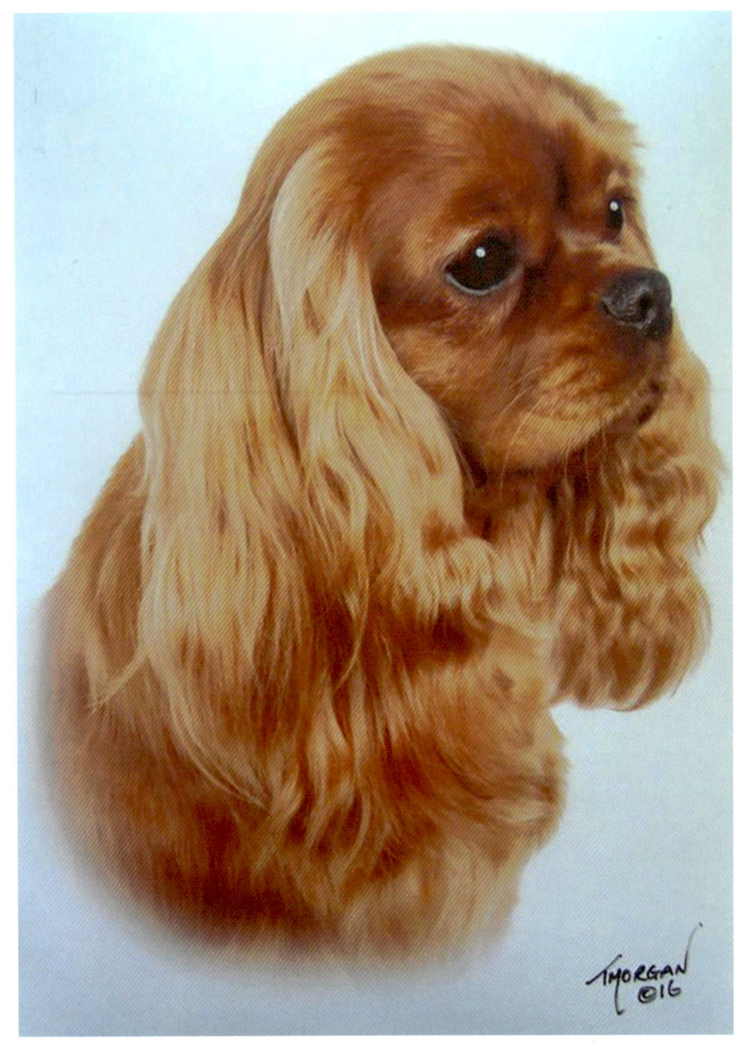

Svena Summer Eve.

Photo credit: Breeder Wholecolour Cavaliers Bridgette Evans, Landrindod Wells, UK

Photography: Tracy Morgan

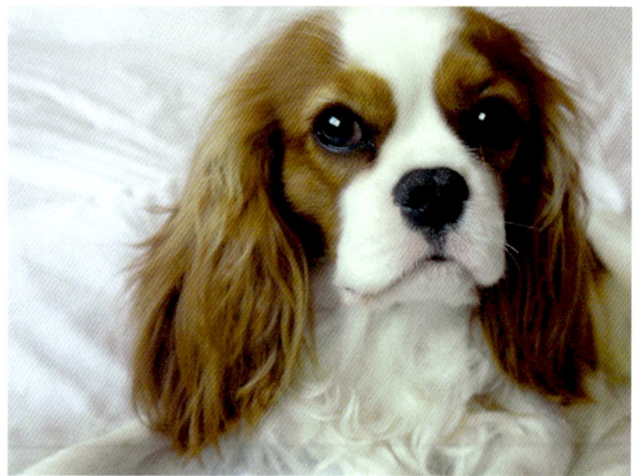

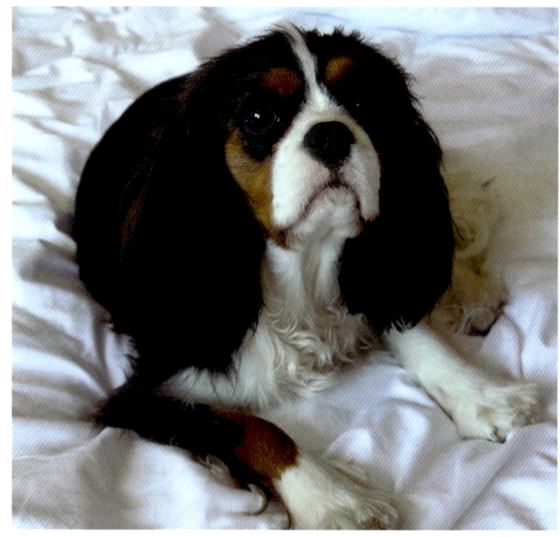

Two-time puppy/jeune winners (Seville and Toulouse) are Dolly and Moonbeam (Blue Moon Cavaliers You Hung the Moon).

Photo credit: Mary Colburn-Green, L'Aude, France

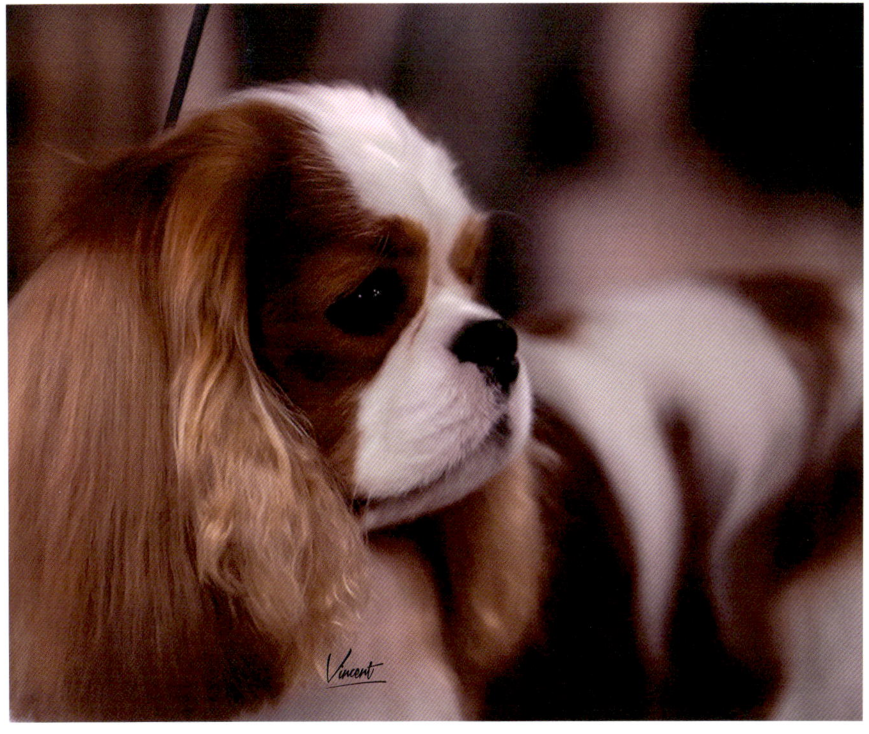

"Robbie" (BIS MBISS AKC GCH & CKCSC-USA CH Bentwood Forestcreek Rob Red (Eng., AKC & CKCSC-USA CH Pascavale Nathan ROM x Maibee Diamond Lil of Bentwood).

Photo credit: Owner Heather Borton, Livelyoak Cavaliers, North Carolina, USA

Photography: Vincent Zuniaga

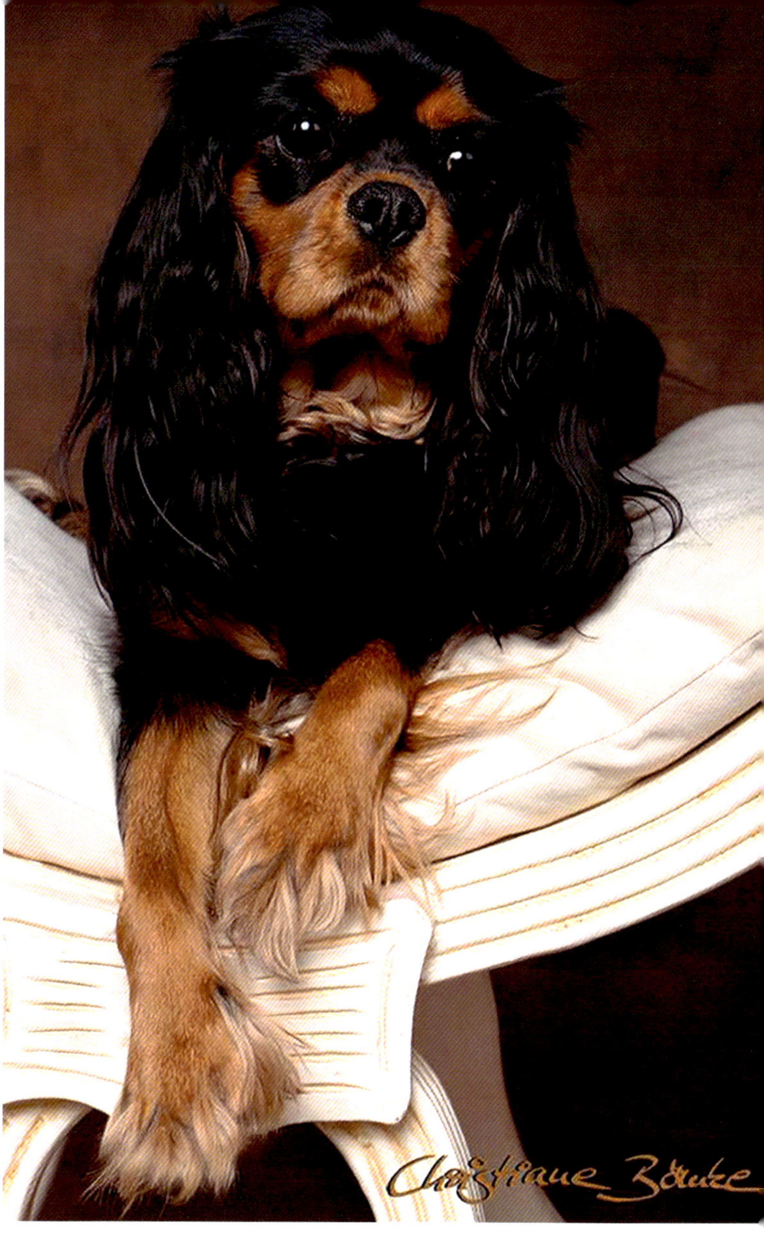

Ronja Blackberry Spark of Hope, bred by Conny Meiboom.

Photo credit: Breeder Conny Meiboom, Germany

Photography: Christiane Bömke

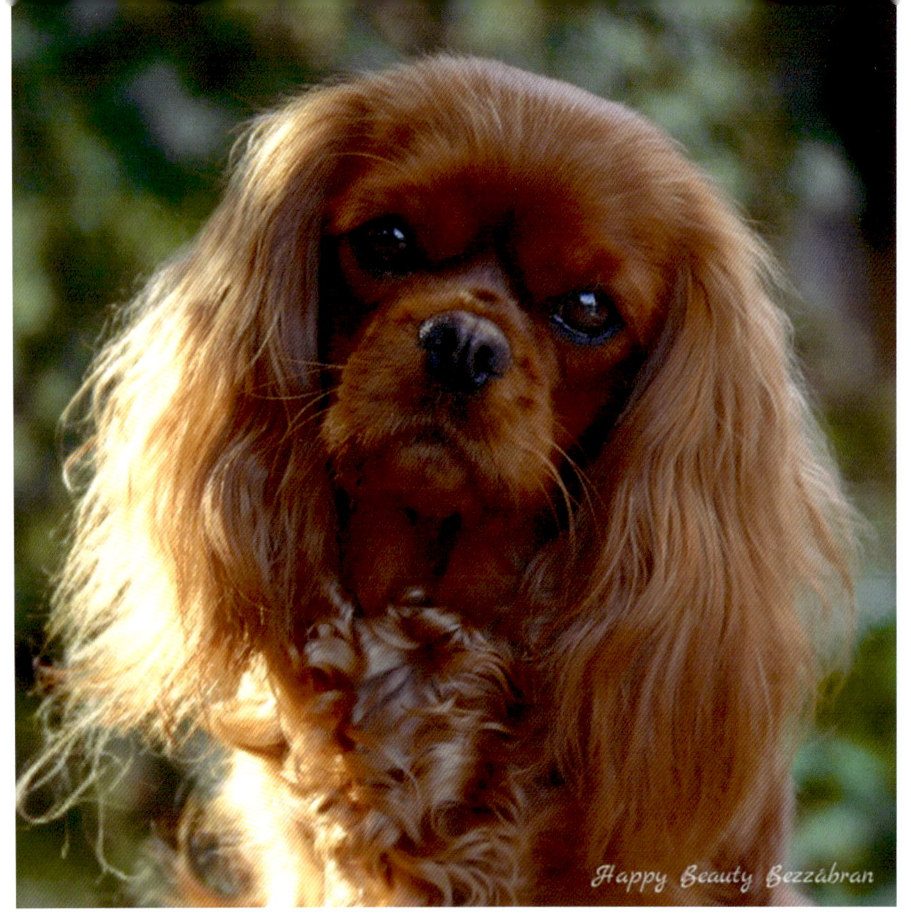

"Bezzabran" Hocus Pocus of Woodville.

Photo credit: Martina Hartmannova, Domazlice, Czech Republic

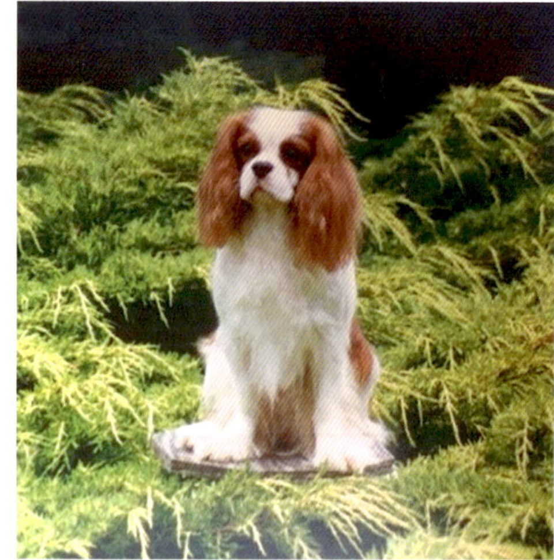

Multi BIS BISS CHAMPION Kewpy's BoDidley, as of this writing, the top-winning Canadian-bred Cavalier in Canadian History.

Photo credit: Karen Wills, Alberta, Canada

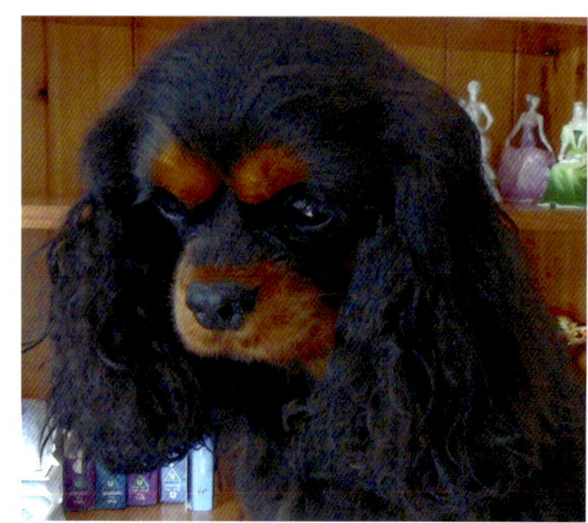

"Lily" Hocus Pocus, bred by Bridget Evans.

Photo credit: Bridgette Evans, Llandrindod Wells, UK

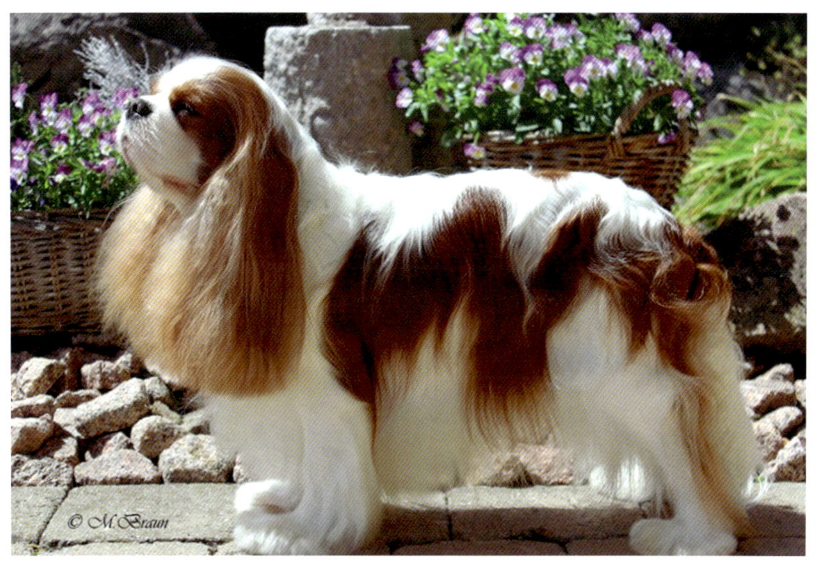

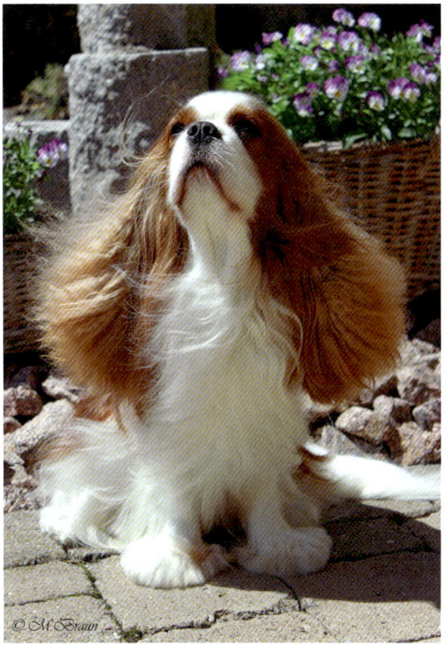

Above and left: CH Tomino of Gillbrook, German Champion VDH, German Champion Club, German Junior Champion Club. Owner Martina Braun.

Photo credit: Martina Braun, Albstadt, Germany

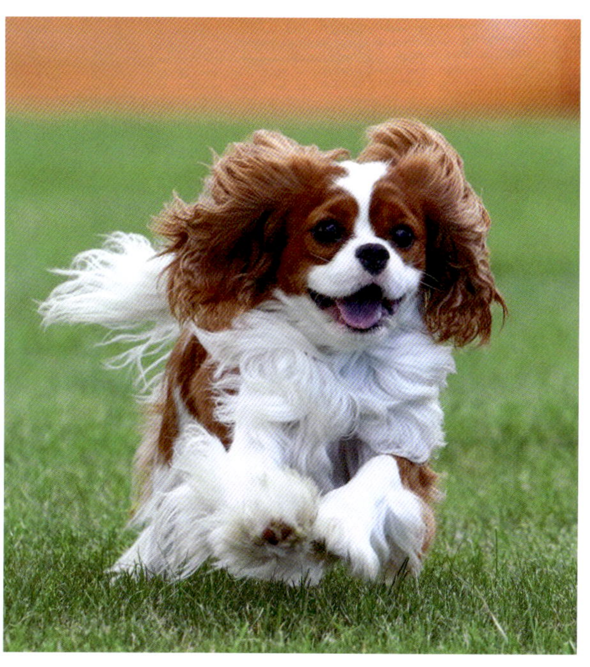

AKC Champion "Niko" Millaray Now or Never.

Photo credit: Malgorzata "Meg" Mlynarska, Illinois, USA

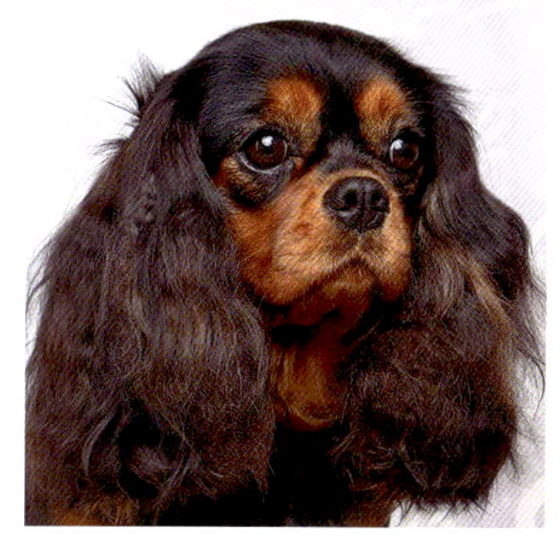

Champion Yasmin Spark of Hope at three years old.

Photo credit: Nicole Sarnowski, Geselkirchen, Germany

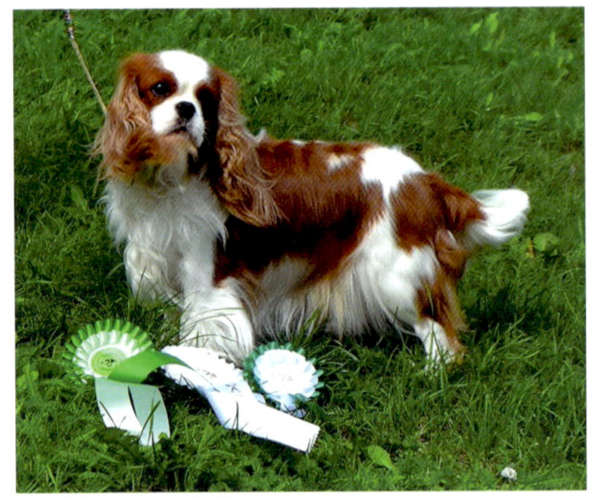

"Tinka" CH Royal Fancy Tinkerbell EST&CZ JCH, BALTW` 16, LTClbW` 16, EST&LV<&BALT&RUS&CZ&HR-CH Ex/1, CQ, BB-1, BOS, CACIB, Crufts Qualified.
Photo credit: Breeder Urve Tipp, Viljandi, Estonia

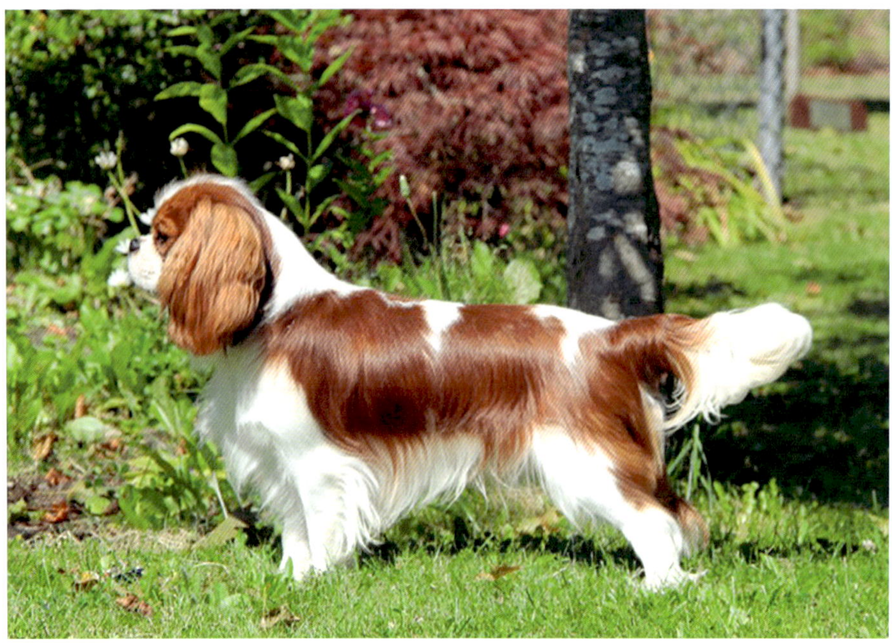

"Benjamin," BISS GCH Can CH Orchard Hill Toy Money, has multiple group placements and is currently a top 20 Cavalier in both the U.S. and Canada. Owned by Julia Johns and Rachel and Erica Venier. Benjamin lives with Julia in Seattle, Washington.
Photo credit: Allison, Lockleer, Washington, USA

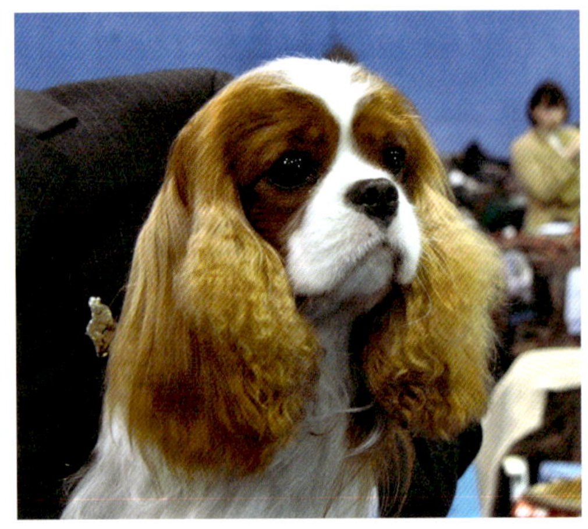

Cosmic, Aranel Cavaliers UK's second Champion, sired by Ch Miletree Nijinsky out of Aranel Arabella.
Photo credit: Rick Aldous and Mark Smith, Suffolk, UK

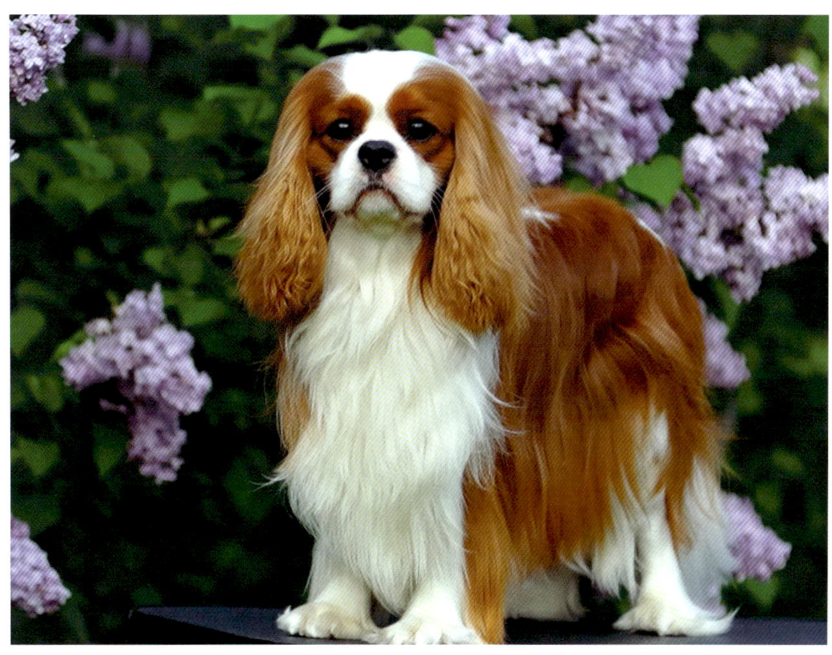

"Leo" GCH Bonitos Companeros Kaleo at Dirchavon, Owned by Dorota Bialek.

Photo credit: Jan Wilusz, JW Kennel Photography, Massachusetts, USA

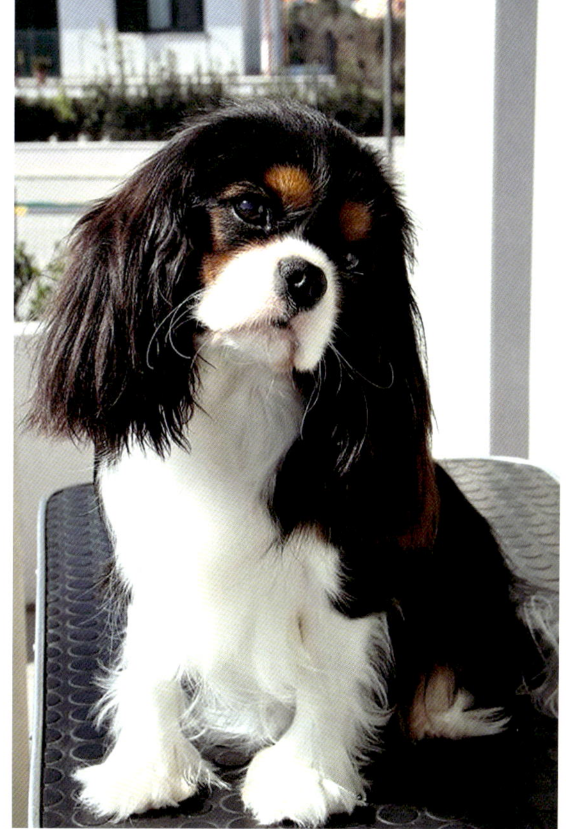

Gallicja Love Me.

Photo credit: Claudia di Bortoli, Termoli, Italy

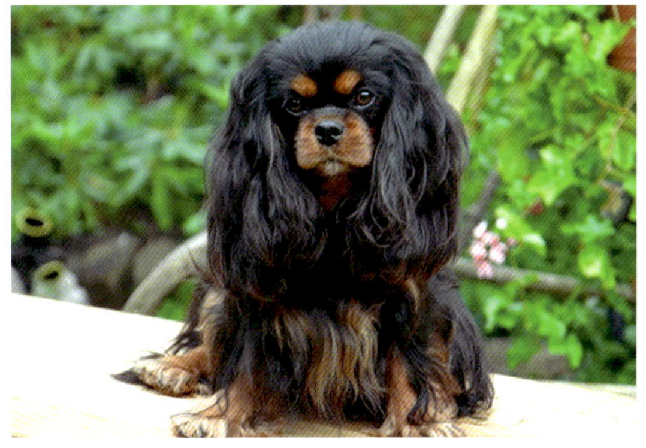

Klopsville San Mateo "Matt" (UK CH Gamble on You Des Contemplations at Pascavale X ClopsvilleSanta Ynez) at stud.

Photo credit: Gaby and Franz Kottmann, Erwite, Germany

Chapter 6 - Regal Cavaliers

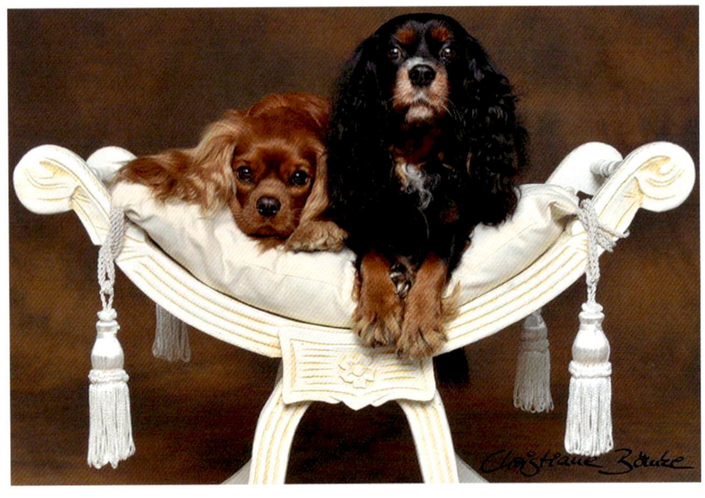

Nia Currygirl Spark of Hope and Maggie look at home on their elegant chaise.

Photo credit: Nicole Sarnowski, Geselkirchen, Germany

Photography: Dr. Christiane Bömke, Gelsenkirchen, Germany

Owing to centuries of affiliation with royalty, Cavaliers innately love the good life. They gravitate to comfortable surroundings and copious attention. They can't get too much petting, pampering, delicacies, treats, and most of all, companionship. They're so much fun to spoil, that their owners may go off the deep end in pampering their pets. But these hearty little souls also love the outdoors and new adventures. Consequently, when the satin and damask are not available or is getting tiresome, they'll happily perch in the middle of a lovely tuft of grass or on a picturesque stone wall, and in the process, still look very aristocratic. They may even waddle in the mud, but that's a whole other chapter *(see Sporty Cavaliers)*.

Entitlement to a Cavalier is like a duck pond to a retriever. They have the soulful eyes and adorable quirkiness that gets them what they want. What's more, the regal Cavalier is only too happy to reciprocate. She will be your dedicated nurse and loyal bed partner should you ever be sick or incapacitated. Spoiling your little prince or princess is really tantamount to treating yourself to endless love.

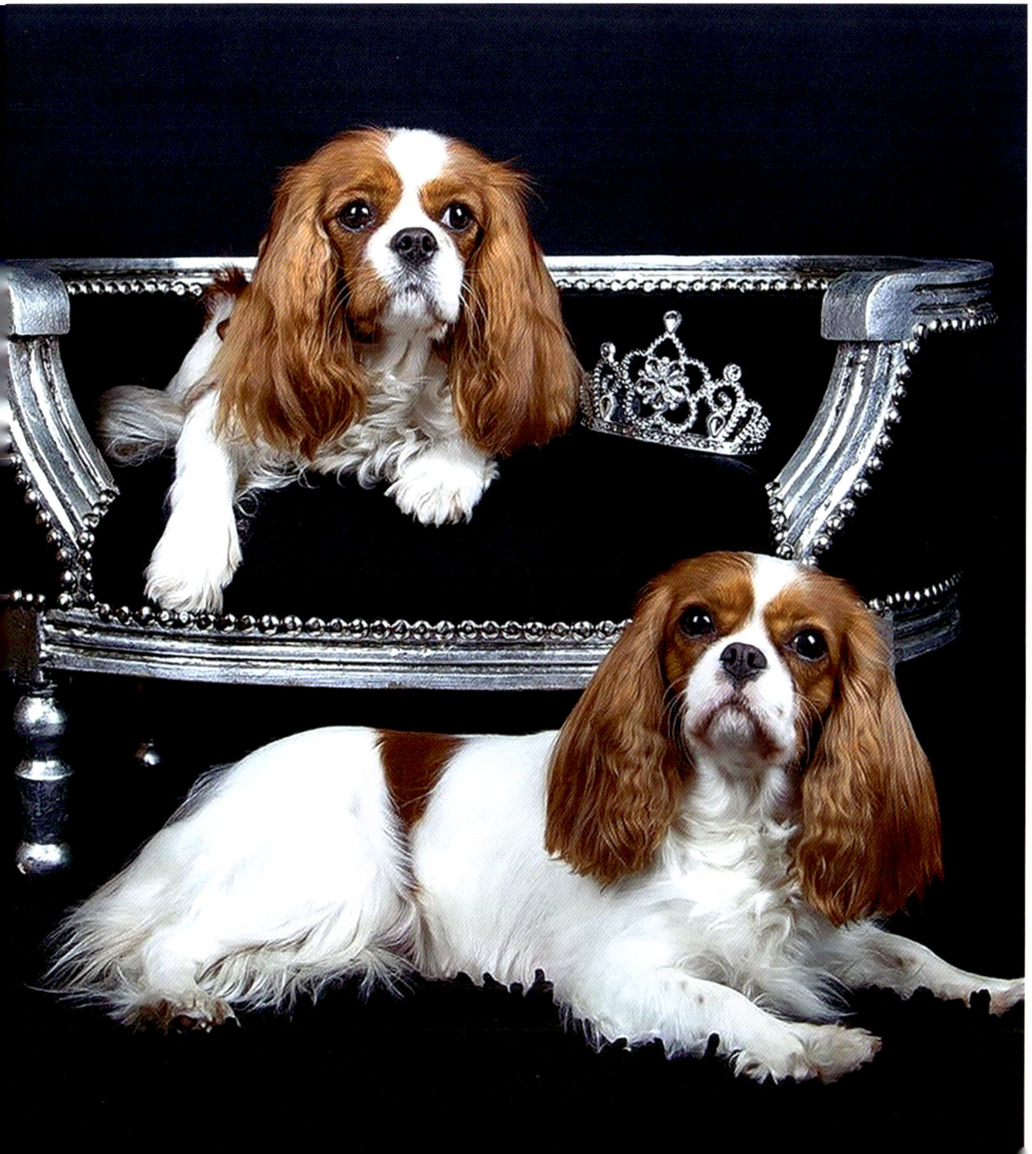

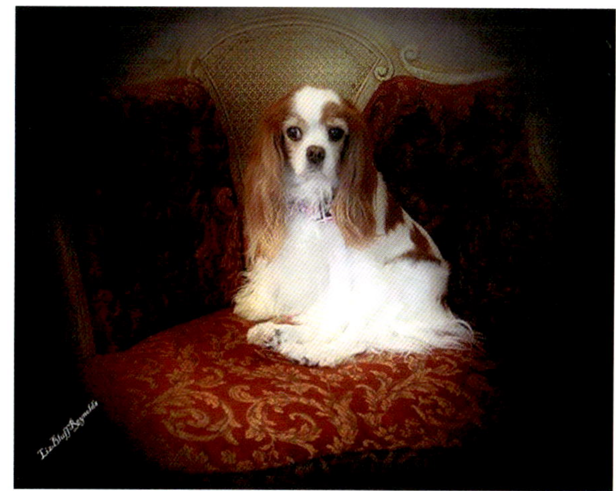

Beautiful Millie is shown here at 15 years old. She recently passed over the Rainbow Bridge.
Photo credit: Susan Clayton Meyer, Illinois, USA

BIS MBISS AKC GCH & CKCSC-USA CH Bentwood Forestcreek Rob Red "Robbbie" (Eng., AKC & CKCSC-USA CH Pascavale Nathan ROM x Maibee Diamond Lil of Bentwood).
Photo credit: Liane Müller, Oranienburg, Germany

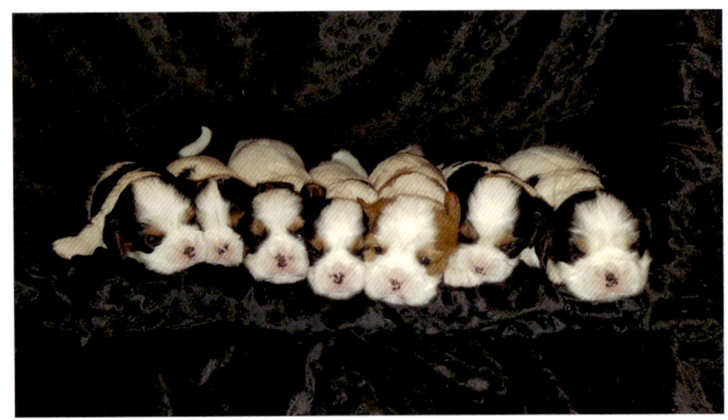

Chanel's fabulous litter of regal puppies are too cute for words.

Photo credit: Gail Sanders, Sanders Sweet Cavaliers, Arizona, USA

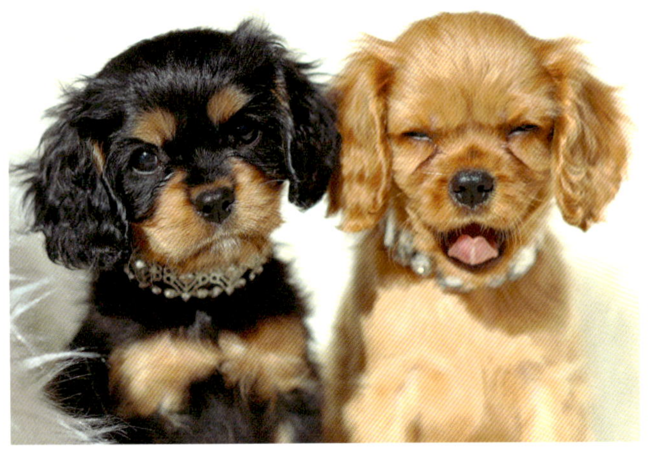

Marino's Precious Cavaliers' puppies are never too young for diamonds.

Photo credit: Heather Marino, Tennessee, USA

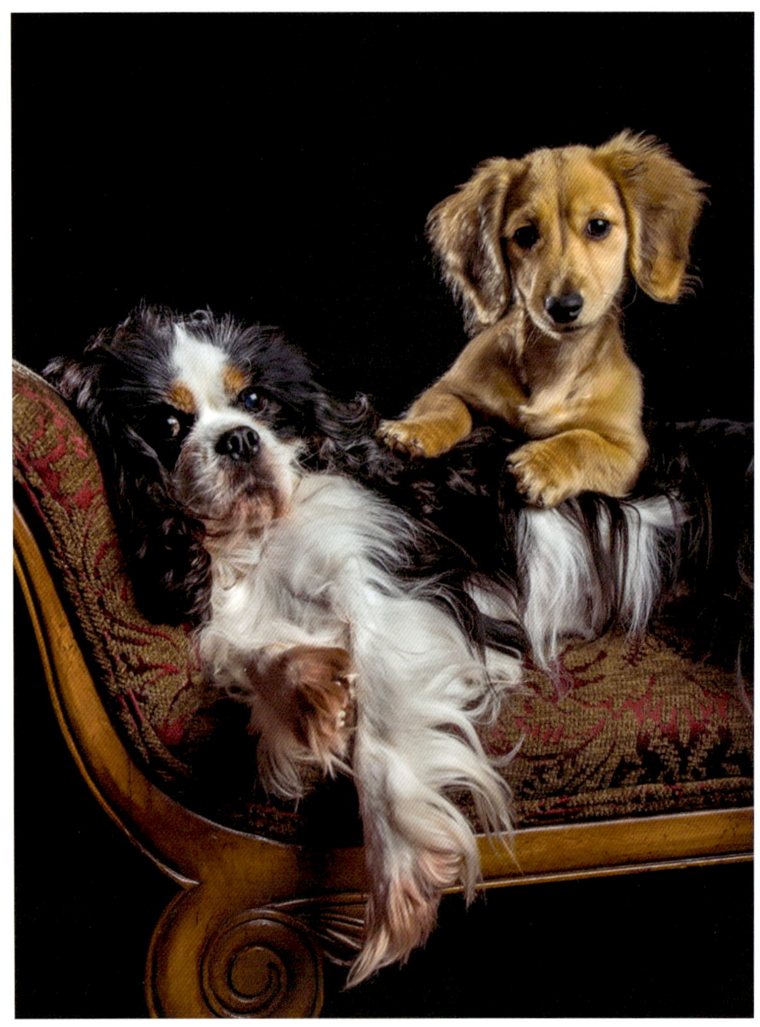

Tri-Color Abbey Shadow of an Excellent Choice, 11 years young, and her Buddy Bailey the Dachshund enjoy the good life.

Photo credit: Michael and Brenda Berg, Studio Berg Photography, North Carolina, USA

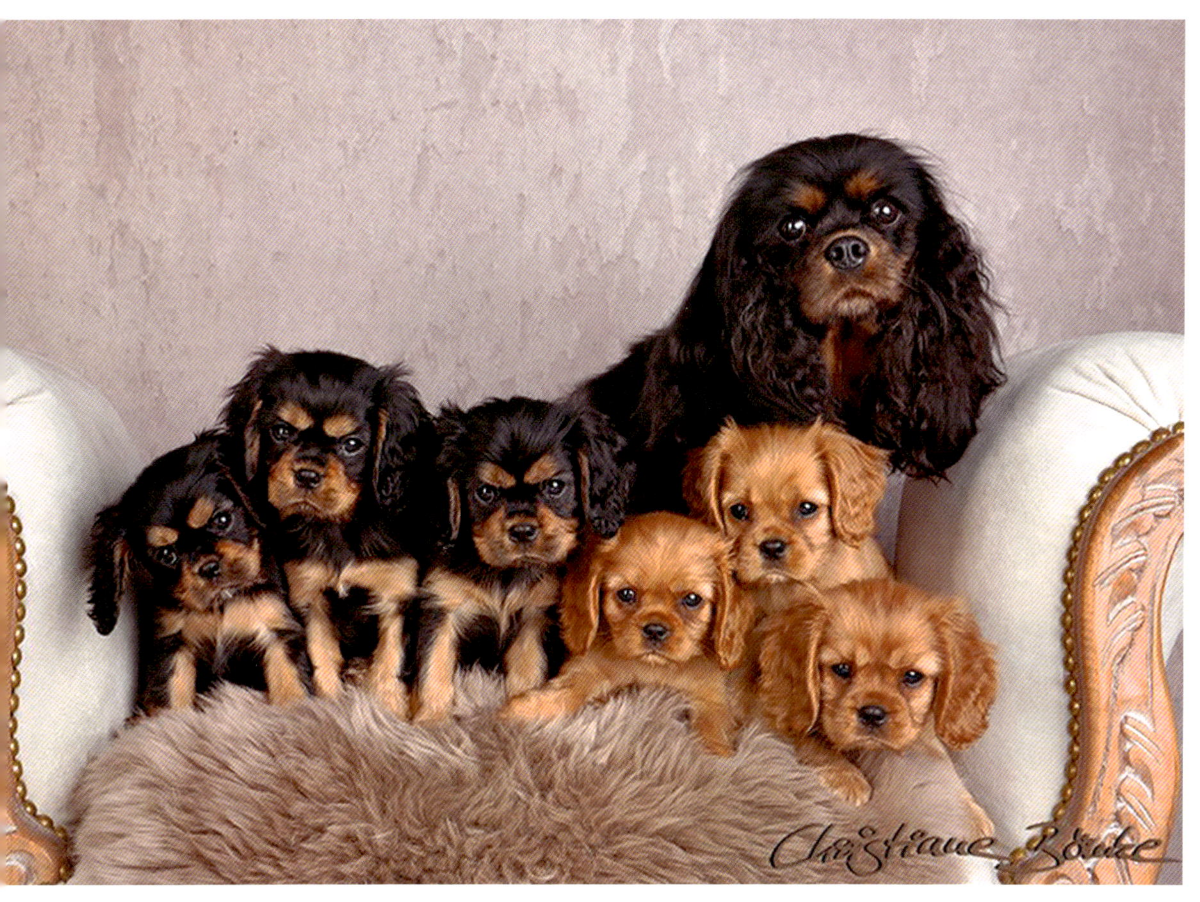

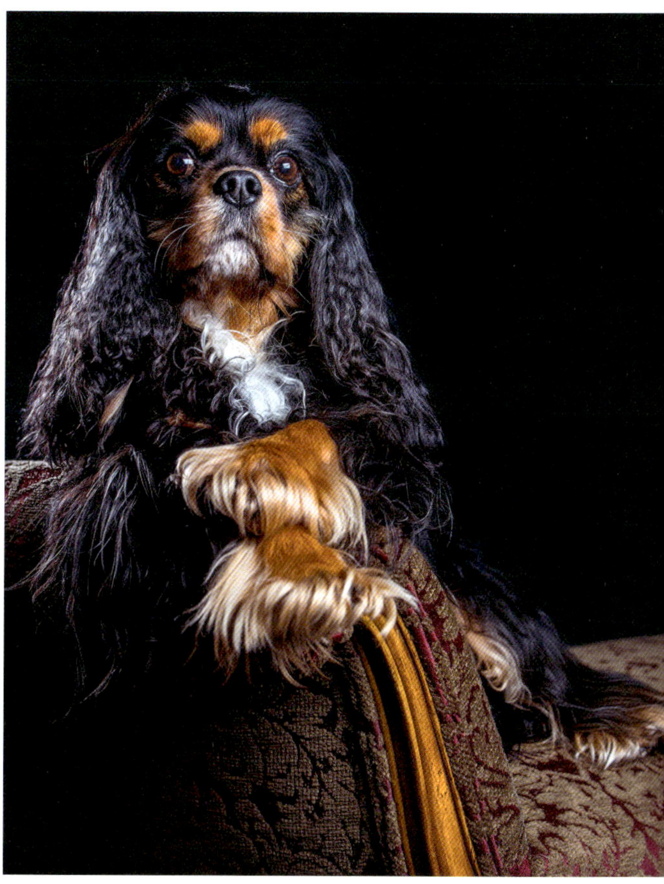

Frenzy's F-Litter from Cavaliere Spark of Hope make a striking family portrait (from the left: Frenzy's Fee, Flyboy Chuck, Famous Joe, Fräulein Smilla, Fiona Norma & Full Metal Jacket).
Photo credit: Conny Meiboom, Xanten, Germany
Photography: Dr. Christiane Bomke

Bandit of an Excellent Choice in repose,
Photo credit: Michael and Brenda Berg,
Studio Berg Photography, North Carolina, USA

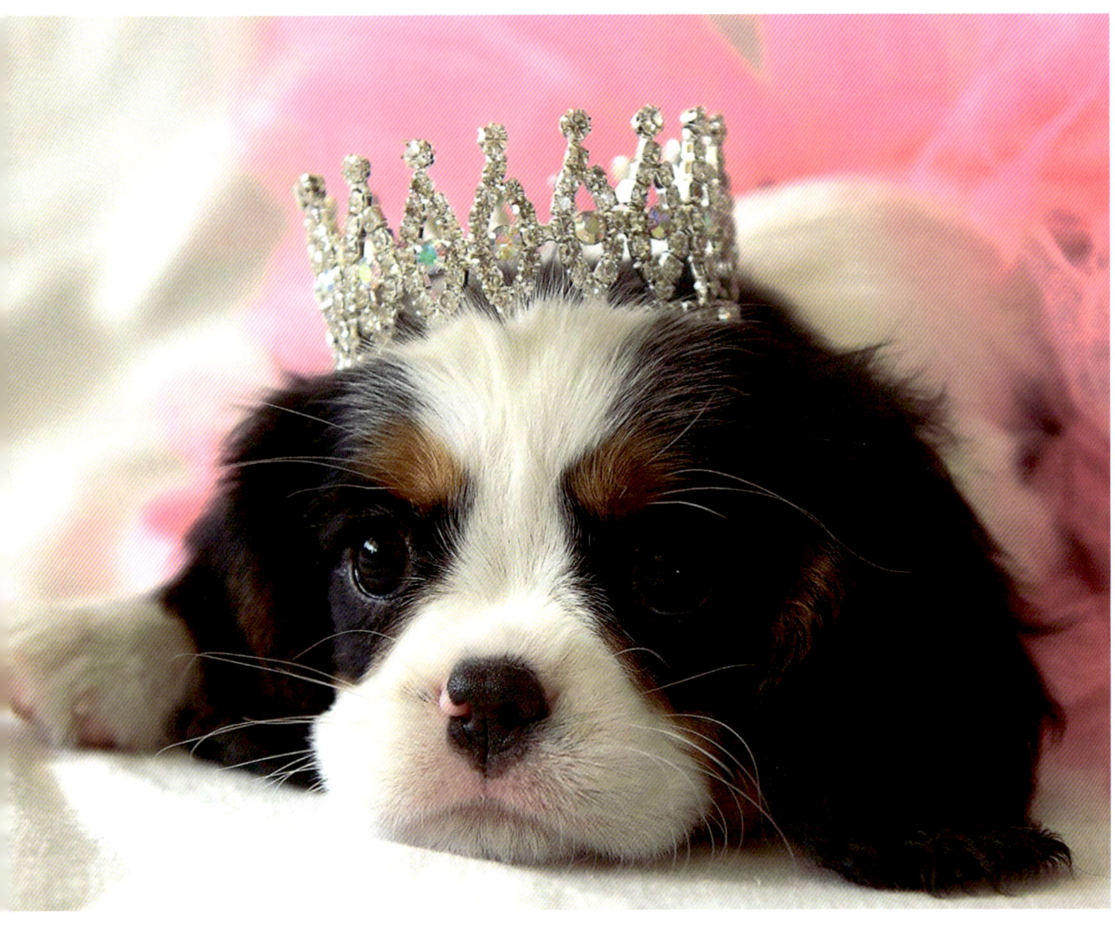

Little Princess Chanel seems slated for the good life.

Photo credit: Gail Sanders, Arizona, USA

Photography: Cathi Cenetiempo

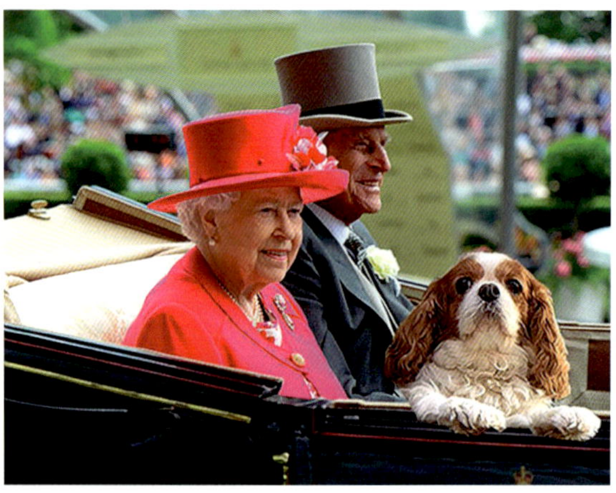

Purdey sure runs with the right crowd!

Photo credit: Artist Alexandra Churchill, Cotswolds, UK

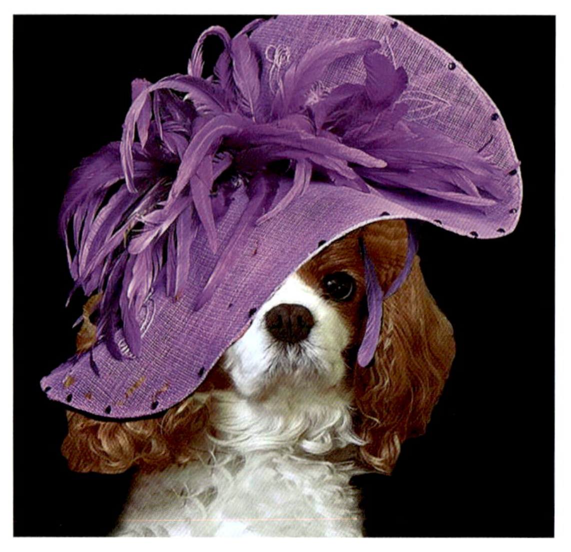

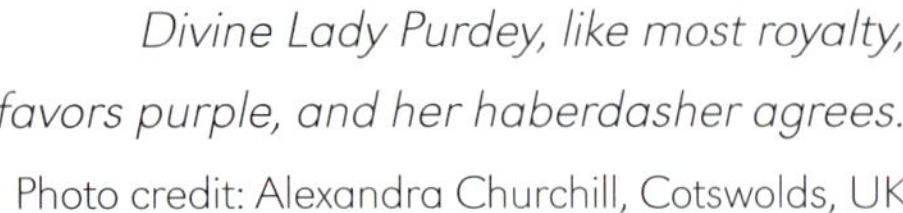

Divine Lady Purdey, like most royalty, favors purple, and her haberdasher agrees.

Photo credit: Alexandra Churchill, Cotswolds, UK

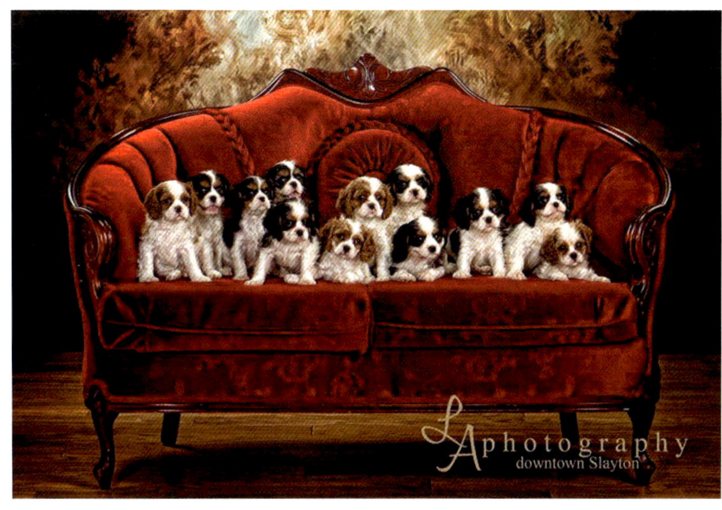

A dozen little princes and princesses from one litter!

Photo credit: Penny Platt, Minnesota, USA

Photography: LA Photography

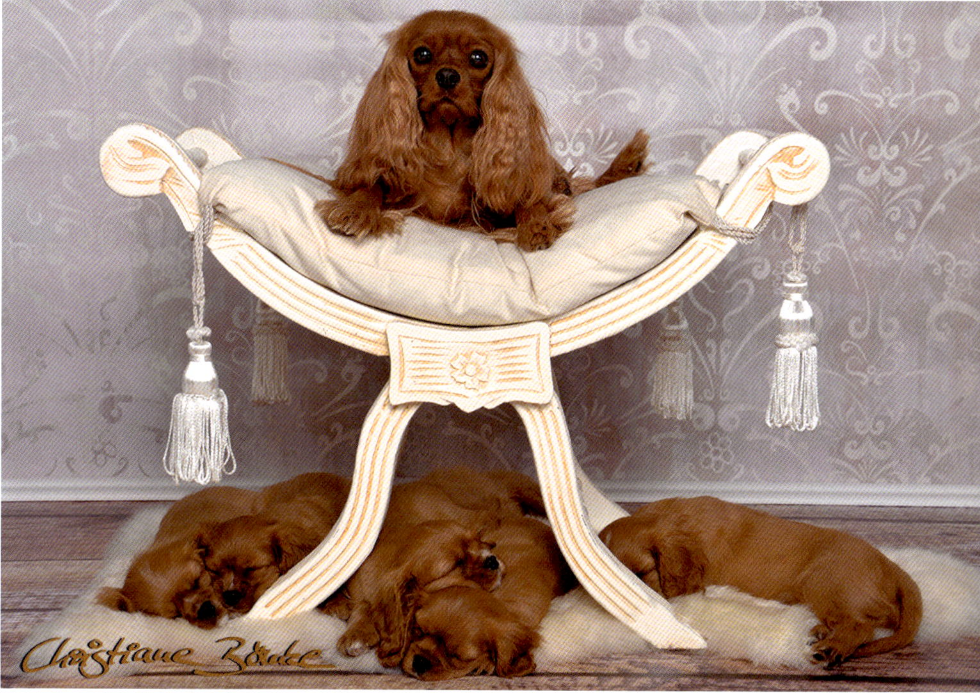

Cavaliere Spark of Hope Cornelia and her pups rest peacefully.

Photo credit: Conny Meiboom, Xantem, Germany

Photography: Dr. Christine Bömke

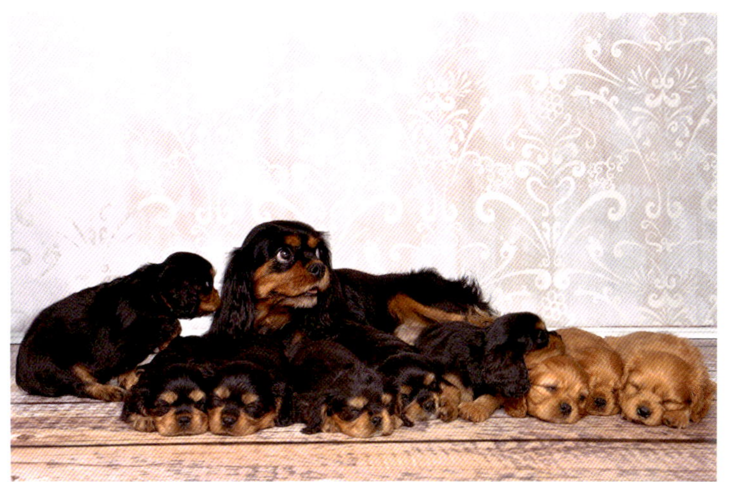

Cavaliere Spark of Hope E Litter looking aristocratic.

Photo credit: Cony Meiboom, Xanten, Germany

Photography: Dr. Christine Bömke

Three darling boys, Geremy (11 months), Eddie (11.5 years), and Caspian Finn (4 years), are enjoying the fresh air.

Photo credit: Radka Barttmanova, Ostravia, Czech Republic

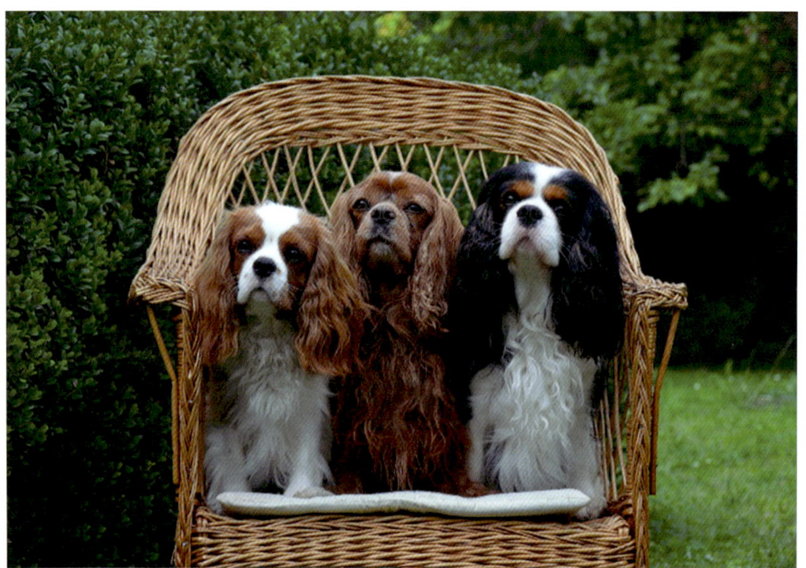

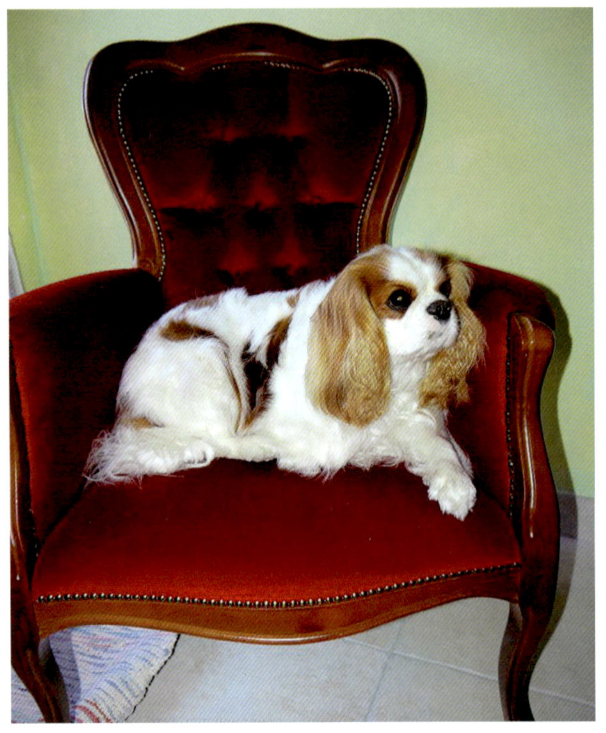

Callie prefers the red velvet Berger Chair.

Photo credit: Mary Colburn-Green, L'Aude, France

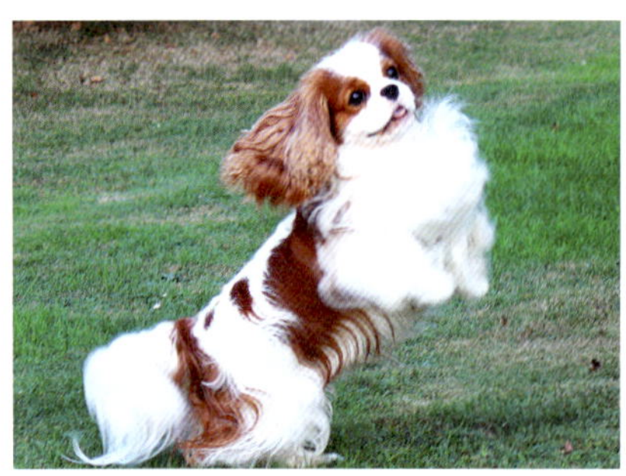

The stunning Klopsville San Mateo "Matt," is showing off his cloud of fluff.

Photo credit and Photography: Gaby Kottmann, Erwitte, Germany

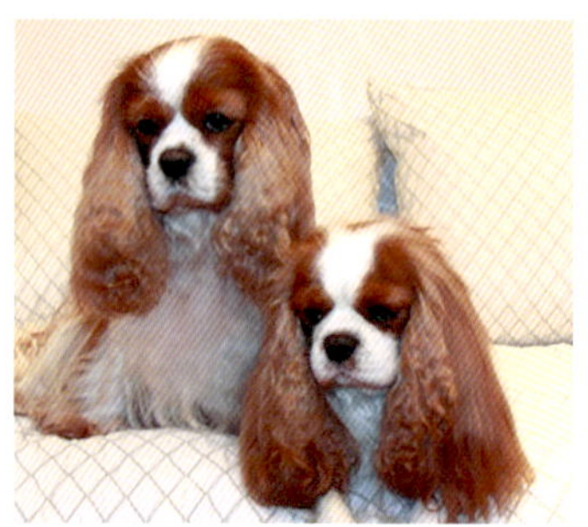

Beautiful show dogs from Nino the Great Kennel.

Photo credit: Natalia Smolenova, Bratislava, Slovakia

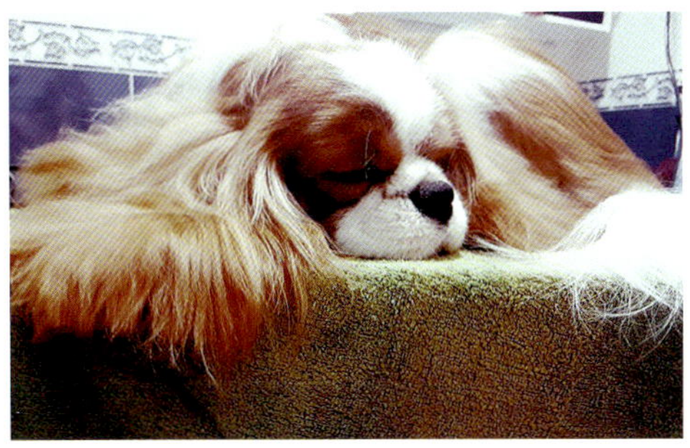

Fly Me to the Moon's Jacomo Salika Soul (Pascavale Buddy X Bonitos Companeros Padme) exudes class.

Photo credit: Eva Rodriguez, Madrid, Spain

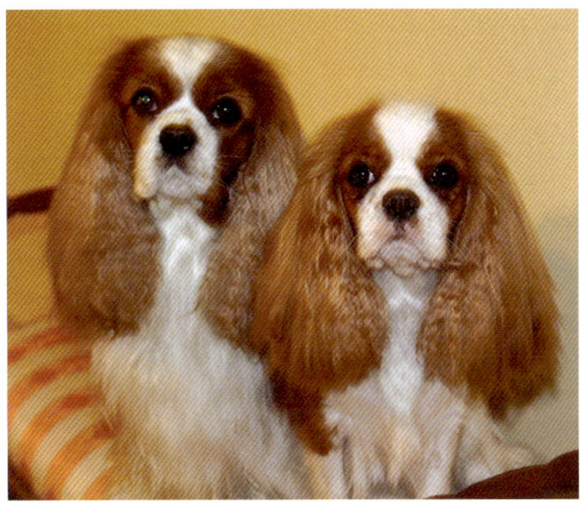

These two are used to posing for pictures (ICH. Multi CH. Grand CH. BIS Kevin Kavaliri Kvarteto and CH. Multi Jch. Liane's Daisy May).

Photo credit: Natalia Smolenova, Bratislava, Slovakia

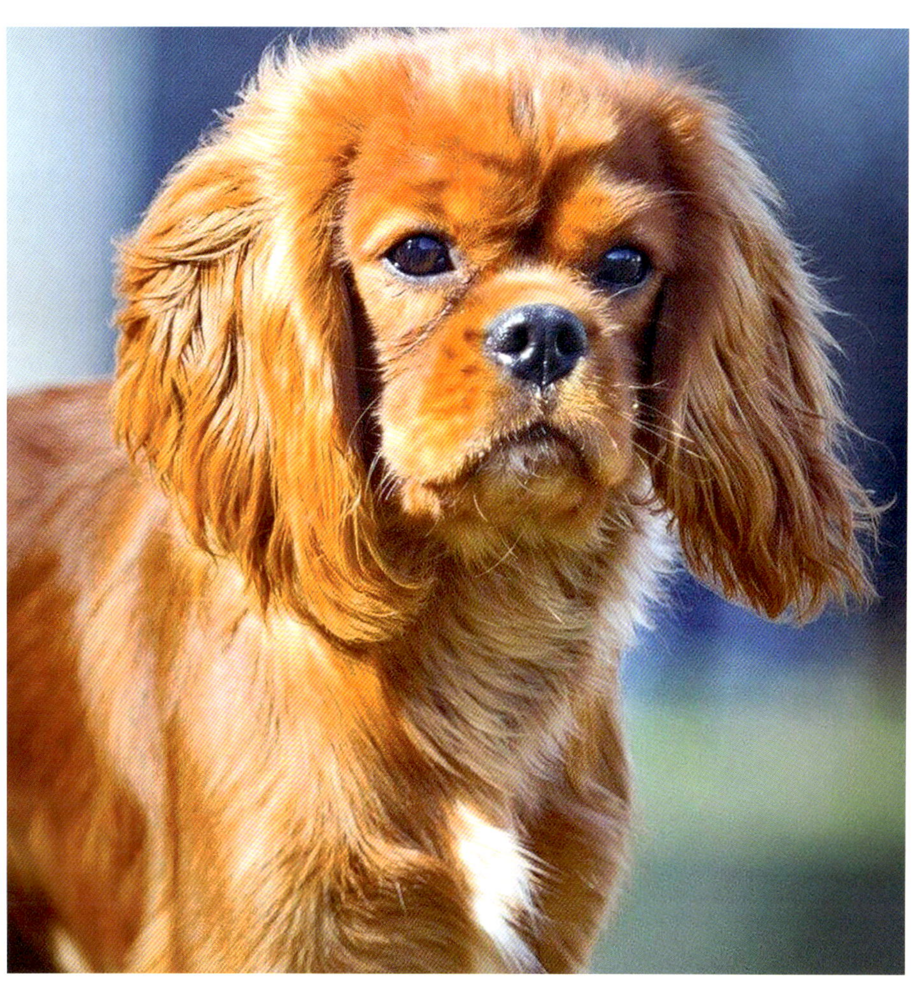

There should be a special movie star chapter for handsome Crème Caramel.

Photo credit: Silvia Marcella Sanchez, Carpi, Italy

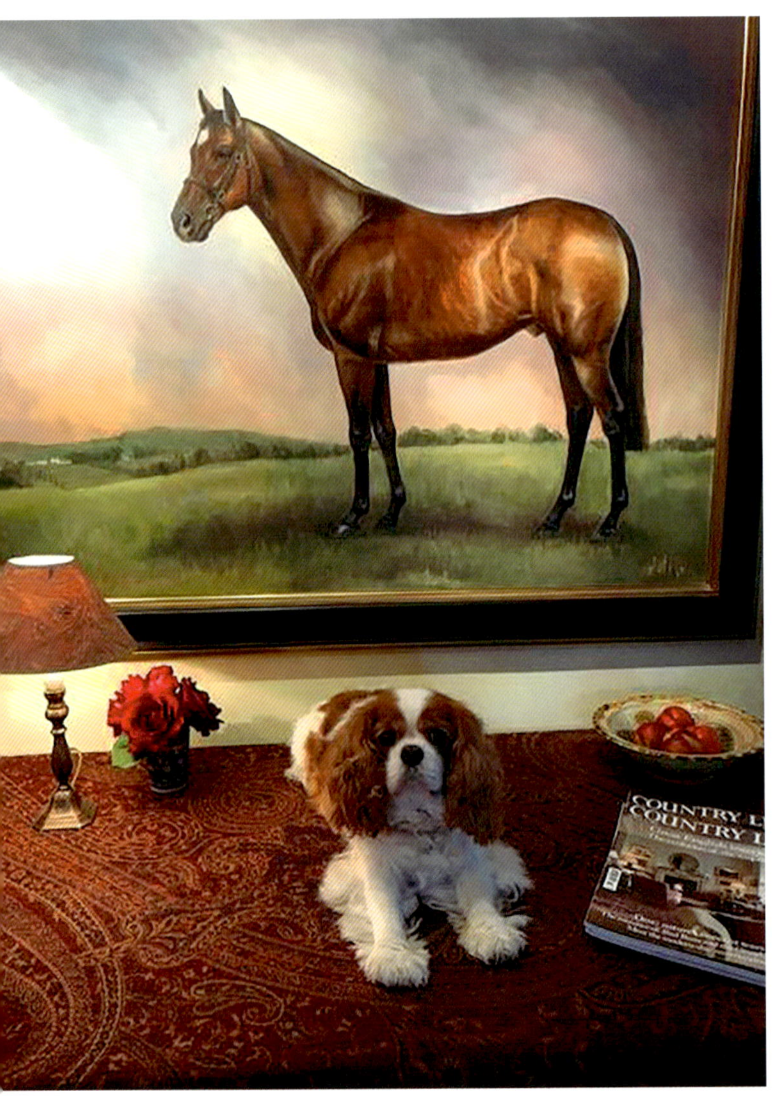

Purdey seems comfortable in her elegant home.

Photo credit: Alexandra Churchill, Cotwolds, UK

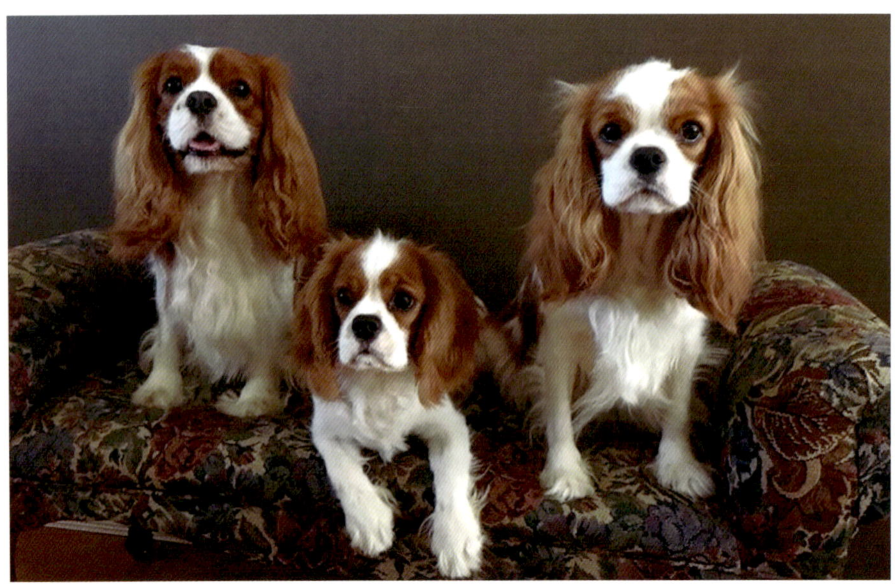

The winsome threesome from Elswyth Cavaliers.

Photo credit: Michele Matheson, British Columbia, Canada

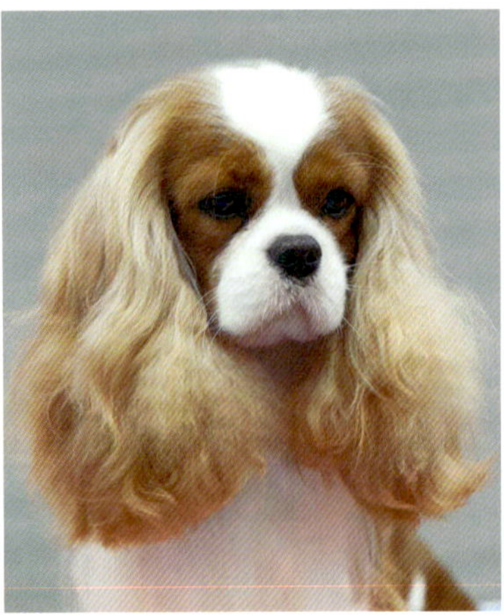

Nathan has Blue Blood for sure.

Photo credit: Kym Brooksby,
South Adelaide, Australia

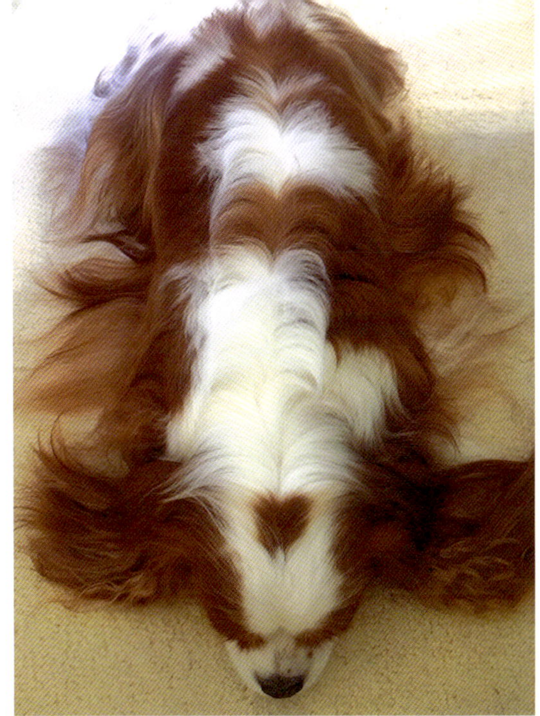

Sweetheart "Legendary" wearing her heart on her head.
Photo credit: Sharon Slobody, Ohio, USA

Purdey must be royalty from the British Isles.
Photo credit: Alexandra Churchill, Cotswolds, UK

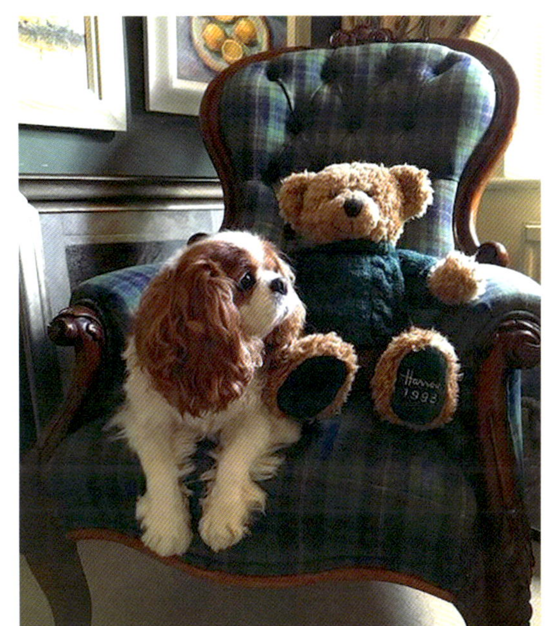

A proper English gentleman or a bit of a rogue? You decide!
Photo credit: Christy Berry, Indiana, USA

Chapter 7 - Funny Posers

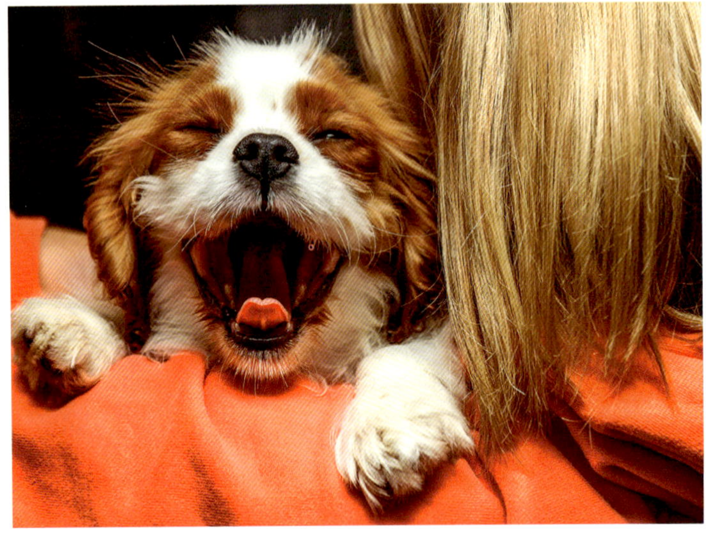

Ollie is just way too tired to think about bubbles.

Photo credit: John Harvey, New South Wales, Australia

Cavaliers are quite comical in the way they sit, relax, and play. They have the cutest repertoire of expressions, and their innocent antics will make you laugh. Their smiles will melt your heart, and their engaging eyes will not be ignored.

These little imps have a number of common poses, such as the "froggy" (lying prone on their bellies with their legs back), the upside-down stretch (a common sleeping position), and the slither (wherein they slide off the couch or bed much like a snake). They'll sleep curled around your head or in your lap for hours.

From time-to-time, your dog will come over and give you a face "schmush," pressing the side of her head on your face for the longest time. The first time your get a face schmush, you'll swoon. It's the most endearing gesture. Cavaliers also like to sit on the back of the couch. Hopefully, yours is against the wall, for they are prone to fall asleep and fall off. They also sit on armchairs with a front leg draped on the arm, like typical aristocrats–very telling about their ancestry.

Like all dogs, they get the sillies and run at top speed around the yard or house for no reason at all, save the pure joy of being alive. And they love chasing bubbles and flies! Ours insist on bubbles at least a couple of times a day. Prepare to be well entertained and don't expect to go to the bathroom alone ever again. Your Cavalier is your new shadow, so get used to it. Unless, of course, your Cavalier is asleep in your favorite chair or snoring in a corner.

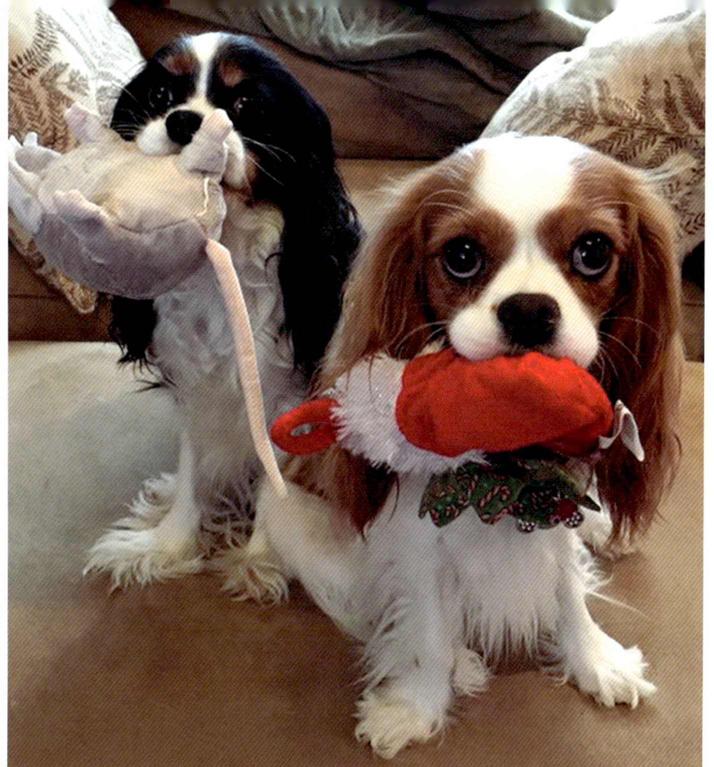

Rhett and Scarlet both want Mom to grab their plushies.

Photo credit: Kaylynn Saunders Steffen, Texas, USA

Rather than complaining about the snoring, realize that her rhythmic background "music" is keeping you company, helping you find her, and/or lulling you to sleep. Our Callie is one of the loudest snorers I've encountered, and after almost 9 years of sleeping with her and hearing her snore for a large part of the day as well, I've grown to relish it. When I realize I don't hear it, I go looking for her. Her snoring also makes for great conversations with strangers. When we go out to eat and she's hidden under the table, people first assume that my husband or I have a massive case of gastroenteritis! When we notice people giggling or talking about us, we quickly point to Callie under the table, and we all have a good laugh.

Too much fun, these Cavaliers! Not to mention that, because of Callie, we've met so many nice people all over the world, some of whom have become dear friends for life. Because she's so cute and friendly, she acts as a natural ice-breaker with strangers, a benefit we hadn't counted on prior to getting her.

People are magnetically drawn to these engaging dogs, who look like living stuffed animals. In fact, most Cavaliers have no concept of a stranger, which includes other animals as well as people. They love everyone and expect the same in return.

Get ready for some giggles with the photos that follow.

Sunny and Maya waiting for their cookies.

Photo credit: Gordana Smith, California, USA

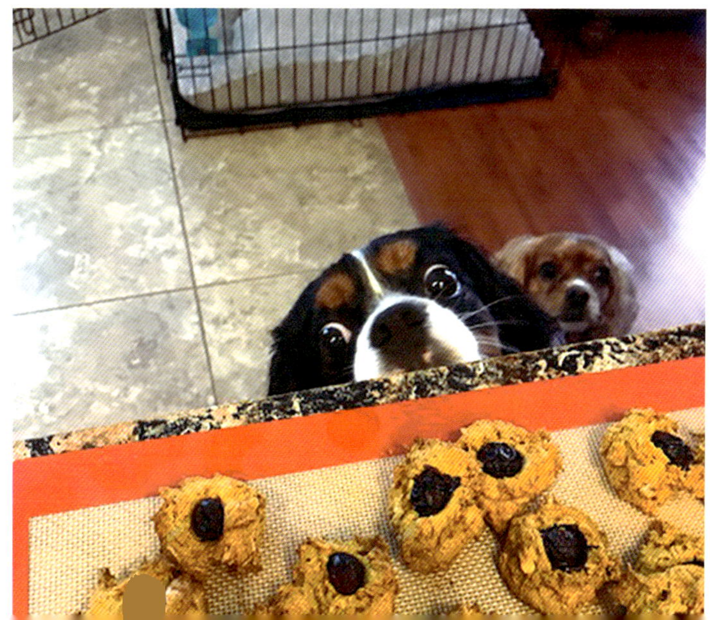

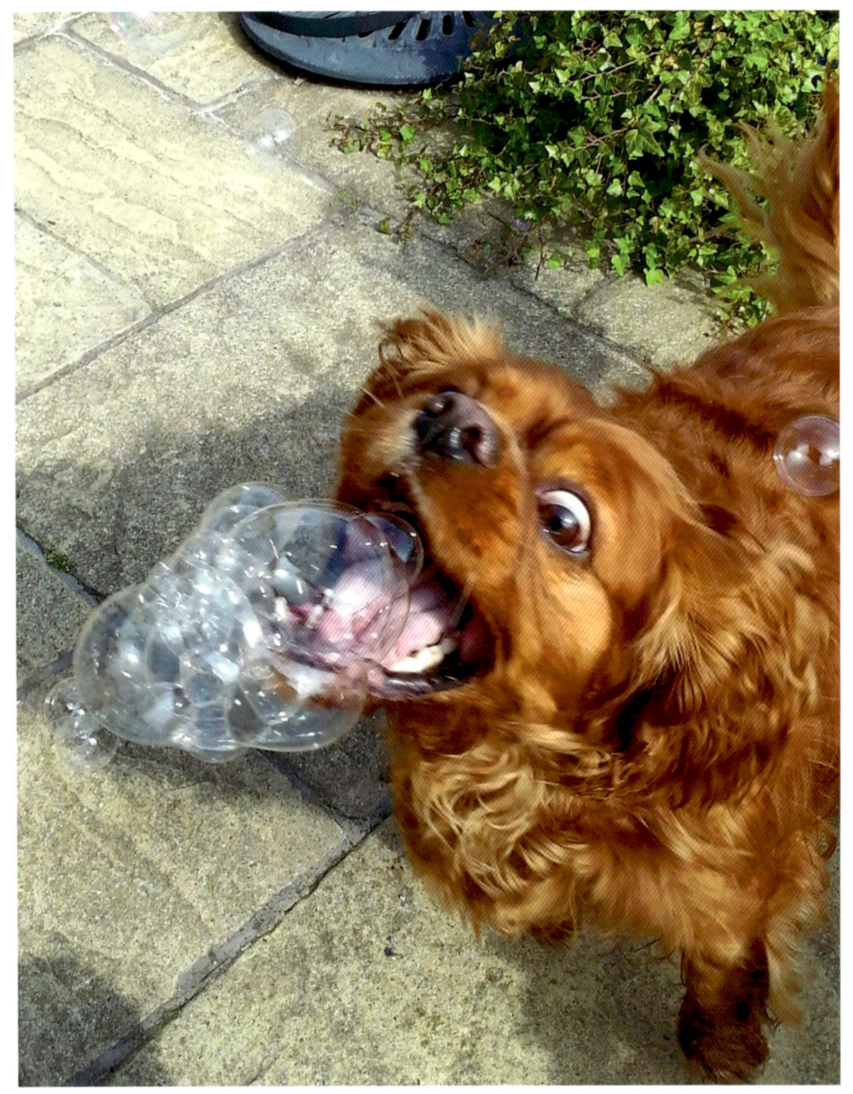

Max thinks this one's going to be bubbleliscious.

Photo credit: Wendy Moss, Georgia, USA

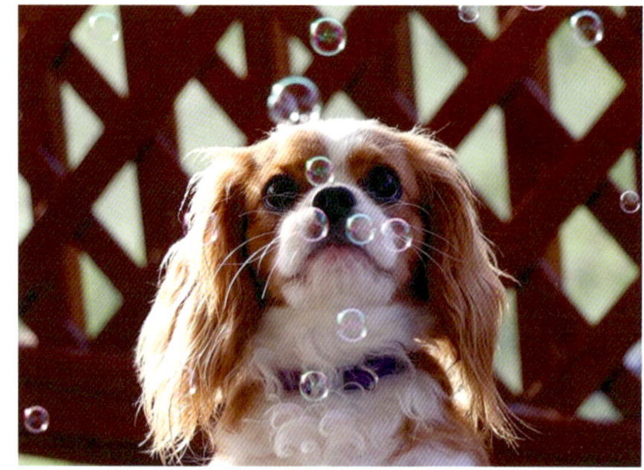

Mango doesn't care that some dogs hunt lions. It's a Cavalier thing to chase bubbles. Flies are good too. Butterflies even better.

Photo credit: Suzy Oliver, Georgia, USA

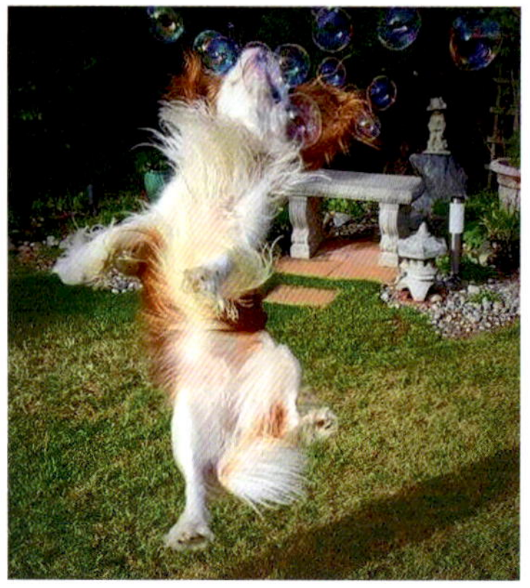

Chasing bubbles is favorite pastime of many Cavaliers.

Photo credit: Michele Matheson, British Columbia, Canada

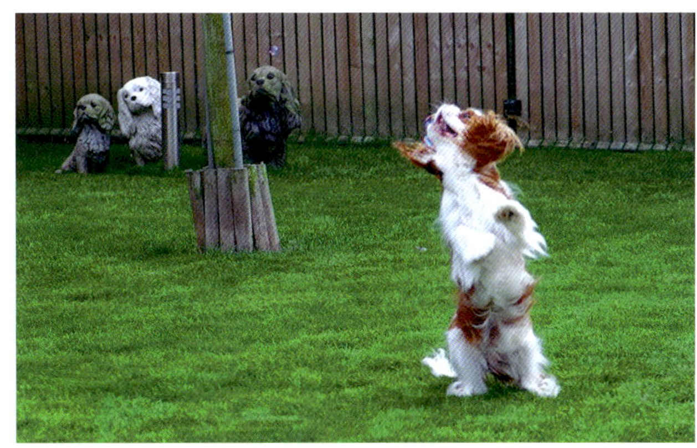

Darn it, Woody. It got away!

Photo credit: Sabine Volkerick, Beveren, Belgium

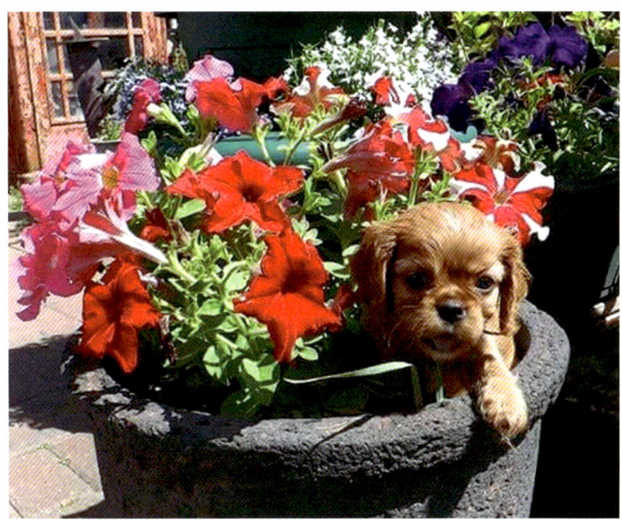

Mischievous Flicki in the flower pot!

Photo credit: Caroline Jane Symms, Wirral, UK

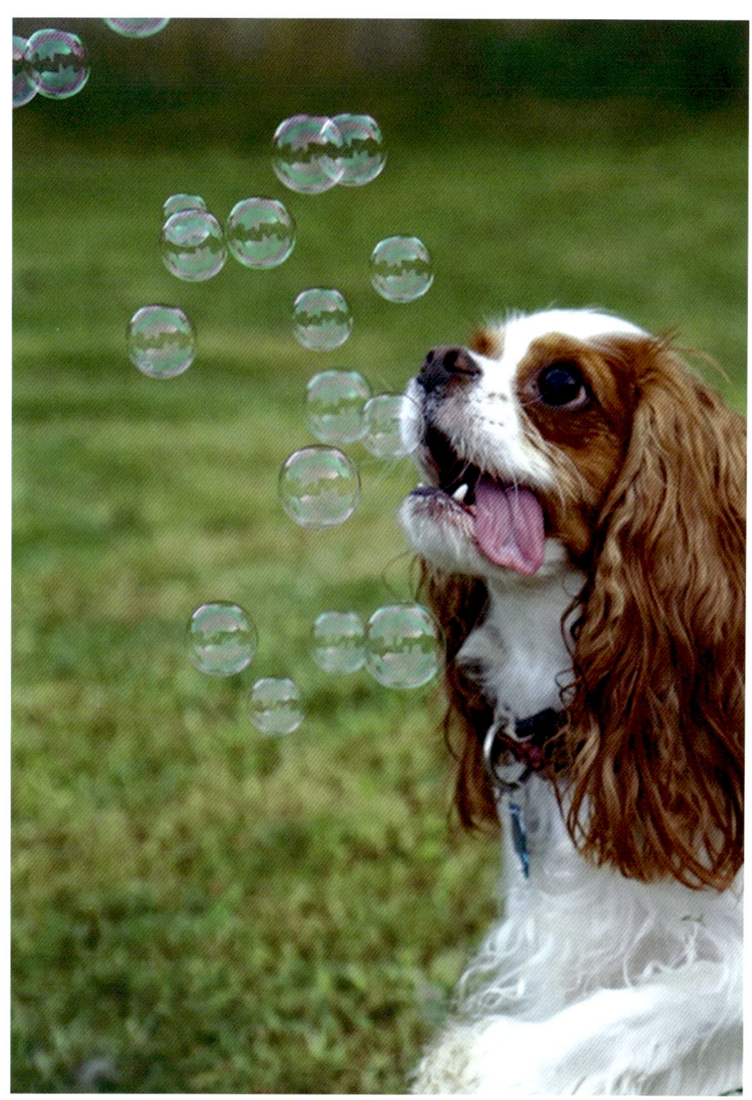

Rescue Lexi Lou has met her challenge.

Photo credit: Tracey Shaffer, Virginia, USA

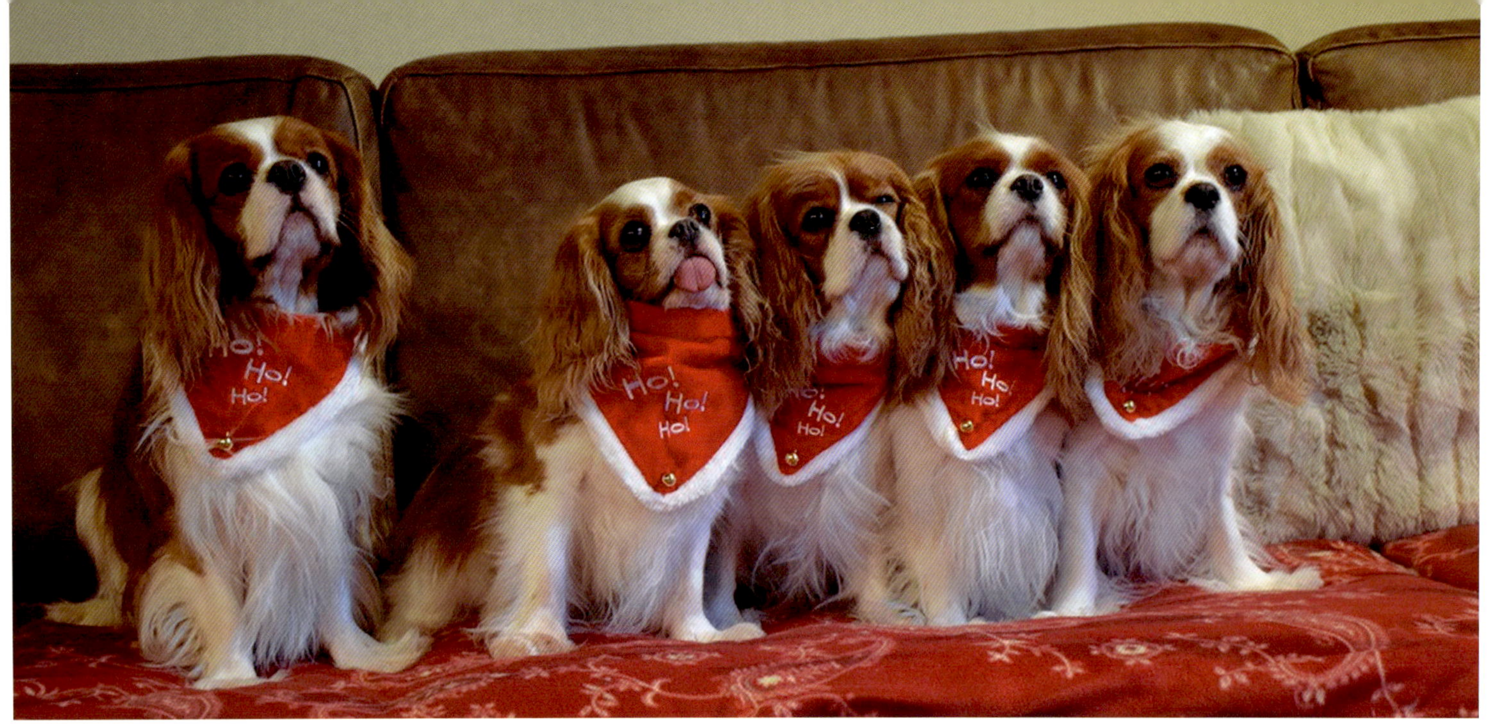

One of the Home White Wings "angels" is just not into this Christmas shoot.

Photo credit: Paola Martini, Savona, Italy

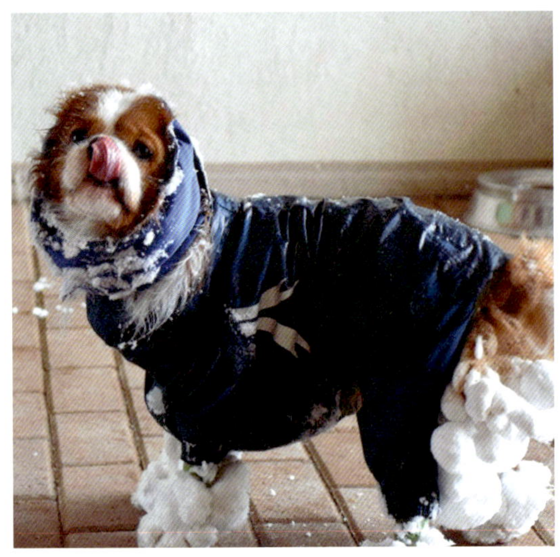

CH Toralac Sebastian of Home White Wings Cavaliers is ready for the blow dryer.

Photo credit: Paola Martini, Savona, Italy

Bad hair, don't care! Ludo is cool with it.

Photo credit: Kitt Huntington, West Yorkshire, UK

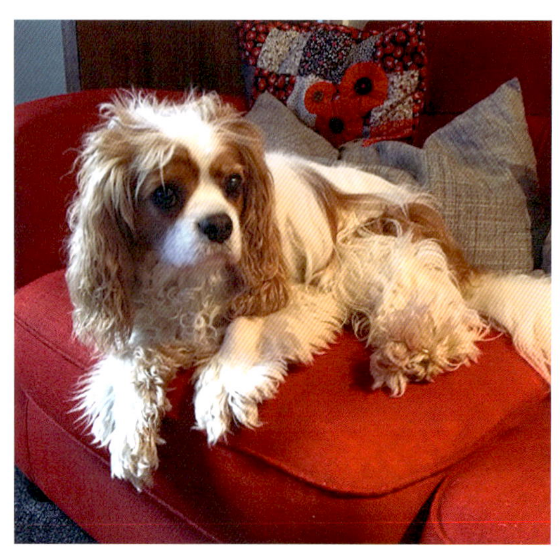

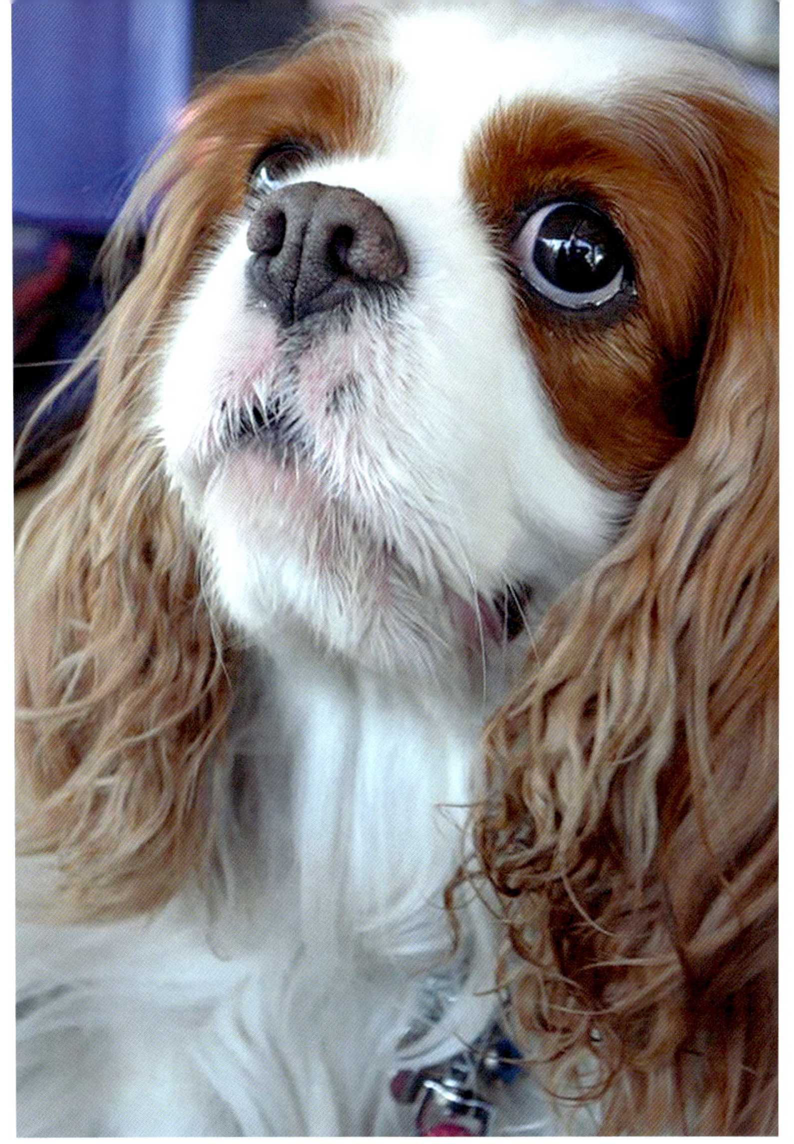

"You're not going to eat all of that," thinks Lindy.

Photo credit: Lia Angelopoulou, Athens, Greece

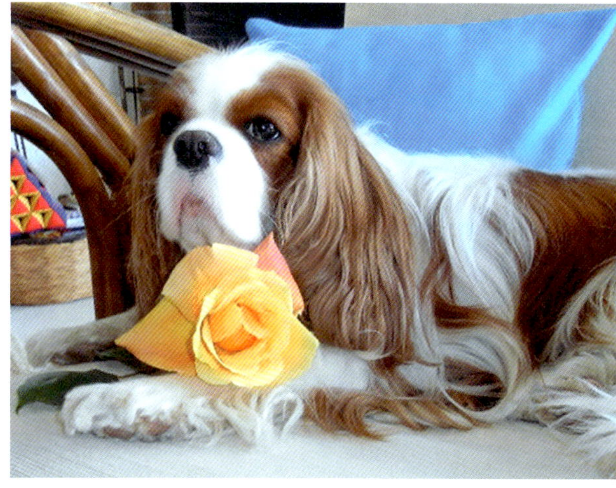

Lindy's weakness is flowers.

Photo credit: Lia Angelopoulou, Athens, Greece

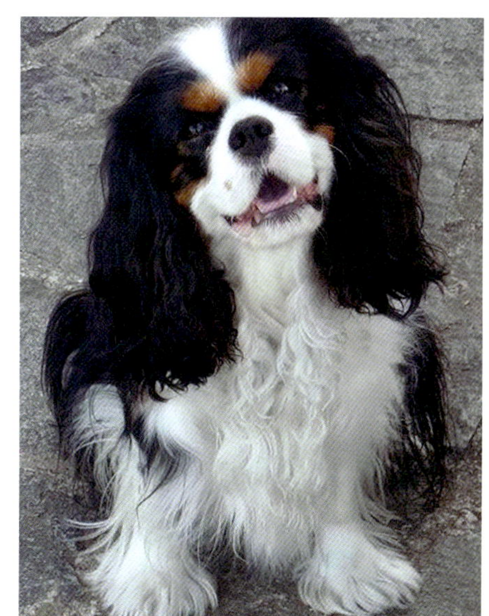

Smiling Max, such a happy companion.

Photo credit: Wendy Moss, Fife, UK

Eight year old "Bobo" is checking out the wildlife.
Photo credit: Kellie Bilston, Country Victoria, Australia

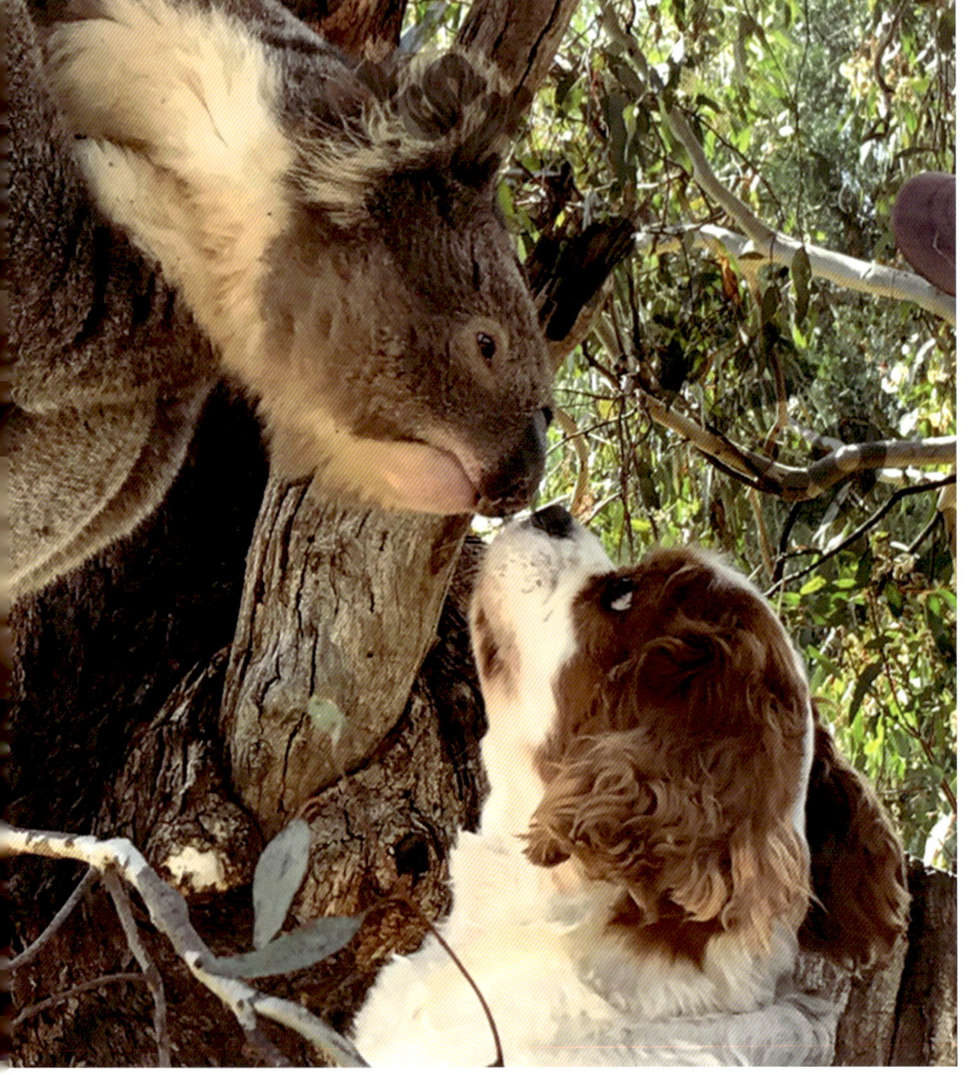

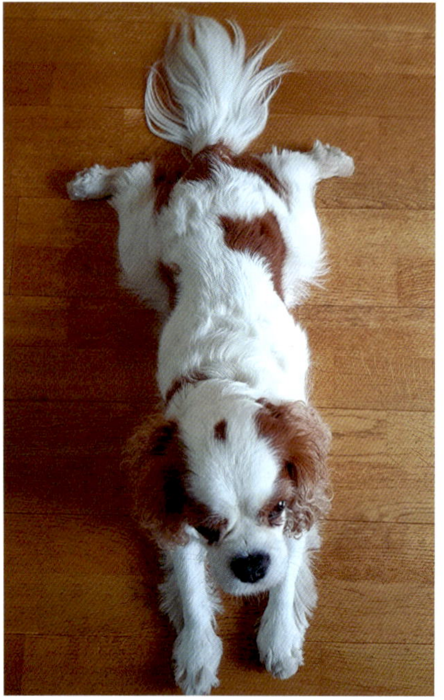

Belle of the Netherlands demonstrating the "Froggy" position.
Photo credit: Bert Wengelaar, Warnsveld, Netherlands

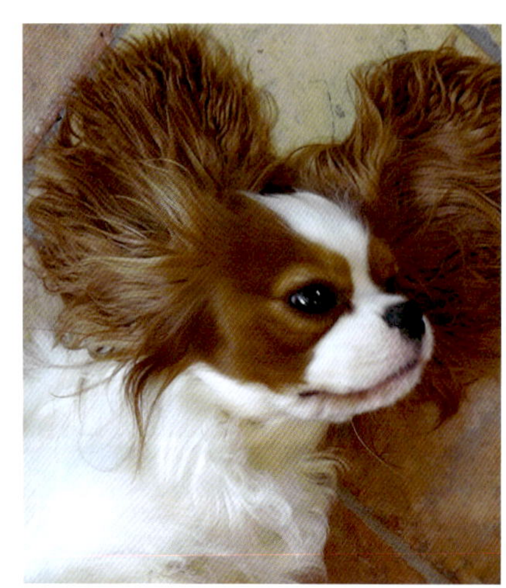

Moonbeam ready to fly away.
Photo credit: Mary Colburn-Green, L'Aude, France

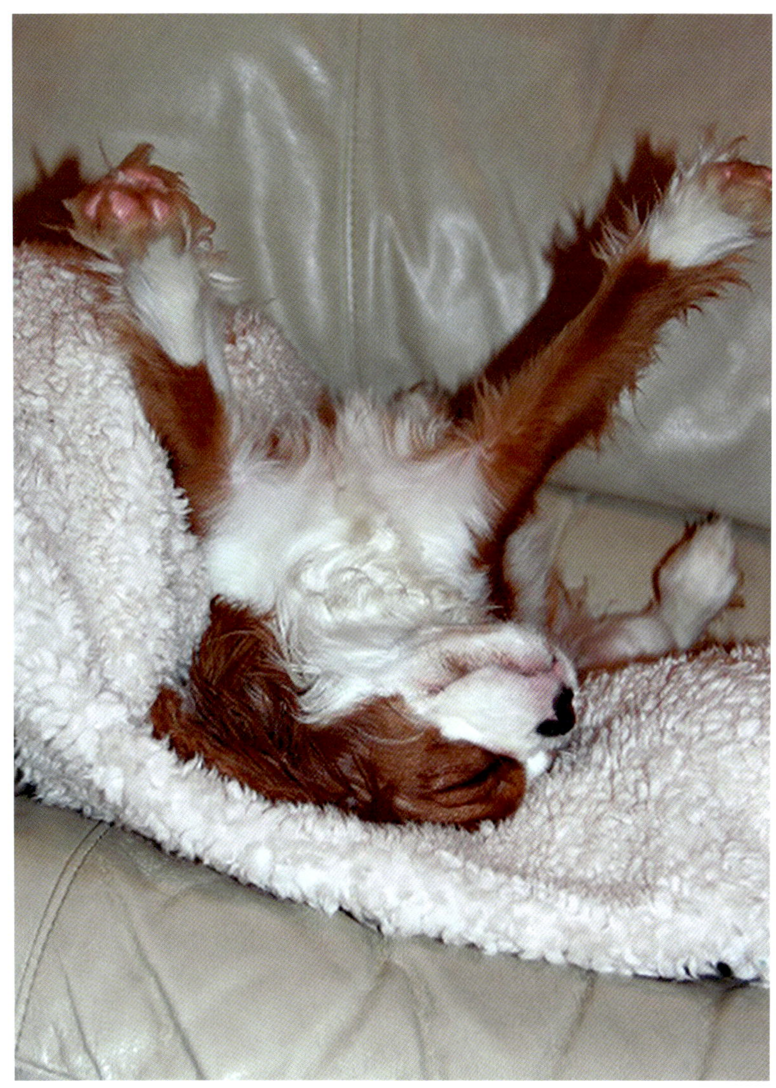

Flame demonstrating a typical Cavalier sleeping position.

Photo credit: Alisha Lockleer, Washington, USA

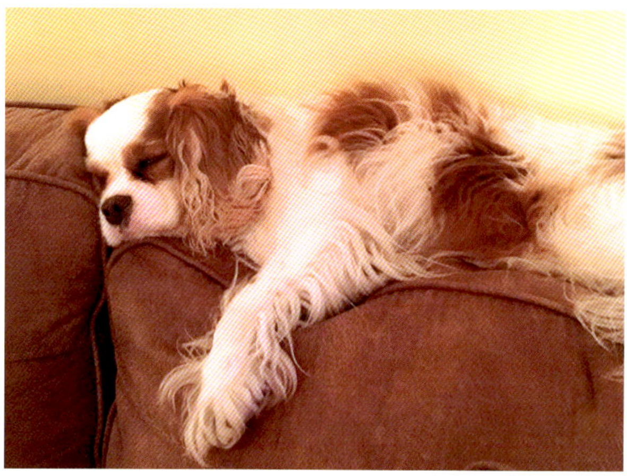

Gracie demonstrates the back of the couch sleeping position. Fortunately, there is a wall behind it.

Photo credit: Tracey Draveck, New York, USA

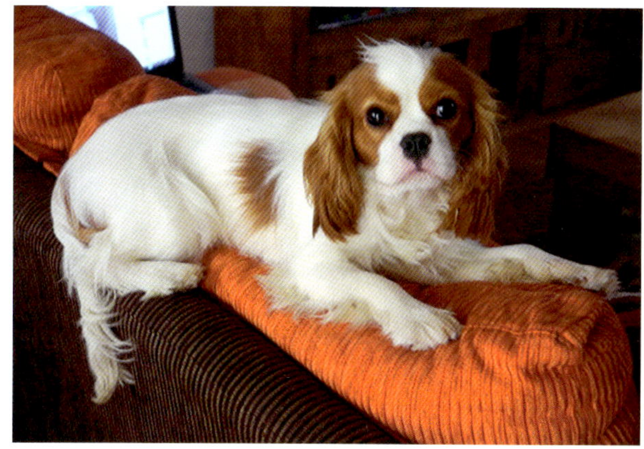

Moonie has no wall...kerplop!

Photo credit: Mary Colburn-Green, L'Aude, France

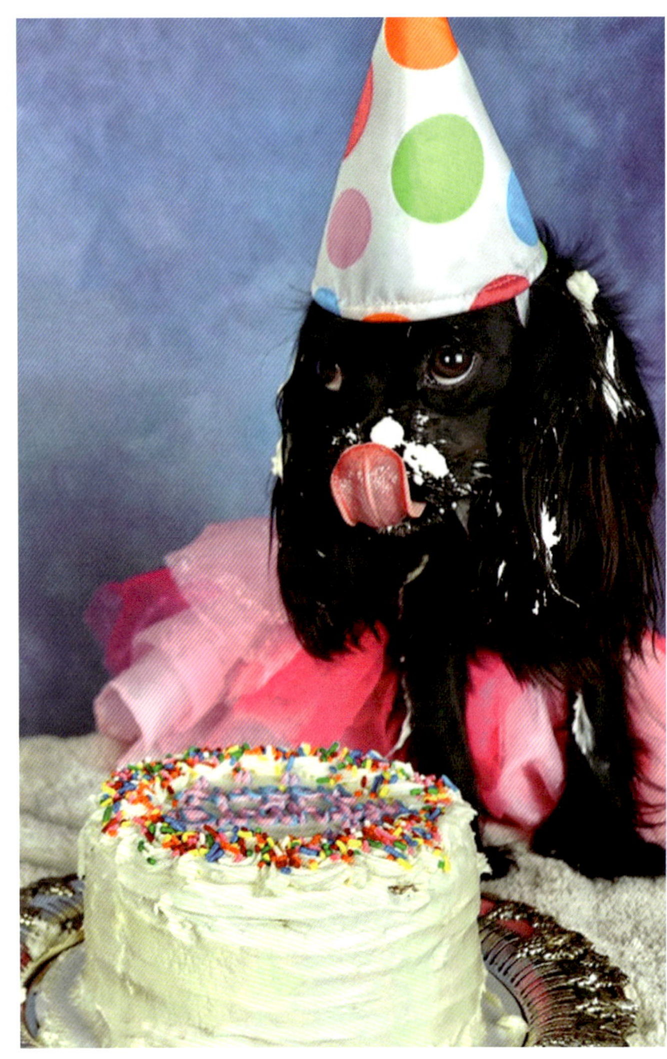

Charlotte, the all-black Cavalier, won't be in the show ring, but that doesn't stop her from enjoying her birthday cake.

Photo credit: Tracey Shaffer, Virginia, USA

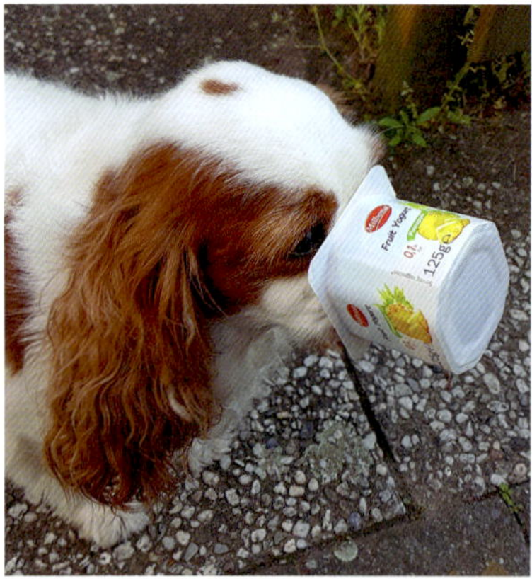

Belle tries to eat healthy foods.

Photo credit: Bert Wengelaar, Warnsveld, Netherlands

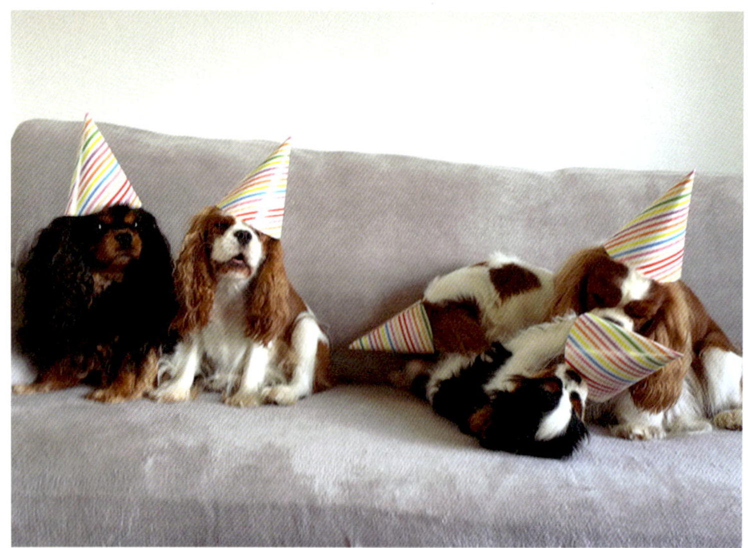

Birthday parties for kids or Cavies, they're all the same. From left: Jazzmina, Betty, Daisy, Peggy Sue, and Pablo.

Photo credit: Christine Bell, Cumbria, UK

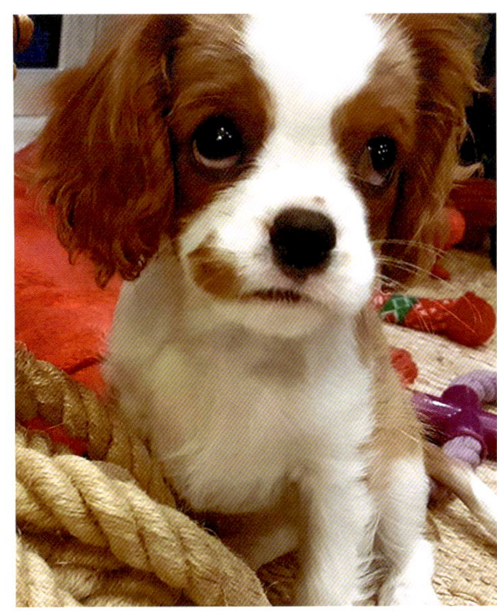

Phoebe might have just peed on the kitchen floor. What do you think?
Photo credit: Liz van Vogt, Salisbury, UK

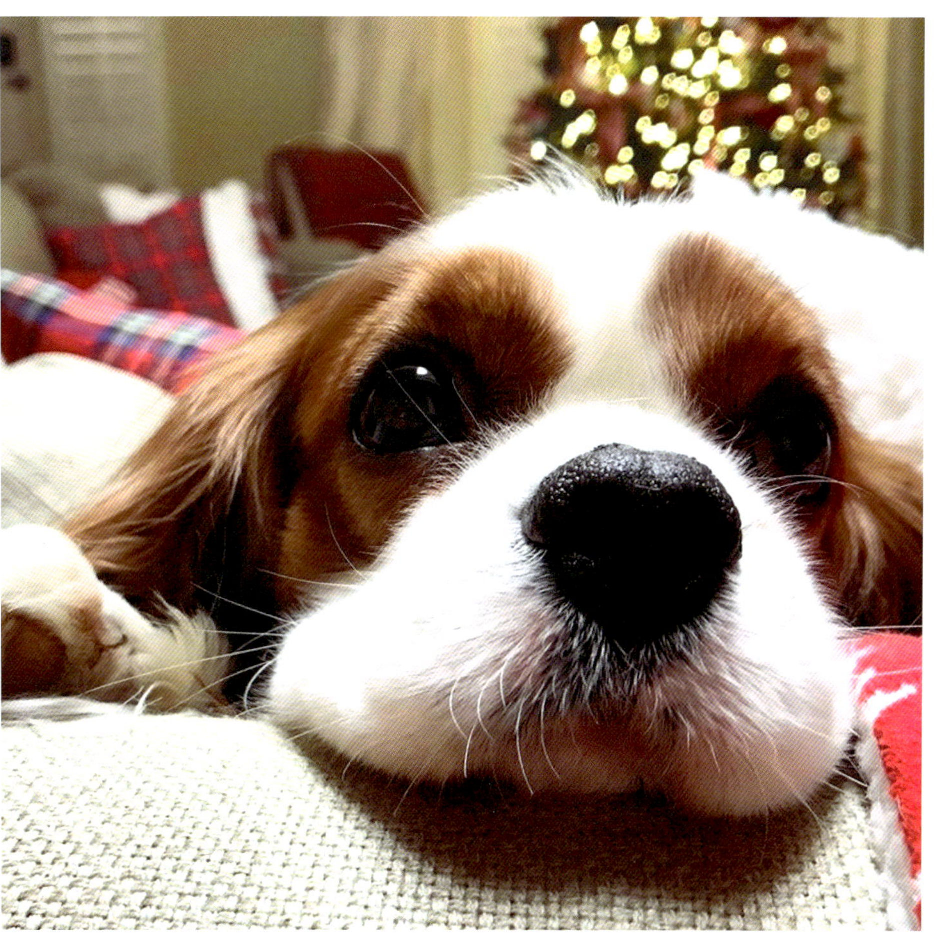

Baxter is a productive daydreamer.
Photo credit: Jenny Rotruck, California, USA

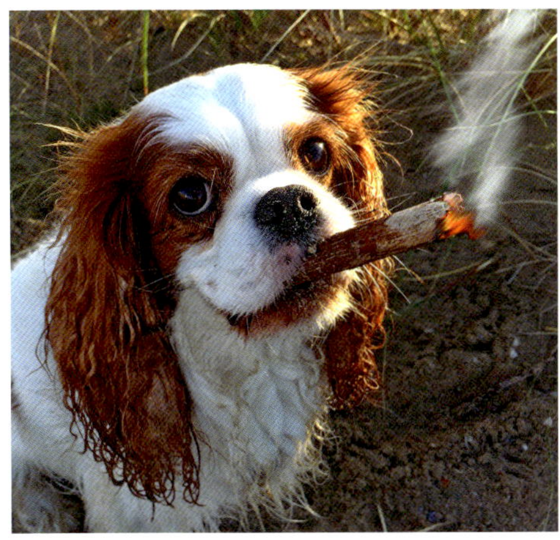

Where there's smoke, there's fire, right, Belle?
Photo credit: Bert Wengelaar, Warnsveld, Netherlands

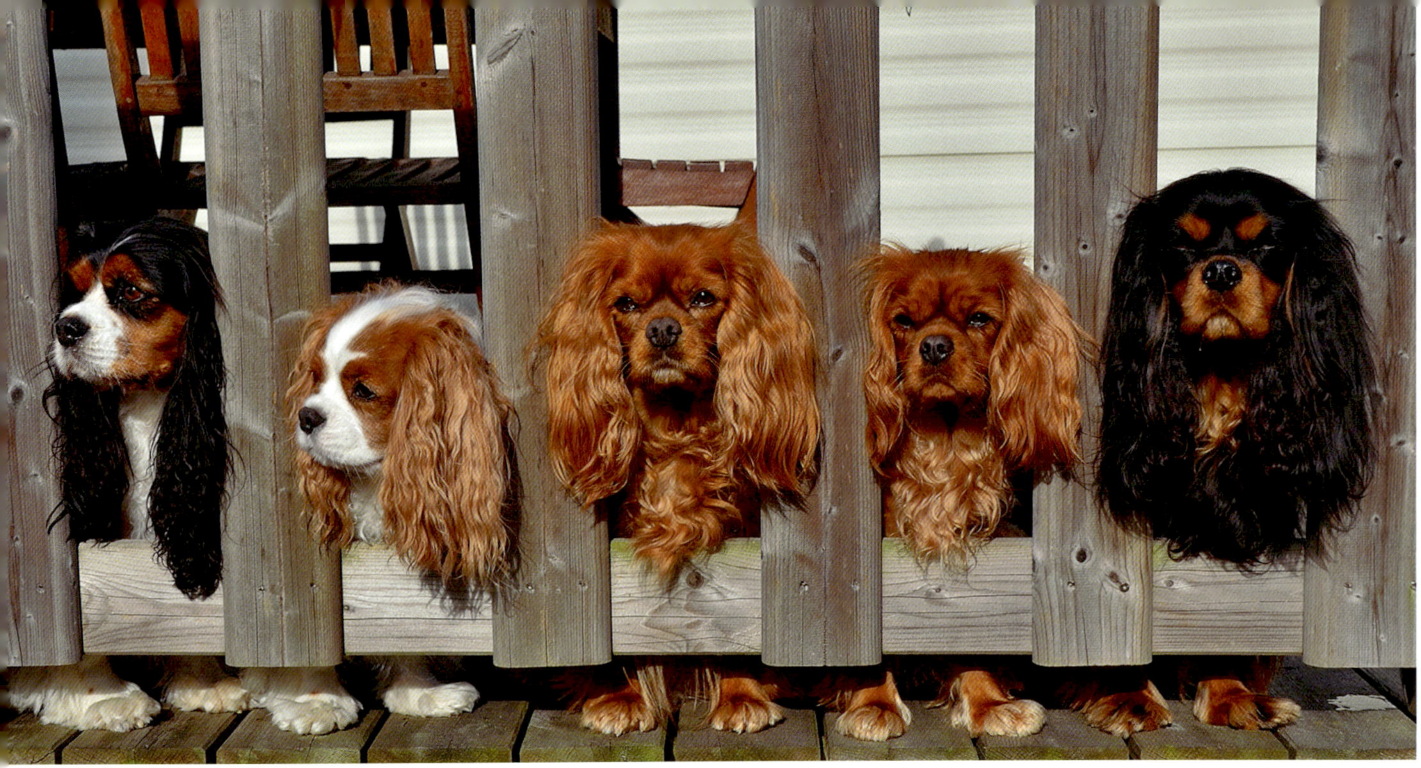

A place for everything,
and everything in its place.
Photo credit: Sandrine Lepoitevin, Fourmies, France

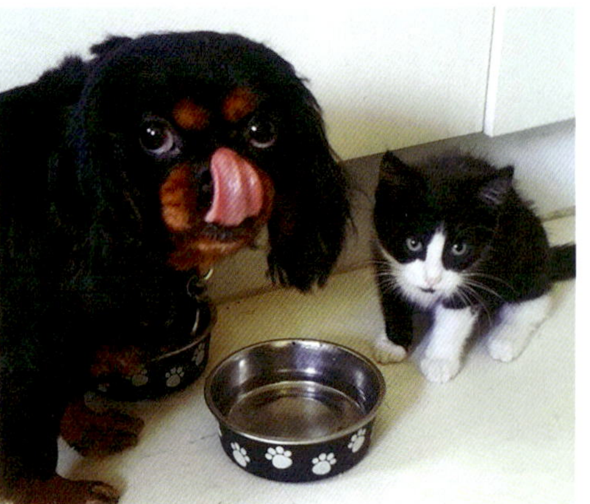

Flo loves her kitty, Ozzy.
Photo credit: Hannah Page, Dudley, UK

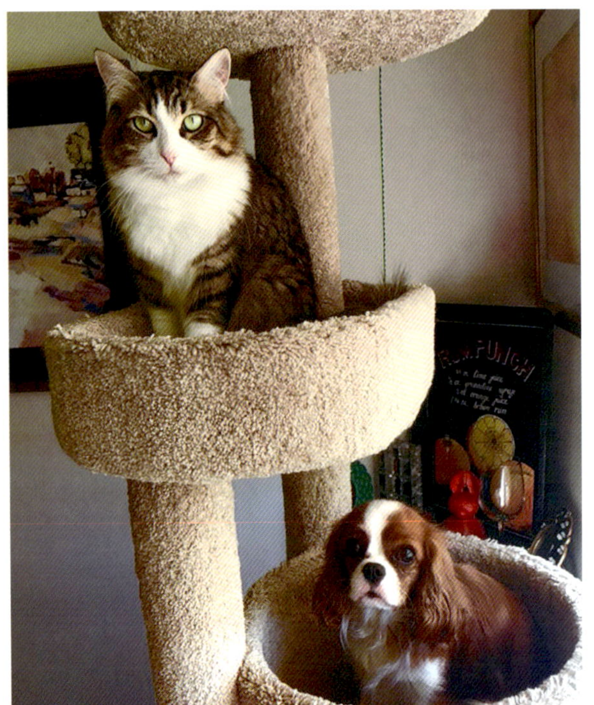

In matters of détente between housemates, the cat's place is always on top. That works for Fiona Kitty and Violet Button.
Photo credit: Mary Padgitt, California, USA

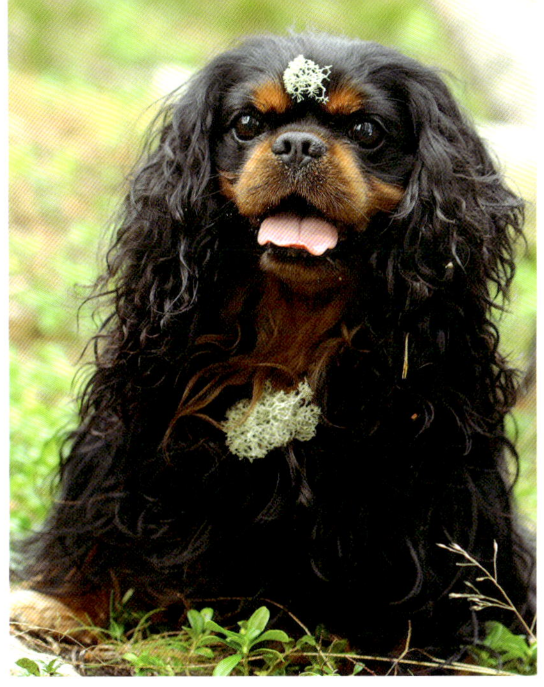

They don't call him Nature Boy for nothing!
(CH Bacchante du Nid du Faisan)

Photo credit: Virpi Laaksonnen, Tarvasjoki, Finland

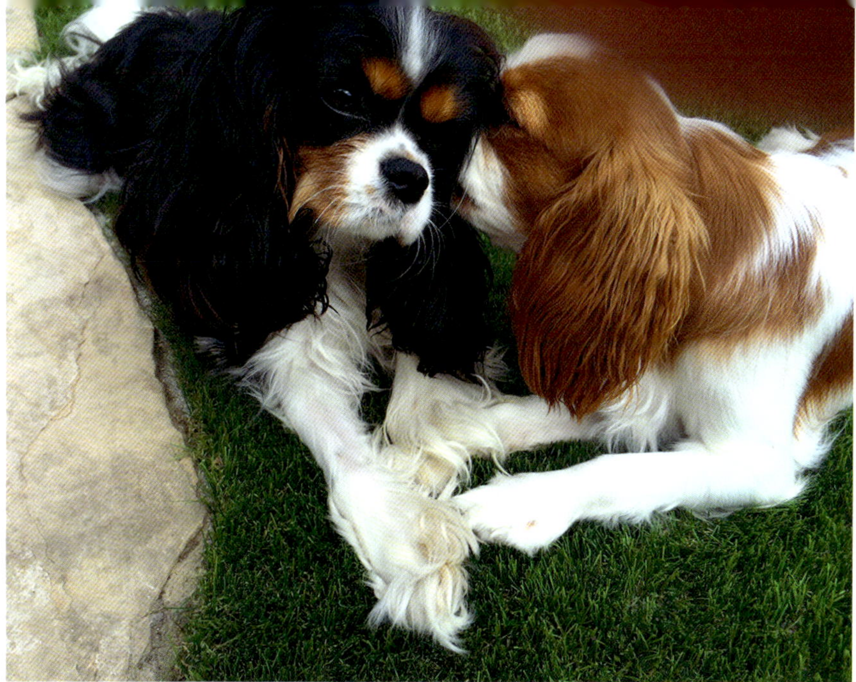

Jezzy likes hearing Grace's secret.

Photo credit: Lisa Falchetti, California, USA

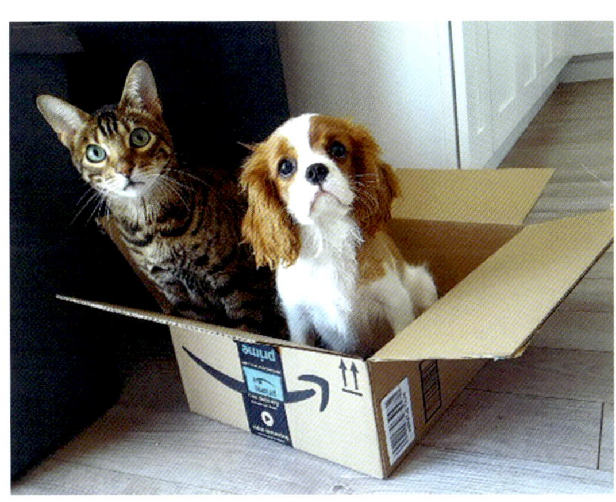

Seems both Savanah and Flame like boxes.

Photo credit: Alisha Lockleed, Washington, USA

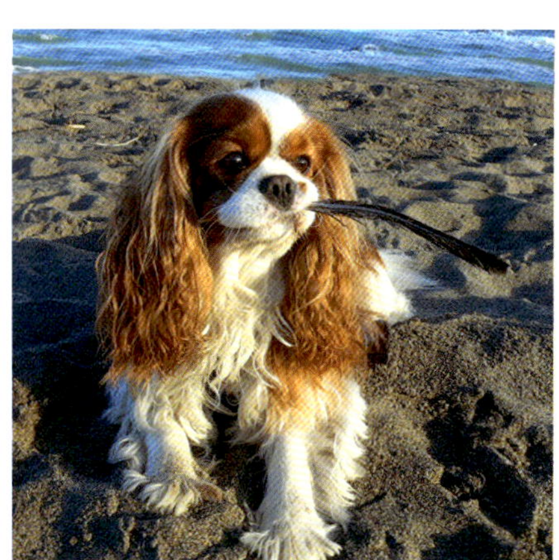

Jack found a feather.

Photo credit: Pat Wood, Liversedge, UK

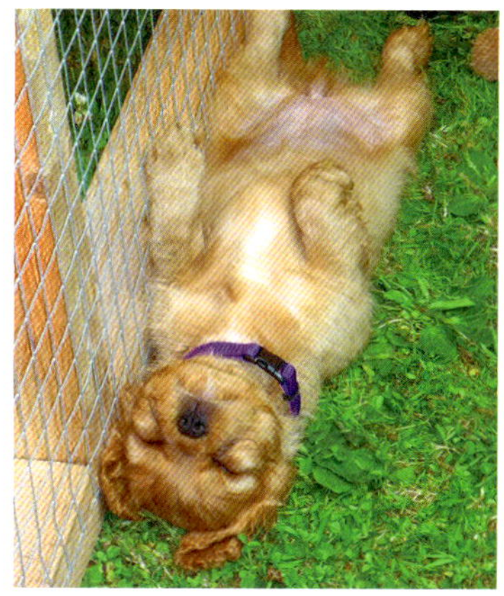

Pups "chill" where they drop.

Photo credit: Kathy Hargest, Gloucester, UK

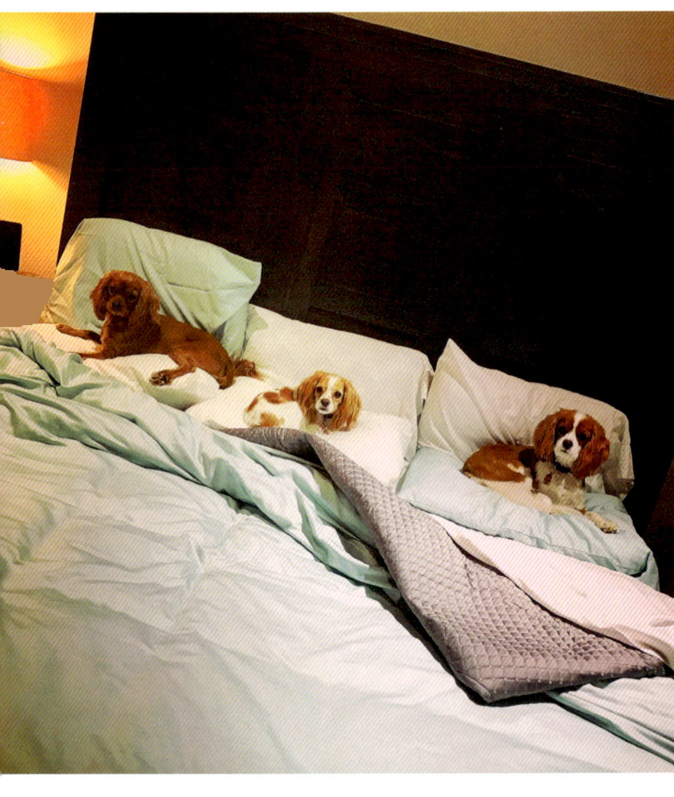

This happens when you get a larger bed!
From left: Siri, Solo and Splash.
Photo credit: Hana Brown, Oregon, USA

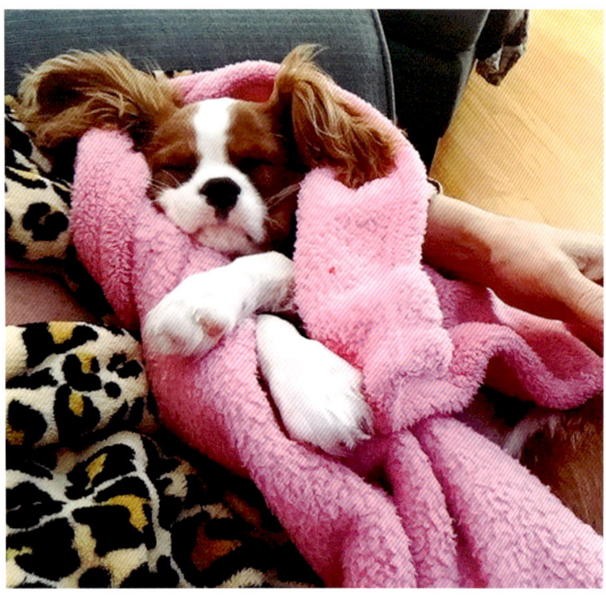

Cavalier or baby?
Photo credit: Tara Reichard Peckitt, Pennsylvania, USA

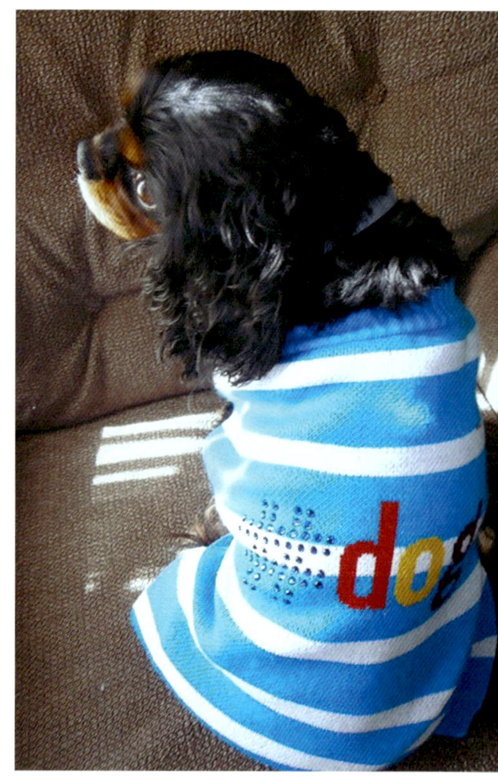

Jackson wants everyone to know he's a dog.
Photo credit: Linda Peracciny, New York, USA

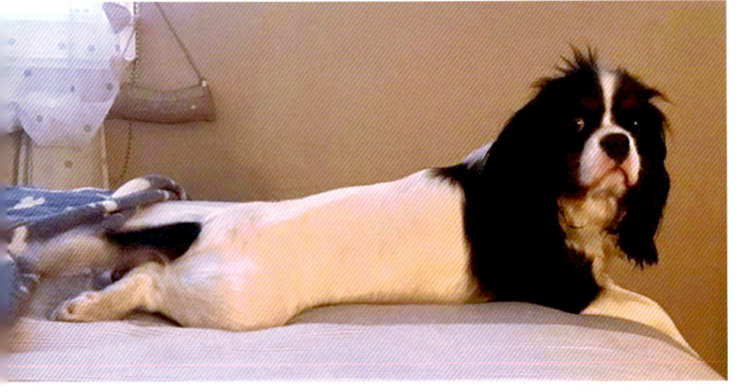

Don't look! Mom washed off Willow's color.
Photo credit: Darcy Wedell, Edinburgh, UK

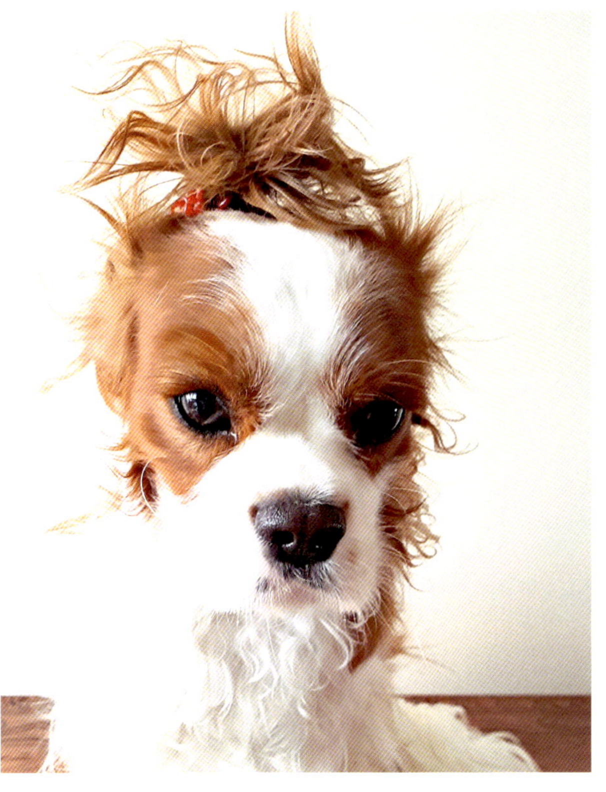

Anuk has a new hairdo, Yeah or Nay?
Photo credit: Sarah Pinto, Penafield, Portugal

"Fleur" Miss Milla says Giddy-up to the couch. She's a cowgirl from Belgium.
Photo credit: Sigrid, Kolenberg, Belgium

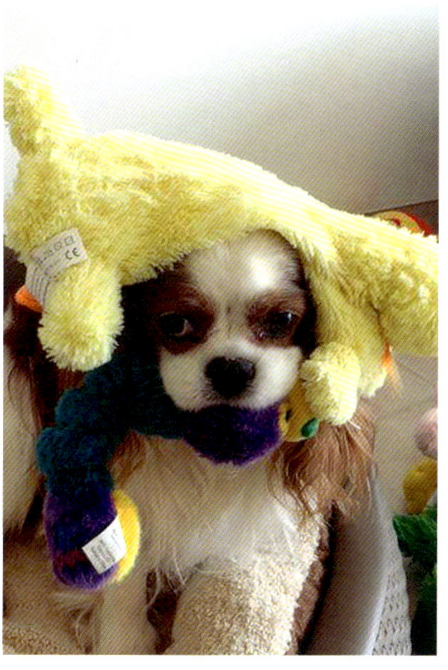

Tobias finds so many things to do with plush toys.
Photo credit: Sabine Volckerick, Beveren, Belgium

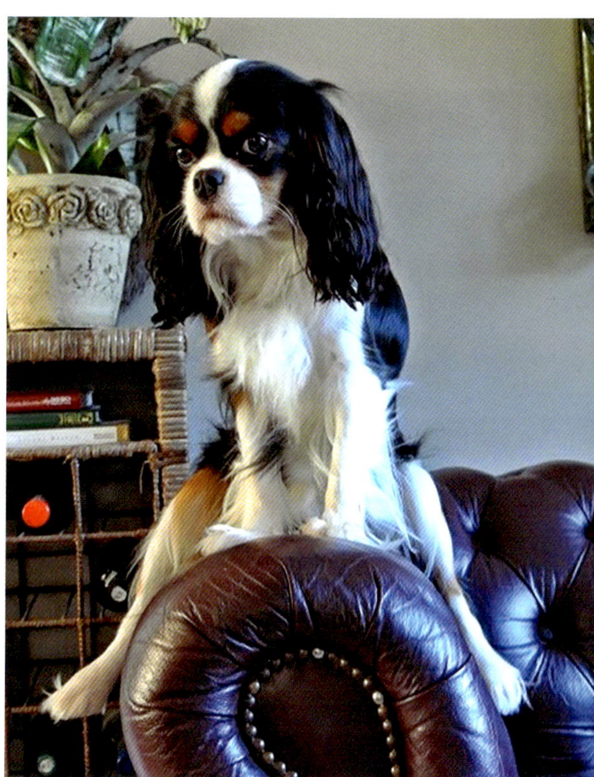

Saturday Night Date Night!
Photo credit: Breeder Michele Matheson, British Columbia, Canada

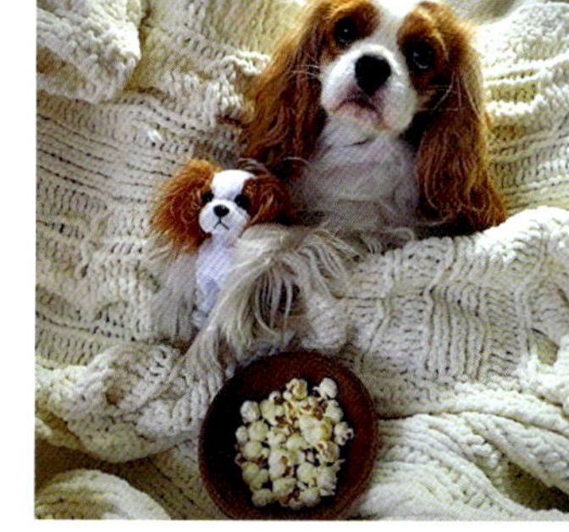

Chapter 8 - Golden Oldies

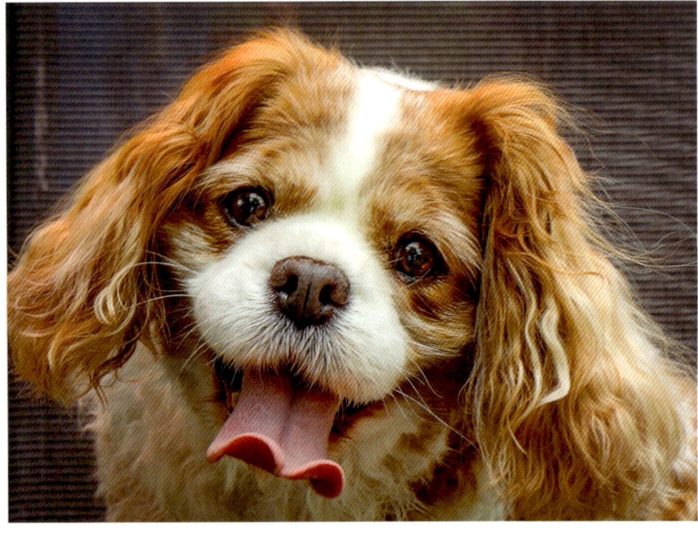

Cindy "Cindoggie," owned by Marie Visser, is a happy girl at 15 and a half years young.

Photo credit: John Harvey, New South Wales, Australia

Our sweet Cavaliers become more beautiful, and frankly, more precious to us with every year that passes. Sadly, many die young, but as breeders improve their methods and use of health-testing protocols, there are bright signs that we can expect longer-lived dogs in the future with fewer health problems.

We share with each of our Cavaliers an eternal bond that lasts beyond their passing over the Rainbow Bridge. With good genes and care, a Cavalier can live to 19 years old, although the average lifespan is between 11 and 14 years.

There's no greater blessing than being able to spend many happy years with these special companions, especially if they can enjoy life to the fullest. Even some of the rescue dogs, who have horrific beginnings, live relatively long lives with the tender, loving care that their adopters lavish on them.

Enjoy these photos of Cavaliers who have reached maturity and are (or were) able to enjoy their golden years.

Veronica Hull talks about her Sasha (right): "As you will see, my Sasha's once-rich, chestnut markings were almost white with age (a sort of blonde, to be exact), but she enjoyed her life to the fullest with no need for medication whatsoever. Food was her passion, and she LOVED to eat. She had a great quality of life. I retired Sasha from maternal duties after she won her first CC (and BIS), and prior to this, bred her to CH Telvara Karbon Kopy. In that first litter, she produced Telvara Top Kopy, who went to Karen Ostmann in the USA at 13 months of age, where he reached Champion and received a Register of Merit award for dogs that produced at least ten champions. Tucker was followed 'across the pond' a year later by his full younger brother, who became CH Telvara Kopyright. Sasha was tightly line-bred and produced champions in each litter. There is so much more to tell, but I'll not bore you with my bragging on this special girl with whom we were blessed to share nearly 18 beautiful years. We still have several of her teenage children here, and the respect they showed this dear oldie was so endearing to watch. Sasha's Sire, CH Telvara Top Hat, died just 5 weeks before his 17th birthday, so she outlived her dad. Until the very end, she still had such attitude, and for me, she was one very special little lady."

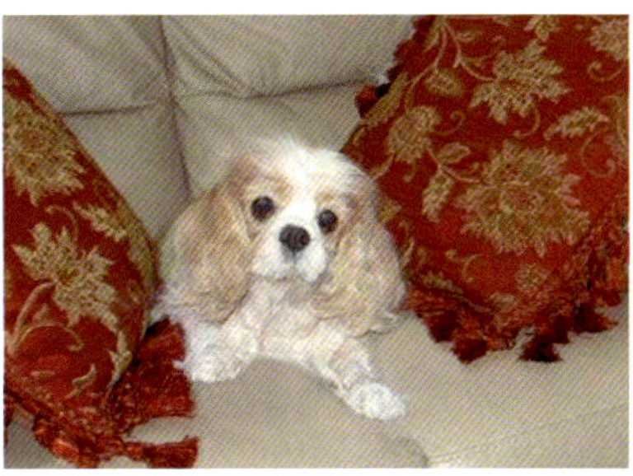

Sasha at almost 18.

Photo credit: Telvara Breeder Veronica Hull, London, UK

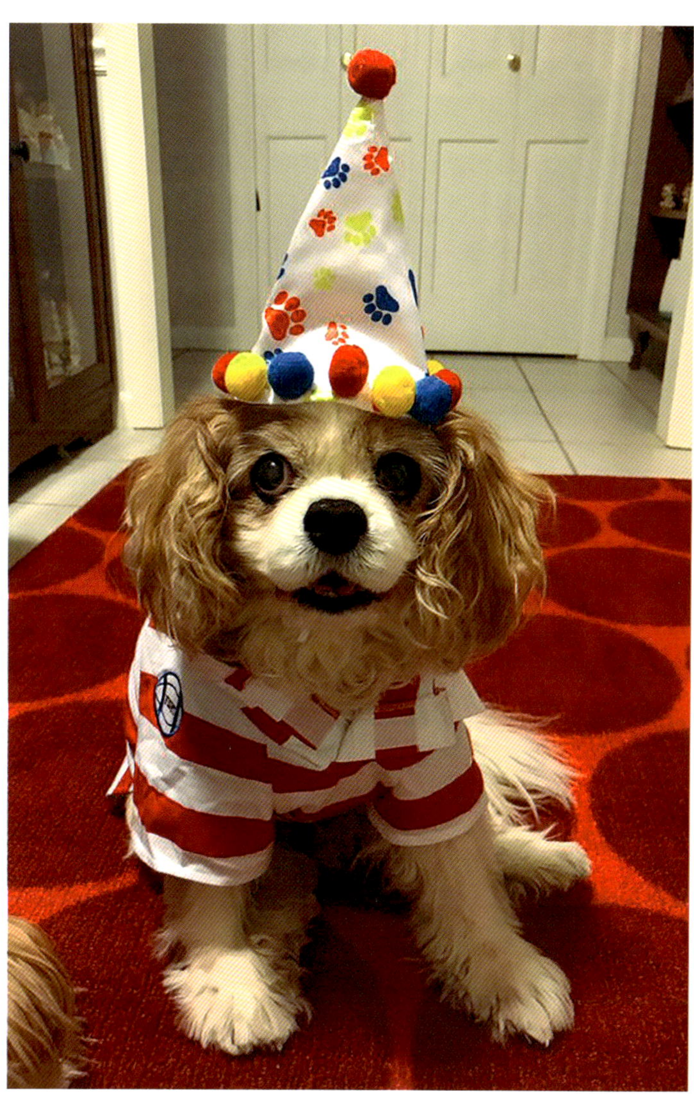

Elvis is thoroughly enjoying his 15th birthday.

Photo credit: Christy Berry, Indiana, USA

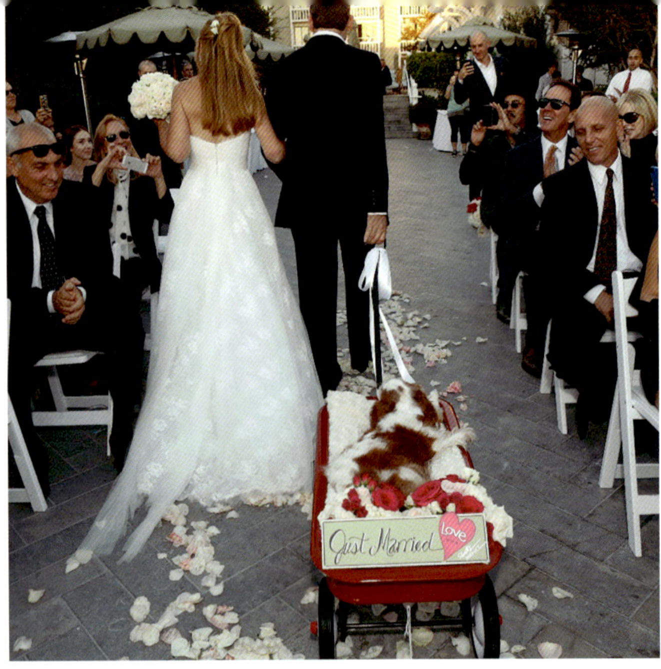

Oliver is guest of honor at Jill and Peter's wedding.

Photo credit: Jill Prives, California, USA

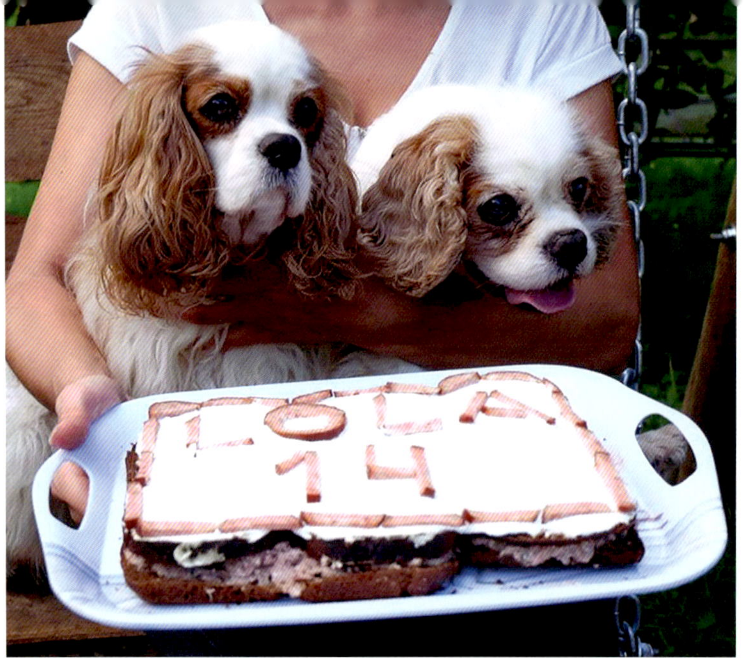

Lola (Helandros Ice Pearl), on the right, is celebrating her 14th birthday with her daughter, Kelly (CH Helandros Vanilla Ice).

Photo credit: Heli Jarvet, Estonia

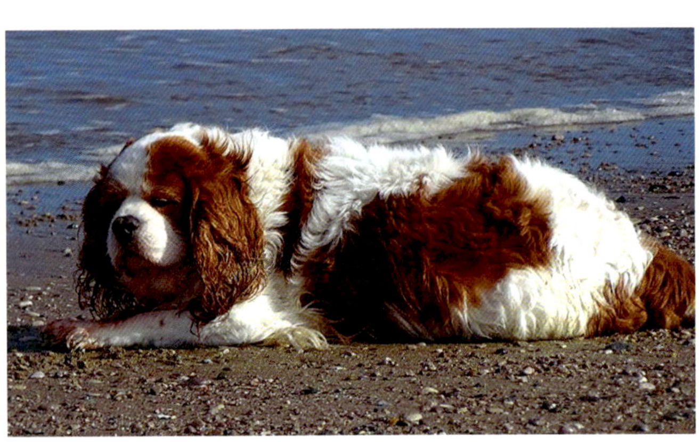

Here is Holly at 15. She was the former companion of Kira and Stan Jackson.

Photo credit: Stan Jackson, Bristol, UK

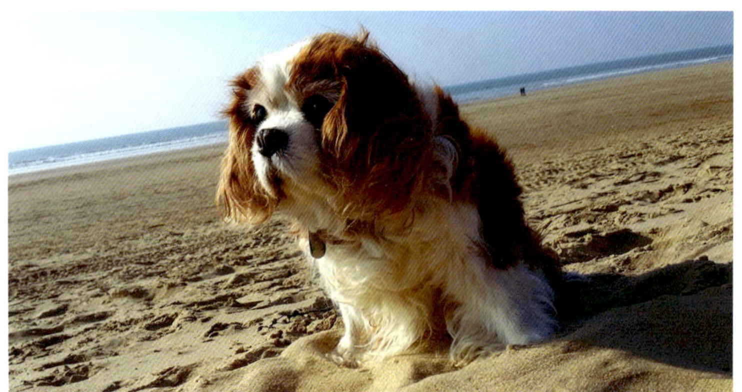

Cassie, shown here at almost 13, is now enjoying the beach over the Rainbow's Bridge.

Photo credit: Christine Lindley, Victoria, Canada

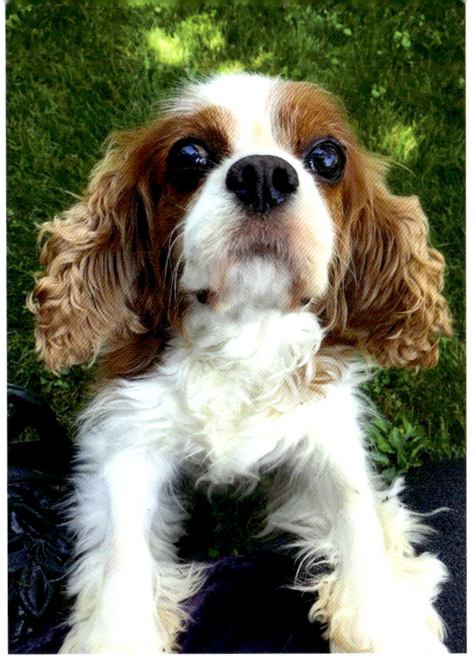

Sevenwood's Highfield Dune (CH SW HF Dune) certainly looks good for 12-years old.

Photo credit: Susan Shidler, Illinois, USA

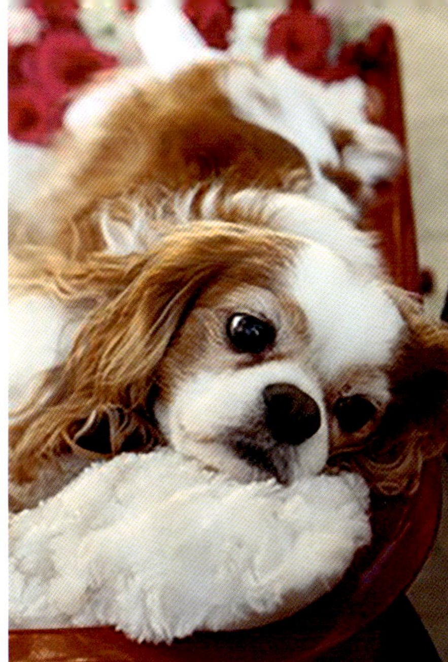

Ellie McMahon is a sweet lass at 15 and a half.

Photo credit: Niamh McMahon, Belfast, Ireland

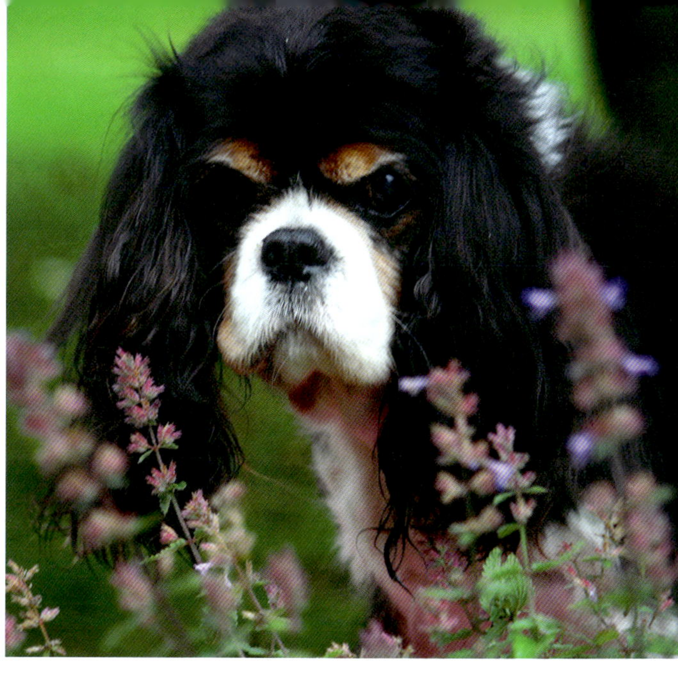

Fifteen-year-old Blumchen (little flower), formally Petite Fleur vom Paulinenhof (by CH Pamedna Waterloo & Crown Hunter Michelle) was bred by and lives with Heidi Jungans. Blumchen had four litters of her own and now helps out with the mothers and puppies at the kennel. All the dogs respect and adore her.

Photo credit: Heidi Jungans, Mecklenburg, Germany

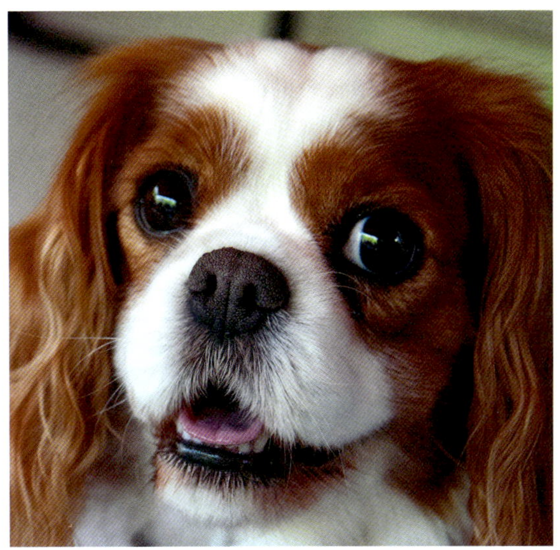

Lady, 11-year-old companion of Ole and Anne Mette Byskov, spends her time in Switzerland and Spain.

Photo credit: Ole Bystov, Malaga, Spain

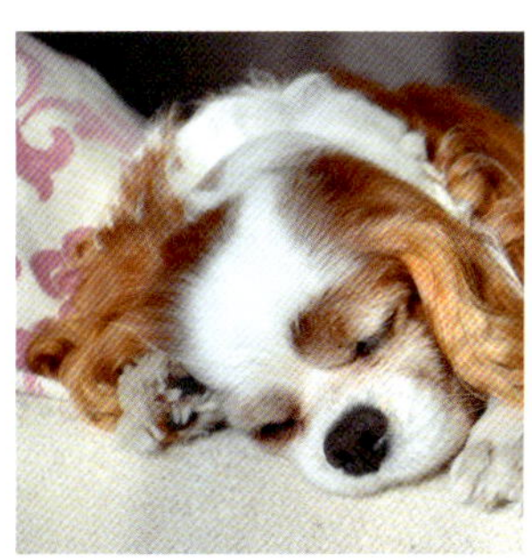

Indy, at 12 years old, is having a little cat nap.

Photo credit: Gordana Lesic, Split, Croatia

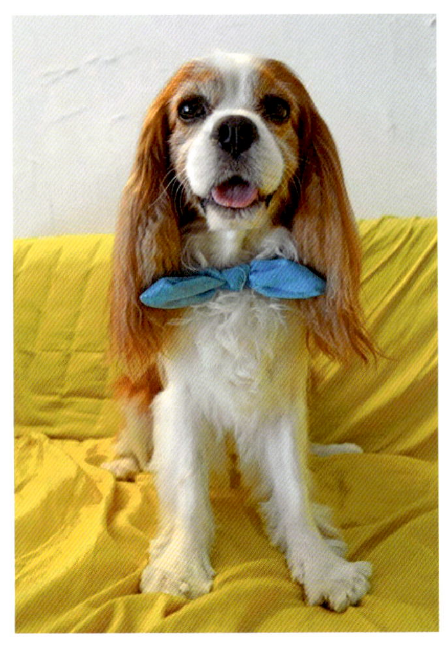

Elvis Alisandrato's Matt, at 12 and a half years old, looks like he drinks from the Fountain of Youth. Or, is it his Mediterranean diet?

Photo credit: Fanny Alisandrato, Kineta, Greece

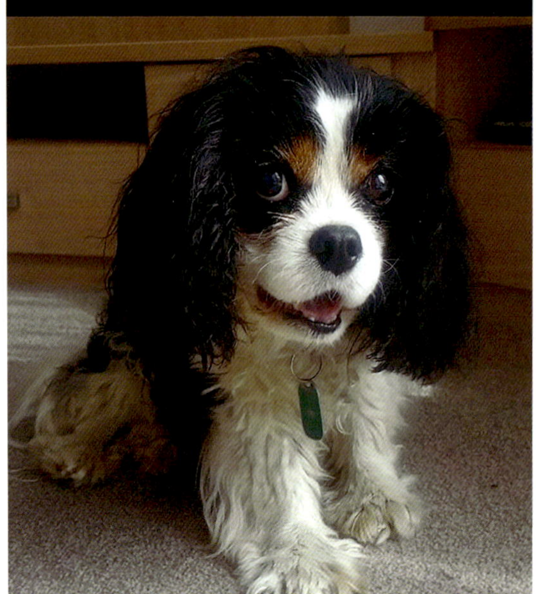

Daddy Stan posts pictures of adorable Kyra, 15, on Facebook almost every day, and we love seeing her.

Photo credit: Stan Jackson, Bristol, UK

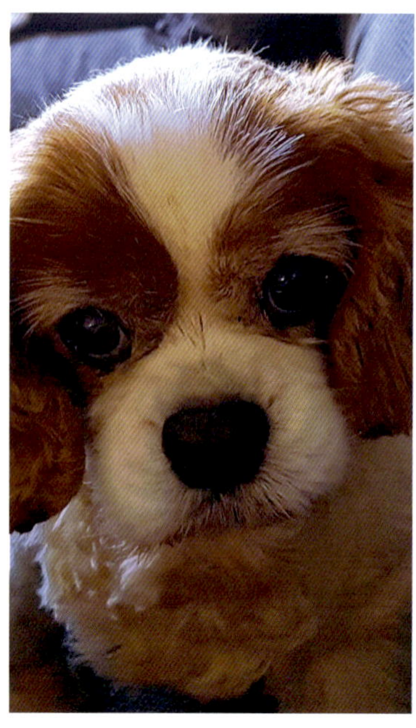

Ellie McMahon is a sweet lass at 15 and a half.

Photo credit: Niamh McMahon, Belfast, Ireland

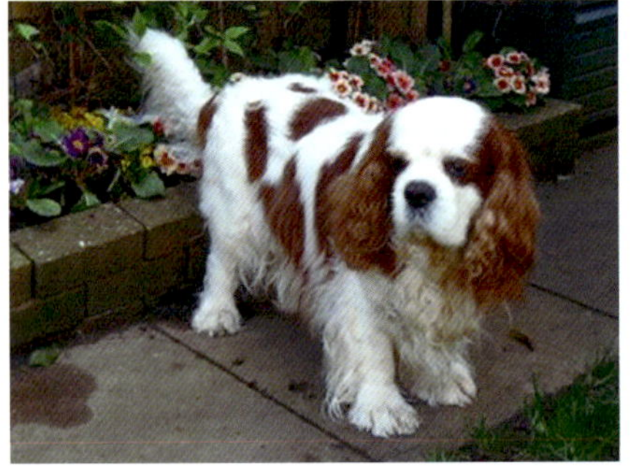

Desi enjoys being in the garden at age 11.

Photo credit: James Defty, Basingstoke, UK

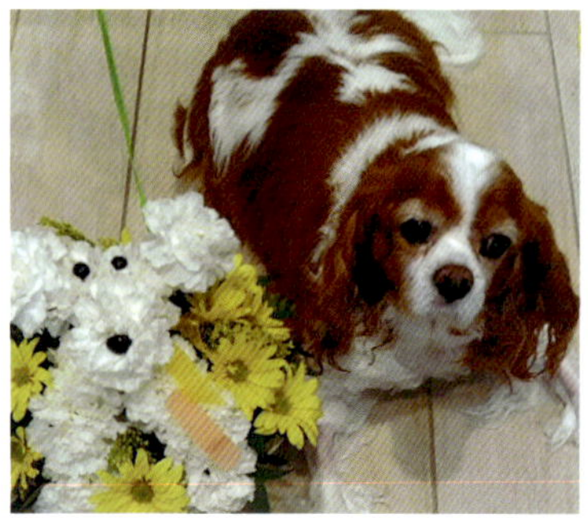

Thirteen-year-old Daisy is enjoying her Golden Years in South Carolina with her owner, Gwen Cover.

Photo credit: Donna Rubendall, Pennsylvania, USA

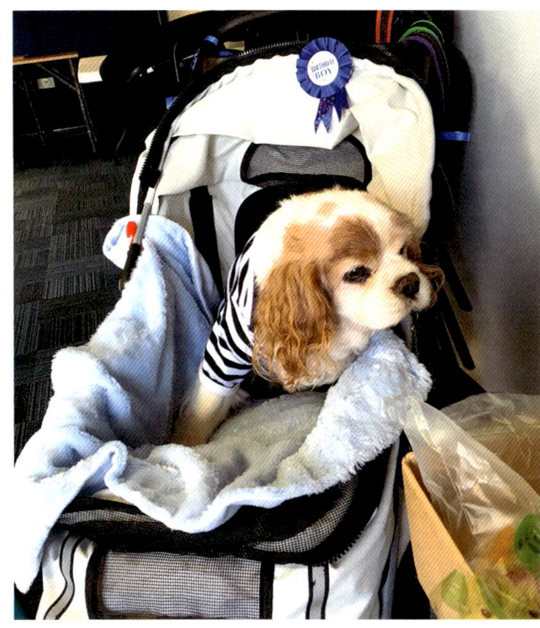

Joanne Holmes is "owned" by Blenheim Josh, who is shown here at his 15th birthday party.

Photo credit: Joanne Holmes, Birmingham, UK

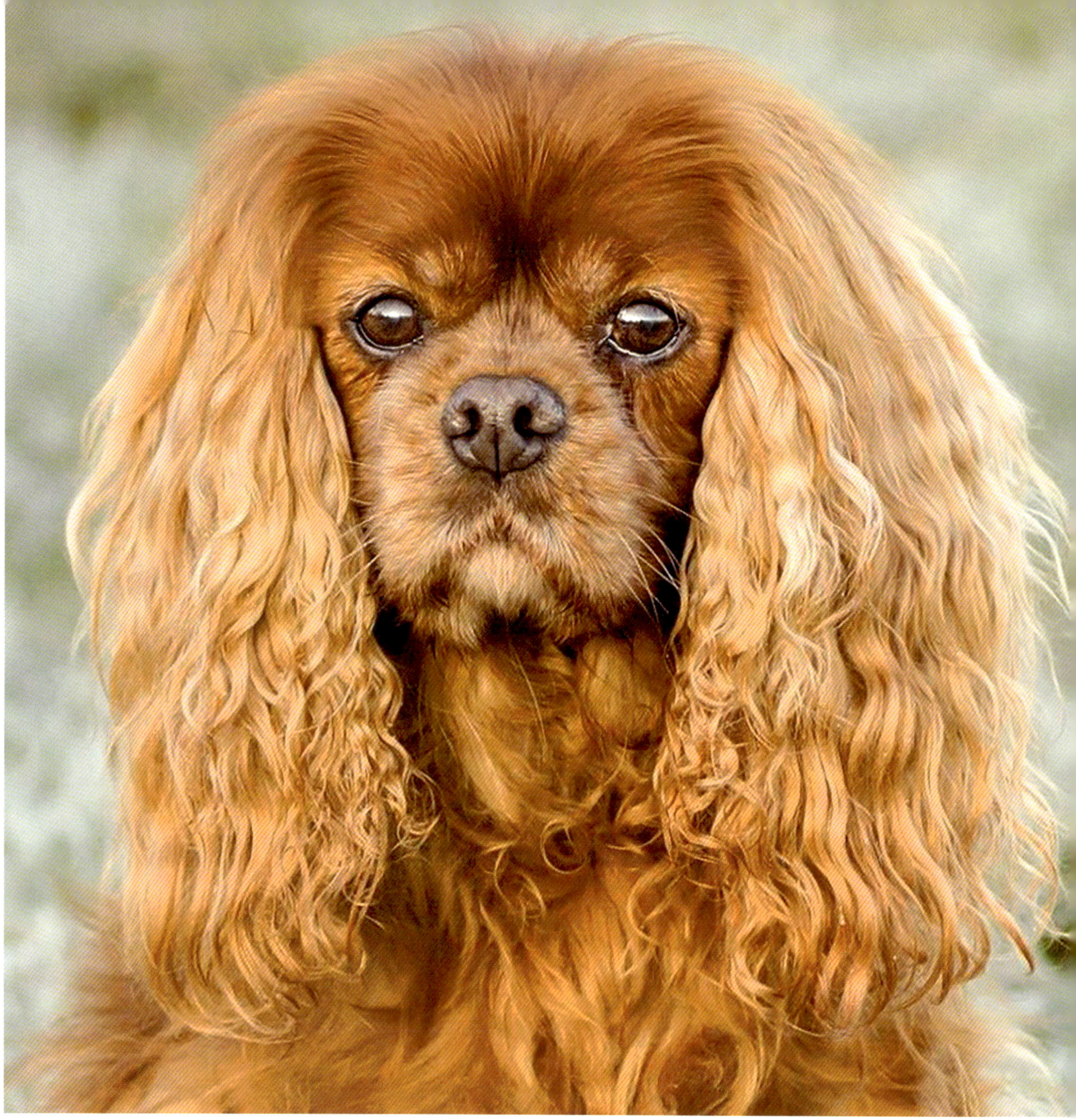

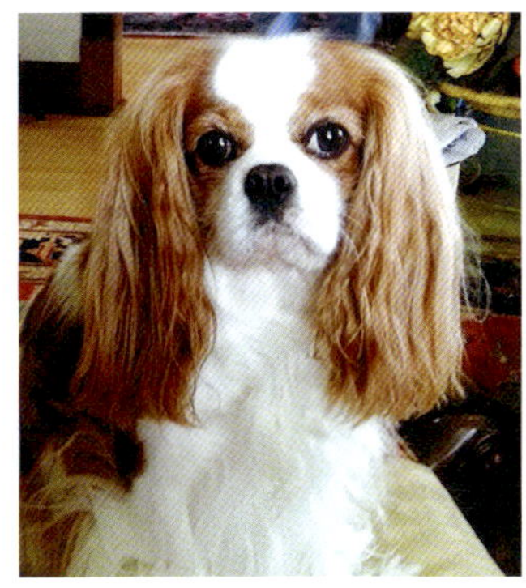

Bu looks wonderful at 11 and a half years old.

Photo credit: Jane Ongaro, Tennessee, USA

Beloved Ruby, Harvey looks very wise at 14 years old.

Photo credit: Ellie Hollingshead, Solihul, UK

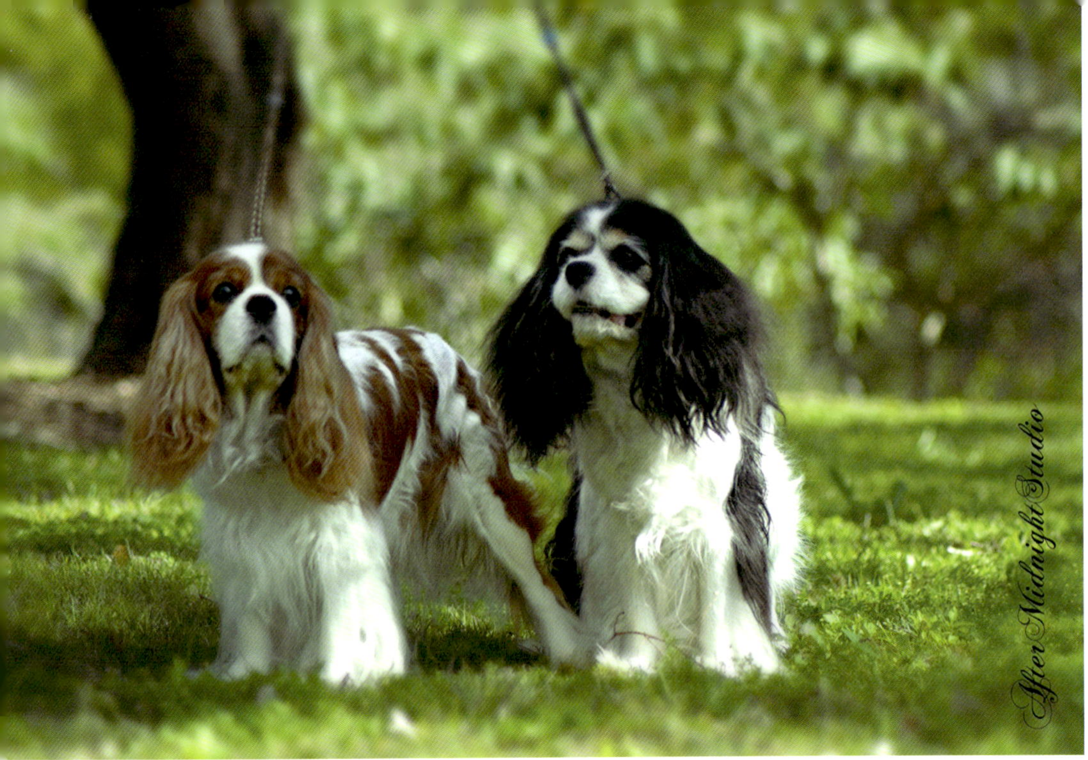

From left: Mr. Darcy, CH/N Kahleyvale Daydreaming is 12 and Bailey, CH Ertae Baileys N Ice is 11. Both are truly golden!

Photo credit: Bronwen Gorden, Brisbane, Australia

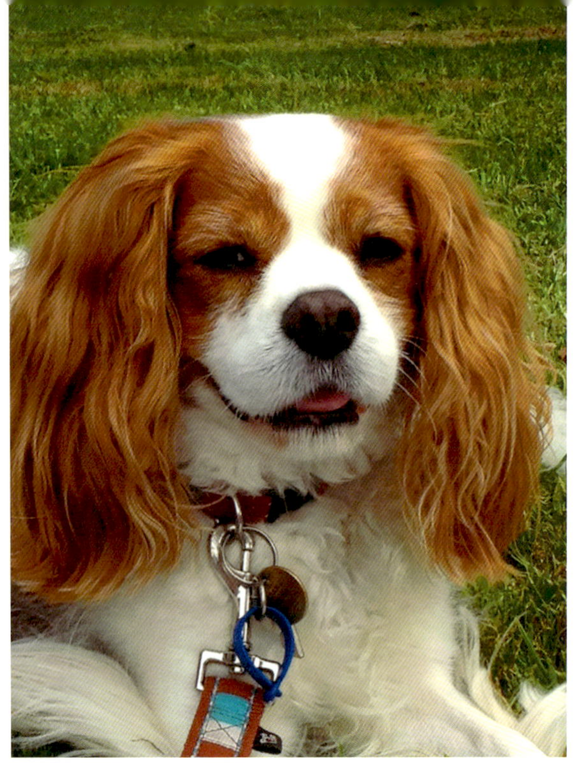

Almost 15-year-old Buckley has been Debbie's only child since he was a puppy, and he's now looking forward to the arrival of a human baby.

Photo credit: Debbie and Marlene Cameron, Victoria, Australia

At 12, Analiese is the picture of femininity with her flowing locks and coquettish smile.

Photo credit: Jennifer Foster, California, USA

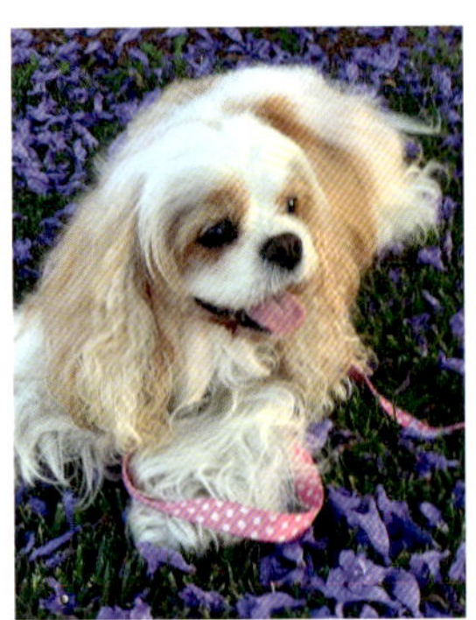

Another Aranel beauty, Bubblicious "Molly" at 14 was the mother of these champions: UK Hh Aranel Scrumptious; CKCSC-USA&AKC CH Aranel With Love; and UK CH Aranel Genesis; and CKCSC-USA&AKC CH Aranel Revelation.

Photo credit: Rick Aldous and Mark Smith, Suffolk, UK

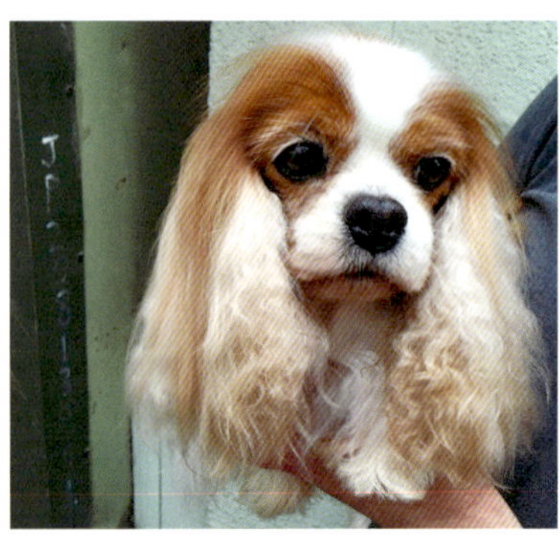

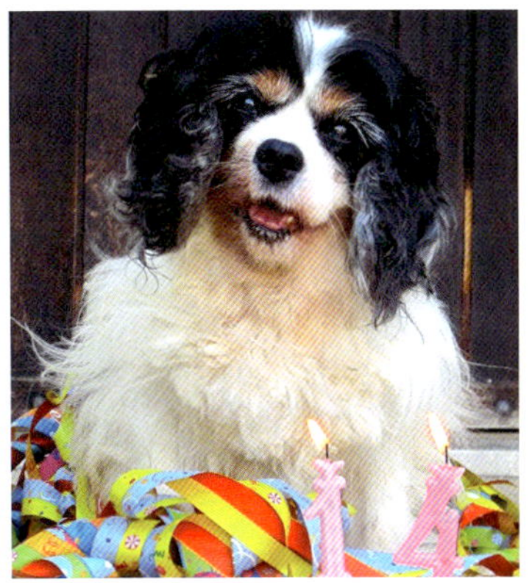

Katie I, who passed at 14 years and 17 days, will always live in the heart of her breeder and companion, Gaynor Davis.
Photo credit: Gaynor Davis, Milan, Italy

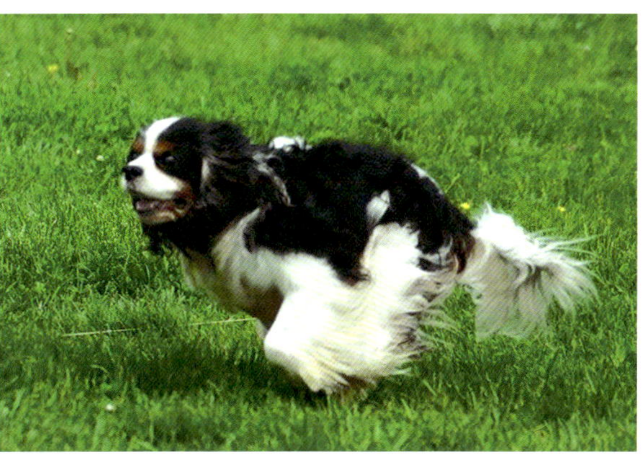

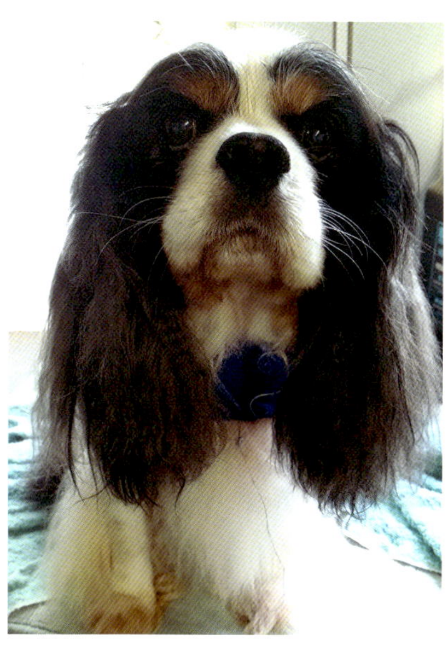

Top: Pierce, CH St. Jon Livewire CA at 12.5 years old, winning his lure coursing title, the oldest Cavalier to do so in AKC history. Left: Pierce at 15 today.
Photo credit: Jennifer Wehking, Tennessee, USA

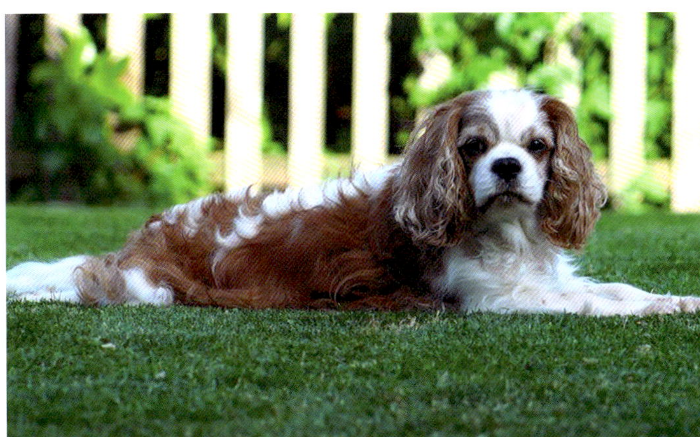

Jack (Lymrey Hi Jack of Narvidar) looks very Zen on the lawn at 11.
Photo credit: Rebecca Wileman, Leicestershire, UK

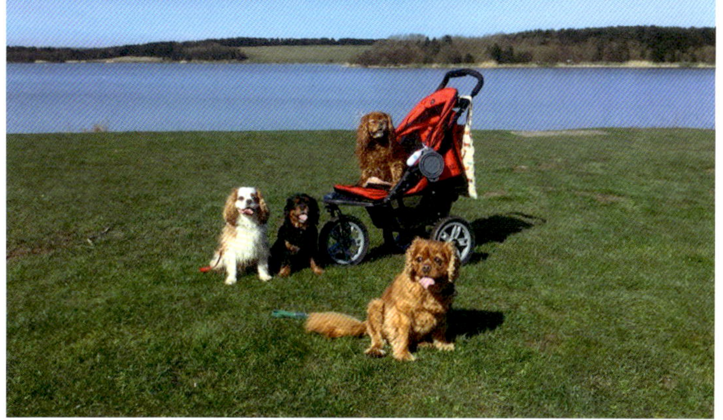

Frodo Cavalier, (in front) at 12-and-a-half and going strong, enjoys outings with his Barking Bugle buddies.
Photo credit: Amanda Knight, Norfolk, UK

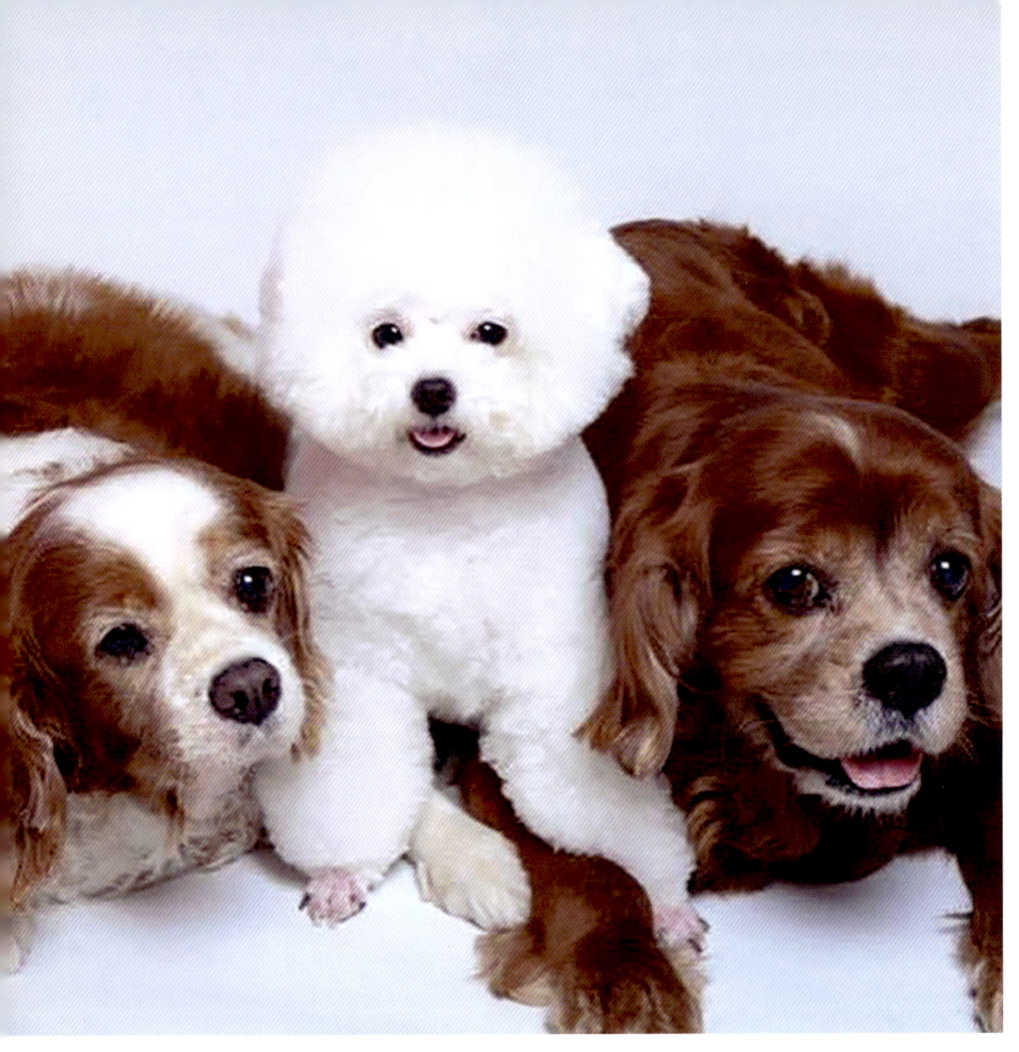

Blenheim Babelo is 14 and Ruby Babel is 16. Sandwiched in between them is 4-year-old Bichon Frise', who is photobombing the oldies.
Photo credit: Jen Chia, Singapore

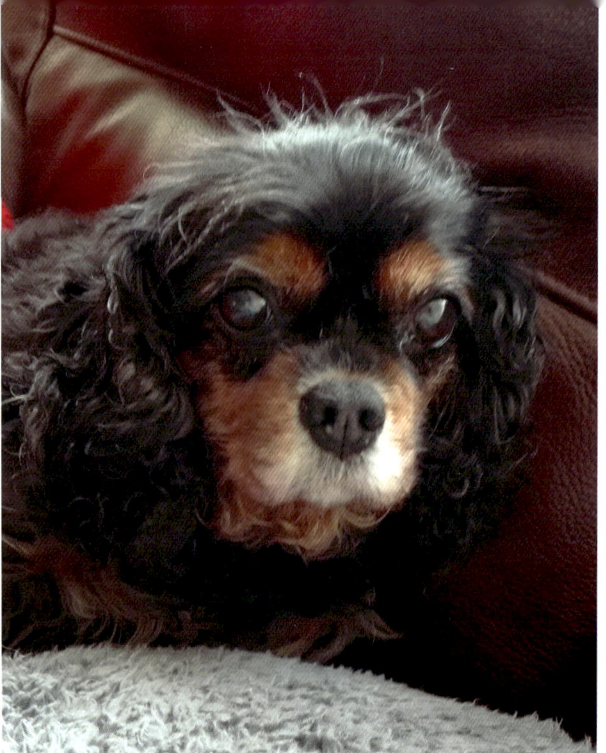

At 14, Chloe from Brnnafrey Cavaliers is a treasured family member.
Photo credit: Susan Pittam, Walsall, West Midlands, UK

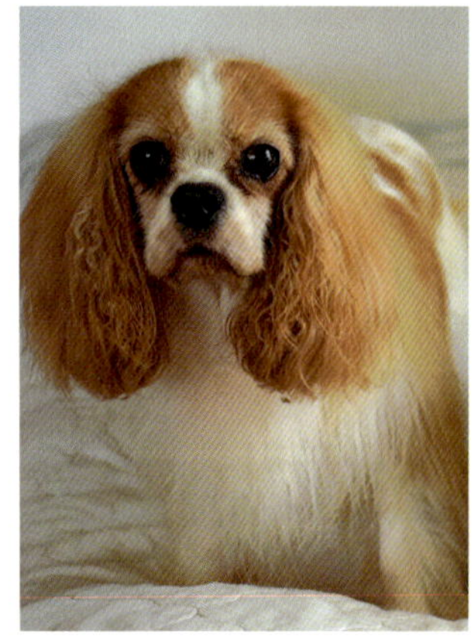

Itaca Aldaha Gold, at 12 and a half, is groomed like a royal prince.
Photo credit: Dana Tosenovjanova, Ostrava, Czechia

Chapter 9 - CKCS Resources

Here are some excellent information resources on CKCS topics and networking:

GENERAL INFORMATION ON CKCS

American Kennel Club information on CKCS
www.akc.org/dog-breeds/cavalier-king-charles-spaniel

The US National Breed Club
www.ackcsc.org

The Cavalier King Charles Spaniel Club, UK
www.thecavalierclub.co.uk

BOOKS ON THE BREED

www.thecavalierclub.co.uk/pay/cavshop.html

Check out *Cavalier King Charles Spaniel — The Origin and Founding of the Breed*, by Dennis and Tina Homes.

CHOOSING A BREEDER

If you decide to purchase a purebred dog, choosing a reputable breeder is the most important thing you can do. The Cavalier Clubs have a list of breeders, but you still need to ask questions to find the right one.

According to Veronica Hull, UK breeder at Telvara Cavaliers and a respected UK Cavalier Club director:

I also feel very strongly about this subject. What makes a 'reputable breeder'? In my book, it's one who strives for the whole package, i.e., keeping to breed type, which is proven by showing to multiple judges who also evaluate structure, soundness in body and mind etc., as they assess the dog in front of them. This should run equally alongside health testing, and only breeding from the healthiest specimens of the breed. SO MANY breeders tick one category, but not the other, and in my opinion, only breeders who engage in both are worthy of the title 'reputable.'

Veronica also gave us a thumbnail of what kind of health tests are essential. They include:

- Eye testing by a Veterinary Ophthalmologist.
- DNA test for both CC/DE and EFS (Curly Coat/Dry Eye, an auto-immune disease, and Episodic Falling Syndrome).
- MRI for Chiari Malformation and Syringomyelia. Unfortunately, these tests have variable results and different interpretations by experts.
- Plus, the age of the sire and dam is important when breeding; both should be more than two-and-a half years of age so that these tests can be done to adult dogs when genetic conditions become more apparent.

The AKC Breeder Referral site
www.ackcsc.org/images/pdf/2017_Breeder_Referralfv2.pdf

The Kennel Club Puppy registry
www.thecavalierclub.co.uk
Click on Puppy Registry in left column for more information.

A list of Questions to ask your breeder may be found at:
www.cavalierhealth.org/questions_for_breeder.htm

HEALTH ISSUES

The Cavalier King Charles Spaniel Club Health Leaflet:
www.thecavalierclub.co.uk/health/KC_LEAFLET.pdf
www.cavalierhealth.org

RESCUE ORGANIZATIONS

ACKCS Rescue Trust Inc. (www.cavalierrescuetrust.org)
The ACKCS Rescue Trust is a national organization dedicated to providing for Cavaliers in need. Everyone in the organization serves on a volunteer basis, so all donations go directly to provide for the dogs. Volunteers are needed.

- To volunteer, submit Volunteer Application on the website.
- To adopt a Cavalier, submit the Adoption Application on the website.
- To surrender a Cavalier or report a dog in need, call 1-888-314-7779.
- Follow the Trust on Facebook: www.facebook.com/CavalierRescueTrust

Cavalier Rescue USA (www.cavalierrescueusa.org)
Every US state has its own chapter doing rescue.

Cavalier Alliance (www.cavalieralliance.org) is a non-profit in the US whose mission is to provide healthcare funding to individuals who adopt senior and special needs Cavaliers.

United Kingdom Cavalier Rescue
Click on Rescue in the directory, where you'll find information on the UKCR (www.thecavalierclub.co.uk) as well as the Regional Clubs' Rescue and Welfare contacts (www.thekennelclub.org.uk/services/public/findarescue/Default.aspx?breed=6149).

Go to www.petfinder.com to access 11,380 adoption groups (close to 300,000 dogs in the registry).

Check your country's Cavalier Club or Kennel Club for its Cavalier rescue organization.

Nadeje Kavalira — Charlie
www.facebook.com/nadejekavaliracharlie/?fref=ts

FACEBOOK GROUPS* AND SITES

- The Healthy Cavalier King Charles Spaniel
- Mitral Valve Disease and the Cavalier
- I Heart Cavaliers
- Cavalier King Charles Spaniel Galaxy
- Cavalier King Charles Stomping Ground
- Make Cavaliers Great Again
- Cavalier King Charles Spaniel Galaxy
- Raw Fed Healthy Cavaliers
- Cavaliers are Special
- Cavalier Life
- Cavalier King Charles Spaniels of the Midwest
- News on dog benefits and events UK (www.thebarkingbugle.co.uk)

*closed groups, ask to join.

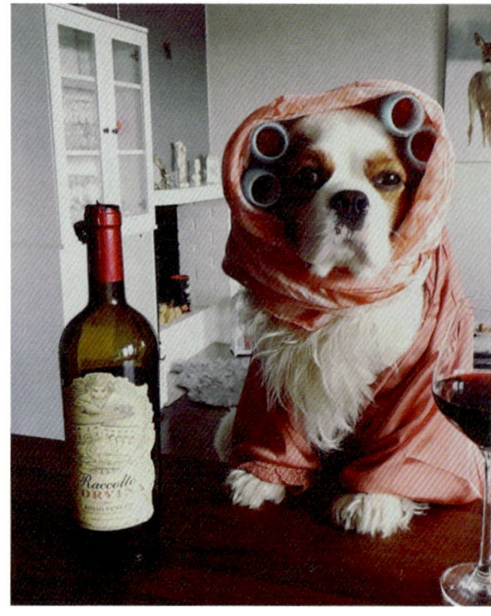

Winston's World, by Line Sletten Larsen from Norway will be a feature of my next book (BTW, this is me upon finishing a book!)